Challenging the Black Atlantic

Challenging the Black Atlantic

The New World Novels of Zapata Olivella and Gonçalves

JOHN T. MADDOX IV

Bucknell University | University Press
Lewisburg, Pennsylvania

Library of Congress Cataloging-in-Publication Data
Names: Maddox, John Thomas, IV, 1981—author.
Title: Challenging the Black Atlantic: the New World novels of Zapata Olivella and Gonçalves / John T. Maddox IV.
Description: Lewisburg, Pennsylvania: Bucknell University Press, 2020. | Includes bibliographical references and index.
Identifiers: LCCN 2019059116 | ISBN 9781684481866 (paperback) | ISBN 9781684481873 (hardback) | ISBN 9781684481880 (epub) | ISBN 9781684481897 (mobi) | ISBN 9781684481903 (pdf)
Subjects: LCSH: Gonçalves, Ana Maria—Criticism and interpretation. | Zapata Olivella, Manuel—Criticism and interpretation. | African diaspora in literature. | Latin American literature—Black authors—History and criticism. | Latin American literature—20th century—History and criticism. | Latin American literature—21st century—History and criticism.
Classification: LCC PN849.L29 M33 2020 | DDC 860.098—dc23
LC record available at https://lccn.loc.gov/2019059116

A British Cataloging-in-Publication record for this book is available from the British Library.

∞ The paper used in this publication meets the requirements of the American National Standard for Information Sciences—Permanence of Paper for Printed Library Materials, ANSI Z39.48-1992.

www.bucknelluniversitypress.org

Distributed worldwide by Rutgers University Press

Manufactured in the United States of America

Contents

Challenging the Black Atlantic

Introduction

This Book, Manuel Zapata Olivella, and Ana Maria Gonçalves

The Black Atlantic is too small, too young, and too blind to encompass the Nuevo Muntu, an American continent founded in slavery but whose branches of freedom spread to the entire world. Ten years before Paul Gilroy wrote one of the fundamental texts of African diaspora studies, *The Black Atlantic: Modernity and Double Consciousness* (1993), Afro-Colombian Manuel Zapata Olivella's historical novel *Changó el gran putas* (*Changó, the Biggest Badass*, 1983) traced a genealogy of the diaspora. It was just as sophisticated as Gilroy's, but it included the entire New World history of Afro-descendants in its 675 pages.[1] Thirteen years after Gilroy's text, in *Um defeito de cor* (*A Color Defect*, 2006), Ana Maria Gonçalves used an enslaved African woman's point of view in her 951-page novel. It tells the story of the Middle Passage directly from the former "Slave Coast" to the largest slave-based nation in history, Brazil. It depicts transcendental moments of Brazilian history, such as a Muslim-led revolt in imperial Bahia and the only slave autobiography to occur entirely in Brazil, that of Luís Gama (1830–1882). Gonçalves's protagonist Luísa Mahin/Kehinde is supposedly his mother, and she loses her son to slavery, travels the country searching for him, and embarks on a bittersweet return to Africa without him. This book examines the tensions and confluences of the Black Atlantic and what I refer to as the Nuevo Muntu. I build on Zapata's concept as well as the challenges Gonçalves's text poses to Gilroy's model of diaspora history and geography. It remains widely influential a quarter century after its publication, and Gonçalves's confluences with Zapata allow me to alter Gilroy for a Latin American context. I then relate the novels and the Black Atlantic to Afro-descent and the New Jim Crow, reaffirming their importance for understanding the diaspora today. Now, as we commemorate the United Nations Educational, Scientific, and Cultural Organization Decade of the Afro-descendant (2015–2024), these Spanish American and Brazilian-based histories point the way to a new understanding of slavery, diaspora, nation, gender, and identity beyond the Black Atlantic.

The Nuevo Muntu is a vision of the Americas, or América, that unifies the history of the continent and makes the African diaspora its protagonist. It is the "New World," but reimagined. Amerindians may be surprised to hear, once again, that their homeland was "new" to others, but the term is an invitation to imagine a radically new future that includes histories of the marginalized in a quest for justice. *Nuevo* is Spanish and *Muntu* sounds like the Portuguese word for "world," *mundo*. Nevertheless, it does not begin with the triumph of the conquistadors. It begins with the story of slavery, which was part of the greater Conquest and provided the third root of the Americas' hybrid peoples: European, African, and indigenous, as Antonio Tillis argues.[2] I am just as interested in the Nuevo Muntu's routes—the diaspora's changes in different cultural contexts. The points of view in Zapata and Gonçalves's texts syncretize the timeless, mythical worldview of traditional sub-Saharan peoples with Western notions of historical evolution. *Muntu* is the singular of *bantu*, or "human," rooting civilization in Africa.[3] However, it is more fluid than "man" is and includes contact between everything surrounding the subject (nature, community) and interaction with the dead and the spirits.[4] Humanity is thus able to communicate with the silenced enslaved of the past in these novels, or at least what these contemporary scholars understand of them, based on archival research as well as an understanding of syncretic oral traditions. In its texts the enslaved's point of view, which is informed by an oral worldview, captivity, and a hybrid of Western logic with non-Western mythology, is represented. It goes beyond the territory of the nation due to cultural mixture and frequent displacement. It empowers the enslaved and their descendants by showing that they have always been part of the experience of the Americas. They have black authors, a twentieth- and twenty-first-century phenomenon with important precursors. This revised view of the Americas from the margins allows the contemporary reader the awareness of slavery's injustices so that he or she can create the truly Nuevo Muntu, a new, just world for all.

This book is part of a resurgence in what I call *zapataolivellismo*, the study of his work as a great author. Zapata's masterpiece, which I abbreviate as *Changó* throughout, was translated into English by Jonathan Tittler (2010).[5] That same year the National Bank of Colombia published the novel alongside the essays of *Manuel Zapata Olivella: Por los senderos de sus ancestros* (*On the Paths of His Ancestors*) on a free online platform to promote his work.[6] Vanderbilt University purchased his archives in 2010 and has begun digitizing them.[7] I worked with them and incorporated materials from the archive into this study. Currently, Colombian scholar Darío Henao Restrepo is preparing a new edition of his complete works, including the previously unpublished novel *Itxao el Inmortal* (*Itxao the Immortal*), which uses a mythical, Afro-indigenous worldview similar to *Changó*'s.[8] The University of Antioquia honored him by creating a *cátedra*, or research and cultural program headed by an academic specialist, in 2017.[9] The Universidad del Valle announced in 2018 that 2020 is the Year of Zapata, honoring the centenary of his birthday with a symposium in his honor, one of a series of events Jairo Torres Oviedo of the Universidad de Córdoba and his team are coordinating.[10] Henao will release Zapata's complete works, an opera adaptation of *Changó* called *Ópera Maafra* will premiere, a black art museum and web space on Zapata will debut, and the black film series Afrocine will promote Zapata and Afro-Colombia. There has been a boom of interest in the author over the past twenty years, and it is in part due to political and intellectual movements regarding Afro-descent, or the African presence in the Americas.

Ana Maria Gonçalves also deserves a close, careful study like this. In 2014 two Brazilian scholars suggested that she receive the Nobel Prize for Literature for her novel, which I will call *Defeito*.[11] She won the 2007 Casa de las Américas Prize in Cuba.[12] She presented at the prestigious Festa Literária Internacional de Paraty (FLIP) in 2016 and 2017 as well as at prominent conferences and universities in the United States.[13] Globo, Brazil's largest television network, is making it into a television "super series" in 2021 that is likely to have an impact similar to Alex Haley's *Roots* in the United States.[14] The series is being adapted in collaboration with screenwriter Maria Camargo and director José Luiz Villamarim, musician and Afrocentric thinker Nei

Lopes, and Eduarda Azevedo.[15] Gonçalves is also a columnist, so this study includes her work for the *Intercept Brasil* as well as other newspapers and blogs to highlight how her notion of slavery and diaspora history informs her thoughts on contemporary issues of race.[16] On a blog she has released a preview of her forthcoming Afrofuturist novel *Quem é Jocenildo?* (2019), of which I will discuss a fragment.

Despite these authors' importance, there is still not enough scholarship on them. Though he had a long and prolific career, Zapata has only seven books dedicated to him worldwide, and only two of them are devoted exclusively to him, in English, and widely available (Captain-Hidalgo, Tillis). I discuss these in my bibliographic overview.[17] Gonçalves has only a handful of articles and book chapters about her work, and even fewer are in English, as my bibliography shows. Zapata should be recognized as a great black thinker and a great Latin American writer. Gonçalves's career is only beginning, but she has already made a powerful contribution to the letters of the African diaspora and Brazil and to international discussions about race and slavery.

In the rest of the introduction, I provide basic information on Zapata and Gonçalves. I include a bio-bibliography of each author and a bibliography of all criticism on them. This will not only familiarize readers with the authors and contextualize my study but also aid future research. While both novels should be read by every scholar of contemporary Latin America, that is not the case, and their length can be prohibitive to teaching and even researching the works.

I include a summary of each novel in this introduction. This will be a valuable tool to students in African diaspora studies and Latin American studies alike. I believe these novels' brilliance will shine forth if readers clearly understand what they are about before they embark on the labyrinthine journey of analyzing each work and comparing them to one another.

In chapter 1 I delve into Zapata's interpretations of myth, truth, and history. Like Gilroy, Zapata uses literature to map the African diaspora and revise its history in a way that challenges historical truth claims. There are two parts to the chapter: one a discussion of mythology and one an intervention in a myth that some consider history. I elaborate on the Nuevo Muntu, which is rooted in his notion of Bantu philosophy.[18] A hybrid thinker, one who mixes Western, African, and, to a lesser extent, Amerindian thought, Zapata created a radically new vision through his novel. I revisit the foundational myth of Changó's anger and exile to rescue the novel from misinterpretations that claim it does not hold whites accountable for slavery and even blames blacks for their own genocide and oppression.

In chapter 2 I further interrogate the play between truth, fiction, and history. It has two parts: an overview of Gonçalves's enslaved Afro-Brazilian protagonist in poetry and a comparison of runaway slave communities in both novels. Until Gonçalves, there was no woman writer who told the story of the enslaved from a female captive's point of view. However, there were important precursors, including the son of Kehinde / Luísa Mahin, Luís Gama, both characters in *Defeito*. It is likely that Gama created his mother's life story; his brief description of her is the only record of her existence. Thus, I discuss his poetry about maternity to develop a picture of what it represented for him. I discuss the evolving representations of Luísa Mahin in poetry and history. I conclude the chapter on truth and fiction by comparing Gonçalves's representation of *quilombos* to Zapata's, noting that there is much more fiction than truth in these tales but also keeping in mind that they each have rhetorical goals in how they present the history of escaped slave communities. While Zapata is more poetic and idealistic, Gonçalves is more realistic. Models of diaspora should accommodate both.

In chapter 3 I engage the debates on the Black Atlantic in three parts: I compare and contrast Gilroy and Zapata, I discuss Du Bois in the text, and then I show the diaspora models of today that Zapata already largely theorized. I provide an overview of select criticism regarding sociologist Paul Gilroy's *The Black Atlantic*, a commonplace in African diaspora studies.[19] In addition to pointing out that Gilroy overlooked the majority of the African diaspora by ignoring Latin America, I analyze his arguments, particularly regarding the philosophical concepts of "double consciousness" and nationalism among enslaved writers in the literature he studies. Central to my argument is Zapata's interest in the life and thought of W. E. B. Du Bois, who is a character in the novel. I compare and contrast Gilroy's essay with Zapata's novel and the Latin American scholarship to which he can be seen as a forebear. I show how Zapata, like Gilroy, challenges traditional notions of the nation and its foundations. I then show how Zapata precedes the current debates on the Black Atlantic's appropriateness for the Afro–Latin American context. I conclude with an examination of how the Nuevo Muntu anticipates Afrofuturism, an aesthetic of cultural production that imagines utopias and dystopias for the diaspora through science fiction.

In chapter 4, as Gilroy does with Toni Morrison, I focus on gender in both novels. This section has four parts. The first is on how a woman's autobiography reaffirms and challenges the Black Atlantic, the second compares the authors' representations of rape, the third discusses their queer characters, and the final section discusses Agne Brown, a prophet of Armageddon. First, I discuss how Gonçalves's telling of an Afro-Brazilian woman's transatlantic voyages problematizes Gilroy's notions of nation and double consciousness. I continue my discussion of women and gender by considering rape as a trope for foundation in slavery and colonialism. In Zapata's case, this is a rereading of Octavio Paz's "Rape of the Chingada" (The Fucked Over), which brought forth a mestizo nation of mixed Amerindian and European "bloodlines," or the "children of the Chingada": Mexicans.[20] Zapata shows that Africans share the trauma of colonization. Gonçalves's depiction of rape is much more realistic and varied since it includes the rape of men. This latter trait is another departure from Zapata: while he confines non-heteronormativity to the spirit world in the form of deities like Olokún and Changó himself, Gonçalves has homosexual characters that add nuance to her realist portrayal of a slave society. I also show that while Gonçalves has been considered to show a more empowering depiction of women than Zapata, and while the latter has been accused of sexism, his Agne Brown is clearly a radical feminist character.[21] She is the persona of Angela Davis.[22] Agne combines a Marxist struggle for the rights of black women—and all oppressed—with decrying the prison-industrial complex that continues slavery by another name.

The conclusion brings *Changó* to the present day; I then discuss Gonçalves's monthly columns in the *Intercept Brasil* from 2017, alongside her other journalism, and conclude by examining Afrofuturism. Zapata, Gilroy, and Gonçalves's texts are, respectively, over thirty, twenty, and ten years old, but they are highly relevant to some of the most recent debates on the African diaspora.

She, like Zapata, analyzes the most relevant issues of our day. The Colombian was criticizing the mass incarceration of blacks as a continuation of slavery in 1983, linking oppression on slave ships to the United States. Like him, Gonçalves also uses the history of slavery in her nation and the United States to unmask racism in two countries that too often refuse to recognize the problem. Unlike Zapata, who died in 2004, her life and works will no doubt continue to depict the most important issues of our time relating to identity: race, class, and gender. Yet nobody has discussed her cultural commentary until now. I view it as the continuation of her novel.

Since my approach is the Nuevo Muntu, or the New World to come that is informed by the slave past of the Americas, I conclude by looking to the future. I explain where these works fit in the recently emerged aesthetic of Afrofuturism. It emerged in the United States and is, generally speaking, black science fiction. However, its precursors include music and other artwork. In Spanish America it is little cultivated, but the novels I study are directly related to the fertile fields of Afrofuturism in Brazil and Latinx literature and cultural production.

This interdisciplinary study is for a diverse audience. Students in undergraduate and graduate literature and Spanish courses can use the summaries. Nonspecialists can use it to study for comprehensive exams. Latin Americanists in literature will use this intervention in contemporary literature and Afro-Hispanic and Afro-Brazilian literature, including those who work in the original languages and in English. Because of the scope of these works, previous literary periods come into play, especially the late eighteenth and nineteenth centuries as they relate to abolitionism and national independence movements throughout the Americas. African American and diaspora studies can use the book in their courses and research on the history of slavery and models of diaspora. I discuss gender and sexuality in both works during my direct comparison of the novels, so it will be of interest to scholars of women and gender studies. Historians, anthropologists, folklorists, and sociologists who specialize in the African diaspora and Latin America can use this book in their work. Its discussion of Catholicism's role in colonialism and syncretic African-based religions will appeal to religious studies. These black authors' representations of race will inform critical race theory debates. These contemporary writers will likely continue to inspire future authors of Nuevo Muntu novels. This book is part of a quickly growing area of study in the work of two great writers, Zapata and Gonçalves, who are only now being considered together in an English-language study.

In the hopes of drawing in new readers for great works, I now give an overview of the authors' lives and oeuvres. The Nuevo Muntu is a reflection upon slavery, the enslaved's point of view, and their importance for imagining a just future for the Americas. This bibliography will be a valuable tool for researchers and other curious readers.

Manuel Zapata Olivella (1920–2004)

Manuel Zapata Olivella is the most prolific and recognized Afro-Colombian writer in history, though his interests and accomplishments do not end there.

He was born on March 17 in the small town of Lorica on Colombia's Caribbean coast.[23] His life is a mixture of conflictive traditions, study, rebelliousness, and wandering.[24] His father, Antonio María Zapata Vásquez, was the son of the Afro-Colombian river ship captain (and Manuel's namesake) Manuel Zapata Granados and an Afro-Colombian woman.[25] Antonio was an atheist, science-loving, liberal schoolteacher who had studied law and loved science.[26] The family raised young Zapata in a remote hamlet on a bog, where his father moved the family to search for oil and precious minerals.[27] Finding none, the Zapata family moved to the poor black community of Getsemaní outside Cartagena in 1927.[28] His mother was the child of a Catalan merchant and a Colombian Carib (Zenu) *mestiza*.[29] She was a homemaker, a devout Catholic, and a trove of indigenous lore.[30] His paternal grandmother and aunt Estebana introduced him to Afro-Catholic spiritual traditions akin to Cuban Santería.[31] Manuel is the brother of playwright and poet Juan Zapata Olivella and anthropologist Delia Zapata Olivella.[32]

When Zapata was still an adolescent, his father forced him to abandon his pursuit of zoology and complete premedical studies at the University of Cartagena in 1939 and the School of Medicine at the National University in Bogotá, where he studied psychiatry.[33] The young Zapata's Marxist consciousness intensified. He abandoned his studies after his qualifying exams to wander Central America, Mexico, and the United States from 1943 to 1946, inspired by literary adventurers and political ideals.[34] While he sometimes went without food or employment, he also wrote for several newspapers, boxed as "Kid Chambacú," and served as a medical assistant.[35] The end of his first U.S. journey came when he met Peruvian writer Ciro Alegría, who helped him publish his first novel, *Tierra mojada* (Wet Earth, 1947), a socialist realist tale of Colombian *campesinos* fighting for their land against the invasive *gamonales*. Upon return to Bogotá, he completed his doctorate with a dissertation on the dialectic and clinical practice.[36] He recorded his travels in his first two autobiographies, *Pasión vagabunda* (*Wanderlust*, 1949), on his trip to Mexico on foot, and *He visto la noche* (*I Have Seen the Night*, 1953), on his U.S. meanderings.

In 1943 he established a Center for Afro-Colombian Studies in Bogotá.[37] He traveled the country with his sister Delia, gathering information on Afro-Colombian and indigenous traditions, culminating in a tour of Europe and China.[38] There he wrote a laudatory travelogue on the Chinese people and the Maoist Revolution called *China, 6 a.m.* (1954). *La Calle 10* (*Tenth Street*, 1960) depicts street life at the margins of Bogotá. In *Detrás del rostro* (*Behind *the Face*, 1963) a street child is killed during the years of the civil war known as La Violencia (1948–1958). *En Chimá nace un santo* (*A Saint Is Born in Chimá*, 1964) recounts the historical, syncretic "Santo" Domingo Vidal, a miracle worker who gave hope to a primarily indigenous village near Lorica.[39] Zapata's most famous novel of this period won an honorable mention for one of the first Casa de las Américas awards in 1962. It is *Chambacú, corral de negros* (*Chambacú, Black Slum*). The work shows that Colombia's conservative government sent poor blacks to be cannon fodder on the U.S. side of the Korean War and sought to destroy the impoverished black community near Cartagena in the process. In addition to these novels, he published four plays and two collections of short stories,[40] among other scattered creative works, though he did not publish a novel for twenty years.[41]

During this hiatus Zapata sought more historical information and more experimental ways of narrating the history of the African diaspora, gathering ten thousand notecards of information from the United States, Spain, Africa, and Latin America.[42] Meanwhile, he studied folklore and taught literature in the United States. He published *El hombre colombiano* (*The Colombian*, 1974), an anthropological study of Colombia's mestizo culture, and later *Nuestra Voz* (*Our Voice*, 1987), a lexicon of popular Colombian speech. He edited a literary journal called *Letras Nacionales* (*National Letters*, 1965–1985).[43] He taught Latin American literature at the University of Toronto (1968–1969), Howard (1969–1970), and the University of Kansas (1970–1971). He organized the First Congress of Black Cultures in the Americas (Cali, 1977). *Changó* was published by Colombia's Oveja Negra Press in 1983.

After *Changó*, Zapata remained active as a writer, teacher, and activist. He traveled frequently between North America and Colombia until the 1990s, when he struggled to recuperate from back surgery.[44] He published the novel as which *Changó* began, *El fusilamiento del diablo* (*Devil's Execution*), in 1987. Its hero, Manuel Saturio Valencia Mena (1867–1897), was a successful Afro-descendant lawyer and judge in the Pacific Chocó region. However, he fell in love with a white woman from the local elite and was framed for arson, a crime punishable by death. The novel displays the leitmotifs of miscegenation, fire, the devil, and rebellion against oppression. Zapata published his bio-bibliography and reflection on his oeuvre *¡Levántate mulato! por mi raza hablará el espíritu* (*Rise Up, Mulatto! My Spirit Will Speak for My Race*) in 1987 in French and in 1990 in Spanish. He continued developing the muntu worldview in *Hemingway, el cazador de la* *muerte* (*Hemingway, the Deathstalker*) in 1993. He tells the tale of Hemingway's suicide, moving it to Kenya and discussing the implosion of colonialism, the Mau Mau Rebellion, and humanity's relationship to nature.

Despite his robust legacy, Zapata lived in poverty during his final years. He died of cancer in Bogotá on November 19, 2004. A cultural center was established in his honor in Washington, D.C. His honors include the Brazilian Francisco Matarazzo Sobrinho Prize for *Changó* (1984), the French New Human Rights Prize (*¡Levántate!*, 1987), and the Colombian national Aplauso 2000; he was named the author of the "Third Best Colombian Novel" according to *Revista Semana* (2007).[45] Zapata is one of the most important writers of the twentieth century in Latin America and a tireless advocate for the oppressed. His biography is documented in María Adelaida López's film *Manuel Zapata Olivella, abridor de caminos* (*Manuel Zapata Olivella, Trailblazer*, 2007). In 2018 the University of Antioquia started a *cátedra* (research group) in his honor, dedicated to the study of ethnicity and Afro-descendants in Colombia.

Zapataolivellismo

The U.S. Context

Changó is Zapata's masterpiece, and it is his most studied work. What follows is an overview of *zapataolivellismo*, a branch of study necessary for the full appreciation of such a multifaceted work. Criticism in the United States and Colombia has been central to promoting and understanding *Changó* and Zapata's work in general since before the novel's publication. What follows is an overview of that criticism, which begins with its landmark translation into English. Before and after this, the *Afro-Hispanic Review* has been at the forefront of zapataolivellismo (studying Zapata Olivella, just as *estudios borgesianos* [Borges studies] refers to criticism on Jorge Luis Borges, for example), a term I am coining to avoid confusion with Mexican Zapatismo. There are only four book-length studies exclusively on Zapata, but there have been scattered articles and book chapters, several of which appear in Colombian and Latin American journals beginning in 2000.

Jonathan Tittler's translation *Changó, the Biggest Badass* (2010) ended a twenty-six-year journey. He translated the work while convalescing from surgery in 1994.[46] In "Catching the Spirit," he reflects on translating Zapata's spiritual, rebellious worldview in *Changó*.[47] The epithet of *El Gran Putas* in the title was perhaps the hardest part to translate. Since Zapata did not like "The Baddest Dude," Tittler suggested "Non plus ultra" and "The Great God," but the University of Wisconsin Press, which nearly published an English translation before Zapata's death, insisted on the former title.[48] I focus on the diabolical imagery of the Gran Putas, since it is a folk devil.[49]

It is appropriate that William Luis introduces Tittler's translation since he has edited the *Afro-Hispanic Review* since 2005, and it was the first journal to promote Zapata's oeuvre vigorously. Luis places *Changó* in the Latin American boom tradition, showing how the novel challenges the canon and continues it in the post-boom period.[50] The journal shaped the ideas I present here.

The *Afro-Hispanic Review* was founded and edited by Ian Smart in 1982 and continued by Marvin Lewis and Edward Mullen.[51] Zapata was active in its founding as a consultant.[52] Zapata's poems "El código guerrero" ("Warrior Code"), "Visión: La travesía" ("Vision: The Crossing"), and "Navego" ("I Sail") appeared in the debut issue.[53] He presents the poems as part of the *Epopeya del Muntu Caminante* (*Epopee of the Traveling Muntu*), which would become the novel's opening.[54] The journal has become the primary venue for *zapataolivellista* scholarship. Recently, Sandra Alzate used the lens of testimonial narrative to approach his socially engaged perspective.[55]

The journal's two special issues on Zapata have been important for his legacy. In 2001 Lewis and Mullen edited the first. It includes critical articles, the poems "El Muntu en América" ("Muntu in the Americas"), a biographical sketch, an interview with him, an homage to his humanism, and the Colombian president's words recognizing Zapata with the Premio Aplauso.[56]

Luis, Laurence Prescott, and Antonio Tillis organized a second special issue of the *Afro-Hispanic Review* (2006) after his death.[57] It includes articles of criticism and unpublished texts.[58] Luis argues that Zapata is the most important overlooked writer of the boom and post-boom eras.[59] Prescott and Tillis note his constant focus on black Latin Americans, his cosmopolitan outlook, and his sophisticated aesthetics.[60] Tillis treats *Changó* as postmodern historiographic metafiction that challenges monolithic truth.[61]

Other U.S. journals have published Afrocentric, Fanonian, and comparative articles on Zapata as well. Lewis, in what may be the first U.S. criticism of Zapata, analyzes violence and myth in *Chimá* (1978).[62] The *Publication of the Afro–Latin American Research Association* has produced seven articles on Zapata, including one by the author. Zapata presents novelists like himself as "herederos de los griots" (heirs to the griots).[63] In *Callaloo,* Prescott discusses cultural whitening.[64] In the *College Language Association Journal,* Smart argues that *Changó* is liberation literature.[65] Cristina Rodríguez-Cabral notes the intersections of postmodernism and postcolonialism in *El fusilamiento* (*Execution*).[66] Edward Waters Hood published an interview with Zapata on his friend Gabriel García Márquez online.[67]

Mainstream journals have not completely ignored Zapata. In *Latin American Research Review,* Prescott analyzes Zapata's U.S. experience.[68] Khamla Dhouti Martínez uses Fanon to discuss *mestizaje* in *¡Levántate!*[69] Margarita Krakusin analyzes Zapata's muntu poetics of space and time.[70] Jackson considers the muntu an Afrocentric "soul-force."[71] John Barry analyzes time, language, and history in the novel.[72] At a 2006 Duke University symposium, Gertrude James González de Allen discussed the decolonizing "performance of memory" in Zapata's essay *La rebelión de los genes* (*Genetic Rebellion*).[73]

Zapataolivellismo has resulted in two book-length manuscripts on his major works in the United States. Yvonne Captain-Hidalgo's (1993) is the first. I disagree with her departure from treating Zapata as one of the "greats."[74] While her target is the Spanish American canon, mine is the emerging inter-American canon Earl Fitz theorizes.[75] Tillis's *Darkening* is an affirmation of the author's black identity and shows how Zapata altered previous Eurocentric models of *mestizaje* (hybridity) to place African elements at the center.[76] His work helps me to discuss how Zapata revises José Vasconcelos.[77]

There have been several scholarly book chapters published in the United States on Zapata. Lewis, in his chapter, provides an overview of violence and racism in Zapata's oeuvre. Smart claims that *Changó* overcomes Alejo Carpentier's exoticism.[78] Smart views Changó as a biblical messianic figure, and he views a "darkened" Egypt as the sole origin of the West.[79] Timothy Cox compares *Changó*'s depiction of the Middle Passage to Carpentier's and those of U.S. and Caribbean black authors, claiming that the magical, spiritual aspects call for change that is more realistic.[80] *Changó* dialogues with Afro-Panamanian Cubena's novel *Chombo* (1981) on disalienation and blackness in Haakayoo Zoggyie's study.[81] William Megenney defines, analyzes, and gives examples of the muntu vision of time, nature, and death in the novel, arguing that it is rooted in the Négritude movement of the 1940s.[82] Jackson claims that Zapata's three major works, *Chambacú, Changó,* and *¡Levántate!,* should be considered great works because they represent a self-determined black voice.[83] Prescott shows that *¡Levántate mulato!* (*Rise Up!*) is among the few black texts in the Latin American essay tradition.[84] Cristina Cabral provides helpful context to *Hemingway*.[85] Patricia Fox mentions Zapata frequently in her 2008 attempt to rethink blackness "as a narrative not about slavery, lack, and open-ended neediness, but rather as a journey propelled by uprootedness and expressed with improvisation, responsively shaping life strategies as much as world views and behaviors."[86] Julia Cuervo Hewitt considers *Changó* a "performative representation and reenactment of the African experience in America" and "a continuation of the *cimarrón* arch-text of the Caribbean."[87] My approach, on the other hand, challenges the Black Atlantic.

Jerome Branche's chapter criticizes *Changó*: "The deification of the historical process, particularly insofar as it subordinates the role of Europeans in modern slavery and capitalist expansion, mystifies the matrix of colonial and postcolonial power and the social, economic, and political relations deriving therefrom. . . . His 'mythical realism' makes them harder to dismantle."[88] I show that *mestizaje* (mixture) is always radically subversive for Zapata. I agree with Branche's statement in another essay regarding *¡Levántate!*: "Zapata Olivella, one of the few Afro-Hispanic creative writers to practice the genre of the essay, confronted the racial bias present in the reflections of his celebrated predecessors, more notably Argentina's Domingo Sarmiento and Mexico's José Vasconcelos, and by embracing and vindicating his own tri-ethnic heritage recast the discussion around identity and diversity in Latin America, underscoring at the same time the elitist tenor of criollo/mestizo versions of Latin Americanism and its ultimate complicity with racialized power."[89] I demonstrate how the novel's complexity and hybridity subvert colonial structures. Now let us turn to Zapata's critics in his homeland.

Recently, part of "Origins" reappeared as "El Muntu en América" in a book on engaged scholarship, which seeks to combine community partnerships for social change with scholarship in higher education.[90] The poem surely inspires activists in Afro-Colombian communities like Arturo Escobar.

The Latin American Context

In Latin America, there are few scholarly books devoted solely to Zapata. José Luis Garcés González synthesizes the author's three autobiographies and interviews the author. Ciro Alfonso Quintero includes chapters on his work in anthropology and literature.[91] He contextualizes Zapata's literary work with his anthropological studies among Afro-Colombians and the indigenous.[92] He states that the three central problems of the novel are the fight against slavery and prison, the desire of the male African for the female, and the struggle to reform a black family after centuries of enslavement.[93] Colombian sociologist William Mina Aragón approaches the life and works of Zapata as exemplifying Colombian triethnicity and a liberation philosophy.[94] He claims that Zapata's categorization as a "black" writer has limited his reception.[95] Mina places him alongside the generation of the boom but questions his marginal position, given the quality of his work.[96] He sees in Zapata an attempt to use the novel to create a new language of the Americas akin to the creole of Palenque de San Basilio.[97] The sociologist states that the muntu notion of nonlinear space-time is akin to the eternal time of Brahma and Nirvana, not the linear time of Messianism.[98] He lauds the novel's historical revisionism and inclusion of black history in Colombian national identity.[99] Mina's book is nearly as important as the International Colloquium in Honor of Manuel Zapata Olivella, which he organized at Popayán in November of 2014. It resulted in the essays of major zapataolivellistas.[100]

Afro—Costa Rican writer Quince Duncan proposes the aesthetic of *afro-realismo* to describe a supposedly new moment in Afro-Hispanic Letters of which Zapata is a part:

> El término *afrorealismo* se justifica porque esta corriente literaria no utiliza los referentes tradicionales de la literatura del "mainstream", como lo hacen los escritores del "boom." No evoca al mito griego, ni al folklorismo. No es literatura negrista ni sigue la corriente de *negritude*. No es realismo mágico. Es una nueva expresión, que realiza una subversión africanizante del idioma, recurriendo a referentes míticos inéditos o hasta ahora marginales, tales como el Muntu, el Samanfo, el Ebeyiye, la reivindicación de las deidades como Yemayá, y a la incorporación de elementos del inglés criollo costeño. ("Afrorealismo")
>
> (The term "Afro-realism" is justified because this literary current does not use the traditional referents of "mainstream" literature like the "boom" writers do. It does not evoke Greek myth or folklore. It is not negrista literature or go along with Négritude. It is not magical realism. It is a new expression, that performs an Africanizing subversion of language, turning to mythical

> referents never before seen or marginal until now, such as the Muntu, the Samanfo, the Ebeyiye, the revindication of deities like Yemayá, and the incorporation of elements of coastal creole English.)[101]

Duncan does not consider the impact of the literary traditions on black authors and others interested in New World slavery. The novel is a form of European origin, but Nuevo Muntu historical novels add African elements and the history of New World slavery and alter this tradition. Nuevo Muntu novels are not purely African. It is clear that Zapata's writing incorporates elements of his work as an anthropologist and linguist. He dialogued with Gabriel García Márquez, and interest in African elements of speech, religion, and music are as evident in the work of Carpentier, Cabrera, and Barnet as they are in *Changó*.[102] Zapata also incorporates European elements, such as *Os Lusíadas* (*The Lusiads*).[103]

Critic Silvia Valero, like Duncan, focuses on a post-boom rupture that focuses on a new black identity. She compares *Changó* to Duncan's *Un mensaje de Rosa* (2004), the first of two novels by him that she considers innovative in their use of a transnational but autochthonous notion of Afro-descent.[104] She ignores the U.S. portion of the novel and claims that its use of the word *negro* instead of the neologisms *afrocolombiano* or *afrodescendiente* shows that its representation of the diaspora is not as evolved as today.[105] She adds that the term *afrodescendiente* has a new political and legal charge to it today, defining a work entirely by its context.[106] She claims the characters can only claim civil rights in the novel, but he is focused on revolution, not civil rights. She considers the questioning of *mestizaje* (hybridity) superior to Zapata's radical redefinition of the term.[107] She defines Duncan's innovations as inspiration in Garveyism, remembering ancestors, racial awareness and solidarity, marronage, and black community. All of these things are central to *Changó*, and he did it all in 1983 without the word *afrodescendencia*.[108] He resignified his own: *zambo* (indigenous / black), *ekobio* (brother), *muntu* (humanity). In another article, she argues that the term/paradigm "Afro-Colombian Literature" should not be used before the beginning of the twenty-first century.[109] Thus, she relegates Zapata to the past for not using the term *afrocolombiano* or *afrodescendiente*.[110] She notes that the Colombian constitution and the United Nations have given political charge to the term, placing a level of trust in government and academic consensus that Zapata does not display in his depictions of the twentieth century or prior. In addition, I see no reason to limit literature to national paradigms, particularly in Afro–Latin American studies. If we are to use only period-specific terms, why not continue to reduce texts to "slave" or "negro" literature, though our views of authors have evolved? How much of this debate is distracting semantics?

Changó received analysis from Roland Forgues, who argues for literature's role in creating a unique Latin American identity. He highlights Quetzalcoatl's role in the novel's mythology.[111] He compares Zapata's masterpiece to Afro-Peruvian Gregorio Martínez's *Canto de sirena* (*Siren Song*, 1971), which also builds an Afro-Indigenous foundation myth and Latin American identity, culminating in the deeds of Vicente Guerrero.[112] He notes the centrality of orality to the plot, marked by an official, written discourse in italics and a subversive, oral counternarrative without any or in asides marked by parentheses.[113] Zapata's blend of history and myth permit an imagination of a *mañana-ayer* that builds on the muntu worldview and the history of the Americas to imagine a utopian future.[114] He notes that *mestizaje* will give birth to a new man personified by Benkos Bioho.[115] Following Mariátegui, he considers a utopia based on non-Western influences possible.[116] Samuel Mate-Kojo argues that Changó's exile is the central myth that lends coherence to the fragmented episodes of the novel, deconstructs colonial-racist paradigms of black subjectivity, and provides agency to the African diaspora. I agree with him, but I delve deeper into Bantu philosophy.[117] Víctor Figueroa's *Prophetic Visions of the Past: Pan-Caribbean Representations of the Haitian Revolution* (2015) has a well-researched chapter on Changó's curse, the root of slavery. It is unclear why Figueroa focuses on the Orisha instead of the Haitian Revolution, the stated topic of his book, but I engage his chapter on Zapata in the next chapter.[118]

As in the United States, Colombian journals produced Zapata criticism, but the earliest widely available critical essay is from 2000. This is not to ignore the author's own foundational journal *Letras Nacionales*.[119] The Universidad de Antioquia's *Estudios de Literatura Colombiana* (*Studies in Colombian Literature*), edited by Ana María Agudelo Ochoa, produced Zoggyie's article.[120] Mario Aguiar argues that the novel represents a continuation of the "New Novel," focused on linguistic experimentation, displays a spiral evolution of time, and combines epic and historic discourses.[121] This evolution of time in the novel culminates in the last novella, in which the development of black empowerment is greatest and described in most detail.[122] Lucía Ortiz contextualizes *Chambacú* in the literary and political history of Colombia and argues that it represents the regional, black "intra-historia" of Colombia.[123]

The U.S.-Colombian Asociación de Colombianistas (Colombianist Association), a venue of zapataolivellismo, was formed at the Kentucky Foreign Language Conference in 1983, the year of *Changó*, and Zapata attended.[124] The 1984 inaugural conference in Quirama resulted in published proceedings, which include three essays on Zapata. Lewis claims there are three types of time in the novel: African mythical time, an interval of the erosion of cyclic time, and the imposition of linear time.[125] Captain treats the novel's time as "un constante fluir en presente" (a constant flux in the present).[126] She compares it to Carpentier's *El Reino de Este Mundo* (*The Kingdom of this World*).[127] Smart argues that *Changó* is a poetic *nueva novela* (new novel).[128] John Brushwood includes Zapata in his discussion of the evolution of "new" and "boom" novels in Colombia.[129] The association has since published three more articles regarding Zapata in its *Revista de Estudios Colombianos* (*Colombian Studies Journal*). María Mercedes Jaramillo analyzes the play *Hotel de vagabundos* (*Hotel for Wanderers*) and reaffirms his humanistic ideals.[130] Captain laments that Zapata died feeling ignored by scholars.[131] She notes that the internet and interdisciplinarity have contributed to a deeper and broader understanding of his work, contributing to his legacy.[132]

In the *Revista de Estudios Colombianos*, historian Pablo Gómez explains how the 150 boxes of Zapata's papers, recordings, and photos arrived at Vanderbilt's Heard Library Special Collections.[133] The author died in poverty. He lived in the Hotel Dann in Bogotá and had many manuscripts confiscated to settle his debts. His daughters and sister housed the collections but did not have the means to preserve them. The Ministerio de Cultura did not offer any compensation for the materials and gave carte blanche to other universities to purchase them, and they went to Vanderbilt.[134] I have been able to include insights from the author's archives.

There are Colombian book chapters on Zapata. Ortiz's edited volume places Zapata alongside other Afro-Colombian authors. It focuses on black and mestizo writers from Colombia's African-infused coasts, from Candelario Obeso and Jorge Artel to Zapata and less studied writers.[135] Liliana Ramírez argues that the subjects of *Chambacú* are cultural hybrids.[136]

Critics are opening up Zapata criticism with comparative approaches. Zapata's novels are part of Raymond Williams's overview of the boom in 1992.[137] Ramírez uses comparative, gender, and postcolonial theories to analyze *Chambacú*.[138] In a Colombian volume, Stefan Hofer uses systems theory according to Niklas Luhnman to analyze ritual communication in *Changó*.[139]

Studies by Chilean critic of Brazilian origin Daiana Nascimento dos Santos has much in common with my own, and she draws a sophisticated comparison between *Defeito* to *Changó*, the first of its kind.[140] Her analysis of *Changó* shows how it goes beyond Seymour Menton's subgenre of the new historical novel.[141] It includes the African diaspora and oral traditions.[142] She notes that the sea structures Zapata's work.[143] The muntu myth challenges the objectification of blacks as people without history and provides the historical basis for universal freedom.[144] She is mistaken in thinking the Benkos Bioho story is true, though.[145] She claims that it advocates for a literal return to Africa like Marcus Garvey's, but I show that he is rooted in the Americas and proposes no such return.[146] She argues that black history has never been told, but I maintain that it has not been told this way—in one that includes the diaspora throughout the Americas.[147] She claims it is an "African" vision of the world, but I view it as hybrid or mestizo with a strong African component.[148] German critic Phaf-Rheinberger proposes, instead of a return to Africa, a new vision of the Americas, since the characters "ya no pertenecen físicamente al África, sino sólo mediante los vínculos construidos a partir de la memoria, lo que permite reelaborar una representación del África en el lado de Acá [del Atlántico]" (no longer belong physically to Africa, but only through the links constructed through memory, which allows reworking a representation of Africa on this side [of the Atlantic]).[149] She agrees that the novel is rooted in the culturally hybrid Americas though deeply influenced by the muntu worldview.

Nascimento dos Santos published a series of articles on Zapata and Gonçalves that are based on her book research. She argues that works by and about Afro-descendants are overlooked in previous studies on the "new historical novel," a subgenre discovered by Seymour Menton, but that they are also ill theorized.[150] She proposes her study of Zapata as a model of an alternative. She claims it is "Afrocentric" and provides a variety of voices for black subjects.[151] She notes the importance of the oral tradition in the text and its narrative form.[152] She notes the intertextuality of *Changó* with the work of Carpentier, for example.[153] The locus of enunciation in these works privileges the marginalized, which grants them agency.[154] She sees the novels as having revolutionary potential for the preservation of the legacy of the enslaved.[155]

Nascimento dos Santos modifies Gilroy's model to place Gonçalves in the tradition of the Anglo-American slave narrative. She does well to note the humanizing force of the historical novel and the powerful pathos evoked by imagining what a slave ship must have looked like to a slave who may have never seen the sea or such a great and horrifying structure. Nonetheless, I believe she should have taken into account the differences between a text from the twenty-first century and those of the abolitionist era.[156]

Colombian critics have illuminated Zapata's texts with introductory essays. Henao contextualizes it in the author's biography and Colombian letters.[157] Henao's edition is the third of twenty-nine digitized masterworks of the 2010 Biblioteca de Literatura Afrocolombiana, the Ministerio de Cultura Colombiana's showcase of Afro-Colombian culture. Dorita Piquero de Nouhaud's introduction to the 2007 edition of *Changó* shows the French influence on his legacy.[158] It discusses the mythology of the return to Africa, the transcendental categories (the Orishas and Ancestors) that unite the novel, the worship of the shadows that links African Americans to their Latin American and African ancestors and transculturation/miscegenation (*mestizaje*).[159] His winning the Matarazzo Sobrinho Prize in Brazil for the novel in 1985 led her French compatriots Claude Couffon and Claude Bourguignon to translate it into their mother tongue in 1991.[160]

The French language was the idiom of the first publication of Zapata's autobiography.[161] It is also the language of the first book-length study on the author's work, François Bogliolo's.[162] It develops a four-part theory of blackness: the origins of the concept in the Americas, an affirmation of identity through "unconscious" black culture (orality, ancestor worship, language), "conscious" blackness (disalienation, political action, and rebellion), and a reappropriation of *mestizaje* (mixture) as a creative force.[163]

In conclusion, zapataolivellista criticism has mostly been focused on concerns of the author's black identity, his Colombian setting, and his Marxist ideals, particularly through the lens of Fanon. Gender studies are beginning to alter his reception. Outside of a few Afro-Hispanic and Colombian journals, he has received little critical attention. While there are comparative studies that place him in an international context, much more work needs to be done if the academy is to treat him as canonical. My study uses a comparative, inter-American approach to show how his text illuminates others that treat the theme of slavery and the subgenre of historical novels in general.

Ana Maria Gonçalves (b. 1970)

Ana Maria Gonçalves is an Afro-Brazilian writer, speaker, and social commentator whose work includes novels, short stories, and blogs. She was born in the town of Ibiá in Minas Gerais, Brazil, an area with a large black population and a reputation for conservative politics.[164] She moved to São Paulo and worked in advertising before realizing her dream of becoming an author. Her first short story was published as part of Portugal's Tribo (tribe) writers, but her work as a novelist began with her personal blog.[165] It led to her first novel, *Ao lado e à margem do que sentes por mim* (*Beside and at the Edge of What You Feel for Me*, 2002).[166] It is a Clarice Lispector–esque, melancholy love story that continues on Gonçalves's blog "100 meias confissões de Aninha" ("100 Half-Confessions by Aninha"), named in honor of the *modernista* poet of Goiás, Cora Coralina.[167] Gonçalves wrote *Ao lado* after she left a relationship and a job in São Paulo for Salvador da Bahia, where she experienced an ethnic and creative awakening while investigating the history of Brazil's first capital. The result is the 951-page *Um defeito de cor* (*A Color Defect*, 2006), her most groundbreaking work.[168]

After *Defeito*, Gonçalves lived in New Orleans for seven years, and she continues to write and speak on Afro-Brazilian history and identity in the United States and Brazil. She recently published a forward to photographer César Fraga and historian Maurício Barros de Castro's travelogue on their journey through the African continent, retracing sites related to Brazilian slavery from Cabo Verde to Moçambique.[169] In it she contemplates the demonizing of the black body and liberating myths surrounding the return to Africa. Barros de Castro's essay contextualizes the photos, which depict many of the places depicted in *Defeito*: Bahia, Savalou, the São Jorge da Mina Fort, the home of the Chachá (African kingpin of the slave trade), the palaces of Dahomey, Vodum priests of the *agudás* (Brazilians like Kehinde who returned to Africa), and the "Brazilian" settlement of Lagos, Nigeria. Her current projects include a novel that imagines an Afrofuturist "racial democracy" in a futuristic São Paulo and a novel about transgender people.[170] She was a columnist for the *Intercept Brasil* in 2017, as I discuss in my conclusion. She is the leading Brazilian voice of historical novels about slavery that rewrite the history of the New World, incorporating black history into its cultural miscegenation, or syncretism, just as Zapata did many years before.

The Bourgeoning Criticism on Ana Maria Gonçalves

There is little written about *Um defeito de cor* (2006) because Gonçalves is a young and previously unknown writer. The novel gained the attention of the academy with her receiving the Casa de las Américas Award in 2007.[171] In Brazil, the first major criticism came in the bound volume *Alguma prosa* (*Some Prose*, 2007). In his chapter, Cláudio de Sá Capuano notes its "singularidade" (singularity) for having a female author, narrator, and protagonist.[172] He relates it to Brazil's Law 10.639 (2003), which requires the teaching of Afro-Brazilian history in schools.[173] He cautions the reader to keep in mind the gulf between the twenty-first-century reader's mentality and that of a slave from the nineteenth century and notes Hutcheon's stance that metanarrative destabilizes historical truths.[174] Critic Idelber Avelar is the first to compare, if briefly, *Changó* to *Defeito* in its originality as a coherent narrative of slave history from enslaved Africans' point of view.[175]

Most scholarship on Gonçalves has been done in Brazil. In 2009 leading Afro-Brazilianists Eduardo de Assis Duarte and Maria Nazareth Soares Fonseca included Gonçalves alongside other young Afro-Brazilian authors.[176] Adélcio de Sousa Cruz analyzes the rape and death of the protagonist's mother, in which a "riozinho de sangue" (small stream of blood) forms beneath the Iroco, a sacred tree akin to the Cuban *ceiba*.[177] He sees the blood as the Middle Passage and the tree as an African symbol of hope. He notes the centrality of orality in the text.[178]

Duarte has led the invaluable *Literafro*, a compendium of essays on Afro-Brazilian themes and authors. In it, he reproduced his 2009 book chapter, which cautions readers to discern what coincides with Gilroy's Black Atlantic and what does not in the novel.[179] He sees the centrality of maternity to the text, much like Maria Firmina dos Reis's foundational *Úrsula* (1859).[180] He notes the text's epistolary form and parallels with the testimonial narrative.[181] Cristiane Felipe Ribeiro de Araújo Côrtes compares it to the epic.[182] Côrtes analyzes DuBoisian double consciousness and the protagonist's constant foreignness in the novel.[183] She traces the novel to the griots.[184]

Critics outside *Literafro* have also analyzed Gonçalves. Regina Dalcastagnè mentions her in the *Afro-Hispanic Review*.[185] She laments that since 1965 80 percent of characters in Brazilian canonical literature have been white and there have been few black authors.[186] Alternatively, *Defeito* is part of a greater phenomenon of black authors populating their works with affirmative black characters that overcome racism, as exemplified by Kehinde's "heroísmo épico" (epic heroism).[187] Ana Beatriz Gonçalves and Clara Alencar Pimentel adopt a Fanonian gaze and note the different roles of black and white women in the text regarding maternity: white women see giving birth as a means to eternal salvation while black women see it as merely reproduction.[188] The focus on the home and domesticity is another element of the maternal.[189] Marcelo Cruz Dalcom Junior and Lícia Soares de Souza argue that the novel tells the story of the oppressed from a political, not objective, stance and rescues that history from silence.[190]

Aline Najara da Silva Gonçalves argues that the novel is part of a surge of interest in Afro-Brazilian culture and the admitting and combatting of racism beginning with the 1970s Afro-Brazilian movement's influence on the state.[191] It presents slaves as rebellious and resilient, not harmonious and happy, to build curiosity toward this history's relevance to the present.[192] Marcos Roberto Teixeira de Andrade uses Edward Said's postcolonialism and Hutcheon's postmodernism to argue that the novel shows the oppressed, peripheral side of Brazil's past and treats history as narrative.[193] This is like telling Gilberto Freyre's *Casa-Grande e Senzala* (*The Masters and the Slaves*, 1933) from the point of view of the *senzala* (barracks), inverting its perspective.[194] The critic finds similarities to Gilroy and notes that Kehinde's depictions of herself are not always heroic.[195] Andrade perceives the contradictory role of the British in slavery, profiting from it even after abolishing the trade.[196] He mentions that Kehinde supposedly inspires Joaquim Macedo to name his foundational Brazilian novel *A moreninha* (*The Brunette*, 1844).[197]

Zilá Bernd celebrates the novel's innovation as the first Brazilian novel narrated from the point of view of an enslaved woman and the first *roman fleuve*, or sprawling page-turner, in Afro-Brazilian letters.[198] She notes Kehinde's devotion to motherhood.[199] Bernd makes comparisons to Antônio Olinto's 1969 *A casa d'água* (*The Water House*).[200] The critic notes the approximation of oral traditions, including the cult of ancestors and spirits, and archival research.[201] She sees three functions of the novel: ancestral memory, the creation of identity through an origin myth, and transatlantic memories beyond the nation.[202] Bernd relates it to Gilroy along the axes of family and historical memory.[203] Her article compares Kehinde's three voyages across the Atlantic: the first of deterritorialization and reterritorialization in Brazil in which her mobility and diversity of comrades make her a *passeur culturel* (cultural observer), the "less interesting" trip back to Africa, and the final one in which Kehinde's blindness assumes a mythical function.[204] She notes the violation of hegemonic taboos around rape and other violence toward slaves in Brazil.[205] The article's conclusion notes the "traces of slavery" Gonçalves gathers: filling the blanks in history, the reunion of mother and son, and the questionable evidence used regarding Mahin.[206] Bernd considers the text an *apokatastasis*, or gathering of souls akin to that of Christian Paradise.[207] She sees this gathering as a subversion of hegemony and a revisiting of national traumas that shows the importance of not only historical knowledge but also emotional reactions to it.[208]

Maria Josele Bucco Coelho's chapter, the first in the United States, reflects on the "novel of historical extraction," noting the emphasis on the "impurity of origins" in the novel.[209] She contextualizes the work in the tradition of historical novels by women in Brazil, beginning in the 1930s' imagining of the nation.[210] She compares the work to contemporary revisions of history.[211] She sees it as a "Black Atlantic in the South," noting that Gilroy focused only on the Anglophone Atlantic.[212] She sees Kehinde's financial independence once she becomes a free woman like Virginia Woolf's *A Room of One's Own* (1929).[213]

Nascimento dos Santos's *El océano* (2016) also compares Gonçalves's protagonist to other black writers and historical figures. These include Mãe Beata de Yemonjá, Conceição Evaristo, Nancy Morejón, and Queen Ginga of Angola.[214] She claims both works share an "African universe."[215] While patriarchs José de Alencar and Gilberto Freyre presented the point of view of the empowered classes in a harmonious relationship with the oppressed, Abdias Nascimento broke with that tradition, and Gonçalves is continuing his work.[216] She claims the novel proposes universal female liberation, but I do not see such a utopian project in the novel.[217] In fact, it is a lot to ask of one woman, even a fictional one. She notes the centrality of rape to the plot and connects it to today's violence.[218] She views the novel as "transcendental violence" to strike back at white oppression along the lines of Davis.[219] *Defeito* is not vengeful. I do share her admiration of Kehinde's resilience: "Pese al contexto de violencia, los personajes femeninos logran resistir y no se dejan abatir por la condición de dolor y sometimiento que los ha marcado a lo largo de sus trayectorias individuales y colectivas" (In spite of the context of violence, the female characters are able to resist and do not let themselves be beaten down by painful conditions and submission that have marked them throughout their individual and collective lives).[220] Kehinde is heroic in her survival, not in her universal liberation of womanhood.

Like me, Nascimento dos Santos doubts Luisa Mahin ever existed. While Elisa Larkin do Nascimento believes she did and Pierre Verger believes there were twenty-six women in the Revolta dos Malês, João José Reis claims there is no evidence of female participation in the uprising.[221] Nascimento dos Santos sees her as an invented hero. Her search for her son is a metaphor for reuniting Brazil with its African past, and her return to Africa is a reoriginalização (reoriginalization) of the black subject.[222] She seems unable to reconcile this utopian return, which she compares to *Changó*, with the "commercial" Africa that Kehinde finds and the involvement of blacks in the slave trade.[223] I, on the other hand, argue that both the search for Gama and her involvement with the traders of Africa are examples of Kehinde's struggle for survival, not a utopian liberation project like *Changó*. She claims the *retornados* (Afro-Brazilians who returned to the Slave Coast) form a "space in-between" relative to the European colonizers and the local Africans.[224] I will show that they are even more like the Brazilian colonizers than she posits.[225]

In an article, Nascimento dos Santos argues that the novel is a metaphor for the contemporary emancipation of black women in Brazil.[226] She notes that the author breaks with the harmonious depiction of the plantation put forth by Gilberto Freyre.[227] This is due in part to the black female protagonist's point of view.[228] This puts her in the tradition of Nascimento.[229] She relates it to contemporary affirmative action efforts in Brazil.[230] Kehinde is, for her, the metaphor of collective feminine freedom.[231] Similarly, Annie Gibson details actions Kehinde takes to resist slavery spiritually and psychologically.[232]

Antônio Luciano Tosta's book mentions *Defeito* and *Changó*.[233] Transnational history and *marronage* (rebellion) are, for him, a confluence of cultures in the Americas. Tosta compares Luís Fulano de Tal, pseudonym of Luís Carlos de Santana, to Ismael Reed.[234] Interestingly, French Guiana enters the analysis, partly because the modern-day narrator of De Tal's novel discovers a manuscript there on which he bases the novel.[235] De Tal's *A noite dos cristais* (*Night of Broken Glass*, 1999) depicts the Revolta dos Malês (1835), during which Muslim slaves attempted to overthrow their oppressors, reenslave their African rivals, and establish a caliphate in Salvador da Bahia.[236] Tosta contemplates the uncomfortable title, which evokes the Nazi Kristallnacht. The Muslims become the "Jews" of the massacre once found out.[237] Likewise, Nascimento mentions Joel Rufino dos Santos's *Crônica de indomáveis delírios* (*Chronicle of indomitable deliria*, 1991), which is another fictional work on the Malês that deserves critical attention and comparison to *Defeito*.[238]

Paulo Thomaz (2015) uses geographer Rogério Haesbaert's concept of multiterritorialization (identification with multiple places due to the scattering of diaspora) and dis-reterritorialization (returning to place of origin) to describe four shifts in Kehinde's fluid identity.[239] First, Kehinde is taken from her village to the Dahomean town of Savalu.[240] The second shift is the Middle Passage, during which the tradition of her grandmother's Voduns (spirits) survive her in Kehinde's memory.[241] The third is the trail Kehinde strikes wandering from the plantation in Itaparica, Bahia, to São Paulo.[242] While in Maranhão, she relearns her first language, Ewe-Fon, which allows her a sense of return to her motherland of Ouidah.[243] The last is her journey from Salvador to Lagos, in which she experiences further cultural mixtures.[244]

Ineke Phaf-Rheinberger first mentions *Defeito* in the volume *AfricAmericas* to show that Gonçalves treats gender issues with more depth than her male counterparts in historical fiction on slavery than Pepetela and José Figueiredo Agualusa.[245] Her single-author chapter shows how Gonçalves's novel is a direct heir to João Ubaldo Ribeiro's *Viva o povo brasileiro* (*An Invincible Memory*, 1984) and Antônio Olinto's *A casa d'água* (*The Water House*, 1969).[246] In the novel, "water spirituality constitutes a broad network that points to hopes for change" through the influence of water deities Yemayá and Ochum.[247] Regarding Ubaldo, "whereas Ribeiro writes a satire of the Brazilian nation, echoing all kinds of prejudices toward 'black' characters, Gonçalves ignores them, introducing instead a rich catalogue of words of African descent from an Afro-Brazilian perspective."[248]

Leila Lehnen argues that the Bildungsroman and epistolary novel, both of which *Defeito* exemplifies, generate awareness of human rights and their violation as well as empathy. Lehnen's approach is informed by contemporary human rights discourse.[249] However, the change has occurred in literary critics like Lehnen, not always in the authors, and certainly not in the nineteenth-century enslaved Africans they represent. While the *Rights of Man and Citizen* (1789) and the *Bill of Rights* (1791) existed when Kehinde lived, they did not extend these rights to the enslaved, as Lehnen herself notes.[250] While the novel creates a form of agency for and empathy with the enslaved, one wonders why a post–World War II notion of "human rights" is applied to the novel.

Fabiana Carneiro da Silva's article on the novel uses its premise as historical fiction to deconstruct the opposition of history and fiction.[251] She notes that Gonçalves borrows heavily from Reis and other social scientists to build her authority, which paradoxically reveals the artifice of her fiction.[252] Silva says so many historical details actually detract from the realism of the plot, since it seems unlikely to the critic that she would remember them so clearly, dispassionately, and linearly.[253]

Luciana da Trindade Prestes and Emília Maria da Trindade Prestes argue that the novel, which they consider the most important of the century, to be an instrument of power. It provides unprecedented, empowering representation of Afro-Brazilian women.[254] They go so far as to say it is the first book by a *mestiça* (mixed) woman, with which the self-affirmed *black* writer would likely take issue, as she indicates in an interview.[255] They see the importance of orality to the text, noting that, when Kehinde reportedly learns to read, over 80 percent of blacks were illiterate.[256] They compare her literacy to Juan Francisco Manzano's and note that the empowering tradition is passed on to Kehinde's adopted child Geninha.[257] I disagree with them that the novel is "otimista" (optimistic), though.[258] I compare the novel to the U.S. "neo-slave narrative."[259] Claire Williams argues that the novel is one of a series of recent Brazilian novels published to work through the trauma of slavery.[260] One could add to the studies on Gonçalves my interview with her in the *Afro-Hispanic Review* and my reference entry.[261] These are all the published works on Gonçalves's novel.

The novelist is not only part of the rapidly expanding field of Afro-Brazilian literature, but also part of a recent renaissance in the study of Luís (originally "Luiz") Gama (1830–1882), who rose from a slave to a poet and an abolitionist lawyer in São Paulo, as several social scientists' studies show.[262] Gama's poetry and letters constitute the closest equivalent Brazil has to an original slave narrative. Gonçalves's novel traces the life story of Gama's mother, Luísa Mahin, who was documented only in these letters.[263] Historian Ana Lucia Araujo shows that she did not exist, a polemic as the Brazilian congress has approved memorializing her in the Panteão da Pátria (National Cemetery) among national heroes.[264]

In sum, the work on Gonçalves has focused entirely on this novel. As with Zapata, the major focus is the questioning of harmonious myths of miscegenation in Latin America. Fanon informs this criticism. Common themes include Gilroy's Black Atlantic, maternity, intertextuality and comparative approaches, and meta-history in the tradition of White and Hutcheon are formal approaches.

With this bibliography in mind, I have chosen to focus on Zapata's notion of diaspora, both as a literary work for analysis, *Changó*, and as a theoretical intervention in the debates over the Black Atlantic and Afro-descent in the new millennium. I will now explain what the muntu and Nuevo Muntu are—Zapata's reinterpretation of Bantu philosophy to fit his revolutionary outlook for the diaspora. His theory will help us understand Gilroy and Gonçalves in a more inclusive way.

Changó and *Defeito*: Summaries

The following section is designed to make more manageable the 1,626 pages of black history that *Changó* and *Defeito* constitute. Both authors resort to this narrative extreme in order to fill the near silence in literature and historiography regarding how the enslaved actually saw the New World. In this way, they compensate for Latin America's lack of a slave narrative tradition, one of the Anglocentric bases for Paul Gilroy's *Black Atlantic*.[265] Historian James Sweet notes that most slaves were illiterate and whites did not find African cultures worthy of much commentary.[266] Pre-1800 documents in Brazil often succumbed to weather and insects, though the Inquisition records, alluded to in *Changó*, are rich in information, as Sweet shows.[267] While the enslaved Manzano told his story in Cuba and Mohamed Baquaqua escaped to Canada after living in Brazil, they are the only two enslaved black voices of the Afro–Latin American literary canon that lived and died before abolition.[268]

As Zora Neale Hurston's *Barracoon: The Story of the Last "Black Cargo"* (2018), shows, even the slave narrative tradition is limited. Its editor, Deborah Plant, shows that only three of the classic slave narratives (Equiano, Baquaqua, and Ottobah Cugoano) depict the ships of the Middle Passage and life on African soil in the barracoons filled with prisoners of war from the point of view who lived them.[269] Of course scholars of Latin America know Cudjo Willis, Hurston's informant, did not provide the last first-person account of slavery: Cuban Miguel Barnet's dialogue with Esteban Montejo in *Cimarrón* (1966) was a famous case, though its communist and Latin American contexts must be kept in mind.[270] Zapata, as a Latin American communist and aficionado of the Harlem Renaissance, no doubt drew on Barnet's ethnographic work and perhaps even earlier versions of *Barracoon* like the article

"Cudjo's Own Story" (1927), which previewed *Barracoon* but found no publisher after its completion in 1931.[271] Recently published, it invites comparison to *Changó* and *Defeito* since the protagonist was enslaved and he hails from Dahomey, where much of the latter novel is set. Both novels adopt the epic telling of enslavement like the African Griot, the role Cudjo/ Kossola plays for Hurston.

Changó el gran putas (1983)

In his preface, Manuel Zapata Olivella describes his work as five different novels.[272] These "novellas" are set in different historical/mythological times and places: Mythical Africa / Historical Slave Coast, Central America; Colombia; Saint-Domingue; Venezuela, Brazil, and New Spain / Mexico; and the United States. A glossary follows the novel. He hopes readers will realize, by the end of the novel, that black and Amerindian history is as much theirs as whites' (36).

The "Origins" novella has three parts (39). The first section lays out the origin myth and transcendental characters: Ngafúa, the griot (sacred storyteller), the Yoruba Orishas ("Loas" in Haiti), and deified ancestors like Kissi-Kama, the spirit that "narrates" through Ngafúa (41). Ngafúa claims that the seed of Africa in order for it to be reborn in the Americas (45). He invokes the unbreakable "knot" between the living and the dead (46). He names major Orishas (48). Odumare Nzare creates the universe (48). The first man and woman were Obatalá and Odudúa. They beget Aganyú and Yemayá (49). The latter is raped by her son Orungán and explodes, giving birth to fourteen Orishas, among them Changó (49–51). Ngafúa tells of Changó's prison and exile. The powerful Third Sovereign of Oyo condemns the muntu, his followers, to suffer the same punishment (55). Changó declared war on his brothers and made love to his sisters (water goddesses) (56). He is served by the warriors Gbonka and Timi (57). Changó conquers territory up to Lake Chad and the Sahara and unites the kingdoms of the Niger (58). But, jealous of his warriors, he has Gbonka and Timi fight to the death. Gbonka kills Timi and goes into exile (59). The victor is then crowned by the people at the behest of the immortal prophet Orno Oba (67). Changó is dragged into exile. He avenges himself by returning and expelling his followers (69). The muntu are marked in exile with the serpents of Tamin, associated with the god of pathways, Elegua (66). At the hands of the White Wolf, the muntu is enslaved and taken to the Americas, where the exiles will forge freedom for all (69–70).

The section "Slave Trade" is narrated in prose. It depicts Portuguese traders on the Slave Coast, including the fictitious governor Diago Dévora and the seaman Coutinho (84–86). Ezili is an African slave trader named for Yemayá. Nagó, Elegba's chosen one, leads an uprising (93). He evades capture until he is placed in a metal mask (96–98). The Portuguese Captain Muñís arrives. Muñís attempts to sexually assault Ezili, but she poisons him (107).

Nagó's leads a mutiny on the *Nova Índia* ship (108). The point of view is split, juxtaposing the ship's log, narrated by boatswain Ruy Rivaldo Loanda, with the point of view of Nagó's rebels (109–111). It is 1540, and Ngafúa's chief Nzynga Nbemba has rejected the ancestors for Christianity. Ngafúa and his comrades do not accept baptism. Ngafúa is *babalawo* (Vodou priest) of Ifá, so he can see the future (115). Sosa Illamba, daughter of Yemayá is among them (121). Kanuri Mai tells how the Muslims enslaved him, despite being a prince of Kanem (129). A priest attempts to drive the devil out of the slaves (132). The ghost of an Ijaw returns to torment Rivaldo, and they enter the Caribbean (133–134). Olugbala then tells the captives to rise up. Fearing a plot, the slavers hang Ngafúa (143). Near Hispaniola, the crew descend to the bowels of the ship to rape the women (140). The ship catches fire, and all perish (145–146). As the ship sinks, Sosa Illamba gives birth to the baby muntu. Nagó delivers the living child to Amerindian mothers on the coast.

The dead spirits reassemble the bodies of the enslaved and lead revolts throughout the Atlantic (151–153). The living cannot see the ship of the dead, but Domingo Falupo speaks with its spirits. His "grandfather" spirit is Ngafúa, who tells him that the destiny of the muntu in their new home is to have no peace until all are free (153–154). Domingo Falupo is summoned to help Potencia Bioho give birth.

The child's Christian name is Domingo, but he is called Benkos (156). Sacabuche is a protégé and interpreter to Pedro Claver y Minguella as he attempts to Christianize the enslaved of Cartagena de Indias (158–159). They discover a babalawo licking the buttocks of a young woman during a ceremony to celebrate Bioho. Melchor Acosta is a slaver (160). Father Alonso de Sandoval, alongside Pupo Moncholo, gives the African Domingo Falupo water as he dies. Two officials of the Inquisition arrive, the Inquisitor

Mañozca and his assistant Salcedo (162–163). Father Claver raises young Benkos at the seminary. Domingo Falupo interprets for Claver as he ministers to the suffering captives (166). The Inquisition interrogates and tortures Sacabuche, accusing him of following Bioho (168–170). Sacabuche tells Claver where Bioho is, the runaway village of Chambacú. Claver recognizes the king's midwife, Orobia. In Chambacú, the babalawo consecrates Bioho at age twelve (172–173). The Inquisition demands all heresies be denounced to them (176–177). Orobia Morelos supposedly denounces the heresies of the Africans. Orobia says she and her masters are good Christians (179–180). She says the enslaved did not plot to kill the whites in their ceremonies, which she witnessed.

The Inquisition adds her testimony to the case against Domingo Falupo / Capelino, the babalawo (181). Pupo Moncholo, free slave in service of Acosta and sentenced to hard labor for leading the rebellion, gives court testimony (166–168). He claims Acosta held orgies with enslaved women and the inquisitors. He supports his testimony with that of the historical Fray Sebastián of Chumillas.

On the eve of Palm Sunday, the maroons of Palenque and Rocha have been promised amnesty during Holy Week but will not come to Cartagena in peace (196–198). On Easter Sunday, the children of Yemayá (Africans) fill the city. The blacks decide to establish a pan-African kingdom in Cartagena. The babalawo crowns Bioho alongside his queen María Angola (201). The governor's troops invade the home and break Benkos's eye with a harquebus (201). Claver gives him the chance to repent of the babalawo's heresies (204). Sandoval is accused of allowing paganism to continue in Cartagena because of the superficial baptisms of Domingo Falupo (210). Despite his arrest, the enslaved can still hear his message (213). The Inquisition tortures Falupo to death (222). The dead slaves of the *Nova Índia* and Nagó join the slaves in revolt (227–228). Nagó frees Bioho from prison. He severs Orobia's tongue (231–232). Morelos poisons the wine Acosta and the Inquisitor drink. The slaves escape to Palenque, where Bioho reigns. Falupo burns at the stake until he flies away (236).

"Vodou Rebellion" opens with Toussaint L'Ouverture in prison at Fourt-de-Joux, France (242–243). He speaks with the spirit of Napoleon Bonaparte. Toussaint regrets aligning with France to fight the British (245–246). The recently dead Dom Petro becomes the "rider" of Bouckman, who speaks for him and marks the beginning of the muntu on the island. Bouckman predicts the Haitian Revolution. The mulatto woman Marie-Jeanne serves the recent arrivals from Paris and feels alienated from the Africans. She joins the slave rebellion (247–248). Ogún Ngafúa tells Toussaint of Bouckman, who arrives from Kingston. He is the coachman of Mister Turpin. In the spiritual realm, Orúnla is given the Ifá Boards, which allow him to see the future (250–251). Mackandal was the first African to teach captives to rebel. He flees the plantation of Lenormand de Mézy but is captured. The maroons cry that Mackandal has not died at his execution (253). King Hénri Christophe is a cook in Le Cap (255–257). He hears that the Black Codes will remain in effect despite their abolition by Louis XVI. Toussaint secretly reads the Enlightenment texts of his enslaver, Byron Lybertat. Mackandal appears after death and tells his followers Toussaint will lead them (259).

Marie-Jeanne seeks the body of her lover, Vincent Ogé, to bury him after the Ogé Revolt (259–260). The Vodou Life Force speaks for Bouckman and sings to the Amerindian and African Ancestors, saying the muntu will return to Changó (263–265). The maroons enact a ceremony to the god Damballah. Father Gallifet considers it heresy. The captives hate Master Le Jeunne, and they have poisoned him four times for torturing and killing his slaves with impunity. The ancestors tell Christophe that Sans-Souci will be his glory and his tomb (268). Mister Byron grants Toussaint his freedom in response to the Le Jeunne case (270–271). All leaders of the revolution gather at Bois-Caïman. Under torture, a slave reveals Bouckman's plot (273). Repressive violence breaks out. Jean-Jacques Dessalines makes Marie-Jeanne his aide (276).

The mulattoes fear the blacks will depose them with the whites (277–279). Bouckman leads the uprising. The rebellion spreads the entire island in four days. The dead join the fight, and Jean-François becomes leader of the maroons. Baron Samedi appears and demands white blood from Christophe to remain alive. Troops from France and Spain besiege Hispaniola (282). Napoleon sends Rochambeau and Leclerc to invade (284–268). Dessalines and Christophe fight to avenge Toussaint's death. Chief Caonabó joins the fight against the whites. Alexandre Pétion is the only great mulatto general of the revolution. Twenty thousand whites die and are fed to Baron Samedi. The more the blacks die, the more undead soldiers they have on their side.

Rigaud joins the fight on the Haitian side (288). The Bourbon king of Spain concedes the Spanish side to the French. Leclerc conquers Fort-Piccolet and takes no prisoners (295). Napoleon betrays Toussaint, saying he will grant peace to the island if he comes to France. The mulattoes demand their land and slaves from Dessalines, but he refuses and defends Toussaint's

Constitution (303–306). Dessalines invades the Spanish side without resistance. Only Santo Domingo, the capital, keeps slavery, and the mulatto conspiracy of Port-au-Prince distracts Dessalines. The latter's own men murder him. Baron Samedi visits Christophe in his palace. The Ferrière citadel begins to fall apart, destroyed by the dead (308–310). He unsuccessfully attempts to quell the uprising. Christophe commits suicide.

"Bloodlines" chronicles four heroes: Simón Bolívar, José Prudencio Padilla, Aleijadinho, and José María Morelos (9). First, the spirit of the Orinoco River visits Bolívar in the form of the manatee man Canaima, who is also Ngafúa (315). Bolívar calls him Nana Taita like his black wet nurse Hipólita and tells him not to go. A seer predicts Simoncito will liberate five nations (318–320). He also says the leader will not reach an agreement with his admiral José Prudencio Padilla to give everyone freedom. Simoncito's father dies and Hipólita raises Simón. Hipólita reminds him of his black grandmother, and that he has "mulatto blood." In the world of the dead, Hipólita and the Ancestors accuse Bolívar of saying he will free the enslaved but not doing so (322). They sentence him to close the wounds of Piar and José Prudencio Padilla, the black leaders he has executed.

Before Padilla was born, Nagó and Yemayá gave Padilla the power to preserve life, and he is born of Sosa Illamba (323–334). Padilla's indigenous grandmother takes him from Caribbean Riohacha, Colombia, after a manta ray stings him (328). Townswomen come to him at night for satisfaction but deny him in the daylight (330–331). Ultimately, he marries the sea.

Padilla becomes a cook on the ship *San Nepomuceno* and is treated unfairly for being black (330–333). Nonetheless, he guides the ship better than the captain, and the crew believe he is possessed. Padilla awakens as a sailor in the Royal Spanish navy. At Trafalgar, his captain, Churruca, dies. His crewmates surrender to the British, but he fights on and loses his illuminated eye. He earns a new "flag" or nation: his race.

The British take him prisoner (333–335). The British sell him as a slave. Abolitionist Thomas Clarkston visits him, and takes his testimony as evidence so that William Wilberforce can fight slavery in the British Chamber of Commons. Clarkston stops the sale, and Padilla returns to Cartagena (336–340). There, he sees the Spanish trading slaves with the Frenchman Louis-Michel Aury while fighting Napoleon's armies. Germán Piñeres gives him lodging. At the Playa del Arsenal, his dead admiral Churruca parades him before the blacks and mulattoes as the first of his color to wear the Spanish Armada uniform. The Mulatto Battalion sees him as Changó. The navy officials condemn him for using a weapon only allowed for a ship's captain.

His official takes the sword and accuses Padilla of conspiracy (340–344). Pedro Romero and Padilla meet with Germán. He claims the two mulattoes seem suspicious and smell of gunpowder. Germán plots to overthrow the Spaniards. Padilla proposes they abolish slavery, but the creole aristocrats disagree. The people rise up and expel the governor, creating a power vacuum. Padilla tries to organize the blacks, but they return to their posts as slaves the next day. Romero, who arms maroons, criticizes Spain for not ending slavery (346–348). Padilla rallies the poor black and mestizo troops under the Revolutionary Board. They invade the Inquisition Palace. Padilla regrets that he did not overthrow the aristocracy to achieve abolition. In Venezuela, only the free people of color rise up.

Padilla and Bolívar compete for the affections of an eighteen-year-old mulatto woman, Francisquita Romero, daughter of Pedro (349–352). Bolívar sings songs learned from captives. Padilla plays the drums to compete. Francisquita was a sugar-cutting slave in Cuba who wanted to escape to Haiti, where the blacks were free. Her mother was married in the church to an African-born slave from Puerto Rico. Romero has bought and manumitted her to marry her. A new woman appears on the dancefloor and Bolívar pursues her; it is his Nana Taita. Padilla runs away with Francisquita and they make love.

When the Independent Province of Cartagena is declared, Padilla takes the bay of Chispatá (352–355). Padilla's victories make his superiors jealous. The creole aristocracy makes a deal with Aury to escape with him when the Spanish attack the city. Padilla fights off the Spanish invaders in their last attempt to retake the continent at Maracaibo. His superiors never forgive his success.

In Jamaica, Padilla writes to Pabla Pérez (359–362). Piar and Bolívar are there with him, and they are all poor. Piar is a maroon leader from Guyana. The three compete for the hand of Pabla, who is twenty. Padilla wins. Aury conspires with them to liberate South America under Bolívar, but they need material support. Pétion is purging Haiti of Vodou. Pétion gives the rebels support, but he asks them to free the slaves (364). In Ocaña, Colombia, the Constitutional Convention members declare that the slaves are incapable of freedom, and they fear an uprising like the one led by Padilla to drive out the Spanish (368–370). He is the first black killed by firing squad in Bogotá.

The crippled sculptor Aleijadinho (Antônio Francisco Lisboa) illustrates the failed attempts at Brazilian independence at the turn of the nineteenth century. He beholds a church in Ouro Preto and the statues he made (375–377). Kanuri Mai, his ancestor, says he will sculpt him in his Christian images. The slave Januario aids Aleijadinho's diseased hands. Agostinho brings him food, but he works constantly. Foremen supervise the enslaved miners to ensure they do not steal bits of gold. They all find relief in Ocaria Mandioca's tavern and her captive women (378–379). The musicians sing against the loudmouth or "Fanfarrón" (Braggart).[273] Aleijadinho was once attractive and danced at Mandioca's. Januario dances capoeira. He tells his master of Ocaria's new slave woman, whom he will surely want to rent. Aleijadinho pays for her with gold from the Church.

The artist's African ancestor, Uncle Antonio, tells him of his mother's lament upon losing him (381–383). Aleijadinho's father wants to make him an esteemed priest, but his skin color limits him. His father's captive tells him of Africa. Aleijadinho hopes the Africa of his mother will reinvigorate his crippled limbs (385). Aleijadinho looks in the mirror and sees African facial traits nobody else can see.

Antônio complains that in Minas Gerais everyone suffers hunger for living only from gold (385–388). That is why slavecatchers explore land in search of wealth. He tells Aleijadinho that his grandmother was captured to fill the hunger of the men who led the gold rush. Antônio joins the Quilombo de Palmares. Palmares's leader, Zumbi, terrifies the locals and is considered the devil Exu. He calls the enslaved, the indigenous, and their offspring to live in freedom and till the soil. They reestablish the cult of the ancestors.

The doctor tells Aleijadinho that the Father Superior is concerned with his illness (388–390). There is an earthquake in Minas. Dead rebels appear and say they were hanged or burned. He learns of an Amerindian *pajé* (herbalist) that may heal him (392–396). The latter "baptizes" him in mud, and he awakens in the church, praying. His uncle offers to take him to the *macumba*, or Afro-Catholic healer. Agostinho reminds Aleijadinho that Tiradentes should come that night. Agostinho tells the enslaved Mauricio that not all the plotters are willing to liberate their captives. Tiradentes rails against the "Fanfarrón," governor of Minas. Mauricio says that unless slavery is abolished, the quilombos will not support the uprising. Aleijadinho celebrates his son with Joana Lopes and recognizes his African ancestors (399–401). Tiradentes is arrested in Rio de Janeiro. The conspirators are sentenced to hanging. Authorities execute Januario (403).

Priest José María Morelos leads a popular revolt during the Independence of Mexico after the execution of Miguel Hidalgo y Costilla (406–408). Nagó claims he rediscovers the lands born of Olodumare, called Anáhuac, since Africans discovered Mesoamerica before the Europeans. The Ancestors call out to Morelos. He sees the Virgin of Guadalupe. Morelos follows Yemayá. Morelos's mother, Juana, reveals the violence of the Church.

Nagó tells Morelos Changó has chosen him to redeem the blacks and Amerindians of Mexico (409–412). The Inquisition sentences Morelos for combining rebellion and religion and hiding Juan Nepumoceno, whom they accuse of witchcraft. Morelos calls for the abolition of racial castes; he claims sovereignty comes from the people, not God, and preaches national independence. The officials blindfold Morelos before the firing squad. Only on the day of his death does he discover his origin (among the Ancestors). The Chingada (Doña Marina) appears and tells him to stop shepherding mules and start being a fisher of men as a pastor (415).

Morelos is taught by the lawyer José María Izazaga. Morelos and Hidalgo, like the generals of Changó, join forces with the poor and oppressed masses to lead the struggle (420–422). Morelos has a job recruiting at the Black and Mulatto Company, but he does not like recruiting troops to kill his maroon brothers. He wants to be a deacon. Pope Clement XII prohibits blacks from being priests. Morelos sees the social contract as the law of the maroons.

Morelos longs to build a church to God and Guadalupe (423–435). The Church chastises him for living out of wedlock with the Amerindian Brígida Almonte and having a child, Juan Nepumoceno. Nepumoceno says he is illuminated by the syncretic Virgin of Guadalupe, which makes the rich fear an Indian uprising. The Virgin represents Quetzalcóatl, inventor of fire, for them. The mulattoes believe she is black. The Amerindian Jacinto Canek leads the Amerindians of Yucatán against the Fourth Provincial Counsel. He allegedly died alongside Hidalgo's troops. Quetzalcóatl gives Morelos his sword and the words to invoke the muntu.

The Ancestors of the slave ship give strength to the revolutionaries under Morelos (427). The Coronel Mariano Matamoros, a white with smallpox sent by Kanuri Mai, is the brightest sword of the army (428–429). Tata Gildo becomes the leader Hermenegildo Galeana, and the blacks Valeriano Trujano and Vicente Guerrero join him. Female soldiers fight and sing. They plan to take Mexico City. Royalists shoot Matamoros (432–435). Morelos begins to lose battles. Ambitious coronels betray Morelos because the

Royalists have divided and conquered them. The new Congress forces him to share power with his ambitious underlings. A traitor turns Morelos in to the Inquisition. Hidalgo taught Morelos that slavery should be abolished. The enslaved of Mexico's history since Cortés, including Ñanga (Gaspar Yanga), gather around Morelos and Hidalgo awards him a medallion with the Virgin of Guadalupe on it. They remain gathered until independence is declared.

Dying of fever, he calls for the lawyer Don Andrés Quintana Roo (435). He claims slavery must be abolished (436–437). Morelos grows larger than the house and the muntu outside call him "Generalísimo de América." By Morelos's time, the river of bloods has formed the Mexican people, all children of Yemayá.

"Ancestors in Combat" concludes the novel (9). While the Latin American portion of the novel was complex and nonlinear, the U.S. section is even more so. Images and the ideas of historical figures take precedent over advancing the plot, which is secondary to the gradual acquisition of a robust black consciousness by the privileged, intellectual Agne Brown and the working-class Joe Stephens. The plot is scattered by flashback and flashforward, making it perhaps the most cinematic novella.

Ngafúa calls upon Agne to remember the Orishas and her ancestors from the *Nova Índia* (443–445). He tells her Changó has chosen her to reunite the broken family of the muntu, now of mixed blood and strengthened by its suffering. She has been adopted as a child by the white Reverend Robert. Men lynch her birth father, Timothy Brown, for reportedly having relations with a mad white woman. In actuality, she obliged him to please her (446). Though adopted by a white, Protestant minister, she uses the pulpit to preach to the black and revolutionary *ekobios* that they must rise up (448–450). At Columbia University, Agne meets with Professor Harrington, an Africanist anthropologist. She once saw his curio treasures as objects of study but now feels them as part of her identity. She reveals to him a plan to have the African diaspora and the oppressed reborn through the Worship of Ancestors and Shadows. Harrington dismisses it. Zaka, her first African ancestor buried in America and Nagó's protégé, is adopted by the Seminole Wild Cat (452–453). Zaka was brought as a captive to South Carolina (453). Zaka is marched to Georgia to aid in the Seminole Wars.

In Lawrence, Kansas, Agne struggles to recall her African past, personified by her lost birth mother (457–459). She hints that she is the illegitimate child of a black woman in Atlanta. Agne was "whitened" by leaving the South. Aunt Harriet, who is white, has a scattered family, so she cares for Agne. But she associates her with the staff (461). Susan becomes Agne's new, white sister.

A detective questions Dorothy Wright at home about the Worship of Ancestors and Shadows while Agne is in jail (462). Agne is arrested for polygamy and prostitution (465–468). In jail, Malcolm X visits her to offer legal aid. Agne accepts when she sees Malcolm die in the future and, beyond death, release her.

Zaka escapes New Orleans with other blacks, but they are captured (469–472). Booker T. Washington defends himself from critics of his visits to leaders of the United States and Britain, saying he is still the son of a slave. He goes to Tuskegee and teaches mothers to read alongside their children.

Agne is looking for Joe when the ancestors call out to her (476–479). She meets Dorothy and joins the Ancestor Cult. She sees Sojourner Truth and Harriet Tubman. Dorothy says Malcolm is her son, killed last August. Seeing the image of Dorothy's father, hanged, causes Agne to recall her own father's death. The abusive Johnson Robb buys Zaka in Mississippi. Zaka kills him. Zaka tells Agne the Americas are hers, so she can share it with the White Wolf but not let it destroy her (482).

Lawrence, Kansas, is founded like Minas (482–485). Masked men burn he integrated church of Agne's stepfather, but white Polish women say the black Muslims that meet there at night did it. Agne studies at the New School. The Black Scorpions, the black Muslims, and the Student Non-Violent Council (SNC) speak out against discrimination. Agne preaches integration against Marcus Garvey's black purism.

Zaka / Wild Cat calls out to Agne at the Fortín Negro (Fort Mosé) (490–491). Zaka hides in Fortín Negro alongside Amerindians. Andrew Jackson attacks the fort, killing innocents.

Joe and Agne embrace after a long separation (493). They make love. Agne assists Harrington at the Natural History Museum in New York, cleaning African artifacts. Hoping to frighten Dorothy, she puts on a Changó mask and is filled with his spirit.

Nicholas Biddle inspires enslaved Africans to fight in the Civil War (495–499). Malcolm claims blacks are children of god like the black Muhammed. Joe is accused of carrying weapons and is interrogated for killing people who died before he arrived in Harlem. Agne seeks Joe's tender soul, which he hides from the cruel whites. Joe sees her as whitened.

Nat Turner promises the blacks of Virginia a New Jerusalem (500–501). Turner and his men killed sixty-six whites. In Chicago's Red Summer, a thousand black families see their homes burned. Blacks fight back, dying and killing whites, but 3,436 blacks were lynched (502–505). The whites of the South fear another Haiti. Turner discovers the serpents of Legba as an eclipse tells him Changó supports his rebellion.

Marcus Garvey meets Langston Hughes (505). Joe becomes a banjo performer (508–510). Richard Allen founds the African Methodist Episcopal Church in Southampton, Virginia. The slaves conspire to revolt, but George Boxley fears a woman will betray him, which occurs, resulting in six hangings.

Anton, Agne's father, builds their house from a tree with two souls and is hanged from it (513–516). A woman from Omaha rejects the redheaded Christ and is called to hear Garvey speak. The spirits and the dead celebrate alongside Malcolm as Garvey rides down Lenox Avenue in New York. Hughes reads a poem to Africa at the Garvey rally in Madison Square Garden, where the latter says that the ekobios will have a free Africa "here" in the United States. Joe cleans at Lawrence College alongside the racist Ernest (517–518). Jonathan, a white coworker, thinks Joe is a Nazi, but black ancestors protect him.

Agne and her classmates protest and bar Dr. Harrington from his classroom and demand black professors (522–523). The police attack the protest. Agne recalls being taken to school with her white sister Susan amid racist demonstrators. Susan abandons Agne in the tumult (526–527). Supported by Reverend Robert, Agne grabs Susan and goes to class.

Nat escapes from his masters and searches for his father (529). Nat performs a Vodou ritual like Bouckman. He sees the red eyes of the Sons of Changó: Gabriel Prosser, Denmark Vesey, his father, and Changó (531–532). His father tells him to lead his rebellion and seek the New Jerusalem, not him. Susan moves west, and Reverend Robert moves to New York, as does Agne. She seeks Joe in Harlem, but he finds his white, red-haired "woman" and gives her a letter from Aunt Anne (535–536). In 1963 W. E. B. Du Bois dies in Accra and a year later is reborn as Malcolm X, who then returns to America. Du Bois tells Agne that life is an eternal return to the future. From Niagara, Du Bois tells Agne the Ancestors have chosen her to lead the muntu.

The muntu's destiny is to remake humanity (537–539). Turner tells of reaching his Jerusalem by resisting slavery and even saving poor whites. He prophesies that women and children will lead the revolution after him. Sojourner Truth takes the lead, arguing for her son to be returned to her.

Susan comes to New York (540–542). Susan convinces Agne to find Joe. They go to the West End Blues bar to hear him. Frederick Douglass speaks to Agne Brown (546–547). He saw a fellow slave commit suicide, which inspires Frederick to fight for freedom.

Shields Green is hanged alongside John Brown (550–552). Brown laments that Douglass did not join him. Harriet Tubman tells Agne her grandmother Margaret is alive (554–557). Margaret Gardner, the woman who escaped Kentucky for Ohio only to kill her children when slave catchers arrive, cries out to Harriet and claims death is a form of freedom. Gardner tells Agne that she is alive in her. Joe's mother, Agne's "Aunt" Anne, fears for his father, Joseph, in World War II. Austerity leads to the closure of Joe's school in Atlanta, so they go to Lawrence, where Joe works in a factory instead of going to school. She tells Joe to take her to the river secretly (562).

After the Civil War, blacks are submitted to the slavery of wages (569–571). The Freedman's Bureau does nothing to stop myriad abuses of blacks. Twenty-two blacks are elected to the U.S. Congress before 1901. Blacks are murdered and terrorized by the Ku Klux Klan and the White Camellias. The cities of the North open their slums to blacks. Du Bois was deaf to the African Legions of Marcus Garvey.

The black socialists who fight for an equal society for all races are the leaders who bring to fruition the freedom that Changó predicted from the beginning (572–574). Garvey buys the old coal/oil ship *Yarmouth* for his fleet. Embargos make the *Yarmouth* a prisoner of its former white owners. The government deports Garvey to Panama. Later, he goes to the Antilles (575–576).

Anton, a black Olmec, tells Agne of his past (576–578). His owner, Molineux, explodes his fists as a boxer as Tom, the Black Beast. In England, he defeats the blonde Tom Cribb to become the greatest boxer in the world. He returns to Virginia to purchase Joe's mother and have free children. Joe is released from prison and joins the National Maritime Union (578–580). Johnny Navajo, who is in the union with Joe, tells him he killed two guards on the Indian Reservation in Arizona. Joe's father shadow died at the Front in Madrid with the Foreign Legion.

The ancestors debate black liberation. The followers of John Brown recall Harper's Ferry (581–583). Nat Turner sits far from Martin Luther King, Junior. Like Brown, King is willing to die for his ideals, but he preaches nonviolence. Malcolm X calls for the violent elimination of all the oppressors. Garvey and his generals surround John Brown and claim that whites cannot liberate blacks; quite the opposite. Turner claims disillusionment with white-led liberation projects. Booker T. Washington disagrees, stating blacks must build their own society through utilitarian technology (584–586). Douglass insists slavery and injustice can be overcome without bloodshed. Zaka translates for Wild Cat, who adds to the polemic the whites' oppression of other peoples and the Mother Earth. Brown grabs his gun alongside the Black Scorpions.

Activists enter conflict over race. Youth march for Black Power, not just for equal rights (586–588). A tank driven by a Klansman appears, and John Brown says he is ashamed of his race and cries to the *ekobios* (brothers) that any form of slavery is an abomination to God. All the shadows realize that their powers to act are limited to the willingness of the living to take action.

The World War has cost Aunt Anne her husband's life and her son's education (588). Joe feels crushed when his employer lays him off. She goes to see Joseph's former commander (591). She refuses to let the army send Joe to the front like his father. Father shadow directs Joe to the court of honor. Aunt Anne has died. The Black Working Class Council convenes in Cincinnati, a center for the Underground Railroad (594). Joseph Curran, president of the National Marine Union, joins the others. Joe Hill, union leader, is killed in Salt Lake (596–597). William Painter, president of the Wales Mineral Workers Union, sings to Paul Robeson. Like in the days of Joshua, the walls of the prison fall. Agne's shadow father communicates with the Afro-Hispanic leaders of the past. The spirits deliver Agne from her cell and bring the dead and Joe Stephens to her.

Blacks were leaders in the U.S. Midwest and seek freedom there alongside Amerindians (600–604). African Americans fought in in the military despite discrimination. Father Shadow (divine Ancestor) reminds Agne that blacks have always struggled to defend the American soil and that no part of America, Africa, or elsewhere will be free while there is still a single oppressed person, black, white, or Amerindian (607).

Protesters cry for the release of Agne (608–611). Prudence, who killed her children, and Zelma Wallcot appear. They cry for Agne to free them. Sosa Illamba's shadow light dissolves the walls. Agne walks out to the streets of Harlem. Forty thousand souls gather at the Temple of Shadows along with Joe and Aunt Anne, who also see the soul of Joseph, Joe's father. Alongside Dorothy, the souls contemplate the muntu's future.

The Harlem Renaissance imagines a future for Afro-descendants in the United States. There are three variations of reaching freedom: art, war, and *mestizaje* (mixture) (614–616). Agne claims the Harlem Renaissance should be a return to African roots. Gladys Bentley and Bessie Smith sing. The slums burn in Watts and elsewhere (620–621). Agne's church, where she preached resignation, has fallen down. Joe rescues her from the flames and tells her to preach to their own group.

Malcolm tells Agne of his pilgrimage to Mecca, which made his vision more cosmopolitan and inclusive (621–624). He speaks in Cairo, stating that blacks' fight will no longer be limited to the United States. He sees his face broken into thirty-two countries and claims that when he speaks of African Americans he is also speaking of Africa. He says the United States is worse than South Africa because it hypocritically preaches integration while finding new ways to kill blacks. He feels solidarity with white Muslims. The Union leaders of the Civil War did not liberate the enslaved. African Americans insisted on fighting and on rebuilding the nation (626).

Agne evolves. As a schoolgirl, she always had to act white even though the white children insulted her black identity (626–628). She learned how to carry herself among whites, and she hears that black oppression is a lie made up by insane white liberals. Agne invites Garvey to A'Leia Walker's house to provoke conflict, since Garvey turns the poor blacks against the intellectuals of Harlem.

Malcolm visits Paris, but his hosts betray him and they trap him in the airport (631–633). The spirits say this is a false imprisonment, since his body is in Harlem, marked "anonymous." In the Audubon Ballroom, Malcolm preaches that Hell is life without justice or equality. As Malcolm is shot, he sees King, Turner, and Garvey (634–635). The Jamaican preaches to the muntu that the days of disunion are passed and that he lives only to gather the family of the muntu; only that way will Changó's society be built, one in which all races will call each other brothers, reunited with their bond to the dead.

Marchers of all races, the family of the muntu, crying for peace, not war, gather around the Washington Monument (635–637). Joe joins them and burns his draft card. King's calls for peace are a late echo of the violence of the two hundred thousand marchers in Washington while the Jim Crows circle the protesters. Garvey distributes weapons among the Black Scorpions. The white troops wear gas masks, but black fighters surround the White House and the "Octágono" (Octagon, Pentagon). Joe protests by burning his uniform but keeping his weapon (638–641). The police arrest him. He compares the prison to the slave ships. The prison unites them, while the slum divided them through crime against one another. They have stopped being rats to become political prisoners. Joe sends a message via the memory of another prisoner to Agne. He tells his lover Agne not to worry about him. He communicates with the others via field hollers. He is arrested for sending coded signals to the protesters via his banjo music. Malcolm lies in the Temple of Shadows in Harlem. Malcolm tells Agne she is Sosa Illamba, who gathers in her breast hundreds of millions of murdered blacks. The muntu fill the temple.

The conclusion is a gathering of spirits in battle. Sosa Illamba wraps Malcolm's body (641–643). Nagó claims that black indecision has cost too many lives. Kanuri Mai appears surrounded by artists and thinkers of the Harlem Renaissance. Olugbala gives strength to the muntu from those who died in battle. The African American revolutionaries and allies join the heroes of Latin America. Antonio Maceo gives Malcolm his sword for action, and Garvey gives him sandals to walk the earth uniting the muntu. Malcolm hopes his ashes are the gunpowder of Changó's revolution (644–645). From his legs spout the baobab tree. Changó emerges and chastises the muntu for delaying in liberating themselves.

Um defeito de cor (2006)

The novel is narrated from Luísa/Luiza Mahin to her absent son, Luís/Luiz Gama, as one long letter. It is divided into ten chapters, a bibliography, and a prologue.[274] The latter describes how Jorge Amado's writings inspired her to leave São Paulo for Itaparica and Salvador to write on the enslaved Malês. She visits Dona Clara in Almoreira, whose son, Gérson, is drawing on the torn pages of Luiza's life story, which is the novel (14–15).

Kehinde is born in Savalu, Dahomey (19). She and her twin Taiwo live with her mother and grandmother. They were born after Kokumo, who was an abiku, or child "born to die." King Adandozan's warriors rape and kill her mother, and they molest Kehinde and her sister (22–23). They kill Kokumo. Kehinde, Taiwo, and their grandmother are moved to Ouidah (26). There they live with a woman named Titilayo, whose daughter is Nilaja, whose granddaughter is Aina, and whose grandson is Akin (30). White men arrive and ask to purchase them from a *chachá* (viceroy), Francisco Félix de Souza (38–39). The three are forced onto a ship and go through the Middle Passage. Before departing, they meet the captive Tanisha. Taiwo and Kehinde's grandmother die (61–63). They arrive in Bahia at the Ilha dos Frades, where they are cleaned, fed, and baptized.

Though Kehinde flees her baptism, she assumes Tanisha's Christian name, Luisa, when she is sold in Salvador (72). José Carlos purchases her and takes her to his plantation on Itaparica, where she is a house slave (74). There, Kehinde meets the *sinhá* (mistress) Ana Felipa and her stepdaughter, the *sinhazinha* (young mistress) Maria Clara (76–79).[275] Maria Clara's mother, Angélica, has already died during childbirth. In Itaparica, Eufrásia mentors Kehinde. Tico and Hilário, captives, are her playmates. She learns of Nega Florinda, a free person of color who is famed for her wisdom and storytelling (89). Ana Felipa miscarries (89, 99). Kehinde meets Fatumbi, a Muslim slave and tutor to Maria Clara (91–92). Kehinde observes the lessons and learns to write. Ana Felipa, after learning that her slave Verenciana was impregnated by the *sinhô* (enslaver), cuts out the woman's eyes with a knife (106). She puts Verenciana's eyeball in José Carlos's food (110). She blames Kehinde for her miscarriage, and sends her to the *senzala grande* (field slave barracks) to work processing sugar (104).

Kehinde and the others are treated like animals, particularly by their foreman, Eufrásio (115–117). They strip a beached whale for oil. There, she learns of the love affair between Belchior and Felicidade (119). Eufrásio chokes to death on meat, possibly cursed by the slaves (126–127). Nega Florinda takes Kehinde to town. She attends a ceremony with Vodou priestess Maria Mineira Naê, who was called Agontimé when she was one of king Agongolo's wives in Dahomey (131). King Adandozan enslaved her, fearing her connection to Voduns (spirits). In Brazil, she escapes and travels among the quilombos of Bahia and Maranhão, where her fellow *jejes* (Fons) live (133–135). She gives Kehinde an Oxum statue. A new foreman arrives at the senzala grande, the mulato Cipriano (137). Kehinde works on the *botada*, where sugar is harvested and processed (139, 148–149). *Quilombolas* (quilombo residents) aid an escape attempt (144). Now she is a "mature" (twelve-year-old) young woman with breasts and a menstrual cycle (160). José Carlos has her returned to the *senzala pequena* (house slave barracks) and the kitchen of the *casa-grande* (plantation home) to "protect" her from the blacks (152–153). In the senzala pequena, the fellow slave Lourenço saves her from the enslaver's advances. Kehinde befriends Lourenço (154–155, 165). Maria Clara tells Kehinde that she will soon marry a law student, José Manoel (163). José Carlos rapes Kehinde and her male friend, then has Lourenço castrated (171–172).

Kehinde learns that José Carlos has impregnated her, and she names her son Banjokô (173). The slaves take their vengeance by placing a snake in José Carlos's bedroom, which bites his penis, making it rot as he dies (174–177). Ana Felipa sells the plantation and moves to the capital with Kehinde (185). Luísa gives birth to Banjokô Ajamu Danbiran/José and has him named officially by Baba Ogunfiditimi (203, 208, 213). As punishment for leaving the house for a ceremony, Kehinde is rented out to a British family in Salvador, the Cleggs (212–213). Her son remains with Ana Felipa.

Her new "renter" is Joseph Edward Clegg (213). Kehinde is well treated and well liked by his family, and the sinhá raises Banjokô (221–223). Concerned for her son's spiritual health, Kehinde leaves the Clegg's home at night to watch her son sleep. She is arrested and the Cleggs return her to the sinhá (228).

Luísa falls in love with Francisco and sleeps with him, beginning a healing process after her rape (236–238). Francisco takes her to a meeting at the Ladeira do Taboão between black slaves and free people of color, a mutual aid society with a lawyer that helps with manumission. Esméria negotiates with Ana Felipa on Kehinde's behalf, and the latter is made a wage slave who can sell cookies, pay her master, and save money for manumission (241–243). Tico and Hilário introduce her to the black streets. After being expelled by the sinhá, Kehinde lives with *padre* Heinz, an abolitionist priest (245, 252, 255–256). She meets the Muslim slaves of the sinhá and the Cleggs, who are educated and make seditious plans at Friday night meetings (258–261). She lives with *alufá* (leader) Ali and his family in the Muslims' store.

Kehinde begins selling cookies to her patron Amleto, a mulatto who was left in charge of a baron's estate. Kehinde and Francisco make love in the sinhá's bed while she is gone (272). The sinhazinha returns from Portugal married to José Manoel, who is now a lawyer (276–277). Padre Heinz allows Luísa to read at his library. An escaped slave, Jacinto, hides at the Heinz residence, a refuge for escapees (279–281). She meets Jacinto, who is fleeing the recently "pacified" Quilombo do Urubu (Buzzard Quilombo) (281–282). She learns that quilombos are communities that aid one another, even when the members are dispersed. She views religious syncretism as a defense among blacks against the white Catholics (290–292). Tico and Hilário become her deliverymen. Padre Heinz, Fatumbi, and Kehinde form a school for children of the poor, primarily blacks.

Following another jeje (Fon) woman, Kehinde joins a Catholic sisterhood (297). Francisco, confounded by Kehinde's alliance with padre Heinz, ends their relationship (302). The sinhá spends much time at the royal court in Rio (308). Baba Ogunfiditimi warns Kehinde that Banjokô will soon die, since he has lived five years without completing the necessary ceremonies for his survival (314–317). Kehinde celebrates with her friends. She forgets her worries, but she also forgets to perform the ceremony on Banjokô. He almost swallows a needle.

Upon learning that the sinhá plans to move to Rio, Kehinde decides to purchase her and Banjokô's freedom (328). The Catholic sisterhood asks her to wait for their aid, but the situation is urgent (336). Kehinde asks the sinhá for her and Banjokô's manumission price, and is concerned that she will be unable to pay (341). She has a vision in which she sees the snake that bit José Carlos's penis and throws her Oxum statue at it. The snake disappears, but she sees gold and jewels flowing from the vagina of the statue, which she can sell (343). She and the other slaves plot to obtain their letters of manumission (345–346). They plan to escape to Minas. Francisco seduces the sinhá and drugs her with marihuana. He then threatens her with revealing their secrets to the padre Notório and forces her to hand over the letters (348–349). Esméria tells Kehinde that she (Kehinde) is pregnant by Alberto, a white man originally from Rio who buys her cookies.

Kehinde and Banjokô go to live with Alberto on his farm and notifies him that she is pregnant (352–356). He gives Kehinde her own house there. Kehinde meets his freed slaves, João Badu and Zola, whom she employs. The sinhá departs for Rio (360). Kehinde miscarries (368–370). Luísa invites Fatumbi to be her business partner, and they invite Sebastião, Felipe, and Rafiki to work for them for wages. José Manoel agrees to support Kehinde's business because they both love the poetry of Luís de Camões. Tico and Hilário buy their freedom (373–375). Wanderers, Jongo and Adriano, show up on the farm, and Kehinde takes them in. They appear to be gay (375–377). Alberto is jealous or indifferent toward Banjokô (377). Alberto impregnates Kehinde (381).

Luísa can now start a permanent and more extensive bakery in Salvador (385). Fatumbi disappears (389–391). Alberto names his child with Kehinde "Luiz" in honor of his Portuguese uncle. Kehinde learns from Aprígio, a black Muslim, of a slave revolt in Salvador, and fears for Alberto's safety. Kehinde learns that Fatumbi was traveling to Recôncavo, putting things in order for another uprising (394). Kehinde gives birth to Luís, and she has Baba Ogunfiditimi perform a ceremony name him Omotunde Adeleke Danbiran (404).

Independence-minded Brazilians are discriminating against the Portuguese, so Kehinde and Alberto change the bakery's name to Pão da Terra (Our Land's Bread) (419). Kehinde recounts the ascension of D. Pedro I and other issues related to Independence, including his abdication and replacement by D. Pedro II (420, 426). There are many independence and slave rebellions in Salvador and Recôncavo (Cachoeira and Santo Amaro) (421). The sinhazinha goes to live with Kehinde on the farm for her safety (425).

Alberto's drinking becomes more problematic and he fights with Kehinde about her friends and how she is raising their child (439). On July 5, 1832, Kehinde returns at night from celebrations for Independence Day, the last time she sees Alberto happy, and she, dressed in the sinhazinha's rich clothing, is surprised by two robbers on the road (445–447). Sebastião, a fellow free person of color, appears and distracts the robbers. Kehinde stabs one to death.

Alberto plans to leave forever (447–449). Kehinde discovers that he is engaged to a white woman. Kehinde divides the bakery with Alberto and goes to live in the rooms behind it (453).

Banjokô is eight years old and Luís is two (456–458). Alberto begins to take the boys for walks, unbeknownst to their mother. Alberto and Kehinde agree to rent out the half of the bakery belonging to Alberto and split the profits; Fatumbi gets Muslim renters for Kehinde (461–462). These renters recently arrived from Africa, and they play an important role in the Malês Revolt. Kehinde hears the voice of Kokumo, her dead brother, and perceives that Banjokô has died (466–467). She finds his body lying in a pool of blood and learns that he died from an accidental knife wound. Kehinde is afraid for Luís as well and falls into a deep depression (471–473). Alberto returns to comfort her.

Kehinde and the Muslims in the former bakery begin to produce cigars (474–476). Fatumbi works as secretary to *mala* Abubakar, a leader of the revolt. Alberto marries the snobby white woman, whom nobody likes. They call her the Ressequida (Dried Up Woman). On December 8, Fatumbi invites Kehinde to the Festival of Our Lady of the Immaculate Conception of the Beach, a Bahian church constructed in Portugal and dedicated to Santa Bárbara, whom the slaves identified with Yemayá, along with other local Christmas ceremonies (480–482). Jongo and Adriano feel a mutual distrust with the Muslims in the cigar business and move out (485–486). Kehinde participates in the washing of the steps at the Church of Our Lord of the Bonfim. Alberto reveals to Kehinde that he and his new wife no longer love one another (494–496). Tico and Hilário carry secret messages for the Malês. Kehinde has doubts about her own participation in the rebellion. She loves many whites and mulattoes (503–506). Padre Heinz restarts his advocacy for blacks, and he is shot in his sleep.

The police inspector and the master of the house disperse a planning meeting for the revolt, and mala Abubakar changes the date (512). The enslaved Sabina tells farm owners of the revolt to punish her husband, Vitório Sule, over a fight (524–527). The rebellion begins late at night. Following Manoel Calafate and Mussé, Kehinde and the Malês storm the streets, fight the police, free alufá Licutan, and take control of the city. Eslebão hides Kehinde in the Medical School (530). Fatumbi is killed (542). Kehinde is carried out of the school on a cart, pretending to be dead (535–538). Kehinde leaves with Luís, Esméria, Malena, Alberto, and the sinhazinha for Cairu, where they hide for two months. When the manhunt dies down, Kehinde returns to the apartment near the tobacco shop, disappointed that she can no longer legally hire Africans to work for her (546–549). The Ressequida kicks Kehinde out of her home and business. Alberto obtains a large sum of money and tells Kehinde to move out, even though Africans cannot own property.

Kehinde falls in love with a doctor, Jorge, who supports the sanitation law that provoked the Cemiterada (Cemetery Revolt) (558–560). In 1837, Kehinde attends a party and sees Alberto crying, perhaps out of guilt for selling Luís (563). Kehinde witnesses a police beating of an old man shouting "viva a República" (long live the Republic) and tries to give him medical care, but she is arrested (566–568). She escapes from prison, but she cannot be with her son in Salvador for fear of the police, so she returns to Itaparica.

In Itaparica, Kehinde dreams that she must take a jar to Nega Florinda (588). Kehinde travels to São Luís (593). She meets Agontimé and thanks her for the statue of Oxum, which was full of riches intended for the construction of the Casa das Minas, her spiritual center (596–597). Kehinde delivers the jar to Nega Florinda and continues her spiritual studies with Agontimé. Kehinde returns to Salvador for her son and Esméria (603–605), but she decides to leave them with Alberto and set out for Cachoeira to prepare a new home for them. She meets Kuanza, a ninety-year-old who wants her to find a way to publish the story of his father, which he has been carrying for eighty years (615–616). His father was enslaved at the Belém Convent, and his story would become José Saramago's *Memorial do Convento* (*Memorial of the Convent*, 1982).

Kehinde learns from Tico that Esméria and Claudina have died, leaving Luís in Alberto's care (630–631). Kehinde soon learns from José Manoel that Alberto has sold Luís. Following a tip from José Manoel, Kehinde travels to Rio de Janeiro in search of him (636).

She rents a room on the Rua do Ouvidor from a woman named Balbiana (639–641). She remains a slave by choice, because the fee she pays her mistress is low. Balbiana and her partner Juan's inn caters to Portuguese businessmen. Jundungo/Piripiri is an *angola* stevedore who lives there (644). Kehinde reads and writes for others in the neighborhood (655–656). Kehinde falls in love with Piripiri.

The Rua do Ouvidor is the Paris of Brazil (656). Piripiri shows her Rio, including a *roda* (fight) of "capueira" (capoeira) in the Morro do Castelo, where she meets the famous Mestre Mbanji (664–666). In 1841, Kehinde witnesses the coronation of Dom Pedro II (674–677). Kehinde opens a *canto* (food stand) with other *baianas*, and she must pay dues to her *capitã* (superior), Benta (681). Kehinde and Piripiri participate in a roda on Corcovado Hill (691). Kehinde meets Joaquim Macedo at the bookstore, and they become friends (699–701). Senhor Joaquim helps her to rewrite Kuanza's story.

Kehinde learns from José Manoel that Luís was sold in a Rio slave market (704–705). There, she learns that he was bought by a man from Santos. In Santos, she learns that he has been sent on to the capital of São Paulo (713). In the city, she stays in a boarding house in Campinas, where Luís had been a slave, but she learns that he has escaped (721). Disappointed and directionless, Kehinde departs for Uidá (727).

On the ship, Kehinde meets several other *retornados* (former captives returning to Africa) (731–735). Acelino and Fortunato dream of an idealized Africa. Vicente, nineteen years old, is Fortunato's son. Juvenal is married to Jacinta, and they have three small children: Tomé, Rosinha, and Ifigênia/Geninha. John is the father of Luís's half-siblings. He is a mulatto who boarded at Freetown, Sierra Leone, a colony of freed slaves established by the British.

She seeks Chachá de Souza's protection so that she can do business in Lagos (741–742). She heads for Ouidah, where her friends Akin and Aina live. Aina, whom she knew as a child, is now old (750). Kehinde and all successful *brasileiros* ("returned" Afro-Brazilians) in Ouidah see themselves as superior to the local *selvagens* (savages), and there are often violent conflicts (757).

John tells her they can invest in the arms trade, which was benefiting from African wars (759–760). With the money, she buys a house in Ouidah (764). In 1848, she has twins and rejects Aina's suggestion of African names (Zinsu and Sagbo), instead opting for Brazilian names: Maria Clara (like sinhazinha) and João (like John) (767).

She tells the story of the Portuguese Forte D'Ajuda (768–769). She becomes friends with its commander, who tells her to get the ear of Chachá, the advisor to King Guezo, who certainly helps her business. Kehinde and John buy a plot of land in Kotonu, near Ouidah (775–777). Kuanza's manuscript is lost. She meets Chachá (781). Kehinde renames herself Luísa Andrade da Silva when she must sign the deed to her new land (789). Selvagens attack Kehinde and Aina (795–798). Kehinde is reminded by a *bokonon* (priest) that she must honor the Voduns, so she builds them a room in her home.

Rafiki and Felipe come to Ouidah as retornados (returned "Brazilians") (803). Kehinde goes with Chachá and a group of slaves and associates of Chachá to visit King Guezo (809–810). Chachá dies of natural causes. Commander José Joaquim and padre José Maria leave the Forte D'Ajuda (818).

Isidoro, Chachá's brother, is appointed Chachá II; Antonio and Inácio receive secondary titles (840). Guezo plans to destroy Abeokutá with his army (844–848). Kehinde meets Domingos José Martins, a Spanish slave trader who has made lots of money trading with Lagos and has worked for Chachá I. He forms ties in Bahia. He then returns to Africa, where he meets Kehinde.

Guezo is the enemy of the king of Lagos, Kosoko. With Domingos, Felipe and Rafiki, Kehinde starts a construction business called Casas da Bahia that makes houses for retornados ("returned") in Africa (853–854, 862). They build a house for Domingos in Aguê (867). Suleimane, a Muslim slave from Brazil, returns to Africa to work for Domingos José Martins as a barber, but he also teaches the *ibêjis* to read (872–874). Geninha learns to read with them. A stranger abandons a baby at Kehinde's house, and she baptizes him Anônio Andrade da Silva (877).

King Guezo dies and is replaced by King Glèglè, who abandons relations with the Portuguese and Brazilians and aligns with the French (878). His Chachá (III) is Antônio de Souza. Chachá II dies and the Portuguese abandon the fort, which then goes to French missionaries, who start a school (879–881). The *ibêjis* (twins) go from the Muslim tutor to this school, along with Geninha and the house servants.

John dies of illness in 1862, and Kehinde moves to Lagos to raise her twins (884). João wants to be a farmer (888–890). Geninha is the one who is writing these letters down, since Kehinde is old and blind. João runs away to farm, but Kehinde reconciles with him. Kehinde sends Maria Clara to study in Paris with the help of Father Borghero in 1895 (898).

In 1899, she is already on the *Aliança*, headed across the Atlantic for Salvador with Geninha, who is writing constantly, by her side, and her twins are in Paris studying (911–914). Maria Clara studies philosophy and João is one of the first Africans to study at the École Poytechnique. Maria Clara becomes a teacher in Paris. Maria Clara and João return to Lagos (920–921). Maria Clara starts a school that integrates brasileiros (returned blacks) and selvagens ("savage" Africans). She marries a Frenchman (923–925). Kehinde finds a wife for João, and there is a double wedding ceremony, planned by Van-van. Political fighting between King Glèglè, France, Portugal, and England leads to the Brazilian community ending in Lagos (929–930). Selvagens defame Julião to Glèglè, and the king loses control of the territory after having his advisor executed along with his male heirs. Kehinde is in ill health (932). Kehinde discovers a forgotten trunk at the Casas da Bahia (Bahian Houses) with letters about Luís. He is found in 1877, and José Manoel has unsuccessfully tried to reach her (945–947). She learns from Maboke that she has been cursed for killing the man on the road and thus must die without ever seeing her son again.

1

Myth, Literature, and History in Zapata

As exemplified through their summaries, these Nuevo Muntu novels tell the history of slavery, have black authors, and tell the history of slavery from the enslaved's point of view. They show the fluid boundaries between myth, literature, and fiction, and national boundaries do not limit them. Like Gilroy's *Black Atlantic*, they trouble but do not abandon the notion of historical truth, especially when it comes to slavery, the transnational nature of the diaspora, and elements of non-Western worldviews that inform it. This chapter discusses Zapata's troubling of history and fiction and his rhetorical project to empower the diaspora through the written word. I begin with political and cultural influences on Zapata's Nuevo Muntu.

The Nuevo Muntu as an overlapping definition for the African diaspora and the Americas is tied to Zapata's identity as an Afro–Latin American writer. He spent years in the United States and was deeply influenced by U.S. black writers.[1] Therefore, his focus was on the Nuevo Mundo (New World), the land that Iberian explorers and settlers came to know. He is seeking the deepest roots for the continent Hispanics refer to as América. He is also trying to overcome the inherent injustices of slavery and colonialism, so he relies on the "New" aspect of a continent where Europeans forced Africans and the indigenous to form new identities. The indigenous are present throughout the novel as the allies of blacks, and the territory is clearly defined as belonging to them before the conquistadors, as is evident in the indigenous mothers that foster African explorers before Columbus arrives and the exploited indigenous characters of the novel's section on Mexico.[2] But the bulk of the characters are black, white, and mestizo, and the protagonists tend to be black. The play on words "Nuevo Muntu" does the diaspora justice by including the largest black population outside of Africa, Brazil, and the most studied population, that of the United States.

Muntu, Nuevo Muntu, and Changó's Curse

Influences

The term "Nuevo Muntu" is used in *Changó* three times. In "Origins" it announces the destiny of the diaspora.[3] The final time it is used is in describing the tears of the raped African mother of the New World, Sosa Illamba.[4] The author also wrote *Tambores para despertar al Viejo Muntu* (*Drums to Awaken the Old World*, n.d.), further exploring the oral history of the diaspora.[5] One could say that the Nuevo Muntu has not yet arrived, but that it lies in the hope of an awakening of the unity of the "three races" in a new consciousness that links the Americas.

Zapata drew on the Harlem Renaissance or New Negro Movement (ca. 1920–1940).[6] His novel is set partly in Harlem, which saw gatherings of the Pan-African Universal Negro Improvement Association of Marcus Garvey and the radical poetry of Langston Hughes. The poet was a friend and mentor of Zapata, who was inspired by his work to visit the author's apartment and stay with him for days.[7] They maintained correspondence afterward.[8] Zapata named his daughter "Harlem" due to his view that it was a "Mecca" of black freedom and expression.[9] Lucía Ortiz reaffirms the inspiration of the U.S. movement on Zapata's ideas of diaspora and muntu because they affirmed a black identity and rejected racism.[10] While I show that there is duality within black subjectivity in black experiences in the famous "double consciousness" theorized by W. E. B. Du Bois, the binary notions of race essential to U.S. segregation were a primary target of the movement. In short, in the context of the color line, blacks had to re-create culture and race.

Writer Alain Locke sought to define Harlem's cultural effervescence, a key inspiration for the "Nuevo Muntu," in "Enter the New Negro" (March 1925): "Subtly the conditions that are moulding a New Negro are moulding a new American attitude. . . . It will call for less charity but more justice; less help, but infinitely closer understanding."[11] Locke continues, "Harlem's quixotic radicalisms call for their ounce of democracy today lest tomorrow they be beyond cure."[12] The "New Negro" is a call for blacks to create their own cultural and political reforms in the United States beyond the North-South division, an expansion Zapata continues to the Americas.

The African American quotes Hughes's poem "Youth" (ca. 1924): "We have tomorrow / Bright before us like a flame. / Yesterday, a night-gone thing / A sun-down name. / And dawn today / Broad arch above the road we came. / We march!"[13] While the past is dark and violent, as the subtle allusion to "sun-down towns" where blacks were sometimes lynched after dark implies, the future is radically different in its progress toward justice for blacks and the Americas. The flame imagery for this struggle returns in the novel as the Yoruba deity Changó's fire, which metaphorically spreads through the Americas as blacks create ways to determine their own destiny. As Locke claims, the African diaspora began as captives but are at the vanguard of an international struggle for a universally just society—for blacks and all. Zapata and Hughes were communists. George Palacios claims he drew inspiration for his own transnational black struggle from the triumphs of the Chinese and Cuban revolutions.[14]

Zapata's focus on black folklore parallels the anthropological and fictional work of Zora Neale Hurston and likely bears her influence. She is represented negatively in the novel, though. She founds the polemic journal *Fire!!* (1926) alongside Hughes and other New Negro thinkers, but it lasted for only one issue before the offices were burned.[15] Like the novel, it depicts prostitution, interracial couples, queer sexualities, and, like the novel, popular black speech.[16] Hurston is taken to task for reportedly practicing phrenology in the tradition of eugenics.[17]

Nothing could be further from the truth. Unlike New Negro thinkers who sought to break with the slave past, she believed that preserving and understanding it would make for a proud future. She considered black folklore "the greatest cultural wealth on the continent."[18] As one can see in her "Characteristics of Negro Expression," she is theorizing, if in a limited fashion, U.S. black culture in order to give it visibility and respectability alongside other cultures. As a student of Frantz Boas, she is using cultural relativism to give dignity to people considered "primitive." She notes the mark of orality on black speech, which the novel exemplifies in the enslaved's testimonies and the songs of the griot Ngafúa.[19] Her portrait of black courting through male bravado evokes "verga de toro" (bull dick), Changó's haughtiness and promiscuity.[20] The novel's avant-garde language, such as the myriad African terms, could be called the "will to adorn" that Hurston sees in black homes and speech.[21] Blacks reject European renaissance ideals of harmony in dance and visual arts in favor of "angularity": the frequent use of flashback, the interruptions of poetry in prose, and the shifts in narrator in the novel exemplify this alongside the constant dancing of the characters from mythical Oyo to Colombia to Minas Gerais to Harlem.[22] "El Gran Putas" is a folk devil, a character from the Colombian analogue of African American folklore.[23]

The irreverent, sometimes grotesque and bawdy scenes in the novel, such as seduction, rape, and torture, exemplify the "absence of the concept of privacy" in its irreverence toward puritan censorship in the U.S. and Catholic guilt in Colombia.[24] Joe Stephens, a self-described "New Negro," performs jazz in a juke.[25] Like Hurston, Zapata shows no shame in recounting not only the illiterate past of Afro-descendants but also the horrors of slavery that inform her vision of the New Negro but that do not limit him/her/them to a plantation past. Just as she is not ashamed to eat watermelon with an illiterate man and treat him like a griot, Zapata is proud to recount the tales of black heroes of both privileged and lower classes, be they workers like Joe or kings like Christophe.[26] Like Hurston's pioneering work *Tell My Horse* (1938) and her criticism of the U.S. occupation of Hispaniola, he sees Haitian Vodou and its revolution as a precursor to the New Negro and a future greater revolution.[27] He also connects Vodou to African American life beyond New Orleans, as she does in *Their Eyes Were Watching God* (1937), which personifies the deity Ezili as Janie, a twentieth-century black settler in Eaton, Florida.[28]

Zapata also had inspiration closer to home in Cartagena. The poetry of Jorge Artel is an important inspiration for the Nuevo Muntu. Artel published a book of poems, *Tambores en la noche* (*Drums in the Night*, 1940), which underwent several revisions and defined him as a poet.[29] Prescott considers Zapata Artel's heir: "elevating and promoting *costeño* [of the three cultures of the coast: Afro-Euro-Amerindian] folklore, reestablishing African nexus, and bringing about an integration of the costal, the African, and the indigenous with the nation's other regions and peoples to ensure an authentic and whole national identity."[30]

Ortiz traces the combination of black pride and *mestizaje* (mixture) in literature directly from Artel to Zapata.[31] Rodolfo Guzmán Morales notes that Artel's poetry is marked by "orgullo en la herencia africana, resistencia social, sensualidad creativa y optimismo para el future" (pride in African heritage, social resistance, creative sensuality, and optimism for the future).[32] Luisa García-Conde argues that though Artel is considered Afro-Colombian, he self-identified as *indomulato*, a mixture of indigenous, European, and African elements.[33] This aesthetic is present in his poetry, and it would be appropriated by Zapata in his vision of the African diaspora as being united with the indigenous by the history of resistance to colonialism.

In Zapata's "Artel, el maestro" (Artel, the Great, 2006), he reminisces on his inspiration. The novelist saw Artel as a rupture with Colombia's other well-known black poet, Candelario Obeso (1849–1884), whose work he called a "merienda cotidiana" (daily snack) for a mulatto elite that denied their blackness.[34] Artel used blackness to foment the overthrow of oppressive structures. His poetry retells oral histories of the black Cuban rebel Pedro Romero and José Prudencio Padilla in Cartagena.[35] They reappear in *Changó*.[36] His "La voz de los ancestros" (The Voice of the Ancestors) speaks of slaves who committed suicide and rebelled against their captors as models for black rebellion in the twentieth century, a rejection of "masks" and alienation.[37] There is a hierarchy of cultural influence in Zapata's work that echoes Artel's: "Aunque en su alma rezongue el llanto indígena de la gaita, y la guitarra española le rasgue el corazón, su credo es africano" (Though in his soul moans the cry of the Amerindian flute and the Spanish guitar scrapes his heart, his creed is African). The enslaved ancestors he praises were free in Africa but will also fight for freedom in their new homeland:

¡Negros de nuestro mundo,
los que no enajenaron la consigna,
ni han trastrocado la bandera,
este es el evangelio:
somos—sin odios ni temores—
una conciencia de America![38]

(Blacks of our world,
Those that did not leave the slogan behind,
Nor those that have switched the flag,

> This is the gospel:
> we are—without hatred or fears—
> an awareness of the Americas!)

Zapata sees in Artel a focus on "una nueva raza que nace en América" (a new race that is born in the Americas).[39] In the only book on Artel, Prescott notes his impact on his student Zapata, who would go on to popularize his work.[40] Prescott considers Artel's "Poema sin odios ni temores" (Poem without Hatred or Fears) to be a precursor to *Changó*'s ancestral memory.[41] It maps the African diaspora throughout the Americas.[42] Zapata sees Artel as a melting pot of cultures like his native Cartagena: "el Renacimiento Negro de Harlem, los negristas antillanos, los primeros alaridos de Cesaire, Senghor y Damas" (the Harlem Renaissance, the Antillean negristas, the first cries of Cesaire, Senghor, and Damas).[43] These inspirations were combined with Latin American Marxism, as in Zapata's own case:

> Sin perder el ancla de los ancestros, Artel va sumando los retos sociales que le plantea la ideología del proletariado. Se sabe poeta y combatiente y más allá de la crítica que impone falsas fronteras entre la emoción y el ideal, no vacila en martillar el poema con claros mensajes de liberación: Martí, Lenin, Fidel, el "Che." Son apenas los cuatro puntos cardinales que orientan la cimarronería (sic) de los nuevos tiempos.[44]
>
> (Without losing the ancestor of the ancestors, Artel adds the social challenges that the ideology of the proletariat sets before him. He knows he is a fighter and a poet and farther from the critics that impose false barriers between emotion and ideals; he does not hesitate to hammer out the poem with clear messages of liberation: Martí, Lenin, Fidel, "Che." They are only the four cardinal points that orient the marronage of our times.)

While none of the four leaders appear in the novel, it is clear that "marronage" means the same thing for Artel and Zapata: a continual black-led struggle from colonial times to the Cold War, which was still raging when the latter published *Changó*.

Ernesto "Che" Guevara's (1928–1967) *El socialismo y el hombre en Cuba* (*Socialism and Man in Cuba*, 1965) lays out a plan for creating a political and psychological "hombre nuevo" (new man).[45] Zapata is creating a "Nuevo Muntu" (New Man). Zapata aligned with the Cuban Revolution, as is evident in its granting him a Casa de las Américas "honorable mention" in 1963, partly for his criticisms in *Chambacú, corral de negros* (*Black Slum*) against U.S. imperialism and exploitation of blacks.[46] Zapata opens his final autobiography, *¡Levántate mulato!* (1990), rhetorically asking himself if he is "¿Híbrido o nuevo hombre?" (A hybrid or a new man?).[47] He is delving into the greater question of his race and identity, which he found in a Marxism revised to liberate Afro-descendants.[48]

Guevara's new man, the Cuban and, eventually, world citizen of the future, is a product of the education and culture that complement reforms in the economic base. For him, Cubans were gaining a collective sense of duty: "el premio es la nueva sociedad donde los hombres tendrán características distintas: la sociedad del hombre comunista" (the prize is a new society where men will have distinct characteristics, the society of communist man).[49] They must express "su propia condición humana a través de la cultura y el arte" (their own human condition through culture and art).[50] This art must liberate the rebellious and define liberty through art that is a "weapon" of denunciation. This art, while communist, should not fall into the mimetic tradition of nineteenth-century "realismo a ultranza" (realism by force) yet embrace formalistic innovations that look to creating a new citizen. One can see the socialist realism of *Chambacú* fall away in *Changó*, which embraces the poetic language of the muntu, a mixture of Bantu and Western worldviews. While Locke and Hughes were creating black citizens through art in a U.S. capitalist context, in the midst of revolution Guevara sets out to make the new humanity of the twenty-first century. Zapata synthesizes elements of Che and Locke: art that is aimed at creating universal liberation by helping to criticize and imagine alternatives to Western capitalism while placing the history of black struggle at its center.

He preceded thinkers like Cuban-American Odette Casamayor-Cisneros, who analyzes films by Sara Gómez and Nicolás Guillén Ladrián to show how they imagine a "New Black Subject" during the years Zapata was writing *Changó*.[51] In the tradition of José Martí, Guevara treats the new man as raceless in favor of national unity.[52] Following Ana Serra, Casamayor-Cisneros claims,

> Since the New Man served as a prototype for the rest of society, he could not embody someone perceived in the social imaginary as "primitive" or "ignorant." As a necessarily virile subject (even if the New Man were a woman), he should also be heroic and brave. Moreover, as a communist, he should be an

> atheist. . . . Cuban religions of African origin, which were considered uncivilized . . . did not factor into the values attributed to the New Man, a creature of the future responsible for leading revolutionary society toward progress.[53]

Zapata corrects these faults, making syncretic religions and black identity central to his revolutionary text. While his protagonists are mostly male, their lives are presented as a struggle to create a new Americas. They are making a Nuevo Muntu that has not yet arrived. He is already able to create this black New Man because he is not "censored or criticized by cultural authorities" as he would have been if he were in Cuba during this time like Gómez and Guillén Ladrián.[54]

Zapata, though a Marxist, is writing in the context of various black liberation struggles directly involving the African continent. As seen in the bibliography, Zapata was politically aligned with Frantz Fanon, whom he knew personally.[55] Zapata himself praises Fanon's theories designed to psychologically and culturally decolonize the African continent in an interview with Ja Johannes.[56] Ortiz reaffirms the importance of Fanon in Zapata's understanding of the transnational African diaspora and its need for liberation.[57] He tells of his affinity for Léopold Senghor in his interview with Krakusin, and Ortiz discusses the influence of the Senegalese thinker on Zapata's transnational vision of black culture and revision of Colombian culture.[58] Senghor's Négritude created a diasporic black identity through art centered on the shared experience of slavery and colonialism.

Zapata was, in some ways, an Afrocentrist, a concept I will revisit in my discussion of Gilroy. The influence of Cheikh Anta Diop is explicit in Zapata's essay *El árbol brujo de la libertad* (*Bewitched Tree of Freedom*, 2002).[59] Diop argued that the origins of civilization, Hellenized by white historians, were actually rooted in Africa, particularly Egypt, as Zapata notes.[60] Zapata mentions the great kingdom of Mali, following Diop's lead in arguing that Africa had sophisticated civilizations before slavery.[61] It is likely, given the African-centered intellectual circles in which Zapata moved in the 1960s and 1970s, that Diop was an influence on Zapata's "Nuevo Muntu."[62]

Zapata's inspiration by Marxist, anticolonial, and black movements is related closely to cultural production of the Tricontinental, which Anne Garland Mahler considers a Cold War precursor to today's political and cultural theories of the Global South.[63] The Tricontinental refers to a 1966 summit in Havana of representatives from Africa, Asia, and Latin America.[64] They had the common enemy of U.S. imperialism, and they commonly used Jim Crow laws as a symbolic microcosm of empire.[65] Garland Mahler traces the roots and aftermath of the ideology the attendees espoused, which for her begins with the U.S. intervention in Cuba's war of independence and culminated in the U.S. invasion of the island in 1898.[66] US racism and imperialism were in many ways one in the Spanish-American War: premised on the eugenic notion that nonwhites could not govern themselves. The conflict also exported Jim Crow laws to the Caribbean.[67] The U.S.-Philippine War and the invasion of Haiti and the Dominican Republic followed. By 1916 southern plantation owners were running much of Hispaniola.[68]

Garland Mahler shows that the U.S. Caribbean interventions led to African American movements and spokespeople, including W. E. B. Du Bois, promoting solidarity with the region. The 1898 victory led him to fear, in 1900, that the problem of the twentieth century would be a global color line spread by a white supremacist empire around the world.[69] Seeking political solutions, by 1915 Du Bois saw pan-Africanism as ushering in a solidarity of working classes across the globe against racism and empire.[70] This kind of union is what I call the Nuevo Muntu, and I believe Zapata's and, in a different way, Gonçalves's novels exemplify it.[71] Garland Mahler insists it is a global unity of subjugated peoples that "foregrounds and emphasizes the struggle of Afro-descendant peoples rather than one that forecloses race-based organizing and dismisses a focus on black political rights as divisive."[72] She contextualizes the Harlem Renaissance with other movements she refers to as *afrocriollo* movements (Richard Jackson's term), *negrismo* / *négritud* / New Negro, which flourished among black and liberal intelligentsia from 1920 to 1940.[73] For her, Garvey belonged to this moment as well.[74] They laid the groundwork for Fanon's anticolonial thought and cultural production of the Cuban Revolution. While likely influenced by it, the Nuevo Muntu is not synonymous with Tricontinental thought. Its reliance on the roots of oppression in colonialism and slavery place it closer to how Garland Mahler presents the *afrocriollo* movement/s since they focused on peoples colonized by Europe, not those negatively affected by capitalism in general.[75] It is like the Tricontinental in its rejection of biological determinist notions of race in favor of "abstract use of color to signify an ideological position of resistance to imperialist subjugation."[76] Blackness is a just rebellion in the Tricontinental and the Nuevo Muntu.

Placide Tempels and the Muntu

Given the impact of Tricontinental thought, Locke and Hughes's "New Negro," Che's "new man," and Fanon, Senghor, and Diop's attention to the African continent in particular, it is clear that Zapata felt compelled to look to Africa to liberate blacks and the Americas from slavery, colonialism, and their legacies in the twentieth century. He also turned to the thought of Belgian missionary Placide Tempels, who wrote a groundbreaking, systematic synthesis of his mission and fieldwork in the Congo called "La philosophie Bantoue" ("Bantu Philosophy", 1945).[77] Tempels had a different aim than Zapata. He wrote to educate other missionaries on how Africans perceived the world so that they could more respectfully and effectively Christianize them and responsibly show them the benefits of colonial "civilization." He wrote it fifteen years before the bloody Congo Crisis (1960–1965) that would see the collapse of the ravaged Belgian Congo.

If the Portuguese brought Catholicism to Central Africa, converting the elite and sending missionaries among the rest, beginning in the fifteenth century, why was it still not taking root in the twentieth?[78] In 1612 the bishop of Congo wrote the king of Portugal, complaining that their "vices are so old and the barbarism is so great that they cannot be cured."[79] Logistically, there were few bilingual priests outside the cities, but there was also a broad philosophical divide.[80] There were parallel worldviews, one Christian, one African, that miscommunicated with each other and allowed Africans to adopt Christian symbols into their nonexclusionary pantheon of spirits and ancestors.[81] They adopted rituals and recognized saints and Jesus, but they did not believe in heaven, hell, or an invisible God that created and ruled the universe.[82] Their gods were human-like, flawed, specific to a region or ethnicity, and invoked for immediate pragmatic needs—or abandoned for others if needs were not met.[83] Colonizers viewed these resistant worldviews as ignorance and things of the Devil (hence *El Gran Putas*, or "great Devil," of the title).[84] Africans used them as a mythology for "explaining, predicting, and controlling things around them."[85] This temporal focus without a mysterious supreme God likely appealed to Zapata, who was raised by an atheist father and trained as a medical doctor, a scientist. Another element of the muntu myth system was that it was the basis of a "Bantu proto-nation with slave Brazil" and the rest of the Iberian world peopled by the Portuguese diaspora, which also had a shared lingua franca (*angola*) and aesthetics.[86] This worldview was transferred throughout the "African-Portuguese diaspora," which is to say much of Latin America, given the central role of the Portuguese trade there.[87]

To appreciate Tempels's influence on Zapata, the reader must see some of Zapata's own explicit definitions of what the muntu or *muntú* are. According to *Changó*'s glossary (1983), the "muntu" is the singular of "Bantu."[88] The latter is "man."[89] However, it transcends "human" to include the living and dead, the animals, minerals, and vegetables that she/he/they use/s. It refers to the "fuerza que une en un solo nudo al hombre con su ascendencia y descendencia inmersas en el universo presente, pasado y futuro" (the force that unites humanity in a single knot with its ascendants and descendants, immersed in the present, past, and future universe).[90] "Bantu" is also a family of languages.[91]

After *Changó*, Zapata revised his definition to make it tamer and more Western. In *La rebelión de los genes* (*Genetic Rebellion*, 1997), he reaffirms and expands this definition, based on Tempels.[92] He adds a biological element. He argues that since the deepest evolutionary origins of humanity lie in Africa, the "filosofía del muntú [*sic*] [resume] los más antiguos conocimientos del hombre para ajustar su conducta a la sociedad y la naturaleza" (philosophy of the muntu gathers man's most ancient knowledge for adapting his behavior to society and nature).[93] He claims that it is not "moralista" (moralist) but focused on survival.[94] He says it is rooted in the oldest traditions, and yet

> en su diáspora por el mundo encontraron otros pueblos con experiencias y filosofías propias, con los cuales, al fusionarse acrecentaron las suyas. . . . Tiene validez más allá de los credos religiosos o políticos. . . . Una filosofía vitalista y existencialista, íntimamente sometida a los mandatos superiores y sagrados de los ancestros [*sic*].[95]
>
> (in their world diaspora, they found other peoples with their own experiences and philosophies, with which they added their own as they fused together. . . . It is valid beyond religious or political creeds. . . . A life-based and existential philosophy, closely following the sacred and superior orders of the ancestors.)

Thus, it is an entire worldview that is not separated into ontology, identity, religion, and politics, and it existed not because of slavery but before it, in spite of it, and in opposition to it. He revises his original definition:

> Ésta es la concepción de la humanidad que los pueblos más explotados del mundo, los africanos, devuelven a sus colonizadores europeos sin amargura ni resentimientos. Una filosofía vital de amor, alegría y paz entre los hombres y el mundo que los nutre.[96]
>
> (This is the conception of humanity that the most exploited peoples of the world, Africans, give back to their European colonizers without bitterness or resentment. A life-based philosophy of love, joy, and peace between men and the world that nourishes them.)

While love is present in the novel, it is not between oppressed and oppressor, so Zapata is adjusting his essay to his post–Cold War context of the 1990s, not the heated conflicts of the 1960s and before that the novel depicts.

In *El Árbol brujo* (*Bewitched Tree*, 2002), he cites Tempels again:

> El pensamiento religioso africano, nacido de las primeras preguntas y respuestas del *Homo Sapiens* para explicarse la existencia de su naturaleza, la vida y la muerte, continúa siendo la fuerza coercitiva que liga su conducta personal y colectiva . . . una religión para interiorizar, para vivir y comportarse. . . . Inspiró los cultos a los astros, dioses y Ancestros. . . . Los negroafricanos, por sus génesis y ámbito geográfico, se sienten más ligados entre sí por la vida, que otros pueblos cada vez más distantes de sus fuentes vitales. . . . Les hace concebir su tierra como un gran templo donde son, a la par oficiantes y devotos de una religión (en el sentido primario del vocablo), para compartirla con los vivos y sus Ancestros. . . .
>
> Este contexto cosmogónico y vital ha inspirado la filosofía del Muntú: la gran familia de los difuntos y vivos, hermanados con los animales, plantas. (Temples).[97]
>
> (African religion, born of Homo Sapiens's first questions and answers to explain to itself the existence of its nature, life, and death, continues to be the coercive force that links its personal and collective conduct . . . a religion . . . to internalize, live, and behave. . . . It inspired the worship of stars, gods, and Ancestors. . . . Black Africans, because of their genesis and geographical environs, feel more bound to one another by life, than other peoples who are

> ever more distant from the sources of life. . . . It makes them conceive of their land as a great temple where they are, much like officiants and followers of a religion (in the primary sense of the word), to share it with the living and their Ancestors. . . .
>
> This cosmological and life-based context has inspired the Muntu philosophy: the great family of the living and dead, in brotherhood with animals, plants. (Temples).

Since *Présence Africaine* (*African Presence*) published Tempels's work in English, it is likely a cornerstone for the worldview underpinning the novel.[98] Thus, the muntu is the African diaspora as well as the worldview that defines it. Like the aforementioned thinkers from Locke to Guevara, Zapata is seeking a model for a future humanity, but he is going back before colonialism to find non-Western models and influences to reform the West. As Zapata puts it in *Rebelión*, which is subtitled *El mestizaje americano en la sociedad futura* (*American Hybridization in the Society of the Future*), he seeks a utopia, the muntu in the Americas—what I call Nuevo Muntu—based on decolonizing and dealienating humanity's mind.[99]

Zapata's selection of myths from the Congo and Yoruba regions is a representation of the three African regions most affected by the slave trade. Zapata's focus on the Portuguese in the African trade is historically accurate, and Brazil is indicative of their practices on both sides of the Atlantic. The first zone, Upper Guinea, was prevalent from 1441 to 1580, and it is represented by the trader Ezili in Mali.[100] The second and most prolific source of human traffic was Central Africa, which included parts of the Congo and Angola, and which is the source of the muntu, Bantu philosophy. It predominated from 1580 to 1770s, spurred by wars the Portuguese instigated and manipulated.[101] Its apex ended when famine and war diminished the supply of human cargo from Luanda and when the Minas Gerais gold rush at the turn of the eighteenth century demanded an influx of labor.[102] The 1770 period to the implementation of abolition in the latter 1800s was marked by trade from Lower Guinea, where wars between Oyo and Dahomey created slaves to exchange.[103] Sweet shows that, in Brazil, religious syncretism was very slow and superficial and that each of these three regions' shared worldviews remained largely intact as captives held to their ethnic identities throughout their lives.[104] While holding onto core beliefs, such as the muntu, Central African slaves did syncretize with other religions, but it was often with other sub-Saharan religions through a process of "Africanization" that began on African soil. A Catholic veneer existed parallel to one's African core at least until the eighteenth century.

Sweet argues that African religions must be revisited without the inferior status ascribed to them by Christians and other Westerners. This must be done to achieve a glimpse at how captives experienced life, both south of the Sahara and in the New World.[105] By comprehending the muntu and similar worldviews below the Christian veneer in the diaspora, one understands the origins of black double consciousness, an idea that is central to Gilroy's Black Atlantic and to which I will return. For now, one must attempt to enter a Central African world of powerful life-giving and life-threatening forces that are not a binary conflict of mutually exclusive notions of good and evil.[106] What powers could have brought the all-engulfing transatlantic genocide? Sweet claims that, for these Africans,

> those who used their religious powers to harm other people or to insure their own success, rather than for the advancement of the common good, were deemed to be malevolent. One of the outcomes of malevolent religious behavior was a growing social and/or economic inequality between the spiritual tormentor and everyone else in the community. Thus, two of the classic symptoms of religious malevolence were unjust suffering on the part of the victims and rapid, unexplained social/economic wealth on the part of the spiritual tormentors. From the African perspective, enslavement and economic exploitation by Europeans fit both of these criteria, but the impacts of these strong and unfamiliar new forms of malevolence radically transformed religious meanings in Africa and the diaspora.[107]

Sweet claims they saw slavery as a "curse" like Zapata does.[108] Like all curses, slavery is a pain or disease that must be cured.[109] To understand how Zapata's muntu-based utopia relates to slavery, let us turn now from the Bantu/muntu ideas in the text to its Yoruba ideas before returning to the muntu so that we understand the interplay of both worldviews as they relate to slavery.

The Curse

The muntu worldview's relationship to slavery has been understudied and misunderstood, particularly regarding the "curse of Changó." It has been secondary to the undeniably important Yoruba and Dahomean deities of the text in criticism of the novel. The emphasis of the Yoruba worldview is understandable since its deities are worshiped in either syncretic or nonsyncretic forms in Colombia, Brazil, and Cuba through religions like *santería* and *candomblé*. Critic Darío Henao Restrepo cites Lydia Cabrera's *El Monte* ([1954] 1993) on Cuba to better understand the work's characters.[110] Her informants' statements about his brutality likely inspired Zapata. They claim he is so cruel that he must travel the world, carrying a slave with him; he is so heartless that he is the spiritual inventor of the nuclear bomb.[111] However, misinterpreting the Yoruba and Bantu roots of the novel has confused some critics, particularly those who debate the spirit Changó's curse, which brings slavery upon his people, the muntu.[112] Changó's curse is, for Daiana Nascimento dos Santos, fundamental to understanding the novel because it circulates through the imaginary of the entire work.[113] Nascimento dos Santos presumes the curse comes from the Senegalese oral tradition; it comes from Zapata himself.[114]

According to the novel, Changó is the spirit who condemns his spiritual children to exile—the "Gran Putas" or "Great Devil" that separated the muntu and brought one of the greatest curses of human history upon multiple continents: the interlocking horrors of slavery and colonialism in Africa and the New World. Víctor Figueroa's *Prophetic Visions of the Past* (2015) argues that the origin myth is inappropriate as an empowering narrative for explaining the scattering of the African diaspora, yet in it he tries to argue for a way that it can be liberating by using black Christian theology. I counterargue that we must focus on the African, not so much the African American, side of the text to understand the myth.

He simplifies the Changó story, saying, "As a result of his subjects' betrayal, Changó condemns them to exile and slavery. . . . It is true that Changó also prophesies that the *muntu* (the African slaves and their descendants) will eventually achieve liberation—by their own efforts—but the reader cannot help being surprised by the callousness of the orisha, by the disproportion of his punishment against his people, and by the central place that that aspect of the myth occupies in Zapata Olivella's narrative."[115] He claims the implication of the myth is that people simplistically accept an African tyrant over a European one.[116] He and Yvonne Captain-Hidalgo claim that he is an "imperfect god," and he argues that "the African diaspora might have good reason to withdraw any allegiance or trust in a god or myth that is capable of so neatly accommodating the callousness of European imperialism."[117] He calls the myth an "Afrocentric Theodicy" in which Changó is a "good and all-powerful god" and "it always potentially justifies the injustice that it tries to explain and even eliminate."[118] He then uses the Christian theologian Anthony Pinn's work to argue for a "black humanism" that leaves "gods out of the equation" of slavery.[119]

Let us set Figueroa's arguments back on his stated track of focusing on African myths, not Christianity. He claims that there is no such tale of Changó causing slavery in Yoruba lore, but he does not consider the important work of the Anglican Priest Samuel Johnson, who gathered Nigerian oral accounts in his *The History of the Yorubas* (1921).[120] He presents tales of Changó as both Yoruba history and myth, an approach Zapata repeats in the novel. According to Figueroa, "When I state that the struggle for freedom starts symbolically with the enslavement of the 'first' African, I refer more precisely to the beginning of the modern/colonial European slave trade . . . [which] evidently cannot be supposed to have instilled a love of freedom to men who were brutally enslaved."[121] I would counterargue that Changó was himself the first slave and that his enslavement originated the archetypical pride, violence, and resistance that repeat throughout the novel.

The Changó story is, in part, one of pride and shame. In the novel he unites the kingdoms of the Yoruba, which is not the case according to Johnson. The latter's account presents him as the son of another kingdom who ruled in Oko but who moved his capital to Oyo.[122] For Johnson's sources, it was, in fact, King Orafiyan who united the Yoruba-speaking peoples at Oyo and led the expedition that extended their territory. The novel attributes these feats to Changó.[123] Changó is thus rewritten as a unifier of the known world, or at least the Niger kingdoms.[124] This must have appealed to a communist attempting to reunite the African diaspora.

While Changó is referred to as beautiful and arrogant, his pride in himself actually seems to be insufficient in the novel, since he is jealous of "ajena gloria" (others' glory), "ciego a su propia grandeza" (blind to his own greatness), and "olvidado de su estirpe sagrada" (having forgotten his sacred bloodline).[125] This is despite being the "Gran Putas": the most fertile, strong, and musical—the greatest.[126] This, despite the novel explicitly insisting that "el negro es bello" (black is beautiful).[127] His personal insecurity drives further disunity. In particular, he is jealous of his faithful (unified) generals, the brothers Gbonka and Timi. He has them fight to the death, which results in Gbonka seeking exile for having killed his brother.[128] The curse of Changó is, in its origin, a curse placed upon Changó for his blindness to his own self-worth.[129] According to Johnson, he pits Timi against Gbonka because the former does not pay him taxes. He hopes both will die, but Gbonka wins.[130] The king has the two fight again, and this time Timi dies, to the king's dismay.[131] Remorseful, Gbonka then appears to commit suicide by setting himself ablaze and disappearing, to the king's delight. Then he magically reappears dancing in the street, shaming the unpopular king among his subjects, and challenges him to do the same. Since the king cannot, he commits suicide by drinking poison.[132] Zapata seems to have chosen the brothers' "duelo interminable" (endless duel/mourning) as a metaphor for jealousy and infighting.[133]

For Zapata, Orunla, who controls the future, and the powerful Ancestors punish Changó for pitting his generals against one another.[134] Orno Oba preaches in the Oyo streets that Changó is a tyrant.[135] He forges the chains and shackles that bind Changó, and a great crowd spits upon him and his family.[136] Zapata does not mention how Changó dies. For him, Changó was cursed before he cursed his followers. It is a spell based on not knowing the future consequences of one's actions or of losing sight of the primary goal: uniting humanity in a just kingdom, which, for Changó, seemed to be the initial goal of his conquests. He pursues justice, since he is the god of this ideal.[137]

Johnson's account is also a story of shame and vengeance. The spirit is "author of his own misfortunes" again, but this time it is for his intelligence. He invents a charm to draw forth his weapon, lightning, but accidentally burns down his palace with his favorite wives and children inside.[138] Inconsolable about losing his family, he hangs himself.[139] The Yoruba then descend into civil war.[140] Like Zapata, he presents Changó as a destructive, divisive king, and Changó's hanging returns in the novel in the leitmotif of lynching.

In another of Johnson's versions of the story, as in Zapata, he was king of all Yoruba peoples, but they expelled him for tyranny.[141] Having lost his homeland and his favorite wife Oya, he committed suicide.[142] Worship of Changó was based on soothing his rage through offerings. To avoid further punishment from Changó, his priests kidnap members of poor families who cannot pay for sacrifices to the god.[143] According to Johnson,

> The unfortunate sufferers already deprived of their all (much or little) by this sudden stroke of ill fortune are often obliged to put their children to service in order to raise money sufficient to meet the demands of the greedy worshippers of this heartless god. The fines obtained are shared between the king or head chief, and the town authorities; but the articles purchased for the

performance of the ceremonies are prerequisites which are appropriated by the priests alone.[144]

Changó, the first enslaved African, according to Zapata's mythology, was already associated with the enslavement of even the most desperate people among the Yoruba. Johnson continues, "This 'descent of Sango' [*sic*] on earth is never done but with a view to show his displeasure on persons who are guilty of perjury and lies. The town for a while is as it were placed under an interdict, and during that brief period the worshippers of the god are allowed to seize with impunity whatever they can come at in the public streets in the vicinity of the catastrophe."[145] Does not the sacking of a village sound like the raids carried out to colonize and enslave Africa?

Changó must have been deeply ashamed to be exiled, a punishment derived indirectly from his initial lack of self-worth and separation of his Yoruba brethren. Zapata adds to his shame of exile by saying his people rose up against him under the noble Gbonka and spat upon him and his family.[146] His retaliation, as a vengeful god—not a loving one, as in Christianity—was to condemn his followers to the same shame and exile he suffered. The roots of slavery are, in the novel, as for the Yoruba, shame, jealousy, lack of consideration for the impoverished, greed, unjust punishment, and the expansion of empire, this time at the hands of the Loba Blanca (White Wolf, Europe).

The Loba Blanca is not Changó, and the myth in no way justifies slavery. In fact, it claims, regarding the Loba Blanca, that "¡las salivas de mil hijos / escupirán sobre tu tumba!" (a thousand sons and daughters will spit on your grave).[147] The European colonizers share the shame of Changó's original sin (a combination of feeling inferior, jealousy, and divisiveness). As the poem states, ambition is their original, covetous, and destructive "sin."[148] But their disgrace is much greater—not only the city of Oyo defiles them, as they did to Changó, but thousands of children (future generations) spit upon them in a great storm of shame. One must not forget that Changó is the god of thunder and storms. In 1896 the Ilorin rebels of Yorubaland described their gunfire as the sound of Changó when they fought the British.[149] The curse of Changó is the curse of shame, and his "children" and followers, the African diaspora, must regain a healthy pride in themselves in order to found the just kingdom that he was on the verge of establishing in Yorubaland.

The Nuevo Muntu is the way. In the novel the American continent is a place of redemption for this African-inspired, self-proclaimed "utopia." Zapata proposes that the fertile muntu (African diaspora) will generate a future generation that is *zambo* (mixed of Indian and blood and culture) as well as mulatto.[150] One must not forget that Changó is a god of war, so slave and postcolonial rebellions are appropriate means to reach freedom, as in "cortarás los puños . . . del amo que te niega" (you will cut off the fists . . . of the master who denies you).[151]

But he does not advocate for being trapped in the past, and by cherishing and fighting for one's family, liberation will come and lead to something like Marx's International, the ultimate goal of communism:

¡Sin fronteras en la sangre
semilla del nuevo hombre vengador de tus padres
vengador de tus hijos
la libertad es tu destino!
. . . .
¡lavarán la terrible
la ciega
maldición de Changó![152]

(Without borders in your blood
seed of the new man
avenger of your fathers
avenger of your children
freedom is your destiny!
. . . .
you will wash off the terrible
the blind
curse of Changó!)

The Nuevo Muntu, founded in the Americas by a never-before-seen mixture of bloodlines and cultures, will impose the just order that Changó failed to create. This society will be free of the racist legacy of slavery. The shame of slavery and five hundred years of being called inferior will be washed away by a unified and just order. In this aspect I agree with critic Samuel Mate-Kojo that the myth is one in which the deified king's subjects establish for themselves a "new beginning by fighting for their own freedom" in the Americas.[153]

Hence, the prophet of black unity against oppression, Malcolm X, turns, by the end of the novel, to a revolution that entails all the oppressed. He preaches to the muntu that the days of disunion are passed and that he lives only to gather the family of the muntu; only that way will Changó's society be built, one in which all races will call each other brothers, reunited with their bond to the dead.[154] Agne Brown is the medium through which all the ancestors of Africa and the Americas speak in order to bring about this reunion of the living and the dead, which concludes with Changó and Legba themselves growing furious that the muntu have not united and fought for a just society. The last successful battle of the novel is a March on Washington (1968), so the characters' impatience must mirror Zapata's upon the novel's publication in 1983. Like the diviners of old, he diagnoses the social problems but leaves it to the reader to resolve them in their time.[155]

Las claves mágicas de América (*Magic Keys to the Americas*, 1989) is Zapata's essay on the effects of slavery and colonialism on blacks, Africa, and the Americas. In many ways it displays the same theses as *Changó*: that the injustices of slavery, racism, and classism must be exposed and that the solution to them lies in Bantu-inspired hybrid thought. He cites the four centuries and three (in U.S. terms, four) continents involved in the radical change of slavery.[156] The muntu is part of enslaved blacks' "mecanismos de defensa y creatividad" (defense and creativity mechanisms).[157] He believes these can be recovered by reading Temples, Senghor, Melville Herskovits, Hubert Deschamps, and Janheinz Jahn.[158] From Tempels he takes the muntu hierarchy of vital forces, pantheism, and permeability between life, death, and nature.[159] Regarding the determinism of slavery, though, he notes,

> la mayoría de las guerras entre las naciones, tribus y familias son inspiradas por la necesidad de sacudirse estas tiranías. En otras palabras, el código jerárquico cuando se trata de guerras entre naciones o castas es cuestionable.[160]
>
> (the majority of wars between nations, tribes, and families are inspired by the need to throw off these tyrannies. In other words, the hierarchical code, when dealing with wars between nations or castes in questionable.)

He then imagines how the captives used religion in defense of "vida" (life): to fight off the encroachment of slavery, preserve life in captivity, and flee slavery whenever possible to preserve and enhance vital force.[161] Regarding enslavement, the captive could have accepted it as a curse for violating natural law, the imposition of foreigners who do not respect such law, or dismiss it as inexplicable, leading either to resignation or to rejection of this fate. His personal response to these options is that blacks always rebelled against slavery and adapted their religions to their new realities. He rejects the notion that Africans' deep religiosity (muntu) was replaced by a Christian doctrine that rejected "la filosofía africana del vitalismo existencial. Tanto más, cuando la nueva religión pretendía justificar la esclavitud" (the African philosophy of existential vitalism. Even more when the new religion was intended to justify slavery).

He reaffirms that the muntu does not excuse European atrocities:

> en mitad de la tormenta, Europa colonizando a la América, el negro debió fabricar su propia brújula, improvisándola a partir de su dolor, de su memoria ancestral, de su poder creador. Fue lo que hizo con su filosofía, sus mitos y experiencias.[162]
>
> (in the midst of the storm, Europe colonizing the Americas, blacks had to create their own compass, improvising it based on their pain, their ancestral memory, on their creative power. It is what they did with their philosophy, their myths, and their experiences.)

Zapata's philosophy incubated for twenty years before *Changó* and remained central to his work until the end of his career. When critic Jerome Branche calls his chronicle of slavery a distortion of it as "black on black crime," he is being flippant.[163]

If the slave rebel is the origin of liberty in the Americas, the ultimate goal is a new kind of mestizo in the tradition of José de Vasconcelos's *hombre cósmico*:[164]

> No reconocemos los títulos colonialistas de latinos o anglosajones. Somos el nuevo hombre de América: ecuménicos por la suma de todos los continentes. . . . No al racismo. Hablamos de una etnia donde se han reencontrado todas las sangres para amarse y no para odiarse.[165]
>
> (We do not recognize the colonialist titles of Latinos and Anglo-Saxons. We are the new man of the Americas: ecumenical for the sum of all the continents. . . . No to racism. We speak of an ethnicity where all bloodlines have been reunited to love one another and not to hate each other.)

I will now return to Zapata's reading of Tempels to explain what the "original" meaning of "muntu" is and how it sheds light on the future in the New World that Zapata's novel puts forth.

Zapata builds on Tempels because the latter proposes a systematic philosophy of the muntu. His work was published in 1945, and its hopeful message must have shimmered for Zapata, who surely knew of the destructive collapse of colonialism in the Belgian Congo Crisis (1960–1965). While Tempels's underlying goal in understanding the Bantu is to ultimately Christianize them, he claims "in the innumbered [*sic*] crowd of the primitive masses, in the faces falsely looked upon as bestial, we see the animal expressions which we lent to these savages fade away."[166] Though a colonizer, his hopes are surprisingly democratic: "We must proceed with the Bantu towards its [philosophy's] sources to the point at which 'the evolution of primitive peoples' was led into a false path by false deductions; and, taking this as our point of departure, help the Bantu to build their own Bantu civilization, a stable and noble one of their own."[167] Zapata, extending Tempels's goal, seeks to build a future of the Americas based on a "wholesome Bantu starting-point" to not only reform the postcolonial societies of the Americas but also return to the original cultures that have been left behind in Africa.[168] Zapata's characters (the Priest on the slaver *Nova Índia*, syncretic priest Domingo Falupo of Cartagena, the Vodou-inspired Haitian army, the heretic Agne Brown, for example) are most often in conflict with Christianity, as many Marxists are.[169] But Tempels's work allows Zapata to create a unique vision of the world for his novel and its ultimate utopian goals of dismantling colonialism. Tempels himself asks if in "vital force, order, law, are there so many Utopias, in contrast to which the Universe, the real world, is only evil, that is to say negation, illusion?"[170] Likewise, the novel depicts slavery, rape, oppression, and one defeated revolution after another. The Bantu answer is also Zapata's: "life is stronger than death."

Tempels cites Herskovits, who reappears in the novel as "Professor Harrington," in a note on similarities between the Bantu and the African diaspora in Haiti, Brazil, and Surinam.[171] Like it is for Zapata, "it is the most primitive of all who have maintained the most pure form of the concept of the Supreme Being," so the least colonized are vital to overturning colonial thought.[172] If the novel tells of black heroes fighting colonialism, then Zapata must also ask, "is it the fear of breaking the mystic bond which, through the chiefs, is established with the ancestors and the fear of the disasters which that may entail?"[173] In the context of slavery and black alienation, this ancestral bond has been severed and first must be understood and then reconstituted to reach "salvation" for the colonized and colonizer alike.[174]

The vital force is a powerful solution to black shame and alienation. Vital force can be increased or diminished in humanity. It is not exclusively a bodily strength, but integrity of the entire being.[175] "A man can . . . be equally actuated by a will to destruction, a wicked will. His evil will (hatred, envy, jealousy) will have repercussions upon the vital force of weaker beings through his mere willing a reduction in their vital power."[176] Changó, by hating himself and feeling jealous of his brothers, diminished his own force as well as that of his followers at the moment of the curse of enslavement, like the curse of a disease.[177] The loss of force is often expressed as death, including illness, fatigue, wounds, depression, injustice, hunger, paralysis, and failure.[178] Thus, it is not surprising that Zapata argues for an African philosophy of vitality that can overcome the diseases of colonialism and black alienation.[179] The same vital force establishes a natural hierarchy in which said force emanates from a distant Supreme Being via the deified clan Ancestors to the political hierarchy of the chief/s on down to the people and from man to animals and the rest of nature. It inverts colonialism's centuries-old project of objectification of black people by making them human and even divine and placing them at the center of the universe. The more alienated subjects like Aleijadinho and Agne become, the more culturally "whitened" they become by being adopted and recognized by their white parents, Lisboa and Reverend Robert, the more they become ill. Aleijadinho physically decays, while Agne remains separated from her family of origin, despite the fact that white society still does not truly accept her. Fanon would argue that they have black skin but white masks.[180] The muntu helps them to take those masks off and to create new ones, like when Agne is filled with Changó's spirit when she wears his visage.[181]

The muntu order of the universe is anthropocentric: force comes from God, then passes through humanity and its hierarchies down to the animal, vegetable, and mineral elements.[182] It is a metaphysics of "reality," not an abstraction.[183] However, unlike in the "West," "being" is a dynamic, changing force that constantly evolves. In this way, it is not static like Western Essentialism. It also informs Bantu natural science, which is based on a universal hierarchy in which animals can be like human kings within their species and habitats.[184] They do not have a Western, binary concept of "good and evil," only strength/life and weakness/death, though injustice and destruction exist.[185] Therefore, Manichaean Christian theodicy is not possible.

Humans (muntu) are tripartite: body, shadow, and breath.[186] When they die, their true selves, free of appearances, leave their bodies. While alive, the muntu is the manifestation of strength, intelligence, reason, and will.[187] The dead provide this force to the living through the wisdom of the elders. In clan societies the deified first fathers have the most divine power, then the other dead of the tribe, based on primogeniture, and then the elders and other living members.[188] This human hierarchy is seen as natural, and obedience to the clan leader is "the source of zestful living," not oppression. Slavery's disruption of traditional African ways of life is not only a moral catastrophe, as in contemporary Western thought, but thoroughly, ontologically unnatural.

Since one being cannot annihilate another (given the flow of energies between temporal and divine realms), the muntu is a brilliant framework for black resistance.[189] Furthermore, the novel's bi-part structure mimics the muntu structure of time: "the present human generation living on earth is the centre of all humanity, including the world of the dead."[190] Though the novel has five novellas, the U.S. novella occupies one-third of the novel. The Ancestors of Africa and Latin America are guiding the forces of the novel's "present" because the protagonist, Agne, has reconnected her energy and understanding with the Ancestors, the forces of Africa and the maroons and the mestizo rebels of Latin America. Their force and wisdom fortify her struggle against racism. The Ancestors make her stronger and wiser, culminating in the maximum strength of the gathering at Malcolm's funeral.[191] This strength is passed on to the reader by the end of the novel.

Changó reverses the colonial ideology that Europeans and their descendants are subjects and that Africans are objects.[192] Changó's curse is not a claim that black people are responsible for their own enslavement but a radical reframing of Europeans who colonized Africa as savage animals. The curse is an invasion by La Loba Blanca (White Wolf).[193] If humans and spirits are superior to animals, then the wolf must be driven by a superior force—in this case, the alienated king Changó.[194] In the muntu, spirits, the dead, and the elders are all superior in force to beasts. They are, therefore, inherently more powerful than she is. A wolf cannot be human because "muntu" (human) implies "excellence or plenitude. Thus, the Baluba will speak of 'ke *muntu* po,' this is not a *muntu*, of a man who behaves unworthily. They will use the phrase of a newly-born who has been begotten outside the normal ontological, moral, and juridical conditions of clan life."[195] The wisdom of the elders holds the solution to all problems, juridical or ontological, so they must hold the answer to the problems resulting from slavery.[196]

The Bantu do not divide soul and body, nor do they have separate notions of soul, mind, will, and sentiment.[197] There are three bases of Bantu psychology: vital force, the increase of forces, and vital influence. Muntu can "grow ontologically" and diminish as a force. Everything that diminishes his force brings him closer to both mundane death and ultimate death: leaving no patrimony and being forgotten.

Zapata's text shows how to be a "*muntu* mukulumpe," a "powerful man who has his part to take in the community" marked by "excellence or plenitude."[198] Thus, Changó occupies the role of king as "the Biggest Badass" or "Gran Putas." He is "mfumu" (leader) due to being "a new, higher vital force capable of strengthening and maintaining everything which falls ontologically within his cure." Hence, public leaders of black history are "children of Changó," possessed by him during their great acts. Naturally, like the *mfumu*, Changó experiences a "growth of procreative potency" in creating and sustaining the black diaspora with every victory. He is also a god of fertility, which explains the rejection of puritanism and bodily shame.[199]

To consider enslavers objects, animals, and diseases and to consider the acts of enslavement and self-hatred "ontological sacrilege" is not to blame the victims of slavery; it is the most radical indictment of it. The massive restructuring of society that came with the colonization and enslavement of Africa constituted a "political set-up which conflicted with this principle," says Temples, and is thus inconsonant with the Bantu mind.[200] Thus, the ancestors judge the betrayals of Simón Bolívar when he betrays José Prudencio Padilla and has him executed, when he and Napoleon betray the leaders of the Haitian Revolution, and when the Union does not liberate the muntu during the Civil War.[201] They are condemned along with the Loba Blanca.

In response, "the community has the right of defense against such an evildoer, who spreads destruction and death, who brings about the annihilation of being."[202] This logic can only condemn slavery. The enslavers, as the "White Wolf," are "the 'not-life,' the force destructive to life, cannot possess rights, it is anti-ontological."[203] Colonialism and slavery's separation of the diaspora is an abomination: "the very existence of children apart from their progenitors is inconceivable."[204] This judgment is not extreme, since "to violate nature incurs her vengeance and that misfortune springs from her."[205] Logically, the unnatural forces of slavery and colonialism can lead only to the reestablishment of homeostasis through their ultimate destruction, making slavery the catalyst for universal freedom, its equal and opposite reaction. This is how the Bantu recognize responsibility: fault is "proportional to the degree of evil will by which harm is done to vital force." Nevertheless, the muntu is also the secret to overcoming slavery and racism: "The tenacity of the '*muntu*' in the defense of his rights is the consequence of his attachment to his fundamental wisdom and to his philosophy. . . . The deeper his thought, the more his arguments are rooted in his philosophical beliefs, in his wisdom and in his ontological behavior, the more tenacious he will be and the more he will rise to defend his precious human rights."[206] The Universal Declaration of Human Rights was signed in 1948. Tempels was brilliant to embrace it in 1945, especially in reference to the ravaged Congo. The Bantu were equally prescient to devise analogous solutions to injustice in times immemorial, as Zapata affirms.

Since Changó is a dead and deified ancestor, "the living are in the position of new-born children in regard to their forefathers. . . . Ancestors and forefathers still stand as the clan itself towards the living clan and towards each member of it as such. From them comes the vital force of the whole clan. Their veneration . . . by elders of the clan to them, are the affairs of the whole clan community."[207] Changó must be worshiped and Bantu rituals are to be restored not because his curse is just, but because his veneration will restore natural order.[208] Changó's fire, a symbol of Black Power and rebellion in the novel, is the same element the Bantu use to purify their clans by burning the bodies of their "pervert brothers."[209] Thus, the fire motif is present throughout the novel as a metaphor for revolutionary action focused on overcoming the legacy of conquest and slavery.

Changó's curse, while it is clearly based on African cosmologies, is relevant to anyone trying to understand the origins of the African diaspora in slavery. Many of us share the shock Zora Neale Hurston expresses in *Dust Tracks on a Road* (1942): "The white people had held my people in slavery in America. They had bought us, it is true and exploited us. But the inescapable fact that stuck in my craw, was: my people had sold me and the white people had bought me. That did away with the folklore I had been brought up on—that the white people had gone to Africa, waved a red handkerchief at the Africans and lured them aboard ship and sailed away."[210] Today's

United States also lives under myths surrounding slavery. To this day, and much more so in Hurston and Zapata's time, the "Lost Cause" narrative reigned and reigns in many southern homes.[211] Today at Confederate sites guides tell tourists that slaves were well treated; some still say it was the best thing for them. On the other hand a myth emerged in the eighteenth and nineteenth centuries that blamed the slave trade on African despots and claimed Europeans were actually civilizing captives by enslaving them.[212] Myths and distortions that justify slavery have made scholars highly skeptical of claims that the trade was anything but a purely European construct.

Nonetheless, it is not true to say that African kings—in some ways, the sons of Changó as much as Afro-descendant rebels—were not agents in the modern slave trade. They were active in it from the start. Herman Bennett's *African Kings and Black Slaves* (2019) is a theoretical meditation on some of the earliest encounters between the Portuguese that initiated the transatlantic exchange of humans and the African sovereigns with whom they negotiated.[213] Despite describing a visit to a colonial fort in Ouidah, Bennett focuses exclusively on European primary texts and uses primarily Western postcolonial theory, but his argument is that Africans were always participants in the negotiation of this trade.[214] The militarily limited Portuguese were forced to negotiate with the African powers to drive the trade, and the powerful Catholic Church of 1441 to 1560 recognized the sovereignty of those reigning the *extra ecclesiam*, those residing outside of Christendom.[215] Bennett considers Paul Gilroy's *Black Atlantic* a "brilliant exegesis" of the Enlightenment, but he seeks the role of Africa in the formation of European modernity in the origins of modern slavery in the fifteenth century, showing how a peninsular focus reveals important information on modernity and double consciousness an Anglocentric focus cannot.[216] His work does not blame Africans for slavery, nor does it simplistically condemn Europeans but gives a nuanced examination of the laws and doctrines involved in using Catholic Reconquest rhetoric to justify the expansion of the Portuguese Empire into Africa.[217] He paints conquistadors and enslavers not as benevolent or hateful but as agents focused on profit and the expansion of empire, particularly that of Henry the Navigator, whom Zapata refashions as the black mutineer Nagó the Navigator.[218] Following the Marxist tradition, Bennett paints slavery as a key moment in the origins of modern capitalism—a racial capitalism that even precedes widespread numeracy in the West.[219]

Zapata's use of the Loba Blanca (White Wolf) to represent Europe is in line with Bennett's. The Spanish *lobo* (wolf) is typically masculine, which draws attention to the feminine term for a decidedly masculine enterprise—conquest by sailors. If rebels and kings are children of Changó, then it is fair to say that, in their own Latin mythology, the conquistadors are the children of the she-wolf like Romulus and Remus. They are children of Rome, the great empire that conquered the known world and enriched itself on the suffering of others. Like Rome after Constantine, the Portuguese slavers represent a Christian empire, and their conquest is the origin of capitalism. Zapata, as a Marxist, condemns the violence of capitalism in colonialism, the nineteenth century, and contemporary times. Unlike Bennett's more nuanced approach, Zapata condemns the White Wolf at every step, just as he celebrates those who rise up against the oppressors: the Spanish, Portuguese, French, and U.S. empires. So why, when describing the origins of slavery, does he move the focus from these new Romans to a mythical Yoruba king? Simply, he is tracing the origins of humanity to their prehistoric origins in Africa, making "human" and "African" one in the same. In this framework, the European invasion of sub-Saharan Africa was a tragedy, but one in which Europe is not the protagonist but a plague wrought on humanity in the name of a foreign god (Jesus). Hence, the original family of the muntu on the slave ship *Nova India* rise up against the priest, and Benkos Bioho and Domingo Falupo, the first heroes of the Americas, fight the Roman Catholic empire to the death. As Bennet notes, the political origin of "black Africa" is synonymous with the origin of modern Europe, which came to understand itself in a new light through the conquest of Africa and relative to the New World, which was previously unknown.[220] Historically speaking, the curse of Changó is the curse of European imperial expansion, against which the Muntu must reunite to resist.

The Origin Myth of Benkos Bioho

Epic battles to throw off Changó's curse define how Zapata represents colonial Latin America. Historian Júnia Ferreira Furtado, writing in 2009, claims that historians of Brazil continue to struggle against the myth of "racial democracy," which, since the 1930s, posits harmonious relationships between blacks and whites in Brazil from the colony to the present due to a uniquely benign, if paternalistic, plantation system and the mestizo nation it formed.[221] Yet "prior to the 1970s, a Marxist historiography rebelled against that conformist vision of Brazilian society, accentuating the exploitative character of slavery; but these studies usually limited interpretations regarding the subject to the so-called Thing or Zumbi binomial. That is, either the slave submitted to the violent coercion of the master (as a thing) or he escaped to the runaway slave quilombos and established a rebellion (as Zumbi)."[222] As Zapata did, they tended to write historiography that accentuated ideal revolutionary characters to support contemporary revolutions. Gonçalves writes in the time of neoliberalism, so it is understandable that she adopts a more inclusive aesthetic.

Zapata's criticism of atrocities carried out by the Church causes him to focus on those stories that confirm his epic narrative. Let us consider rebel Benkos and heretic Falupo's struggle against the Church. David Wheat's history of Cartagena and the Spanish Caribbean notes that they were, at best, exceptions, not the rule:[223]

> On an even more basic level, Caribbean Spanish and Iberian Catholicism served as a lingua franca and a public set of cultural reference points respectively, enabling Africans to communicate with other peoples—including other Africans—with whom they did not share mutually intelligible languages or similar belief systems. In short, most African migrants actively participated in their own acclimation to Iberian customs as a means of addressing practical matters or advancing their immediate interests. Many would serve as intermediaries for subsequent generations of forced migrants, especially those with backgrounds similar to their own. During the late sixteenth and early seventeenth centuries, as successive waves of captives flooded into Cartagena and other ports, this cyclical process of African acculturation fueled the expansion of Spanish Caribbean society, facilitating the growth of stable populations in key ports and reinforcing Spanish colonization of the region.[224]

Thus, one can presume that Zapata is presenting conflict where Africans often lived in pragmatic fluidity as regarded their spirituality, using the institutions and codes at hand. In the Hispanic Caribbean, they were indoctrinated, often thoroughly, and the "bogus baptisms" Cartagena were a myth spread by the historical Father Alfonso de Sandoval, a character in *Changó*.[225]

But did the heroic maroon Bioho even exist? There is no evidence he founded it in 1603, which is the myth immortalized by a statue of him breaking the chains of slavery in the town's main square, but that this myth emerged from contact with the first scholars to visit Palenque.[226] This myth is widely propagated today, as in *palenquero* Víctor Simarra's interview.[227] Zapata spreads the same myth in *Changó* and his *El árbol brujo* (*Bewitched Tree*).[228]

Linguist Armin Schwegler, the first outsider to learn the creole language of Palenque, has labored to understand the origins of its people. In his recent Technology, Education, and Design (TED) talk, he describes his work in population genetics searching for the origins of the palenqueros in Africa. This has complemented his study of history, which relies heavily on Maria Cristina Navarrete.[229] She claims,

> El relato de la gesta de Domingo Bioho [Benkos Bioho] es una construcción de los pocos documentos escritos que mencionan la revuelta conducente a la existencia del Palenque de la Matuna. El hecho de tratarse de fuentes escritas no garantiza absoluta claridad. Hay discordancias y vacíos en cuanto a la fecha de la huida del caudillo y sus acompañantes, de quién y de dónde se fugó, cuantas veces fue atacado, y los términos y causas de los tratados de paz. Tampoco se conocen los motivos de su sentencia de muerte.[230]
>
> (The story of Domingo Bioho [Benkos Bioho] is a construction of a few written documents that mention the revolt that led to the existence of Palenque de la Matuna. The fact that we are dealing with written sources does not grant absolute clarity. There are discrepancies and lacunae regarding the date the leader and his followers fled, from whom, and where he fled, how many times he was attacked, and the terms and causes of the peace treaties. The motives of his death sentence are not known, either.)

The foundation myth of Benkos Bioho dates back to Camilo Delgado.[231] Escalante, who "rediscovered" Palenque, brought this myth with him during his fieldwork in the 1950s.[232] At this time, palenqueros, a community without historical documents, had no recollection of events prior to 1900.[233] While a Benkos Bioho existed and was captured and executed between 1618 and 1619, there is no evidence that he founded Palenque de San Miguel, present-day San Basilio de Palenque.[234]

Like Bioho, there is no apparent historical basis for Falupo other than the existence of numerous heretics arrested and tortured by the Spanish Inquisition, which had a palace in nearby Cartagena de Indias, the primary slave port for the Spanish colonies until the end of the eighteenth century.[235] However, he does represent the 30 percent of Inquisition cases filed against

Afro-descendants in Cartagena, since it focused on "crypto-Jews."[236] Henao notes that Falupo is also a name for Bioho, so creating two fictional characters that link African political rebellion with African spiritual beliefs fits Zapata's revolutionary goals of continuing Palenque's manifold rebellions.[237] Falupo's role in the tragedy of Bioho fuses the legendary uprising of 1603 with the historically documented Cartagena Holy Week Conspiracy of 1799.[238] While I disagree with Branche that the lack of "foregrounding of black bodies under the thrall of forced labor" makes it "more romantic than radical," it is clear that Bioho and Falupo are primarily a foundation myth that praises constant rebellion as the alternative to objectification, a continuation of the Thing-Zumbi binary.[239]

Wheat notes that, by 1600, the Hispanic Caribbean was primarily populated by black people.[240] While the entire region had roughly forty thousand African captives and their descendants in the seventeenth century, Cartagena had twenty thousand in 1622.[241] The slave trade was the city's primary source of income during the 1590s.[242] Wheat juxtaposes the port's population with the quilombo of Palmares, which I will discuss next chapter, and notes that the latter had only eleven thousand people at its height.[243] To limit one's scope to maroons is to ignore the majority of colonial black experiences. In addition to forced labor, blacks were part of colonial society in multiple ways. Some governed other Africans and Afro-descendants, black militia leaders, and supervisors of free work crews. Wheat notes black majorities and populations of 30 to 50 percent in Cuba, Puerto Rico, Florida, and Guatemala, to name a few, in that century. Many were active in the Catholic Church. With so many blacks occupying the role of "settler"—usually by brutal force—Zapata's selection of slave revolts in and around Cartagena like those of the seventeenth century is less a representation of historical fact and more the representation of a desire that the majority throw off their African curse and rule the colonies they inhabited. If blacks and mulattoes were so numerous, why did they not rise up to overthrow the Church, state, and economy that oppressed them? The answer the novel conveys is that they were divorced from the traditions of justice of their ancestors. Those who preserved them rebelled, if unsustainably.

2

Afro-Brazil in Gonçalves and Zapata

While Zapata details the intersection of history, myth, and literature, Gonçalves draws on a different kind of mythology based on poetry, oral tradition, and recorded history. Black authors have struggled to create a representation of slavery that is empowering to Afro-Brazilians. Perhaps no other writer has embodied this connection between activism, representation, and black identity more than Luís Gama. He can be seen to be the creator, in a postmodern sense of challenging truths, of Luísa Gama, his mother and the narrator-protagonist of *Defeito*. First, in many ways, Luís Gama "created" his own mother's life story, inverting the mother-child relationship. Then, feminist poets of the 1980s re-created her life story, including elements of another revolt leader Zeferina. All these alterations share the common desire to fill the gaps in the history of slavery from the slaves' point of view with empowering myths to support the political movements of the moment. These creations are highly relevant today, since the Brazilian congress has approved memorializing her in the Panteão da Pátria (National Cemetery) among national heroes, although there is no evidence she existed.[1] I conclude the chapter by comparing Brazilian runaway slave communities called *quilombos* in Gonçalves and Zapata's works. Both authors bear the impact of Abdias do Nascimento's political philosophy of revolution inspired by slave rebellions, called *quilombismo*.

Luís Gama: History, Myth, and Literature

Luís Gama's (1830–1882) life story is pivotal to *Um defeito de cor* (*A Color Defect*), not only because the latter's plot revolves around it, but also because he paved the way for a self-affirming black literature in Brazil. He was a poet, an abolitionist lawyer, a political activist, and a former slave. What follows is a more detailed biography of him to help the reader understand Gonçalves's novel as well as my own arguments about Gama's life and works. Little is written about Gama, though critic Lígia Ferreira's 2000 edition of his masterpiece is part of his recent rediscovery.[2] Aside from her, those who have resuscitated Gama studies through book-length studies have been historians and sociologists. They have gathered and circulated the documents that tell of his life. Gonçalves's reception places him again at the heart of the Afro-Brazilian canon.

Gama's story is tied to Brazilian abolition. The nation had the largest enslaved population, and its economy was dependent upon the institution. Ricardo Henriques notes that Brazil has the second largest black population in the world, after only Nigeria.[3] Britain outlawed the transatlantic slave trade in 1807, but illegal trade continued. The Haitian Revolution and U.S. Civil War made many in Brazil fear a violent end to slavery. A compromise between the Brazilian monarchy and the planter class, the Free Womb Law of September 28, 1871, stated that children born to enslaved mothers were required work the land with their mothers (and masters) until the age of twenty-one. The law was ignored mostly. Princess Isabel of Brazil signed the May 13, 1888, Golden Law, abolishing slavery fully in the eyes of the law. Gama was born one year before the November 7, 1831, law that declared all Africans brought to Brazil (not born there) and their offspring to be free.[4] This law was enforced by only a select group of liberal lawyers, particularly those associated with the Freemasons, whom he would join upon gaining his freedom.

Gama's autobiographical narratives, a letter and his poetry, are the only known sources on Luísa Mahin, so he wrote the woman Gonçalves would call Kehinde into being before Gonçalves did. Historian Ana Lucia Araujo shows that her life is fiction, and Ferreira is working to bring his story into focus.[5] The most important document on Gama is his widely published

July 25, 1880, autobiographical letter to abolitionist lawyer and founding member of the Brazilian Academy of Letters Lúcio de Mendonça.[6] Here he claims he was born in Salvador on June 21, 1830, and baptized in Itaparica.[7] Nonetheless, no records exist to prove his baptism.[8] He leaves out the name of his white father, who belongs to a rich Bahian family, and whom Gonçalves dubs "Alberto."[9] He states that his father sold him on November 10, 1840, to settle gambling debts. He was stored for sale by the trader Vieira in Rio de Janeiro. He was well treated by the women of the household, whom he mourned when he was sold in December of 1840. His new owner was Antonio Pereira Cardoso dos Santos of Campinas, who would commit suicide once his abuses toward his slaves—jailing, starving to death—were revealed. Gama befriended Cardoso's houseguest, the student Antonio Rodrigues do Prado Júnior, who taught the slave to read at seventeen. In 1848, the enslaved young man reportedly learned of his freedom and escaped. Questions surround how Gama learned of his being born free in 1848 after being able to read for only a year and living in Campinas, many miles from Bahia, where he was separated from his mother at ten years of age.[10]

Upon gaining his freedom, Gama became a lawyer, activist, and writer. He joined the military and served as *ordenança* (primary, but servile, assistant to an officer) for Conselheiro Francisco Maria de Souza Furtado, chief of police, law professor in São Paulo, and his patron for many years.[11] He became secretary of the São Paulo Police. In 1859 Gama and his then common-law wife Claudina Fortunata Sampaio (whom he later married) had a son, Benedito Graco Pinto da Gama. That year he published the first edition of *Primeiras trovas burlescas de Getulino* (*Getulino's First Humorous Ditties*). In 1861 he became a professional journalist due to the success of the revised version of the collection. He participated in several satirical periodicals: *Diabo Coxo* (*Devil with a Limp*, founded 1864–1865), *Cabrião* (*Big Goat*, contributor as "Barrabás" or "Barrabas," 1866–1867), *A Província de São Paulo* (*The Province of São Paulo*, 1875), *O Coaracy* (1876), and *O Polichinello* (*Open Secret*, owner-editor, 1876–1882).[12] His civic activity was formidable. He helped found the Republican Party in 1868, a free public school for all children and adults in 1869, and a public library in 1871. His patron fired him for defending slaves in 1869. In the 1870s he was alienated from the Republican Party by the landowners he reviled, and he was accused of being a communist in 1871.

His legacy has not gone unnoticed. His was perhaps the biggest funeral of his day, and all strata of São Paulo attended it.[13] After Gama's death, in

1904, the final and expanded edition of *Trovas burlescas* was released. *Modernista* (avant-garde) poet Manuel Bandeira praised "Quem sou eu?" (Who Am I?) and "Meus amores" (My Loves) in his 1937 literary history of romanticism.[14] A Masonic lodge in São Paulo was named after him in 1894, pilgrimages were made to his grave until the 1930s Vargas regime, and 1930 saw his centenary marked with many publications.[15] His biography has undergone many revisions: the 1881 letter to Mendonça was the only one published during his lifetime, and Sud Mennucci's 1938 bio-bibliographical study was the only one for most of the century.[16]

Journalist and writer Raul Pompeia took up the abolitionist flame after Gama's life and made the poet the center of his work.[17] He shows that the press, which boomed at the end of the nineteenth century, was a means of controlling public honor and shame.[18] Gama became a symbol of Brazilian honor in the face of the shameful institution of slavery. Pompeia met Gama at the São Paulo Law School a year before the latter's death in 1881 and molded his career around him.

Gonçalves's recovery of Gama's legacy mirrors Maria Consuelo Cunha Campos's.[19] The critic includes Gama's description of his mother and his relationship to her, part of his affirmation of a black identity.[20] She notes his literary recognition, including his friendship with Machado de Assis and José de Alencar. Sílvio Romero and Edison Carneiro anthologized him.[21] The poet Lino Guedes was born to former slaves and is a direct link between the poetry of Gama and the international African diaspora.

Critic Emanuelle Oliveira considers Guedes the beginning of Brazil's version of *négritude* (black consciousness) in literature.[22] His essay *Luiz Gama e sua individualidade literaria* (*Luiz Gama and His Literary Individuality*, 1924) celebrates Gama as a black poet. Otherwise, critics have only recently reevaluated him as a precursor to today's black writers. Gonçalves's imagining of his family's compelling story fills important gaps in his autobiography, particularly regarding his mother.

Luísa Mahin: From Poetry to History

Let us examine how Gama used literature to tell the story of his mother and his view of black motherhood in general. Gonçalves presents her in a way that, unlike Zapata, includes the forced labor of slavery alongside more banal interactions with those around her. Gama describes her explicitly only once, in the only historical record of her existence, though, and it supports the abolitionist argument that the law must be changed regarding slavery or face revolt. He mentions Luiza Mahin by name, stating that she was an unacculturated slave/*boçal*, Mina (Nagô de Nação [Yoruba]), and someone who always refused Christianity.[23] *Boçal* means "muzzle," making her a symbol of the silenced and animalized enslaved.[24] She was an enslaved food seller (*quintandeira*) and participant in failed slave revolts:

> Era dotada de atividade. Em 1837, depois da Revolução do dr. Sabino, na Bahia, veio ela ao Rio de Janeiro, e nunca mais voltou. Procurei-a em 1847, em 1856, e em 1861, na Corte, sem que a pudesse encontrar. Em 1862, soube, por uns pretos minas que conheciam-na e que deram-me sinais certos, que ela, acompanhada com malungos desordeiros, em uma "casa de dar fortuna", em 1838, fora posta em prisão. . . . Era opinão dos meus informantes que esses "amotinados" fossem mandados pôr fora pelo governo. . . . Nada mais pude alcançar a respeito dela.[25]
>
> (She was always active. In 1837, after Dr. Sabino's Revolution [Sabinada], in Bahia, she came to Rio de Janeiro, and never returned. I looked for her in 1847, 1856, and in 1861, at the Court, without finding her. In 1862, I learned, from some Mina blacks that knew her and that gave me clear indications that she was taken to prison, along with some disorderly comrades, at a "fortune-telling house," in 1838. . . . It was my informants' opinion that these "rabble-rousers" were sent away by the government. . . . I found out nothing else about her.)

This description leaves much to the imagination. It seems even Gama wanted to know more about her, since he searched the Royal Court for her and likely searched legal records for her, since she was imprisoned. Who was she? What was her specific role in these rebellions? Gama does not or cannot reveal these details, either because he does not remember them, having been sold into slavery as a child, or because he is playing with the truth to create and conceal aspects of his mother's identity and his own for a public of slave owners and abolitionists. While he claims she was of "nagô" (Yoruba) ethnicity, her last name indicates a specific region: "mahi," a confederation of tribes that was, tragically, the area Dahomean kingdoms like Agajá and Glele used as a primary region for the wars where people were taken and sold as captives.[26] In Bahian Candomblé circles, there is a *nação jeje-mahi* (jeje-mahi ethnicity), which would explain later claims that she was jeje, and which

Gonçalves also claims.[27] Impressively, the literate, creole, and highly acculturated Gama refers to his mother's comrades as *malungos* (brothers, shipmates), showing impressive black solidarity for his time and station as an influential mulatto.

As in the letter to Mendonça, a text of close parentage to the slave narrative, he uses poetry to create and/or portray a mother with abolitionist ends. In his only book of poetry, Gama devotes a work to a mother (perhaps his) in "A minha mãe" (My Mother).[28] Gama uses short, rhyming verses (abbcdeec . . .), a simpler, more popular, more childlike verse, to recall his mother with "saudades" (longing). It is unclear how much of the poem is based on lived experience. In the text, the speaker peers in his memories into the eyes of his mother:

> Os olhos negros, altivos,
> Dois astros eram luzentes;
> Eram estrelas cadentes
> Por corpo humano sustidas.
> Foram espelhos brilhantes
> Da nossa vida primeira,
> Foram a luz derradeira
> Das nossas crenças perdidas.[29]
>
> (Her proud, black eyes,
> Two shining stars were;
> They were falling stars
> Held up by a human body.
> They were shining mirrors
> Of our first life,
> They were the lasting light
> Of our lost beliefs.)

His mother's eyes are renowned by the son not for what they see but for what they reflect: the implicit author's own desires, his own mourning, his own *saudade* for lost childhood hope. For an enslaved African, the historical context makes mourning the maternal body take the form of a common foundational trauma: the imagined "loss" of an idyllic "Africa" that was never there. His "lost beliefs" are faith in humanity, stability, and unity for himself and his family, which are dashed by the loss of his mother when he is enslaved. These projections make the eyes more than mimesis. They are starlike, providing light instead of absorbing and interpreting it. She is the moon, not the sun, reflecting the light the speaker has imagined for himself.[30] Her voice forms not words but

Brandinha a voz sonorosa,
Sentida como a Rolinha,
Gemendo triste sosinha
Ao som da aragem faceira.[31]

(Soft was her sweet-sounding voice,
Felt like a columbina [bird],
Moaning sad, alone
to the sound of the breeze.)

His mother is a beautiful absence. Her kisses are life itself, versus the "death" of losing her when he was enslaved.[32]

An allegory of Mother Africa alters the interpretation of his once-mentioned brother. As in Gonçalves's novel, Gama has a (half) brother, whom she calls Banjokô.[33] For Gama's voice, the only details given are that his mother cared for both:

Era mui bella e formosa
Era a mais linda pretinha,
Da adusta Lybia rainha,
E no Brasil pobre escrava![34]

(She was very fine and beautiful
She was the most beautiful negress
Queen from arid Lybia,
And in Brazil a poor slave!)

The Lybia referred to is all of "Africa." Other terms for it were "Guinea" and "Ethiopia," for example. If one brother is Lybia and the other is Brazil, remembering the happy family together is a means of "recalling" or imagining a time when Africa and Brazil were joined in peace like a presubjective state. Hence, "Ella sorrindo brincava" (she would play smiling) would signify a joyous union of the two lands the mother represents: Africa and

Brazil.[35] She is historically impossible: the two were bound by bloodshed, oppression, and conquest, but she is poetically imaginable. Thus, she is a saint in stanza 7 and in stanza 8 has a "prece infinita" (infinite prayer) and her tears are "pérolas sentidas" (aching pearls), making her like a Baroque Madonna. However, her tears (reflections of his tears?) pour onto the land of slavery, becoming commodities, bought and sold as Gama and Mahin were. In this poem the enslaved "pearls" of the past hold an undiscovered, unappreciated beauty that was overlooked by their initial role as commodities. The person one might expect to have the most information on Mahin, her son, records her only in a few cryptic lines of prose and poetry that may be about her (or Africa) in relation to him (or an imagined poetic voice).

The poetic re-creation of Mahin would continue throughout the twentieth century and ultimately the twenty-first, so Gonçalves's text is merely the most developed monument to this legendary woman. Dulcilei da Conceição Lima notes the lack of evidence regarding Mahin.[36] In fact, the leading historian on the Revolta dos Malês, João José Reis, claims that there is no evidence that there were any female leaders in the revolt and that there is evidence only that women had servile roles in the rebellion.[37] The heroic inflation of Mahin to rebel leader is "um misto de realidade possível, ficção abusiva e mito libertário" (a mixture of possible reality, abusive fiction, and liberating myth).

Mahin was given new life by the eugenicist-inspired author and historian Pedro Calmon in his historical novel *Malês: A insurreição das senzalas* (*Muslim Insurrection in the Barracks*, 1933).[38] While the novel exemplifies naturalist determinism and the ultimate argument of the novel is that the Revolta dos Malês failed due to blacks' inability to organize themselves, Calmon did add much detail to the character of Luísa Mahin. The Malês were superior to the Yoruba/*nagôs* for him, but they were all inferior to the civilized white elite of Bahia.[39] In Calmon's novel, her name is Luiza Princesa (Luiza Princess) and would have been crowned queen had the revolt been successful.[40] She is a *quitanda* (enslaved food vender), which allows her mobility. The rebel stores weapons and leads the *batuques* (drum circles) that unite and inspire others.

Calmon's depiction of Mahin was so convincing and interesting that it inspired Arthur Ramos. His posthumous book *O negro na civilização brasileira* (*The Negro in Brazilian Civilization*, 1971) includes the chapter "Insurreições negras no Brasil" (Black Insurrections in Brazil), which argues against the previous presumption that blacks passively accepted slavery, unlike the warring Amerindians.[41] Luísa is a leader in the revolt, and the conspirators meet at her home to plan. He calls the "princess" a "símbolo do valor da mulher negra" (symbol of the black woman's bravery) and praises her important role as a mother and a fighter in a noble cause.[42] Nonetheless, he still portrayed blacks as culturally inferior to whites.

With these academic precursors, the Black feminists of the 1980s re-created Luísa Mahin for their own political purposes, which would later align with Gonçalves's own. In 1986 Alzira Rufino, Nilza Iraci, and Maria Rosa Pereira formed the Coletivo de Mulheres Negras da Baixada Santista (1986) that wrote the *cartilha* (booklet) *A mulher brasileira tem história* (*Brazilian Women Have a History*, 1987), which includes her biography alongside strong black women such as Anastácia, Aqualtune, Laudelina de Campos Melo, and Luísa Mahin.[43] The booklet was an internal document not published elsewhere. The writers lived in a period of great change in Brazil. The Movimento Negro Unido was formed in 1978 under the leadership of Abdias do Nascimento, alongside Leila González, who sought to fight sexism within the black movement itself, dating back to the Frente Negra Unida (United Black Front, est. 1931) and to "darken" feminism to include voices beyond white heterosexual women of the middle to upper classes.[44] The myth of the *mãe preta* (black mammy), which dated back to the time of domestic slaves who served as nurses to white families, was the demeaning stereotype these activists sought to problematize and substitute. Hence, they embellished previous accounts of Mahin. Rufino, Iraci, and Pereira claim Mahin was either *jeje* (from the former Slave Coast) or born free in Brazil in 1812.[45] She participated in every revolt in Salvador and led the Revolta dos Malês. On the face of it she is a virtually impossible character, given the limitations of her time. However, Reis, the historian who denies female leadership in the Malês, does note that Zeferina, a maroon woman and Candomblé priestess, was a leader of the Urubu (Buzzard Quilombo) and that she was called "queen" among the rebels when she led her people as an archer when the colonial forces invaded their territory.[46] In the oral tradition the stories of Mahin and Zeferina were combined. Mahin became the symbol of black female rebels in general.

As with Gama's depictions of her, the black feminist version of Mahin was re-created through the poetic imagination. In 1978, the same year as the consolidation of the Movimento Negro Unido (United Black Movement), Afro-Brazilian writers published the first issue of the journal *Cadernos Negros* (*Black Notebooks*), the catalyst for the Quilombhoje literary circle.[47]

The journal's goals included creating a self-conscious black literature and granting visibility to the black history that "official history" denied.[48]

Alziara Rufino and Miriam Alves are the two Quilombhoje poets who re-create the biography of Mahin in their works. In Miriam Alves's poem, Mahin is a vision of the past and the future, giving the work its title, "Mahin amanhã" (Mahin Tomorrow, 1986), which I quote in full:[49]

Ouve-se nos cantos a conspiração
vozes baixas sussurram frases precisas
escorre nos becos as lâminas das adagas
Multidão tropeça nas pedras
Revolta
Há revoada de pássaros
Sussuro, sussurro:
———é amanhã, é amanhã.
Mahin falou, é amanhã.
A cidade toda se prepara
Malês
Bantus
Geges
Nagôs
Vestes coloridas resguardam esperanças
Aguardam a luta
Arma-se a grande derrubada branca
A luta é tramada na língua dos Orixás
———é aminhã, aminhã
Sussuram
Malês
Bantus
Geges
Nagôs
———é aminhã, Luiza Mahin falô.[50]

(The conspiracy is heard in songs/corners
Low voices whisper precise/needed phrases
The blades of the daggers drip in the alleys
A multitude stumbles on the stones
Revolt

The birds fly away
Whisper, whisper:
"It is tomorrow, tomorrow."
Mahin said so, it is tomorrow.
The whole city prepares
Malês
Bantus
Geges
Nagôs
Colorful clothing conceal hopes
They await struggle
The great white tumbling is set
The fight is planned in the language of the Orixás
"It is tomorrow, tomorrow."
They whisper
Malês
Bantus
Geges
Nagôs
"It is to-Min-o," Luiza Mahin has spoken).

The "tomorrow" of the title and refrain notes the centrality of time to the poem: the past is being reimagined to create a new "tomorrow." Nevertheless, in both the past and the present, a revolution is awaited and hoped for, but it is not yet carried out. The collective action of the MNU is clearly a part of Alves's poetics, driving her to put a call for future revolution into this leader of the past. Also, unlike the historical record of the Malês revolt, all Afro-Brazilians are united in the struggle, not under Allah but under the Orixás, the Yoruba deities that inform her poetics and worldview and that of many present leaders in the struggle, including Nascimento himself. She is molding the life of a woman who may not have existed to create community and implement political change for women in Brazil. The neologism "aminhã" combines "tomorrow" with "Mahin," but also with "a minha" (mine), indicating a collective black struggle for "a grande derrubada branca" (the great white toppling). Revolutionary violence seems to be an option, as the bloody daggers of the Bahian streets indicate in the poem, but the political will seems dissipated in a constant state of procrastination.

Rufino's "Luiza Mahin" (1988) reinforces feminist and revolutionary ideals:

Filha de gêge
na escravidão
Luiza Mahin
sofria os negros
Luiza de gêge
mulher em luta
todo dia toda noite
em espadas
Mahin dos Malês
posição ao sol couraça
Luiza revolta a noite
vermelho o chão da Bahia.[51]

(Daughter of a gêge
In slavery
Luiza Mahin
Suffered the blacks
Luiza of gêge
Woman in struggle
Every day and every night
In spades/swords
Mahin of the Malês
Breastplate facing the sun
Luiza revolt the night
Red the ground of Bahia.)

Never the passive, benevolent *mãe preta* (mammy), she is a woman who leads, fights, and kills. She is born of Africa. She embodies strength and continued militancy for black liberation in the twentieth century and beyond.

In addition to poetry, Mahin was the topic of several other texts at the turn of the new millennium. A Wikipedia article presents her with the face of Carolina Maria de Jesus to tie her to literature and black female leadership.[52] São Paulo dedicated a square to her in 2011. It is in the "Freguesia Ó" (O Parrish), which is primarily Afro-Brazilian, and it was the initiative of the Coletivo de Mulheres Negras de São Paulo.[53] The poster for the inauguration depicts a drawing of a woman with neatly trimmed natural African hair, unlike any previous depictions of her, so she is the embodiment of black pride. The square reaches the Brazilian masses and instils pride in them, as is the case of Fábio Malavoglia's *radionovela* (radio drama) *Luiza Mahin*, supported by the Palmares Cultural Foundation, a branch of the Brazilian Ministry of Culture.[54] The protagonists are Mahin and the creator god of Yoruba mythology Olodumarê, who stands as judge for Mahin's life and acts. They also speak to Dandara (a feminization of the male Malê warrior Dandará) and queen Nzinga of Angola.

This account exemplifies how much heterodoxy there is in the recording, creation, and re-creation of Mahin's existence, acts, and identity. As Afro-Brazilian feminist Sueli Carneiro argues, Black feminism had to rely on oral traditions and the collective imagination to recover the lives of "mulheres batalhadoras" (women warriers).[55] Thus, like Bioho, she is a liberating myth for multiple authors and readers. Gonçalves's sprawling and human narrative sometimes confirms and sometimes challenges this background of constant heroism and rebelliousness.

In her prologue Gonçalves admits that she is re-creating, or creating, a unique life story:

> Mesmo porque esta pode não ser uma simples história, pode não ser a história de uma anônima, mas sim de uma escrava muito especial, alguém de cuja existência não se tem confirmação, pelo menos até o momento em que escrevo esta introdução. Especula-se que ela pode ser apenas uma lenda, inventada pela necessidade que os escravos tinham de acreditar em heróis, ou, no caso, em heroínas, que apareciam para salvá-los da condição desumana em que viviam.[56]
>
> (Maybe because this is not just a story, maybe it is not the story of an anonymous woman, but that of a very special slave, someone whose existence has not been confirmed at least by the time I write this introduction. It is speculated that she was only a legend invented by the necessity slaves had to believe in heroes, or, in this case, heroines, that would appear to save them from the inhuman conditions in which they live.)

It sounds like this introduction was written for one of the superhuman depictions of historical figures like the previous "Mahins," but the novel's plot shows a very different figure. Gonçalves is writing after the "Thing-Zumbi" binomial. She is depicting more than a revolution, and she is showing details of the rebellion that might have escaped a more epic telling like that of Bioho.

First, the fluidity of work, celebration, and liberation is evident in Kehinde's role in the plot. Her home and place of business houses the Malês, who make cigars to survive, to free mala Abubakar, and to finance their rebellion. She delivers the cigars, which contain messages in the African Haussa language and in Arabic characters:

> Mesmo com todos os preparativos para a rebelião, os muçurumins não deixaram de enrolar charutos. Os pedidos aumentavam e tínhamos que trabalhar dia e noite, na oficina ou em casa. Foram bons aqueles dias de dúvidas sobre a minha participação, porque quase não saí do seu lado, e nem sei o que fizeram com os recados que precisavam ser entregues. Mesmo tendo muito trabalho, havia dois momentos do dia em que eu fazia questão de estar com você, que era no desjejum e na hora de dormir. Você não dormia sem ouvir histórias, e eu costumava inventar muitas sobre a África, dizendo que lá era bom e que todos os pretos viviam livres.[57]
>
> (Even with all the preparation for the rebellion, the Muslims did not stop rolling cigars. The orders grew and we had to work day and night, in the shop or at home. Those days of doubts about my participation were good, because I never left your side, and I don't even know what they did with the messages that needed to be sent. Even with a lot of work, they were two moments in the day when I made sure to be with you, which were breakfast and bedtime. You would not sleep without hearing stories, and I used to invent a lot about Africa, saying that everything was good there and all the blacks were free.)

The central role of motherhood in her participation is also a part of this discussion, as is the self-conscious rejection on the author's part of Africa as a romantic homeland, one of Gilroy's arguments and a difference from Zapata's more ambitious muntu philosophy. Also, unlike Zapata's characters' constant rebellion, here and elsewhere Kehinde records domestic life. The rebels' profession also has a contradictory element: much Brazilian tobacco was sent to Lower Guinea to buy slaves like these characters, so they are continuing the slave system even as the subvert it.[58]

Zapata, in his novel, aspires to unite all of the oppressed under black leadership and overthrow the oppressors, but the historical record is much more fraught with internal ethnic conflicts. Navarrete shows that there were many conflicts between African groups in Palenque (San Miguel) and its surrounding black strongholds, and there was strife between African-born and Colombia-born blacks.[59] Likewise, the Malês also have a story of disunity:

> Todos tinham muita fé nos trabalhos de proteção do mala Abubakar, pois ele era um dos únicos na Bahia que já tinham ido a Meca. O Fatumbi disse para eu não contar a ele que podia ser chamada de gente de santo, ou seja, que eu cultuava os orixás. Entre os muçurumins que não tinham a importância do mala, os pretos da religião dos orixás eram até suportados, mas os grandes mestres nos desprezavam. Eu sabia que muita gente de santo também desprezava os muçurumins, a quem chamavam de malês.[60]
>
> (They all had great faith in the tasks to protect Mala Abubakar, since he was one of the only ones in Bahia that had been to Mecca. Fatumbi told me not to tell him that I could be called a "saint person," or rather, that I worshipped the Orishas. Among the Muslims that did not have the Mala's importance, the blacks of the Orisha religion were even tolerated, but the great masters looked down on us. I knew that lots of saint people also looked down on Muslims, whom they called "Malês.")

The Revolta dos Malês would not bring about the Nuevo Muntu. In fact, religious and ethnic divisions, which were a driving force that united these jihadis, made their collaboration with other Africans and Afro-descendants almost impossible outside the fact that they had a common enemy. They are the continuation of Muslim blacks who rebelled against slavery using military strategy and even horsemanship they learned from their Muslim captors in Africa.[61] There are parallels here with black Christian Jubilee, a Christian trope of the U.S. slave tradition Gilroy studies, that rids these blacks of their oppression, but it is only for some.[62] It points to some of the fissures in Zapata's uniting the muntu: how are Christians like Martin Luther King Jr. to unite with the faithful of Bantu and Yoruba religions? Or with black Muslims and Rastafarians? Religion can be both a resource and a barrier to revolution, and Gonçalves shows that.

Another dividing factor for the Malês and Kehinde is gender:

> Eu adoraria ter ido, mas só os homens foram convidados. Não haveria somente a reunião, mas também uma festa, um grande jantar para comemorar a data que eles chamam de Lailat al-Miraj, a ascensão ao céu do profeta Maomé. A

> Fátima, a Binta e a Safyia não quiseram ficar sozinhas na loja e foram para a nossa casa, levando um pedaço de carneiro assado que comemos todos juntos. Para nós era um sábado comum, vinte e nove de novembro, mas, no calendário diferente que os muçurumins seguiam, era o dia vinte e seis de Rajab.[63]
>
> (I would have loved to go [to the meeting], but only men were invited. There would be not only a meeting but also a party, a large dinner to celebrate the date they call Lailat al-Miraj, the ascension of the Prophet. Fátima, Benta, and Safyia did not want to be alone in the house and went to our house, taking a piece of grilled lamb that we all ate together. For us it was an ordinary Saturday, November 29, but, on the different calendar the Muslims followed, it was Rajab 26.)

While it is anachronistic to expect nineteenth-century African Muslims (or many other groups, for that matter) to have female leadership, it is important to point out that there was no Mahin at the helm.

Another example of fluidity between the public and private spheres is the denunciation of the conspiracy to the police. One of the participants, Vitorio Sule, makes his wife Sabina very suspicious will all his secret activity.

> Ao retornar, já de noite, encontrou a casa toda revirada e os filhos sem saber do paradeiro do pai, que tinha saído de casa levando algumas roupas. Achando que tinha sido abandonada, a Sabina resolveu ir até os lugares que ele costumava freqüentar, como a loja do Manoel Calafate.[64]
>
> (That night, upon returning, she found the house a complete mess and their children not knowing where their father was, only that he had taken some clothes and left the house. Thinking that she had been abandoned, Sabina decided to go to the places he used to frequent, like Manoel Calafate's house.)

The simple observation that a domestic dispute can imperil a whole revolution makes the analysis of them more nuanced than a Manichaean discussion of "supporters" and "traitors." Sabina does not betray the revolution—she is angry because the thinks her husband is betraying her!

Another issue that betrays the rebellion is desertion, which again accentuates Kehinde's humble heroism as they descend on Salvador: "Já éramos muitos, mas também era grande a quantidade de pretos desertando, e eu tentava convencê-los a continuar" (There were a lot of us then, but there was also a large quantity of blacks deserting, and I tried to convince them to continue).[65] So while she may have been excluded from top leadership, she showed leadership in a more humble fashion.

Kehinde's personal sacrifice in participating in the revolt is evident when she becomes aware that it will soon fail as they charge through the streets of Salvador:

> Pelas palavras de ordem gritadas em línguas de África e respondidas por todos, dava para perceber que quase não havia crioulos entre nós, que aqueles homens e mulheres que rumavam para Itapagipe tinham feito a mesma viagem que eu. Mas a grande maioria provavelmente não tinha firmado laços, não tinha filhos nem casa e, portanto, quase nada a perder. Depois de tudo começado, não pensei em abandonar o grupo, mesmo sabendo que muita coisa não tinha dado certo, que a precipitação nos tinha impedido de contar com boa parte dos pretos e com a maioria das armas.[66]

> (From the orders shouted in African languages and answered by all, one could tell that there were almost no creoles among us, that those men and women that made their way to Itapagipe had made the same trip I had. Yet the great majority probably had not formed connections, had no children at home, and, thus, almost nothing to lose. After everything began, I didn't think of abandoning the group, even knowing that a lot had gone wrong, that haste had stopped us from counting on a large part of the blacks and the majority of the weapons.)

By emphasizing a woman's perspective, Kehinde includes the expectations of the time that women constantly care for their children and not take huge risks in the public sphere like marching in an armed revolt.

Her role as a mother no doubt contributes to her adoption of remaining a survivor and not adopting an attitude of "libertad o muerte" (liberty or death) like Zapata's novel or a "turn toward death" like Gilroy's theory.[67] As the authorities gain ground on the rebellion, she turns to her mentor Fatumbi, the Muslim teacher she has known since her first days on the plantation.

> O Eslebão tentava me puxar pelo braço na direção da praia, e eu disse que não iria sem o Fatumbi, que encontrei ajoelhado junto com quatro ou cinco pretos, orando. Corri até ele e disse que precisávamos sair dali, mas antes que ele pudesse responder o que eu já imaginava, que dali só saía morto, uma bala bem

> no meio da testa o dispensou de falar. Não sei se saí correndo de susto ou para não ver meu amigo morrer, ou para não ter o mesmo fim que ele.[68]
>
> (Eslebão tried to pull me by the arm toward the beach, and I said I would not go without Fatumbi, whom I found kneeling by four or five blacks, praying. I ran up to him and said we needed to get out of there, but before he could respond with what I already imagined, that he would only leave there dead, a bullet right in the middle of the forehead stopped him from speaking. I do not know if I took off running in fear or to not see my friend die, or to not meet the same end as him.)

Kehinde's survival instinct and dedication to family no doubt are factors in her not staying and dying a traditional masculine hero's death in war. She is a different rebel from Zapata's.

Kehinde overcomes some of the divisions in the Revolta dos Malês and saves her own life and those of others with the help of the mulatto Dr. Jorge. They are trapped and hunted by the authorities.

> O Uzoma quase me convenceu quando disse que àquela altura todos já sabiam que a rebelião tinha o propósito de, mais adiante, matar os brancos e escravizar os mulatos, e que, portanto, um mulato não poderia estar bem-intencionado ao nos oferecer ajuda. Mas minha intuição não costumava falhar, e algo me dizia que aquela era nossa única chance de sair logo dali, e quando eles disseram que iam embora naquela noite mesmo, pulando o muro, eu disse que ficaria e me responsabilizaria caso quisessem ficar também, e acho que minha segurança os convenceu.[69]
>
> (Uzoma almost convinced me when he told me that at that point everyone already knew the rebellion had the intent of killing the whites and enslaving the mulattoes later on, and, therefore, a mulatto could not be well intended in offering us help. But my intuition did not tend to fail, and something told me that was our only chance to get out of there right then, and when they said they were leaving that very night, jumping the wall, I said I would stay and be responsible in case they wanted to stay too, and I think my security convinced them.)

So Kehinde's survival instinct saves lives and overcomes divisions. She ironically feigns death in her fight for life: "E foi disfarçada de cadáver que fui carregada para fora da faculdade e colocada em uma carroça. Suspirei aliviada quando percebi que ela estava se movimentando, e mais ainda quando reconheci as vozes do Tico e do Hilário" (And it was disguised as a corpse that I was carried out of the college and placed in a cart. I sighed with relief when I sensed that I was moving, and even more when I recognized the voices of Tico and Hilário).[70] The irony of her sigh, the physiological sign of life, accentuates her constant will to live. Also, her allies are the other humble foot soldiers of the revolt who could not even read, but who delivered the messages that made it possible.

The Revolta has a devastating end like the overwhelming destruction through fire and torture that follow the rebellions of the *Nova Índia* and Benkos Bioho. The hopes, plans, work, and risk end in a

> verdadeira devassa, que centenas de pretos tinham sido presos e seriam condenados à morte. Na noite do acontecido, enquanto ainda lutávamos em Água de Meninos, um grupo apareceu na loja e recolheu todas as coisas dos muçurumins, que também tinham desaparecido sem deixar vestígios.[71]
>
> (true routing, that hundreds of blacks had been arrested and would be sentenced to death. On the night of the occurrence, while we were still fighting in Água de Meninos, a group appeared at the house and gathered all the Muslims' things, which had also disappeared without a trace.)

Gonçalves's attention to minute details, like who cleans up after a revolt, reveals important elements pertaining to history's revolutions. Repeatedly, heroes like Benkos and Falupo die and that is the end of the story, at least until they become part of a disembodied spirit world. She survives to know the aftermath of the bloody battles that tend to end when the fire burns out in *Changó*.

Quilombos in *Changó*

Up to this point I have been discussing the fluid boundaries between black literature, myth, and history. I now turn to the Brazilian *quilombos* described and mythologized in each work. For Zapata the quilombo is an animistic, communal, and African-rooted alternative to the greed of colonialism and capitalism. For Gonçalves the quilombo is a space of female liberation that does not reject capitalism but incorporates it into a mixed system that includes African and Afro-Brazilian practices. Zapata's takes place in the eighteenth century boom-towns of Minas Gerais.

The Afro-Colombian seems to see in the mulatto sculptor Aleijadinho the embodiment of the African diaspora's struggle to overcome oppression through creativity. He named a short-lived black cultural center in Mexico for Aleijadinho in the 1940s.[72] In addition to his race, what stood out to Zapata, a medical student at the time, was his illness. The artist's name means "little cripple" because he was afflicted with a degenerative disease that caused him to gradually lose toes and fingers. He had to be carried, and his tools eventually had to be tied to his fingerless hands for him to work. Much, if not all, of Aleijadinho's life has been (re)fabricated by each of his biographers.[73]

Gilroy claims that slavery is at the heart of capitalism.[74] Zapata, an anti-racist Marxist, already shows this to be true. The leitmotif of hunger in Brazil, popularized in cinema by Glauber Rocha, shows the perversion of slavery during the Americas' first gold rush around Ouro Preto (Black Gold). Zapata falls into the "thing-Zumbi" paradigm of representing the enslaved, but he does so in a complex manner that continues Abdias do Nascimentos *quilombismo* utopianism.

Nascimento was a Cold War exile from the Brazilian military dictatorship. Censorship was the law, and Freyre's "racial democracy" and "lusotropicalism," which posited that Portuguese colonialism and slavery were more benevolent than elsewhere and that miscegenation created harmonious societies, were the dominant narratives in history.[75] Nascimento counters these sweet dreams by speaking of a "genocide of blacks," which includes forced miscegenation—rape—of black women, the hunger of the poor, and cultural genocide through assimilation to this harmonious *mestiço* myth.[76]

In the quilombo, Marxism, anticolonialism, Afrocentrism, and Brazilian nationalism find their utopia for Nascimento. His goal was to revise Western history, that of Brazil in particular, to overcome its Eurocentric bias and reveal the horrors of slavery and the nobility of the struggle against it, which transcends the colonial context and Brazilian borders to include the entire African diaspora.[77] He uses the bellicose boomerang metaphor to describe how Africans in Brazil can use tools of oppression to fight the oppressors, such as education and performance like "culturally *mestiço*" samba schools, both of which became ways to preserve African traditions. He would use education, particularly the revision and dissemination of history, to undo the distortions of the past. This would culminate in 1978 in what is celebrated now as Black Awareness Day, the commemoration of Zumbi's valiant death in battle. This would replace the previous celebration of abolition in Brazil, May 13, 1888, with an homage to black self-liberation. Nascimento envisions it as the culmination of the Week of Afro-Brazilian History. The seven days were to teach black history and organized into the following daily themes: (1) pre-slavery African history, (2) the Portuguese invasion of Africa, (3) the Middle Passage, (4) the slave markets of Brazil, (5) slave life on the plantation and in the city, (6) black resistance from quilombos to today, and (7) homage to Zumbi and celebration of all of Afro-Brazil on November 20.[78] Nascimento dreamed of establishing a new Palmares where there would be no private property, Afro-Catholic religions would be treated as equal to all others, work would be based on civic duty, leadership would be black but all would be welcome, and half the jobs would be reserved for women. Nascimento would go on to become a Brazilian senator and mollify his rhetoric, but his radicalism in *quilombismo* is clear.[79] Zapata's revision of Brazilian history is just as uncompromising.

Zapata's chapter on Brazil tells the life of mulatto sculptor Antônio Francisco Lisboa. Hunger is omnipresent, and allusions to it continue throughout the section.[80] Starvation defined Brazilian slavery, leading to chronic disease, early death, and low birth rates; economic slowdown often caused masters to deprive their captives food.[81] As the chapter on Aleijadinho opens, the captive Agostinho gives his master food and wine, symbols of the Eucharist on the other, indicating the church's role in colonialism. This is the only meal described in the chapter and a symbol of an emerging black community, since it is his slaves who feed him and with whom he grows in solidarity.[82] The Africanized Eucharist is in keeping with the eighteenth-century slave belief that the wafer itself was a powerful talisman in the African tradition.[83] The lack of food is surprising since a key scene takes place in the fictitious Ocaria Mandioca's tavern, a venue for eating and drinking.[84] Mandioca represents the historical figure of the *nhara*, or merchant woman of the Atlantic World, much like Ezili did in Africa, especially since she appears to own the establishment.[85]

While there are no explicit descriptions of eating, food-related terminology is used for exploitative sexual encounters, or *comer*, Brazilian slang for coitus. The teeth are pulled from suffering, enslaved prostitutes' mouths and replaced with gold.[86] Their bodies are moved "a gusto" (to taste) under Ocaria's clients. Aleijadinho comes in search of a Mandinga that Ocaria drags through the market, and his slave salivates: "¡Aunque la cubrían las enaguas, sus caderas me dieron dentera!" (Even though her petticoats covered her, the woman's hips made my teeth chatter), to which the sculptor replies "¿Qué perro rabioso te persique?" (What rabid dog is chasing you?).[87] Later the slave Januario grovels: "Me contentaré con olisquear las manos del mestre después de que él se haya relamido los dedos, tras de almorzarse a la cabocla" (I will be content to sniff the master's hands after he has licked his fingers, after having dined on the cabocla). Again, there is an indirect allusion to food (the fingers, lunch), but only sexual exploitation is described in detail. The *bandeirantes*, enslaver-explorers from São Paulo, enslave indigenous, Africans, and *cafuso* (black-Amerindian mixed, *zambo*) people to work in the mines, but they do not care if their teeth fall out.[88]

Aleijadinho's free white father finds him stricken with illness as a young man.[89] A quote from Aleijadinho's Uncle Antonio sums up the hunger:

> Cuando me desprendo de las entrañas de tu abuela, la gente por estos lados de Minas Gerais padecía una hambruna que desde entonces, acá nunca más se ha terminado. Castigo que reciben los hombres por atragantarse de oro. . . . El estómago siente más hambre por los minerales de la tierra que por los frutos que en ella se cosechan.[90]
>
> (When I come loose from your grandmother's entrails, the people on this side of Minas Gerais suffered from a hunger that since then has never ended. A punishment that men receive for swallowing gold. . . . The stomach feels more hunger for the minerals of the land than for the fruits that are harvested from her).

The consumer of human flesh for gold is the personification of the colony and the slave masters enriched and "fed" through the Minas Gerais, the gold and diamond mines that financed the beautiful churches Aleijadinho beautified. This confirms the African notion of slavery as European cannibalism of black bodies.[91]

Comer as sex is present in the work. However, in Minas Gerais it is not a carnivalesque orgy but a rape of nature and human beings. In addition to the selling of women's bodies for money at the inn, other blacks' bodies are constantly violated. Overseers search *garimpeiros* (miners) for gold, including in the cracks of their toes and anuses.[92] The Johns pay Mandioca, but she searches the girls' teeth and vaginas to make sure all the money goes to her. Aleijadinho is born from the purchase of a sex slave as well. His white, landed father bought a black woman and had relations with her in an alleyway, not unlike the prostitutes whose services Aleijadinho later seeks.[93] Their madame Mandioca's name means "Manioc," a comestible tuber. She never eats or copulates—she only sells those who are eaten and penetrated. Thus, Zapata denaturalizes the violence of the Americas' first gold rush. Due to his Marxist philosophy, Zapata reviles the brutality of an unnatural, savage capitalism that exploits blacks, both in the eighteenth century and in the twentieth, when he is writing. The hoarding of women and exploiting them sexually for money are also historically accurate—there was a very high male-to-female ratio in the mining town, where males were preferred for physical labor.[94] In addition to gender imbalance, malnutrition, disease, and exhaustion led to low birth rates among the enslaved in Brazil.[95] Many captive women prostituted to feed their children, and some were prostituted by their masters.[96] Enslaved prostitutes were as young as ten years old, and Minas Gerais was a popular destination for trafficking them.[97] By the end of the chapter Aleijadinho's lover has a child, a personification of divine African fertility and resistance to the barren slave system.[98]

The slave Januario dances *capoeira*, which is presented as being able to break an arm or neck and feared by the *bandeirante* slave catchers.[99] His violent, rebellious dance gives him something in common with Gunga Zumbi. The authorities consider demonize the rebel: "Para unos Gunga Zumbi es el mismo Exú, oricha de los truenos en quien los frailes veían encarnado al demonio" (For some, Gunga Zumbi is Exú himself, the Orisha of thunder that the friars saw as the devil incarnate).[100] This makes him an earthly appointee of Changó, the Great Devil. Zapata blends him with Brazilian folklore: "Los caboclos afirman que es el mismo Sací, errante y solitario, a quien su amo cortó una pierna para que no huyera. Se aparece de noche en las senzalas, en los mercados de Vila Rica de Albuquerque, y aún en los atrios de las Iglesias donde predicará a los esclavos" (The caboclos claims he is Saci himself, wandering and lonely, whose master cut off his leg so he would not flee. He appears at night in the barracks, in the markets of Vila Rica de Albuquerque, and even in the atriums of the Churches where he preaches to the enslaved). The syncretism of the text has combined the spirits of the historical Gunga Zumbi with the Brazilian equivalent of Elegua, Exú, who is commonly associated with the devil. He is simultaneously an indigenous figure. Sací was popularized through the comics of Ziraldo as Saci Pererê, a lovable, flat black humanoid with a red hat and a pipe. He has parallels with the U.S. minstrel tradition in his stereotyped representation of black people. He is a monopod, but in Zapata's text, like the suffering Aleijadinho, he is missing a body part, which handicaps him. His enslaver cut off his leg as punishment for escaping.

Minas is fraught with corruption, which affects the church that pays Aleijadinho. Franciscan monks train the slaves in diamond cutting, which allows them to gain freedom and riches but not a sense of a unified black community due to status and class differences.[101] The Franciscans who pay Aleijadinho are so famously wealthy that the prostitutes of Mandioca are thrilled to lie with him. However, he does not purchase her services; he sublimates his desires into chiseling his saints.[102]

Like Agne Brown would later do in the novel, Aleijadinho must overcome the alienation of forgetting his black identity and his black ancestors. The sculptor also learns of his past from his Uncle Antonio, including the *pai-de-santo* (priest) and rebel leader Luís Bengala. The whites feared him as a "Demonio negro" (black Devil), but in the spirit world he is crowned king with a paper crown.[103] For this *pai-de-santo*, slavery itself is likely an illness, and the infertility of Minas was likely a divine curse that destroys African families.[104]

In the novel Aleijadinho's statues of saints at the Basílica do Bom Jesus de Matosinhos in Congonhas in the boom town of Vila Rica (Ouro Preto), Minas Gerais, represent conspirators of the first attempt to liberate Brazil from colonial rule. This was called the Inconfidência Mineira (Minas Conspiracy) of 1789. Inspired by the recent American Revolution and, more directly, by the French Revolution, a group of primarily white men in positions of power conspired to overthrow the Portuguese. However, the plot was discovered and its conspirators arrested. Reportedly, the government executed only one: Joaquim José da Silva Xavier, called Tiradentes because he was a dentist. He was allegedly drawn and quartered and his body parts spread throughout the towns that supported the conspirators, though Siva challenges the veracity of the account. The artist was aware. The short-lived Inconfidência enjoyed popular support and Tiradente's head was displayed in Vila Rica (Ouro Preto) while the sculptor was working there.[105] Martin Dreher argues that his masterpiece, the twelve soapstone prophets of Conghonhas, is a veiled monument to them. They are all exiles from their biblical homelands, as were the surviving conspirators, and they all hold verses of Holy Scripture condemning empires. For Zapata, Tiradentes is portrayed in the statue of the prophet Isaiah.[106] In notes on an early manuscript of

Changó, the author shows he was developing a historical argument similar to Dreher's, claiming that the twelve prophets were clandestine monuments to the conspirators.[107]

In the novel, the light-skinned Mulatto Aleijadinho, who lives a life as a trained, well-paid sculptor, has a life that could be considered "white" in his context. He learns through the Ancestors of the Inconfidência, but his slaves will not support it since Tiradentes will not liberate the slaves. Black and mulatto people, the majority of those living near Ouro Preto, were closely watched and arbitrarily punished. Having lost his slave Januario to the negrophobic colonial guards, he fears death without finishing his saints.[108] If the mulatto Aleijadinho's physical decay parallels Vila Rica's moral decay, then his loss of black Januario represents the loss of Minas Gerais's independence due to myopic leaders like the white Tiradentes who could not conceive of a Brazilian society without slavery.

The author uses the failure of the Inconfidência to highlight the importance of captives' self-liberation. A subsection of the chapter describes how Tiradentes supposedly attempts to convince Aleijadinho to send his slaves to fight for independence from Portugal in 1789.[109] Tiradentes's racism places him in stark contrast with Gunga Zumbi, who emerges as the spirit who might have lead the "Quilombo Grande de Minas Gerais" (Great Quilombo of Minas Gerais).[110] After the revolt is quashed, Januario is arrested and executed, leaving the sculptor without anyone to carry his frail body, but it may be implied that it was always Januario who made the sculptures at Minas Gerais, translating his master's will into stone for him.[111] If this is true, it does not contradict Aleijadinho's supplication to Ancestor Kanuri Mai: "Escúchame en esta noche de mi primer encuentro con el África de mi padre. La olvidada, la postergada, la alejada, regresa a mi vida con sus angustias de difunta. Será ella la que me devuelva los potentes brazos y los puños talladores" (Listen to me on the night of my first encounter with the Africa of my father. The forgotten, postponed, pushed away one returns to my life with her anguish of a dead woman).[112] If Africa is a violent origin like rebirth, then the bond with Januario is one in which they create art through a community. This is not unlike the community formed by Gunga Zumbi in the quilombo of Palmares: "Un pacto entre los vivos y los muertos para subsistir todos unidos. Los difuntos nos ayudan a escoger al sargento Siembra, al cabo Diligencia, al general Defensa, al mariscal Armas" (A pact between the living and the dead to subsist together as one. The dead help us to choose Sergeant Planting Seeds, Corporal Diligence, General Defense, and Marshal Arms).[113] The colonizers are a foil to Gunga Zumbi, who leads the people of his quilombo to plant crops of the Americas, corn and manioc, so they are black but culturally hybrid.[114] He calls his maroons to attack when the mines are exhausted. They will still eat during Lent, presenting the church's dogma as part of colonial decadence in comparison with Afro-Brazilian vitality.

The historical Palmares was a Brazilian re-creation of an all-male Central African warrior society.[115] It was a new start for maroons to start their own kinship bonds, free from previous bloodlines. It was "new" like the Nuevo Muntu. However, unlike in Zapata's romantic depiction, food in quilombos was in short supply and they lived under constant military threat.[116] They were not seen as a realistic solution for most slaves, but they are inspirational to many today.

Zapata's Zumbi is clearly influenced by his friend and collaborator Abdias do Nascimento. His tragedy *Sortilégio: Mistério de Zumbi Redivivo II* (*Sortilege: Black Mystery*) was published in 1979 while Zapata was finishing *Changó*, but its first version was completed in 1957, so the novelist was most likely aware of it.[117] The play opens with the protagonist saying "quero ver se o demônio dos negros é pior que o demônio dos brancos" (I want to see if the blacks' devil is worse than the white's devil), linking blasphemy to rebellion and liberty.[118] Like this novella, the play's characters and are based on Yoruba Orishas. Nascimento shared with the Afro-Colombian a rejection of the harmonious version of Latin American slavery that hides the abuses that permeated the system.[119] His Teatro Experimental do Negro played a key role in the establishment of an Afro-Brazilian movement under the 1964 to 1985 military dictatorship, which left little room for dissidence. Zumbi became the symbol of black resistance in the face of denied racism. Beholding the warrior's vitality and Aleijadinho's suffering is, for Afro-Brazilians, a look into a collective mirror.

In "Sortilégio II," Exu (also Eleguá and Legba in *Changó*) is both the devil and the god of doorways and crossroads. Like Changó, he is a diabolical figure that reminds the reader of a hidden or distorted African side to the history of Latin America. Niyi Afolabi argues that Nascimento's theater was a syncretic aesthetic based on Yoruba-dominant Brazilian folklore.[120] In the second version of the play, the spirit of Zumbi becomes, along with Emanuel and his wife, a symbol of tragic death, sacrifice, and transcendental spirit in the struggle for black liberation, since Emanuel dies fighting off "mental slavery." For Nascimento and Zapata, the passive, harmonious *negro bom* (noble savage) stereotype is abandoned for a rebellious, wild representation of Afro–Latin Americans.[121]

In Nascimento's *O Quilombismo* (1980), a collection of essays based on speeches from the 1970s and published three years before *Changó*, Nascimento explains what quilombos, Palmares, and Zumbi mean to him and his vision for the recently consolidated Movimento Negro Unificado. Under Zumbi, Palmares remained sovereign until 1695, but he was also a symbol that repeated in various contexts afterward.

Nascimento's *Quilombismo* is

> Objetivamente, essa rede de associações, irmandades, cofrarias, clubes, grêmios, terreiros, centros, tendas, afochés, escolas de samba, gafieiras, foram e são os quilombos legalizados pela sociedade dominante; do outro lado da lei se erguem os quilombos revelados que conhecemos. . . . Foram uma unidade . . . integrando uma prática de libertação e assumindo o comando da própria história.[122]
>
> (Objectively that web of associations, brotherhoods, fraternities, clubs, unions, temples, centers, stores, carnival groups, samba schools, dancehalls, were and are legalized quilombos by dominant society; on the other side of the law lie the aforementioned quilombos that we know. . . . They were a unit . . . integrating a liberation practice and assuming the command of their own history.)

For Nascimento, Zumbi was the epitome of a just leader who rejected colonialism and preserved African practices and a struggle for freedom. He served as the model for those like him who sought to create a unified black consciousness in opposition to the capitalist and neocolonial realities of his day.

Changó has much in common with Nascimento's *Quilombismo*. Denilson Lima Santos has compared *Sortilégio* and *Changó*'s incorporation of Bantu and Yoruba cosmologies into their texts.[123] Zapata teaches the history of the African diaspora as self-liberation, beginning with Afro-Catholic beliefs and Nagó's revolt during the Middle Passage. Like Nascimento, he focuses on the national, Palenque de San Basilio, before proceeding to a pan-African scale. Instead of Zumbi and Palmares forming the liberation movement that reappears throughout black history, it is Bioho and Palenque, Colombia, that are the founding freedom fighters.[124] Nascimento's description of miscegenation as rape is evident in the chapter, and his disdain for capitalism is evident in the suffering enslaved of Minas. Like Nascimento, he envisions a utopian future, a worldwide quilombo where all would be free. This utopia is the Nuevo Muntu.

Through the awareness of his enslaved ancestors and his rebellious comrades in Palmares, Aleijadinho discovers his Afro-Brazilian side. Like Agne, once his black identity is rediscovered or re-created, he is able to celebrate African fertility. Just as Agne eventually finds her black lover Joe, who leaves her for a white woman, Aleijadinho discovers his own fertility and sires a child.

Quilombos and *Terreiros* of *Defeito*

Like Nascimento and Zapata, Gonçalves also challenges simplistic "racial democracy" myths. In *Defeito*, Yoruba and Dahomean faiths are an alternative to a restrictive form of Catholicism. They give her commonality with other captives. They illuminate leitmotifs and the characters' actions. They provide spaces of sanctuary in tumultuous times.

African religions are seen as a form of cultural resistance. One example is the altar buried in the *esconderijo* (hiding place) beneath the *casa-grande* (big house). Statues dedicated to the Voduns/Orishas include Xangô, Naná, Oxum, the Ibêjis, and the pendant that represents her twin Taiwô, lost at sea.[125] The hidden altar is a parallel to the purist interpretation of Catholicism that marks the interior of the plantation home. These spirits come out when the legendary but historical priestess Agontimé visits São Salvador, when Verenciana must be healed, and again when the slaves gradually subvert the plantation's order, such as Kehinde's lashing out at her master in dreams.[126]

The text not only presents the destruction of Freyre's celebrated plantation but also depicts matriarchal orders (communities governed by women) within the history of Brazil. These are the Urubu (Buzzard Quilombo), the Casa da Mãezinha (Momma's house), the Casa das Minas (House of the Mines), and the last is the Roça de Baixo (Low Country).[127] These provide alternative orders of Brazilian society that might have led to a more just society had they been allowed to thrive beyond the limits imposed upon them by slavery. Their position at the margins makes these temples centers of resistance, respite, reflection, and respect at the borders of the plantation, altering the Brazilian landscape.

Before we analyze the novel further, some information on an enslaved Dahomean in similar circumstances, Domingos Álvares, will shed light on the female-led communities in the novel. Historian James Sweet claims that Africans traditionally sought to gain power and prestige by accumulating dependents and forming community, not merely gathering money, a process distorted by slavery: "The glue that ultimately held together these 'new' communities of exiles and refugees was the belief that healing was the most viable means of addressing the misuse of power."[128] This held true in African wars and American plantations. "In short, a person was a person only insofar as he or she was a member of a kinship group, and the kin group was defined by the number and quality of people in its ranks," so Kehinde had a religious and psychological compulsion to seek these communities.[129] She builds community based in part on religion. Her belief in Vodou is integrative and flexible, so adopting elements of Yoruba beliefs and Catholicism is natural for her.[130]

Vodou cosmology illuminates the knife motif. Blades rip the captive Verenciana's eyes out, castrate the enslaved Lourenço, and kill Luís's brother Banjokô.[131] Kehinde uses one to kill an apparent black robber.[132] They are symbols of Ogum. This deity, the spiritual archetype for the Banjokô, controls war and iron. As the child is initiated into Candomblé (the dominant faith in Bahia), spiritual leader Nega Florinda says he will win battles and open paths, though these hopes are dashed when he accidentally kills himself with a blade.[133] Kehinde's fluid faith is still marked by the Voduns, and Gu (the analogue of Ogum) can cause knives to clear obstacles and break the bonds of slavery in that faith.[134] The Fon word for slavery means literally "to be tied by cords," which a blade can cut.[135] However, they can also symbolize death and rebirth. Pathways and ambivalence are a part of Vodou faith, including the ambivalent nature of Legba. The latter is often called "the Devil" by fearful Christians and is another commonality with Changó el Gran Putas (Great Devil).

The snake leitmotif in the novel relates to the worship of the snake god Dan in Dahomey. First, a snake bites the penis of sinhô José Carlos, ending his cruel reign. One could surmise that the slaves have poisoned him with the help of Dan, according to Kehinde's beliefs. Poisoning owners was a common accusation against slaves when masters suffered illness.[136] Poison was a more common, more effective form of resistance than open combat, the favored form of resistance in *Changó*.[137] Later, Kehinde sees a vision of that snake and throws a jar at it. Inside, she finds the gold Na Agontimé was saving to build her house of worship to the Dahomean gods in Maranhão.[138] In the novel, Kehinde recalls her grandmother weaving a rug that depicted Dan. She syncretizes him with Oxumaré, the androgynous god of the sky.[139] They live half the year as a man and dwell in the forest as a man, and the other half is female and lives in water. She assumes the form of a snake eating its tail and is called Dani, not unlike the serpents of Legba in *Changó*. Dani is the feminine form of Dan, and both snakes are made of iron, Ogún's element. They symbolize the cycles of life, of death and rebirth, of day and night. Dan's cycles are also present when Doctor Jorge saves her from the crackdown that ends the Malês Revolt. She must hide among rags and pretend she is a cadaver to be smuggled away from the chaos.[140] Her death and rebirth are like the initiation rituals of Dan in which initiates "die" before assuming their new identities.[141]

Now, let us turn to gender and myth in the novel's depiction of Dahomey. Kehinde's faith in the Dahomean Voduns displays considerable balance between entities viewed as masculine and feminine. Sweet describes the religion's views on gender as he details the life story of the enslaved healer Domingos Álvares:

> A more compelling explanation for women's prominent roles in Dahomean vodun [*sic*] is the actual cosmology, which emphasizes harmony and balance between male and female. This ideology is succinctly summarized in one version of the Fon myth of origins, which begins: "The world was created by one god, who is at the same time both male and female." This androgynous creator gave birth to twins, one male (Lisa) and one female (Mawu), who were given equal domains - sun/moon, day/night, hot/cool.
>
> Though this creation myth likely did not enter into Dahomean monarchical "orthodoxy" until after Agaja's death in 1740, the monarchy's embrace of these ideas was a reflection of existing realities of a gender-balanced priesthood and a broader cosmology that placed women at the center of the belief system. Moreover, it was a woman, one of King Tegbesu's wives, Kpojito Hwanjile, who is credited with introducing the Mawu/Lisa myth into the Dahomean cosmos in the 1740s. In practical terms, sexual balance and gender fluidity characterized most congregations in the 1720s and 1730s. Domingos' parents, Afnage and Oconon, shared leadership over their ritual community. In

> addition, male voduns regularly mounted female initiates, and vice versa, rendering initiates their sexual opposites, at least in their ritual guises. In many respects, androgyny was the ideal expression of balance and reciprocity exemplified in the concept of *axê*, the life-giving force of empowerment desired by most vodun communities. Male and female had to share equally in order for this power to be achieved.[142]

Thus, it is easy to see why an enslaved woman of this belief system would seek out a female-led community, be it a quilombo or, more commonly, a *terreiro*, or another house of worship. Through the healing power of Vodou, women could contest patriarchal power in the spiritual and political realms in Dahomey.[143] "Witches" were commonly enslaved by both Africans and the Portuguese.[144] While the Catholic Church barred women from serving as priests, by the end of the nineteenth century roughly a quarter of Dahomean women were Vodou initiates, and it offered one of the few paths to power for black women in Brazil.[145]

Afro-descendant women were also secular leaders. Like Reis, Gonçalves shows that she is aware of Zeferina, the maroon warrior, who is not Mahin. Like the black feminists of Quilombhoje, she presents Zeferina as a proto-feminist. The quilombo allows the author to resolve the conflict regarding Verenciana, whose eyes the sinhá Ana Felipa has torn out and whom the mistress has threatened with taking away her child.[146] Though the patriarchal order of the plantation has crumbled for a moment with the death of *sinhô* José Carlos, a new master has purchased the plantation and can easily violate previous verbal agreements, such as the promise to grant Verenciana her freedom. Urubu is an alternative society where both men and women have leadership roles. The free woman of color Nega Florinda takes the refugees there, reaffirming her leadership and solidarity as an elder in the black community.[147] There, Zeferina is the governor.[148] In addition to leading the secret community, she is also a leader in the Urubu revolt. During the conflict, she fights off Portuguese-Brazilian soldiers with a bow and arrow and shouts orders to keep her troops from surrendering or fleeing. Her plan was to head a slave revolt in Salvador and be crowned queen of a "novo império nagô" (new Yoruba empire) alongside a king that Gonçalves's former quilombola witness, Jacinto, does not know. In this manner, Gonçalves continues the tradition of "pretos fujões e valentes" (brave escaped slaves) that dates back at least to Nascimento's quilombismo and adds black feminists' intervention.[149]

One can also see the quilombo as a precursor to turn-of-the-millennium black activism:

> [O Jacinto] Disse também que não deveria me preocupar com meus conhecidos porque um esconderijo nem era tão importante assim. Importantes eram as amizades feitas nos quilombos, onde todos formavam uma grande família que continuava se ajudando, independentemente do local. Depois de uma rebelião esses laços ficavam ainda mais fortes, pois a luta unia os pretos e fazia com que se importassem mais uns com os outros, pois muitas vezes a força estava na quantidade de gente reunida em busca de liberdade. Eu me surpreendi com a inteligência e o propósito das palavras dele, o que me fez entender perfeitamente porque não aceitava ser escravo.[150]
>
> ([Jacinto] also said I should not worry about my acquaintances because a hideout was not that important. What was important were the friendships made in the quilombos, where everyone formed a big family that continued helping one another, regardless of the location. After a rebellion those bonds became even stronger, since the struggle united the blacks and made them care more about each other, since many times strength lay in the quantity of people reunited in search of liberty. I was surprised by the intelligence and purpose of his words, which made me understand perfectly why he did not accept enslavement.)

Hearkening back to Quilombhoje's project to present indocile blacks, the quilombo is once again a space where blacks are united in one purpose. While the Yoruba rule in this community, religion is overcome by the struggle for unity. It is a model for black activism in the present. The extreme of this single-minded struggle is that the quilombo is a space of "liberty or death": by the time Jacinto tells Kehinde of the community, it has been destroyed. Valiantly, Zeferina and her partner face execution, and in the ultimate military defeat of the revolt, the last five warriors of Urubu commit mass suicide rather than return to slavery.[151]

Once again Gonçalves's depiction of the Urubu revolt is more nuanced than Zapata's Manichaean struggles. Its downfall is due to the all-too-human errors of a few of its residents. They are caught stealing food a few days before the revolt was planned. They panic, kill, and rob residents of Salvador.[152] This precipitates a government crackdown on the quilombo, which leads to a rushed attempt at rebellion. The quilombolas go to war shouting "morra branco e viva preto" (death to the whites, long live the blacks!). However, the first three *capitães-do-mato* (slave catchers) to invade the large encampment are called "courageous." They are not all white. In fact, one is a mulatto that the rebels torture for being a traitor. One wonders if Kehinde, whose children are mulatto and who is a concubine of a white man, Alberto, would survive the litmus test of fidelity to the revolt. In addition, one of the families killed by the thieves is mulatto, so the binary of noble blacks versus cruel whites is harder to maintain. As the battle draws to an end, Jacinto escapes into the bush, only to be helped by two whites who are good Samaritans: Father Heinz and his friend Dona Maria Augusta.[153] Gonçalves presents the church not as only a colonial force but as a community of individuals with free will regarding the conditions of Afro-descendants.

Kehinde joins other alternative communities. The chaos of the Revolta dos Malês (1835), followed by the Cemiterada (1836), leaves Kehinde on the run. She returns from Salvador to Itaparica. Traumatized, instead of going back to the plantation, she goes to the Casa da Mãezinha (Little Momma's House).[154] It rekindles Kehinde's African side. Here she is acquainted with the *gelédés*, Yoruba women who worship the seven birds, one of which flies between good and evil. Only women can practice this religion.[155] The New Year is Yemayá's day, showing a re-Africanization of the syncretized saints. Christmas celebrates Oxum's day, the spirit that protects Kehinde like a mother. Today, Gelédés is the name of the Instituto da Mulher Negra in São Paulo established in 1988, reaffirming the foundational role of these societies in providing models for the present.[156]

The Itaparica sanctuary reconnects her with the Voduns and similar spiritual traditions of her grandmother. It is led by Mãezinha, whose name refers to her role as a *mãe-de-santo* or *ialorixá* (priestess).[157] Festivities to the Orishas, marked by music to Exu, Yemayá, and Xangô, distract her from her missing son.[158] It bears the same name as her secret altar to the Voduns buried under the manor and the place she hides when escaping the Revolta dos Malês with her life: *esconderijo* (hiding place).[159] This accentuates its subversive, outlying nature. She has dreams of her mother and grandmother that augur her departure for Queen Agontimé's temple, which Mãezinha must interpret for her.[160] It is a place where she becomes "naked," stripped of the surfaces of Christianity and slavery that she "put on." It is telling that, when her "whitened" (privileged) former mulatto lover Doctor Jorge visits, she feels self-conscious and wants to put on her best clothes to receive him.[161] African healers were converted to Western medicine en masse in Brazil in the nineteenth century, as represented by Salvador's Medical School in the novel.[162]

Kehinde continues her spiritual growth through a pilgrimage to São Luís do Maranhão and the Recôncavo. This journey is at the behest of Nega Florinda. Mãe Assunta, of Mãezinha's *terreiro* (temple), has Kehinde take a special container to Nega Florinda at the Casa das Minas in São Luís.[163] She travels there by sea in an otherwise all-male commercial ship.[164] The captain, Tibúrcio, is a son of Yemayá, the mother goddess, and he protects Kehinde. Her previous giving birth to Banjokô unites the waters of Kehinde's body with that of Yemayá, so this is a matriarchal spiritual protection for a treacherous journey through a patriarchal land.[165] Ineke Phaf-Rheinberger notes Kehinde's devotion to Ochum.[166] This continues in Africa, where she prays to her once again to save her daughter during childbirth. Ochum binds Kehinde to the sea (Yemayá) and to other women.

The Casa das Minas and its matriarch, Agontimé, are the height of feminine strength in the novel. According to legend and in the novel, she was queen of Abomé in Africa until Adandozan usurped her late husband's throne and expelled her and the Voduns she served as a priestess from the kingdom of Dahomey.[167] In the novel her cerebral beauty is empowering for Kehinde from their first meeting in Salvador: "Como se fosse feita só de palavras, como se conseguisse se esconder por trás do sentido das palavras, fazendo com que elas tivessem uma força e uma presença muito maiores do que qualquer pessoa que eu tinha conhecido até então pudesse dar a elas" (As if she were only made of words, as if she had been able to hide behind the meaning of words, making them have a force and a presence that were much greater than anyone I had met until then could give them). During her exile Agontimé learns from the Vodun king Zomadonu that her destiny is to continue worshipping the Voduns in Brazil and that she will be served by his followers, the *têxossus*.[168] She comes to Salvador seeking these special deformed servants, since their name refers to a child born to an Dahomean king but, as was the custom, discarded in a river and granted magical powers. In Brazil they are all females.[169] Kehinde's servile role in following Agontimé makes her journey one of a têxossu, an "ugly" servant (if she listens to how her mistress Ana Felipa defines her) who is given new importance through serving Agontimé.[170] While Kehinde is still enslaved, it is she who tells her of the freedom of escaped slaves in quilombos, a place where blacks take care of one another beyond the bonds of slavery.[171] The priestess's itineracy during this time is indicative of colonial authorities' project of isolating healers like her, as was the historical case of Álvares.[172]

The Casa das Minas is financed by profits the queen, renamed Maria Mineira Naê, gained in the mines of Minas before traveling to São Luís among the quilombos along the way. It is a "convento" (convent) owned and operated by black women who have passed directly or indirectly through slavery.[173] There, Agontimé's name has changed to Noche Naê, which means "spiritual mother" in Ewe-Fon, Kehinde's first language, and she is called *gaiacu* (mother and owner of the house).[174] Kehinde feels so happy that she wishes to bring her son Luís and her mentor Esméria to live there with her forever in this matriarchal commune.[175] This raises the question: how might the life of Luís Gama, one of the greatest abolitionist poets, been had he grown up in this re-created African matriarchy? Interestingly, when Kehinde stays there, she describes her own role as that of a sort of secretary. This term implies not only serving and obeying, but like "ethnographer," one of writing things down. In her letter she explicitly chooses to reveal certain aspects and conceal others, as well as her limited knowledge of these rituals, as is the case in the other temples where she resides, reaffirming African ways of knowing beyond the West.

Kehinde's spiritual growth requires that she travel to Recôncavo to be initiated in the ways of the Voduns. This is her final service to matriarchy before the turning point that precipitates her being cast out of these joyous, safe, life-affirming, free societies. She goes to Roça de Baixo, the place where initiates are trained for the Casa das Minas and the larger Roça de Cima.[176] Because of the requirement that she not leave the center for three years of study, she does not bring Luís there, which can be seen as shirking off the maternal responsibilities imposed by the patriarchal family. It is the chance to be a daughter again after being orphaned by slave traders and defined, in Brazil's patriarchal system, as a slave, a lover, and a concubine. She details festivals led by related organizations, such as the Roça de Cima and the syncretic Afro-Catholic Irmandade da Boa Morte (Sisterhood of Good Death), which has close ties to these African religious centers.[177] It is historically questionable if Kehinde, as a Gege, could be initiated into this sisterhood since they were usually divided by African ethnicity, this one being Yoruba from Ketu.[178] Nonetheless, she has adopted Yoruba faith at this point, so they may have overlooked her origins to build kinship ties.[179]

She reaches the climax of her journey in 1839: "O meu ritual de iniciação foi um dos momentos mais felizes que já vivi, quando finalmente pude receber meu vodum, que me disse coisas lindas por intermédio de uma das hunjaís da Roça. À noite, sonhei com a minha avó e a minha mãe" (My ritual of initiation was one of the happiest moments I have ever lived, when I could finally receive my Vodun, which told me beautiful things through the medium of one of the Roça's *hunjaís* [initiated]. At night I dreamed of my grandmother and mother).[180] She feels complete, reunited with the women she has lost, but also with nature itself, since the spirits come from the elements. Sweet notes the "common experiences of initiation and worship. It symbolizes the security of a spiritual home. In Brazil, the attraction of such a space for those who were forcibly uprooted from their natal homelands, or who were otherwise marginalized or enslaved, was powerful indeed."[181] This closeness is like the muntu's animism, but uniquely focused on women.

This positive climax clearly crumbles when she learns of her happy friend Claudina's miscarriage and death.[182] Kehinde learns that her perceived safety and peace have been an illusion. During the confusion of Luís's caretaker Claudina's funeral, Alberto sells the boy to settle gambling debts, beginning the next section of the novel's plot: the unresolved quest to reunite mother and son. The fact that a father, Alberto, can sell his own son to settle a debt is a glaring example of patriarchy.

While it would serve a legitimizing purpose, marriage to Alberto might not have helped Kehinde or given her custody rights. Up to 90 percent of enslaved Brazilians did not marry.[183] Masters saw marriage as an impediment to the free sale of their property (separating families), and even manumission of a family member provoked jealousy and sometimes encouraged runaways.[184] If marriages occurred, the master often arranged them and then ignored such ties if deemed inconvenient. Jealousy often contributed to domestic abuse between slaves. As an enslaved or even manumitted woman, Kehinde could enjoy very few benefits from the institution of marriage.

African temples are alternative, healing institutions. Spiritual work is the driving force of the Casa da Mãezinha, a Casa das Minas, and the Roça de Baixo (Momma's House, Mina Slave House, and Low Country). Kehinde's rebelliousness as a slave makes her a lover of this kind of activity, a drastic departure from her labors in slavery. Additionally, her role as a mother, particularly in this conservative society, demands that she be constantly present to care for her children Banjokô and Luís, in addition to those who come later in the book, in a way that is not expected of her male partners. A "bad" slave and mother becomes a "good" student and pious follower of these syncretic faiths. She leaves her cruel master and undependable partner to serve a just and nurturing queen, Agontimé, the high priestess who turned the lucre from the brutal mines of Minas into a shrine to feminine spirituality. These faiths are taboo on the plantation due to sinhá's prohibitions, but in these centers Kehinde is free. It is a meritocratic system in which one can study and rise through the ranks of the temple.

These centers of faith, while not an explicit or military affront to the plantation system as the quilombos often were, are by their mere existence inconformity to the spiritual and legal bases of patriarchy. One wonders what the kind of matriarchal Brazil or Africa Agontimé or Mãezinha might have led, had they become the dominant force. In the novel Agontimé refuses the chance to return to Africa once her son is instated as king.[185] As I show in the next chapter, this is not the most common telling of Agontimé's story in Africa, where she is believed to have triumphantly returned as Queen Mother. Gonçalves's choice to keep Agontimé in the Americas expresses her desire to focus on representing and rooting the Afro-Brazilian community in the nation, thought in alternative spaces.

Kehinde's flight to these refuges is a major factor in her losing her son, Luís, likely forever. Claudina's lifeless body can be read as a metaphor for the narrator-protagonist's loss of her son and the "death" of her time at the life-affirming, matriarchal temples.[186] Since the novel is a series of letters to Luís, she states her opinion clearly:

> De repente, tudo o mais perdeu a importância, os muçurumins, os federalistas, a Cemiterada, a fuga para Itaparica, a viagem para o Maranhão, a Roça da sinhá Romana, os voduns. Tudo aquilo só tinha feito com que eu me afastasse, permitindo que você fosse tirado de mim. . . . Talvez a esperança fosse apenas o meu axé, o emi que fazia a vida circular dentro de mim.[187]
>
> (All of a sudden, everything else lost its importance, the Muslims, the Federalists, the Cemiterada Revolt, the flight to Itaparica, the trip to the Maranhão, sinhá Romana's Roça, the voduns. All of that just made me stray from you, letting you be taken from me. . . . Perhaps hope was only my *axé*, the *emi* that made life circulate in me.)

Upon being sold, Luís no longer belongs to his father. In an emotional and spiritual sense, he belongs only to his mother. Thus, the maternal bond and its loss marks Gama's writing.

Gonçalves adopts a realist aesthetic not unlike that which prevailed in late nineteenth-century Brazilian prose, with carefully researched details and "objective" representations of Afro-Catholic faiths and the daily practices of Africans and Afro-Brazilians. As Roberto González Echevarría notes, the ethnographer's case study heavily influences realism in Latin America, recorded by ostensibly invisible viewers, pen, and paper.[188] But Gonçalves adopts the "I" of Kehinde to tell this story, making her as much one of the observed—dancing, praying, traveling, having sex, living—as the observer who writes down these practices.

Conclusion

Unlike Afro-Colombia, Afro-Brazil has a robust literary and historiographical tradition with which to dialogue. It is so famous that Zapata had to choose a new image from many to avoid creating another cliché of Afro-Brazil.[189] He settled on the Aleijadinho, but alongside him continues to laud Zumbi in the spirit of Abdias Nascimento's *quilombismo*. Gonçalves's work is special though because it uses the novel to portray the lives of ordinary, enslaved people in Brazil's Black Rome. It links these stories to the urban centers of the nation, and it ties them to their ancestors in Africa. Her portrayal of Kehinde is fictional, but it is a means to tell the stories of hundreds of other characters. She shows that women have always had an active role in the history of the nation, even when they are imperfect people and face the most harrowing of circumstances. Gender informs Kehinde's survival instinct, and it causes her to leave the quilombo and terreiro spaces of refuge since she must live to care for her children, and for herself. For Zapata, the quilombo is a place of health while the colonial city is a place of exploitation and suffering.

3

Double Consciousness and Nation in Gilroy and Zapata

The last two chapters compared the novels to show their different treatment of myth, literature, legendary black heroes, and runaway slave communities. These communities exist to this day, as in the cases of Palenque, Colombia, and the *quilombolas* of Brazil. The quilombo of Palmares coincides in Zapata's text with the Inconfidência Mineira (Minas Gerais Conspiracy), which the French and American revolutions inspired. The Age of Revolution brings to mind the emergence of national "imagined communities."[1] The nation was a source of freedom for some, but for people of color it often involved a continuation of slavery in different forms. Nation, reason, and capitalism, three pillars of what can be called modernism, or Enlightenment thought, were seen to be limiting by the 1990s when Paul Gilroy was writing his seminal *The Black Atlantic: Modernity and Double Consciousness* (1993).[2]

Although there were cosmopolitan black thinkers before him, the British scholar's most important contribution to the study of literature and culture was to open the ports between nations with a sophisticated black globalism that engages the Western philosophical tradition. Judith Newman describes it as "catalytic."[3] Elizabeth Maddock Dillon states that Gilroy's "paradigm shifting" work enabled "a shift in the mode of analysis of New World literary texts from the proto-U.S. teleology of a previous generation to the new Atlantic model of circulation," a claim Newman seconds.[4]

The Black Atlantic and the Nuevo Muntu

Gilroy's impact is too far-reaching to summarize here, but I provide some representative Anglophone critics. Newman provides a panorama of his impact in history and literature.[5] Eric Slauter showed that the "Atlantic" framework of cultural history was already common in the 1970s, but that it boomed by the end of the 1990s, inspiring other "Atlantics," such as a conference on the Indigenous Atlantic in 2010, a representation of the term's flexibility.[6] Christine Chivallon and Karen E. Fields believe Gilroy's book "embodies" 1990s cultural studies.[7] Bénédicte Ledent and Pilar Cuder-Domínguez consider the Black Atlantic a "necessary bridge between the work of African-Americanists and post-colonialists."[8] Nevertheless, popularity can chip away at Gilroy's initial intent, for better or worse. "The suspicion lingers that the phrase has become a tag to sell books."[9] It often speaks to a "utopian" notion of globalization that redraws maps in the interest of celebrating multiculturalism and hybridity.[10] Another example among readers of Gilroy is Simone Pereira Schmidt, who considers Gilroy an alternative to the Luso-African colonial ideologies Gilberto Freyre supported.[11] Newman claims Gilroy's "most important" impact has been on "creative work," such as Bernardine Evaristo's parallel universe based on white slavery in *Blonde Roots* (2008).[12] Peter Erickson shows that "new visual work shows that the conception of the Black Atlantic as a special focus is still relevant as an analytical framework capable of generating new images, insights, and critical perspectives. . . . These artistic ventures allow us to continue to imagine and to invent revisionary alternatives for—in Julie Mehretu's eloquent phrase—'this new possible world.'"[13] Also in the article is Afro-Cuban exile María Magdalena Campos-Pons's "Everything is Separated by Water" (2007).[14] The latter artist plays a central role in Kimberly Juanita Brown's *The Repeating Body* (2015), which includes intellectual borrowings from Gilroy for, as her introduction states, "Visualizing the Body of the Black Atlantic."[15] She devotes her work to slavery's "afterimage" in texts on black women, particularly mothers, which includes representations of the legendary enslaved Brazilian queen Blessed Anastácia and novelist Octavia Butler's depictions of Brazil.[16]

Gilroy remains one of the most-read black intellectuals. In 2008, scholars cited him more than any other critic.[17] His relevance for humanities and social science scholars is still evident in an international, interdisciplinary conference titled "African Diaspora beyond the Black Atlantic" at the Administrative Staff College of Nigeria on August 22, 2017, an indicator of Gilroy's reach.[18] His ideas laid the groundwork for the British Institute for Black Atlantic Research. Feats like these show that the term he coined has become synonymous with interdisciplinary, transnational studies on the African diaspora. He expresses a global viewpoint in at least three aims for the *Black Atlantic*. Understandably, today's black cosmopolitans look to Gilroy as their forebear.

The Black Atlantic: Summary

Gilroy presents Black Atlantic culture as a "counter-culture of modernity" that does not always conform to Enlightenment or nationalist ideals.[19] It is a "changing same," part of a diaspora.[20] Unlike nationalist projects that tie groups to the land where they are born, Gilroy proposes the ship as a "rhizomatic" (ever-changing) alternative chronotope (setting) for blacks.[21] For Gilroy, scholars have treated African American culture as provincial and limited to the U.S. territory, so he discusses the travel to Europe of Martin Delaney, Frederick Douglass, W. E. B. Du Bois, and Richard Wright. He notes the centrality of slavery to capitalism.[22] He criticizes Molefi Kete Asante's Afrocentrism for overlooking slavery in favor of a purist, idealized, simplistic relationship with preslavery Africa that reflects more about U.S. notions of race than the disparate cultures of the continent.[23] He frequently mentions the enslaved's desire to die for freedom, as in the case of an enslaved mother killing her child to keep her from captivity.[24] Gilroy discusses the diaspora's evolution of arts, music, and culture, all of which transcend borders like the sea.[25]

After *The Black Atlantic*

One could argue that since the Black Atlantic is now over twenty years old, Gilroy has moved on, but it is indubitably central to his way of thinking, as is evident in his Du Bois Lectures at Harvard University, *Darker Than Blue*.[26] Most of his books between *Black Atlantic* and *Darker* return to his focus on Europe. *Small Acts* devotes only one-third of the book to dialogues with U.S. thinkers like Toni Morrison and bell hooks.[27] His *Against Race* seeks to erase "the bonds of all raciology in a novel and ambitious abolitionist project" to produce a "radically nonracial humanism," but that humanism has not taken hold in academia the same way the "Black Atlantic" has.[28] *Postcolonial Melancholia* analyzes Britain's mourning of its lost empire and adjustment to multiculturalism.[29] The book does return, however, to Du Bois's double consciousness and cosmopolitism. He looks simultaneously to a diasporic past and to a raceless future.

Speaking at Harvard in 2010, he remained focused on Du Bois and humanism. *Darker* is about Black Atlantic culture in relation to human rights and neoliberalism's commodification of blackness. Only two pages are devoted to Haiti, and Caetano Veloso is the only Latin American mentioned.[30] He devotes discussion to Guantanamo inmates but not to the millions of Afro-Cubans on the island.

In 2016 Gilroy published an interview on the Black Atlantic.[31] The interview shows the late impact in France of the *Black Atlantic*, his only work translated there, and only in 2003.[32] Despite his work's impact, he considers the Black Atlantic to have already died when it was theorized. It ended in 1981 with the death of Bob Marley, the last "etiopista" (Ethiopianist).[33] He still thought black movements would continue along that direction in 1993, but after the book he perceived a movement toward Islam, the waning centrality of politicized black music to social movements, and the rise of the internet. He notes Latin American influence over his cornerstone text, including the Brazilian Roger Bastide and the Mexican Roger Bartra. Nevertheless, he mentions neither of them in the *Black Atlantic*. Interestingly, he argues that "el desafío a partir de ahora debería ser dibujar un mapa del 'Atlántico negro' que comprenda la bahía de Guantánamo" (The challenge now should be to draw a map of the "Black Atlantic" that includes Guantanamo Bay).[34] Furthermore, he sees some African Americans' xenophobia toward "latinos [*sic*]" and admiration of conservatives like Condoleezza Rice as examples of the Black Atlantic's demise. Even Gilroy sees the need to reimagine the Black Atlantic in a way that includes Anglo- and Latin America.

The year 2019 marked what was perhaps the apex of Gilroy's influence in academia. He became the founding director of the new Centre for the Study of Race and Racism at University College London, institutionalizing his interdisciplinary vision through graduate programs.[35] That month Gilroy received the Holberg Prize, Norway's most prestigious award in humanistic endeavors.[36] In his acceptance speech he rejects provincialism in approaching the complexity of racism. He acknowledges his focus on Northern Europe, but he also notes the importance of looking to other spaces, arguing that "the dialogue that results from these interventions now extends eastward and into the global South. It has moved further into Africa, to Latin America and the Pacific, all locations where struggles over the racial *nomos* assumed forms that differ sharply from the patterns characteristic of the north Atlantic." He notes the importance of Haiti in this effort. In addition to his perennial focus on cosmopolitanism, he calls for a return to humanism. As I have shown, the notion of the Nuevo Muntu or "New (Black) Man" that encompasses the Atlantic does just this. Gilroy adds a new sense of urgency to Black Atlantic ethics: "Seafarers and others acquainted with the traditions of maritime life know the primal responsibility towards others that gets discovered amidst the elemental perils of storm and shipwreck. Similar obligations sometimes emerge in other settings: from flood, drought and the effects of pollution. Clear, ethical and juridical obligations are associated with the interrelated practices involved in human salvage, naming the drowned and promoting dignity by burying the bodies of the dead." Manuel Zapata Olivella names the enslaved and oppressed and focuses on humanity's relation to nature. His focus on helping the most oppressed and his criticisms of the capitalism, nationalism, and imperialism that support racism begin to address many of the concerns that have defined Gilroy's work, but it delves deeper into the Global South than the laureled Briton does.

Representative Critics of Gilroy in the Anglophone Tradition

My study is part of the critical tradition that has challenged the British thinker. Natasha Barnes criticizes his overemphasis on men from the United States. She claims that including more women and Caribbean thinkers like Marcus Garvey would provide different contours to a Black Atlantic.[37] *Changó* does all of this, and Gonçalves delves deeper into women's points of view.

On one hand, James Clifford sees it as a "hybrid diaspora" that joins "contraries," occupying a space within modern categories and outside of them.[38] On the other, William Boelhower claims that the Black Atlantic must be treated not as a "single unit of analysis" but as an "ecosystem," a setting where there is no "inside" or "outside."[39] It creates "continuities" between cultures where there are actually radical differences. One could argue that the transcendental categories of ancestors and spirits create nonexistent continuities in Zapata's utopian worldview, but his novel uses cultural particularities such as nationalisms (Haiti, Colombia, Mexico), languages (Palenquero, Haitian Creole, English), and religions (Muslim, Christian, Yoruba). By linking disparate projects like those of Zumbi dos Palmares, Toussaint L'Ouverture, and Garvey, he is developing lessons for the twentieth- and twenty-first-century reader, particularly the Afro-descendant reader, to follow their examples. Gonçalves's combination of the *retornados* with the historical realities of Bahia and the urban centers of southeast Brazil serves to develop the apocryphal story of Luísa Mahin, who may be a creation of Luís Gama, but who is certainly a model of resiliency.

Gilroy leaves out Afro-Europe and Africa too. Daria Tunca notes the absence of African cultures in the Black Atlantic, which Zapata and Gonçalves address with the continent and Latin America.[40] On the other hand, Richard Follett, who writes on Afro-Brazilians and soccer, redresses Annalisa Oboe and Anna Scacchi's criticism that Gilroy ignores Latin America.[41] Ledent and Cuder-Domínguez criticize Gilroy for treating slavery as a metaphor, often overlooking historical realities, and they note that the Black Atlantic does not include European blacks.[42] Historian James Sweet, following Paul Lovejoy, is part of the "revisionist school" of the Black Atlantic, which marks a shift away from studying creolization (hybridity) toward placing African and Afro-descendant individuals at the center of their own stories and using Africa as a starting point for the study of diaspora, especially during the slave trade.[43] They use historical and cosmological specificity to break up the "static, homogenized notions of an essentialist Africa," but they do so by charting social change from specific ethnic homelands.

Laura Chrisman criticizes Gilroy's "anti-economistic approach" to blackness.[44] It keeps him from noting the fluid relationship between labor and ludic activities such as music and sports, two arenas where Afro-descendants have excelled, and which Zapata celebrates in his boxers and his musicians. She finds Gilroy's antinationalism in favor of diaspora fatalist, since it leaves ethnically homogeneous national identities like Britain's intact. Zapata constantly celebrates the mixing of bloodlines and cultures.

She believes showing "black debts to European philosophy" is not a widely useful means of social transformation, but that critics should seek "to emphasize black U.S. intellectual, political, and cultural cross-fertilization with the Caribbean, Latin America, and proletarian cultures (white, Hispanic, trade union), as well as Third World liberationist thought. And a way to counter the problematic racial purism of Afrocentrism might be to emphasize and explore the significance of mixed race intellectuals and cultural texts."[45] Zapata's novel does all of this: including Latin America and the United States in dialogue with one another. Its radical emphasis on cultural and biological miscegenation is central in the combination of African elements with indigenous and European ones to create a new, just hybrid humanity. She also criticizes Gilroy for emphasizing "blues" (melancholy, suicide, and fatalism) in black history to the detriment of acts of resistance based on "rational calculation."[46] The Marxist Zapata writes before the postmodernism debates. He emphasizes rage over fatalism, and his characters constantly sabotage the plantation, whether it is through organized revolt like Benkos Bioho (maroon resistance) or Toussaint (enlightened and maroon resistance) and, yes, suicide. Sweet shows slave births in Brazil were commonly celebrated by the enslaved and abortion was rare.[47] The optimism of a future revolution prevails over the nihilism Chrisman sees in Gilroy.[48]

Zapata's negotiation of nationalism and transnationalism is central to understanding his entire oeuvre. Lucía Ortiz says it "hace referencia a la hibridez, el hiper-espacio, el desalojo, el descentramento, y a la vez cuestiona los significados tradicionales de raza, etnia y nacionalidad definidos por las ciencias sociales" (relates to hybridity, hyperspace, displacement, decentering, and at the same time questions the traditional meanings of race, ethnicity, and nationality defined by the social sciences).[49] Alfonso Múnera claims that he uses the diaspora to reinterpret local racial oppression in the tradition of Négritud.[50]

Gonçalves's novel, while more pessimistic—the novel ends before Kehinde finds Gama—presents a relatable protagonist with no special qualities who overcame great struggle to survive and raise a family in bondage and on both sides of the Atlantic, which cannot be described as "nihilistic," Chrisman's charge against Gilroy. Both novels precede Stephen Best's call to abandon the lachrymose approach to black history that *The Black Atlantic* exemplifies in order to imagine a better future.[51]

Chivallon and Fields claim that the book can be summarized as a rejection of nationalist Afrocentrism rooted in a premodern, pre-Western racial tradition (Asante).[52] But neither of these models considers the Latin American third path of maintaining hybrid identity (*mestizaje*) and premodern traditions (Orishas, Voduns, muntu). Zapata renders homage to Garvey and

Rastafarianism, which Chivallon and Fields praise for its rejection of all hierarchies, community building, and its basis in the lived experience of ordinary people, not the intellectuals Gilroy gives as examples of the Black Atlantic.[53] Zapata's inclusion of the essentialist Garvey, despite criticizing his purism, precedes what A. L. Reed Jr. proposes: "The notion of 'double consciousness' is highly variable—not for Du Bois, but for succeeding generations who have appropriated it, from the 'assimilationists' at the beginning of the twentieth century to the most up-to-date intellectual circles in the academy, and, along the way, the militants of Black Power and of ethnic pluralism."[54] David Scott calls for theorists to consider a diaspora model's political strategy and epistemology.[55] Scott claims that diasporas should be discursively constituted, not based on a "veridical" character, but cites the example of the Du Bois versus Garvey debates over integration and hybridity of black identity versus purism, black nationalism, and segregation.[56] Chivallon and Fields argue that scholars should return to the modernist project of objectifying or defining the diaspora using an empirical basis, but with postmodern skepticism.[57] Zapata does this, since he includes the same debate Scott cites along with a majority of documented historical figures, not purely discursive creations. The Nuevo Muntu covers more history than Gilroy's Black Atlantic, though it does not present the diaspora as "objectively" or disinterestedly constructed. On the contrary, it is an explicitly revolutionary project.

Ineke Phaf-Rheinberger worked with Gilroy on the *Black Atlantic* project in Berlin in 2004.[58] She builds on Gilroy's transatlantic focus of the diaspora using Ángel Rama's "lettered city" paradigm to understand the cultural evolution of port cities in the South Atlantic.[59] The writers she studies concentrate on these doorways of the trade between Africa and America. "The authors' rhetorical inquiries take up the 'double consciousness' of modernity that Paul Gilroy (1993) wrote about, but now with its roots in the mercantile philosophy."[60] In the same book, Tiago de Oliveira Pinto uses Gilroy's Black Atlantic to theorize the music the enslaved brought with them to Brazil.[61]

Paul Tiyambe Zeleza claims that Gilroy oversimplifies the African American experience and applies that experience to the rest of the diaspora.[62] Gilroy is largely "androcentric" and "Eurocentric" and implies an African American "minority" framework will apply neatly to majority-black nations on the Atlantic. He sees Anglo-U.S. global hegemony as the cause.[63] Zeleza views Gilroy's hunt for an "overriding sense of double consciousness" to be homogenizing. Gilroy, in his estimation and mine, forecloses "relationships and connections among the black diasporic cultures themselves beyond the Anglophone world (the largest African diaspora population is in Brazil and speaks Portuguese) and between them and African cultures."[64] He argues to include Portuguese, French, Spanish, and Arabic languages in the study of the diaspora, and, while Zapata and Gonçalves write in Spanish and Portuguese, they include terminology from these languages.[65] They represent marginalized nations like the ones African scholars Zeleza believes should play a stronger role in theorizing diaspora. Zeleza cites Kim Butler, a Brazilian historian who argues that there are actually five dimensions to diaspora: reasons for dispersal, relationship with homeland, relationship with "host lands," interrelationship with "diasporan" groups, and comparative study of different diasporas.[66] These novels do all this.

Charles Piot appears to answer Zeleza's call by turning the Black Atlantic on its head: while Gilroy argues against a static, preslavery African origin of the diaspora in favor of the foundational nature of the slave trade, Piot shows that slavery created key aspects of the history and cultures of the African continent itself. For example, he considers Togo "diaspora-derivative."[67] Hence, Zapata and Gilroy were already looking beyond the "old parochialisms" that Gilroy could not overcome.[68]

Yogita Goyal went even farther to redress Gilroy's lacunae with a special issue on "Africa and the Black Atlantic."[69] In her introduction she challenges the notions of nation as static and diaspora as flexible. She also hopes to foment studies that include Africa in models of modernity, and *Changó* does just that with the Nuevo Muntu, a new "collectivity" beyond the colonial and national.[70]

Gilroy continues to hold great sway in African American studies, as is evidenced by Marlon Ross's article. He dialogues with *The Black Atlantic* regarding Wright's travels abroad.[71] He shows that the novelist maintained a Eurocentric worldview that colored his perceptions of Africa. Apparently, he was a tourist who wanted to bolster his pedigree as a writer.[72] Zapata, through his travels, created a postcolonial masterpiece.

Du Bois in *Changó*

Zapata was as indebted to the Harlem Renaissance as he was to African and Latin American thought. The intellectual debates he dramatizes have at their heart many of the ideas of Du Bois, who was the patriarch of the black intelligentsia and whose relevance has yet to be overcome, as Gilroy's subtitle, *Modernity and Double Consciousness*, attests.

Zapata claims direct inspiration by Langston Hughes and Du Bois to write *Changó* in his autobiography *¡Levántate mulato!* (*Rise Up, Mulatto*).[73] He summoned the spirit of Hughes and told him that he wanted to write a "novela total" (all-encompassing novel) on African Americans. Hughes's first command was to remember the thousands of lynching victims, but he proceeded to say, in Zapata's words,

> Vete a las Cataratas del Niágara y escúchalas. Es el discurso más auténtico de la lucha de nuestro pueblo por su libertad; las voces reunidas de los pequeños y grandes gigantes en la innominada historia de nosotros los negros. Lo que no entiendas, el viejo Bourhard Debois [*sic*] te lo contará.[74]
>
> (Go to Niagara Falls and listen to them. It is the most authentic discourse of our people's struggle for their liberty; the collected voices of the small and great giants in the unnamed history of us blacks. Whatever you do not understand, old Bourhard Debois [*sic*] will tell you.)

While Zapata's novel goes beyond the scope of *The Souls of Black Folk* to encompass Latin America, it is clear that his thought inspired him.

Zapata's Du Bois

Let us review Du Bois's role in *Changó*: World traveler Du Bois dies in Accra, Ghana, and a year afterward he comes back as Malcolm X, who then returns to America.[75] Du Bois was born the year of the Fourteenth Amendment, and African ancestor Kanuri Mai orders that his rebellious spirit inspire, die, and be reborn at Niagara. No doubt, this refers to the *Niagara Manifesto* (1905), which founds the Niagara Movement, the precursor to the National Association for the Advancement of Colored People, in 1910. Du Bois tells Agne that life is an eternal return to the future, returning to African roots to rethink the West through a mestizo approach.[76] Du Bois tells Agne she has been chosen to lead the muntu.[77] He claims to have drawn too close to the sun and that he or she must listen to the cloud and mud, the *pueblo* (popular movements and thought). Du Bois can be accused of this himself, since he focused on the "talented tenth" of African Americans.[78] He admits he was deaf to the masses in a way Garvey was not.[79] He sings a spiritual of leaving his body to join God, one of the foundational "spirit songs" that perform double consciousness for him and for Gilroy.[80] He announces to her that she will encounter the "combatant sons of Changó."[81] These are Agne's ancestors and the reader's. Only Agne can see Africa living in the soul of America/the Americas, her "double existence":

> Examina tu alma a la luz de dos lámparas y te explicarás la penumbra de tu doble existencia. Nadie, sino tú, escogida por Legba, podrá tener conciencia de tus dos mundos: África viviendo en el alma de América. El destino de nuestra sangre es encender un nuevo renacimiento en el corazón anciano de la humanidad.[82]
>
> (Examine your soul under the light of two lamps and you will understand the darkness of your double existence. No one but you, chosen by Legba, will be able to have an awareness of your two worlds: Africa living in America's soul. The destiny of our bloodline is to light a new renaissance in the ancient heart of humanity).

This quote shows Zapata's understanding of "double consciousness" as an understanding of the West that is complemented by a counternarrative that includes not only African knowledge, such as the muntu and Agne's mediumship granted her by Legba. She has her own black experience to build upon, and her goal is to include African and Afro–Latin American thought in a new renaissance that will radically reshape humanity.

In "The Civil War Gave Us Freedom, Freedom Returned Us to Slavery," blacks are sent to capitalist slavery, says Du Bois.[83] Agne responds "Te escucho, Abuelo Burghardt" (I am listening, Grandfather Burghardt), a sharp departure from the opening of the novella when ancestor Ngafúa must shout to her to grab her attention in the shower, a modernized water flow that contrasts with the gushing Niagara.[84] After this dialogue, the novel notes his mestizo blend of French, German, and African ancestors; the latter is the spirit of the African king Kanuri Mai, so he recognizes modern-colonial influences in his thought alongside Africa. Du Bois, in Zapata, does not deny the classic double consciousness imposed by the color line: Jim Crow is, for the United States, two colors, two bodies, and one head, the height of cruelty in the country, which the novel represents by using upper-case letters for Black and White in this section, unlike in Spanish.[85] He charts a history from the Civil War to the ills of 1900 as in *Souls*.[86]

Double consciousness is lived not only by blacks but also by all oppressed people who constitute colonized countercultures in the novel. Du Bois agrees with Turner in that Changó forged the muntu with a rebellious spirit.[87] He states that the muntu is not a black body, as the White Wolf claimed, but the muntu's face reflects all of humanity, just as all that feed from its spirit are human. Zapata adds to the debate the indigenous chief Wild Cat and a black maroon Zaka, who became his close ally. He adds other colonized people and a concern for Mother Earth to the struggle against oppression, which returns the black renaissance to its African roots in natural forces but by means of similar pre-Colombian beliefs. While Du Bois debates forms of black liberation, Zapata allows him to reach consensus with his black rivals in that there are three variations of reaching freedom: art, war, and *mestizaje* (cultural mixture).[88] Du Bois disappears as Malcolm takes over as the synthesis of an enlightened, eloquent, and uncompromising leader and one who had substantial popular support from marginalized African Americans.

Du Bois's role as one of the first recognized historians and intellectuals of the Black diaspora is reaffirmed, though Zapata, Gilroy, and Du Bois note that the slaves' songs were themselves a type of oral history.[89] Agne and the reader walk in Du Bois's footsteps through the history of U.S. blacks, which is contextualized by the Latin American section of the novel.

Double Consciousness

Du Bois, in his *Souls of Black Folk*, argues that African Americans have a "double consciousness." He explains that black people view the world both through the eyes of the enslaved and the enslaver, which allows them a critical vision of the country:

> The Negro is a sort of seventh son, born with a veil, and gifted with second-sight in this American world,—a world which yields him no true self-consciousness, but only lets him see himself through the revelation of another world. It is a particular sensation, this double consciousness, this sense of always looking at oneself through the eyes of others . . . two warring ideals in one dark body, whose dogged strength alone keeps it from being torn asunder. The history of the American Negro is the history of this strife,—this longing

> to attain self-conscious manhood, to merge his double self into a better and truer self... to be both a Negro and an American.[90]

For Du Bois the internal struggle to the death between slave and master creates a unique perspective for the African American subject, both excluded from yet supplementary to Enlightenment ideals of consciousness, freedom, and nationalism. Surviving the struggle meant not assuming the master's vision of him, but creating a new, synthetic view from both the master's point of view and the slave's. Du Bois was exceptional in his vision of diaspora, and he is part of a black intellectual tradition that allowed Zapata and Gilroy to look beyond the nation to an international African diaspora.

Gilroy wrote *The Black Atlantic* because he was dissatisfied with the absence of black history from debates on modernity/postmodernity.[91] He revisits Du Bois's "double consciousness," using a wider lens to capture the international influences and ramifications of this concept.[92] Gilroy rereads the master-slave dialectic in light of plantation slavery and black history. The British author shows that Du Bois, like him, embraces "the fragmenting of self (doubling and splitting) which modernity seems to promote."[93] Du Bois, like Zapata and Gilroy, was an advocate of cultural hybridization, not purity.[94]

Zapata maps the history of the diaspora through a split consciousness with parallels to Du Bois's ten years before Gilroy. The Colombian incorporated not only the Anglophone but also the Lusophone and Hispanic sectors of the diaspora, beginning with a unique explanation for slavery as a curse from the gods. The Yoruba Orishas and Dahomean Voduns are the magic beliefs beyond Western rationalism that the Europeans first encountered in Africa at the beginning of the explorations that would lead to the creation of the Americas. However, even in Africa the impact of indigenous beliefs is present in references to alleged (Afro-)Olmec ancestors with special powers, Carib beliefs that guavas are the food of the dead, African and Carib cannibalism, and the ghosts of Incan princesses.[95] The mythical Africa that opens the novel even has Manatee Men from Native American lore, since Africa does not have this species.[96] Unlike "mulatto" beliefs, these are not just a mixture of "white" and "black" but a mixture of indigenous and African peoples under a name given them by the Spanish colonizers as part of a complex series of *castas*. *Zambo* (black and Amerindian) and *mulato* (black and white) for Zapata are not biological determinist notions of race but a spiritual consciousness beyond Western logic.

The diaspora in *Changó* is first performed in the most limited space possible, the hull of a slave ship; then it grows to a transatlantic scale, constantly moving and changing. Changó's individual exile and itinerancy in a mythic past is repeated on a virtually continental level as a vast group of sub-Saharans, reduced to the term *muntu*, and again to the characters in the dark bowels of the Portuguese vessel, the *Nova Índia*. The muntu are shackled not by a transcendental race of whites but by a transcendental spirit, the "White Wolf" or "la Loba Blanca."[97]

The mutiny of the *Nova Índia* is simultaneously an indictment of the colonial slave trade and an affirmation that the New World can be liberated from its tragic past. By overcoming the fear of death by dying, Nagó the Navigator's spirit transcends its bondage and commandeers the ship in the name of the entire muntu, replacing the Portuguese Prince Henry the Navigator as the leader of discovery.[98] The confines of the slave ship are followed by the Spanish slave port of Cartagena, Colombia.[99] There, rebel slaves escape and form the Palenque San Basilio, supposedly first led by Benkos Bioho.[100]

The struggle continues on land in the New World. The colonial rebellion of great local importance for the Afro-Colombian is followed by a rebellion of great global importance in the novel and in history, the Haitian Revolution.[101] The uprising spread Changó's fire throughout the Americas, striking fear in the hearts of slave owners and creating a sign of hope for the enslaved everywhere.[102] It combined Africans' struggle for liberation with national struggles, which the work then transfers to the Hispanic and Brazilian independence struggles of the nineteenth century with Simón Bolívar, José Prudencio Padilla, Aleijadinho, and José María Morelos at the center.[103] Luis has shown that these sections appear out of chronological order, since it should be Aleijadinho-Bolívar-Morelos-Padilla.[104] The progression in the text shows the ever-expanding fire of Changó in the Americas, which begins with Lusophone enslavers like Henry the Navigator and ends with liberators like Zumbi de Palmares. The Haitian Revolution is followed by Padilla's failed struggle to right Bolívar's betrayal of the enslaved, but the Aleijadinho shows that artistic creativity is another, more sophisticated form of liberation that complements the Inconfidência Mineira. Morelos's project shows that the indigenous are part of blacks' struggle for liberation in the Americas. The chronological order of facts is subservient to the lesson that freedom is spreading, imperfectly and partially, throughout the Americas through progress. The work ends with "Ancestral Combatants," which, while set in the

United States, encompasses voices from the previous revolutions.[105] Scenes take place throughout the North, South, and West, depicting slave escapes and rebellions (Nat Turner, Douglass, Harriet Tubman, and black settlers in Oklahoma) and portraying these as part of the same struggle as diaspora thinkers of the twentieth century (Garvey, Du Bois, Malcolm). The spiritual language of the text allows this transcendence of national histories to occur and yet for the narrative to remain coherent. In it, the diaspora is simultaneously united by yet also fragmented by historical traumas. The implicit author's perception of the diaspora's invisibility in hegemonic imaginations of national history, the product of a master conscious unaware of the slave's consciousness, is what necessitates this myth and this new imagined community. However, Zapata recalls that "Africa" did not imagine itself as a collective until slavery forced a new identity, "slave," or "black" onto sub-Saharans that often had no other connection. "Africa" is a longing for a home that never existed as it was imagined by the enslaved, so the dispersal of seeds, the metaphor of "dia-spora" is insufficient in this sense, since the "spora" (seeds) were never "together" until "scattered" (dia-).[106]

For Gilroy, Asante's Afrocentrism treats slavery as "a cluster of negative associations that are best left behind" in favor of "ornate conceptions of African antiquity."[107] The muntu is a way out of this binary. There is an "ornate" Africa in the novel, but it is one based on spirits that exist within and without the space-time of modernity. This is an element in Zapata's diasporic double consciousness that differs drastically from Gilroy's and Du Bois's because the consciousness of the enslaved in Latin America was not only double but radically religiously syncretic. The duality of space-time in the novel is historical and mythical, but this changes drastically given the setting of the diaspora phenomenon. While in Africa, on the slave ship, and in the port of Cartagena, slaves are split between African faiths and an imposed temptation to slip into slave consciousness. However, the indigenous mothers who rescue Sosa Illamba's child, the muntu, give their customs and spirits a new centrality to the muntu. These in turn are different from those of Morelos in Mexico and from the African and Native Americans of the novel, but they all have in common that they lie beyond a Western worldview.[108] The muntu is a spiritual consciousness beyond Western reason and a counternarrative to the evolution of nation-states.

An Africa beyond slavery is simultaneously everywhere and nowhere at once in the novel. It is a belief, a narrative that gives coherence to the fractured world of the novel and the vision of the diaspora it creates. One cannot say that Africa is a lost paradise, as it was for Gilroy's depiction of Asante, since the world of Changó and the Orishas is as fraught with struggles to attain a master consciousness as the world created by slavery and the Conquest. In this way, Zapata uses a DuBoisian approach to correct the Eurocentric histories: he makes men of "objects," but he does so through a unique, syncretic poetizing of Bantu notions of time, space, and death—all of which can be transcended through language—Ancestors and Spirits of Yoruba, Dahomean, and Native American origin. He shows that a linear, Eurocentric, and nationalist vision of progress is unfounded and that African, indigenous, and, perhaps most of all, hybrid consciousnesses are a space from which to criticize, complement, and refine the spirit of humanity in the name of self- and world liberation through understanding. Because Zapata can draw on the syncretic traditions of Latin America, he can perceive of a New World that not only is binary but also synthesizes many cultures and traditions. These traditions have been marginalized since the Conquest, but Nuevo Muntu novels show their importance as a counterdiscourse to dominant Eurocentric ideas of modernity.

Marked by these beliefs, *Changó* novelizes a series of revolutions in the New World. The result is a revision of José de Vasconcelos's introductory essay to *La raza cósmica* (1925) that gives new recognition to the African diaspora in the New World, as Antonio Tillis argues.[109] Zapata views black culture, particularly music, and understanding its hybridization with modern colonial culture as part of the "espíritu cósmico de América" (cosmic spirit of the Americas), a hybridity that will lead in the future to overcoming the oppression of the past.[110] He claims that black culture must not be treated paternalistically by dominant culture but as part of a community deserving a place at the table of national history. Vasconcelos posits that the Latin American "race," with all the eugenic weight of this word, had its "growth" stunted by Napoleon's invasion of Spain and the resulting chaos that led to the foundation of most of the independent Spanish American republics, though the historical reality was more complex than he presents it.[111] Later, the monarchy under Fernando VII could not reach an agreement with the liberal Cortes de Cádiz, which designed a new Spanish constitution in 1812 as Spain struggled to liberate itself from Napoleon with British and Portuguese aid.[112] This led to the chaos of the Wars of Independence in Spanish America. *Changó* follows Vasconcelos's trajectory from a new transculturated perspective. As in Vasconcelos's essay, Napoleon is responsible for the downfall of the Americas, but it is for the execution of Haitian liberator

General Toussaint, not for invading Spain and losing Louisiana to the "Saxons."[113] This inhibition of the American Muntu's evolution is reflected in the fragmentary theater of memory in "Rediscovered Bloodlines," where the growth and triumph of America continues, but in an incomplete manner: some fight off oppression while others remain colonized. However, reversing Vasconcelos's voyage south to Brazil and Argentina to devise the *raza cósmica*, Zapata's muntu, generally speaking, heads north to the United States. This path is identical to almost all U.S. slave narratives. The battles of old between black and oppressor continue in the form of slave revolts, the fight against Jim Crow, and the partial triumphs of the Civil Rights and Black Power movements.

For Gilroy, Black Atlantic thinkers periodize modernity by starting with the ships of the Middle Passage.[114] Zapata does something similar, though he contextualizes the Middle Passage as part of the greater tragic collision of the Conquest. *Changó*'s first chapter, "Land of the Ancestors," sings almost exclusively of a mythical Africa with only the loosest references to history.[115] The only historical depiction of Africa is that of the arrival of the European slavers, the Africans with whom they deal, and the slaves who fight back against their captors. Historical Africa does not reappear until Du Bois and Malcolm return to the motherland in the late twentieth century. Preslavery "Africa," in the novel, is useful because it creates an origin for a community, the African diaspora, but it does not present this origin as something static or retrievable. In *Changó* Africa is a mobile spirit, not a stable, historical place. Historical depictions of colonial Africa are almost entirely absent after the voyage of the *Nova Índia*, following the notion that, if an individual does not rebel from his or her slavery, he or she is not a historical consciousness but an extension of his or her master's consciousness.

Gilroy chooses the metaphor of a moving ship on the Atlantic to represent the African diaspora because it is mobile and international, like Zapata's muntu. For Gilroy, ships evoke the Middle Passage as well as black sailors. Changó's avatar, Nagó the Navigator, the protagonist of "The Trade" who overpowers the slaver and pilots the *Nova Índia* around the Atlantic throughout the novel, coincides with this international vision. However, he is able to transcend life and death, showing the usefulness of African spirits in recalling the past. *Changó*'s poetic language calls attention to the multiplicity of origins of the African diaspora. The novel creates three origins: a mythical Africa, the Middle Passage, and the indigenous-African collaborations that create a uniquely hybrid American people. Another fact missing from Gilroy's text is that, before the British, the Spanish colonies of the Caribbean and scattered Luso-African empire were defined by predominantly black ports to the point that historian David Wheat considered enslaved and free Africans "surrogate colonists" of the early Caribbean.[116]

Gilroy's work is not devoid of spirits, religion, or magic beliefs, however. He recalls that Anglophone slaves dreamed of a "return to point of origin" in Africa after death.[117] He notes that Douglass, when faced with the life-or-death struggle of his brutal foreman, was inspired by a conjurer who remembered the "old ways" and gave him an amulet.[118] Douglass's spirituality is part of his double consciousness for Gilroy, which *Changó* also demonstrates. Gilroy praises the Black Church in the Anglophone world as a preservation of tradition where "the dramatic power of narrative as a form is celebrated."[119] The black novel is a transition from oral culture to written culture, from Du Bois's notion of the marginalized black consciousness, captured in Negro spirituals and sermons, to the written culture of modernity. Unlike Du Bois and Gilroy, *Changó* clearly shows that syncretic religious traditions, largely absent from the Anglophone world outside of Catholic Louisiana (both U.S. traditions being shown in *Changó*), are a wellspring of narrative traditions. This is evident in *Changó* from the written summons imitating an oral call to the reader: "¡Oídos del *muntu*, oíd!," linking body, sound, community, and language, as in oral discourse.[120] The music of Afro-Catholic religious traditions is constant in the novel, which is tied to the syncretic oral traditions it emulates. Returning to "Origins," Luis notes that the first part of this narrative triptych mimics an invocation of Changó, the Orishas, and the Ancestors.[121] It begins and ends with a greeting to the demigod of openings and closings, Eleguá.[122] Eleguá's symbol, an Ouroboros of Yoruba origin, is written on the body of all the novel's heroes from birth and indicates the transition from oral to written discourse.[123] Critic Kameelah Martin has shown that iconic conjure women, from practitioners of Vodou and Santería to those who believe in "root work" remedies, display double consciousness, negotiating African vestiges alongside Christian and other Western secular worldviews.[124] She calls this negotiation an example of double consciousness.[125] These traditions are inseparable from the body, music, and dance.

Music, Orality, and the Sea

Like Zapata's text, music unites the African diaspora and forms part of its unique consciousness as double consciousness does in Gilroy's Black Atlantic.

For the Briton, "Music and its rituals can be used to create a model whereby identity can be understood neither as a fixed essence nor as a vague and utterly contingent construction to be reinvented by the will and whim of aesthetes, symbolists, and language gamers. . . . Lived as a coherent (if not always stable) experiential sense of self . . . it remains the outcome of practical activity: language, gesture, bodily signification, desires."[126] Gilroy claims that performers and vinyl records being shipped around the world would eventually replace the slave ship as the means of giving visibility to the diaspora by popularizing U.S. black music. Though Zapata wrote his novel before hip-hop had the global audience it did for Gilroy in 1993 and even more so today, the Colombian also notes the role of music in creating and revitalizing the diaspora. The U.S. novella "Ancestors" makes constant allusions to Negro spirituals and U.S. jazz as well as to the *poema-sones* of Afro-Cuban Nicolás Guillén, in imagining a transnational community.[127] Gilroy claims that black sophistication in music challenges the privileged conceptions of both language and writing as preeminent expressions of human consciousness, though he reminds the reader that literacy was forcibly out of reach for most slaves.[128] These fluid, transcendental aspects of diaspora identity are all present in *Changó*, and they are all intimately linked to its infusion of a written text with the music, gestures, and orality of the Orishas. The "moral basis" of black music of which the Afro-Briton speaks is inseparable from Afro-Catholic religions in the Latin American context, which are much older than the British Empire Gilroy studies, and this longevity makes it instrumental in community formation and resistance from the beginning.[129] Gilroy sees African American music from its origins in slavery as a means of imagining Jubilee, a Christian utopian quest for justice.[130] Zapata presents the creation of ideals through musical performance as part of the reconstruction of history, sharing with Douglass, Du Bois, and Gilroy a respect for a musical double consciousness. According to Lucía Ortiz, popular black music of the coast, appropriated to represent other countries like Cuba and Brazil, was highly radical when Zapata toured his country and the world performing it.[131] The music was rejected by Colombia's purist white elite, so folklore is cultural resistance for Zapata. Likewise, George Palacios shows that he used music and folklore to give visibility to Afro-Colombians through performance.[132]

In the novel, history will end in a syncretic "Jubilee." The novel's final prophet and heroine, Agne, reveals,

> El hecho de que el pueblo Negro haya podido sobrevivir a tanta ignominia, recreándose siempre más poderoso, es una prueba irrefutable de que estamos señalados por Changó para cumplir el destino de liberar a los hombres. El culto a los Ancestros, la ligazón entre los vivos y los muertos, pondrá fin al mito de los dioses individuales y egoístas. ¡No hay Dios más poderoso que la familia del Muntu![133]
>
> (The fact that the Black people has been able to survive so much ignominy, always re-creating itself and becoming more powerful, is irrefutable evidence that we are chosen by Changó to carry out our destiny to liberate all men. Ancestor worship, the bond between the living and the dead, will end the myth of individual, selfish gods. There is no God more powerful than the family of the Muntu!)

Gilroy, citing David Biron Davis, claims that overcoming slavery is, for Hegel, the source of true emancipation, and so it stands to reason that blacks' fight for liberation is vital to the Hegelian search for universal liberty.[134]

Zapata presents a history of the most transcendent of African diaspora thought. For example, it praises the pride of the black nationalism that would lead to Asante. This begins with Jamaican Marcus Garvey's attempt to gather Africans from the Americas and "repatriate" them in Africa. The Colombian synthesizes the ideals of flamboyant Garvey with his intellectually refined opponent, Du Bois, a gesture he repeats with Du Bois's historical antagonist Booker T. Washington.[135] In all cases the African respect for supernatural Ancestors, which all three thinkers become, forms a new consciousness.

Garvey's dream of the diaspora's return to Africa is presented as part of the same spirit as Malcolm X's evolving notions of Islam. Like Garvey, Malcolm reaches blacks of lower socioeconomic status like the "anciana" (old woman) who sells copies of the Black Islam Newspaper *Muhammad Speaks*.[136] Agne equally inspires her because she is imprisoned for her Ancestor Cult, which the racist media calls, in the old woman's words,

> Mañana, cuando el Muntu despierte con sus prédicas y coreen por las calles el glorioso nombre de Changó, repetirán las mismas monsergas lanzadas contra el profeta Garvey: "el Culto a la Vida y las Sombras es una explosión irracional de negros ignorantes y fanáticos."[137]

> (Tomorrow, when the Muntu awakes with its message and sing in the streets the glorious name of Changó, they will repeat the same mumbo jumbo they threw at the prophet Garvey: "the Worship of Life and Shadows is an irrational explosion of ignorant, fanatical blacks.")

The muntu and the Worship of Life and Shadows is a substitute for the red-haired, white Jesus (the spirit of the "Loba Blanca," the continuation of oppression) that evangelization forced upon blacks.[138] Garvey's message is that of a space on earth for the muntu, a quixotic challenge to the colonizers of Africa that they leave or face his people's wrath. The threat is followed by a shift in setting for his vision: "Nadie sabe cuando llegará la hora de la redención de nuestra África. Pero se oye el viento. ¡Está llegando! ¡Un día, como una tormenta, la tendremos aquí!" (Nobody knows when the time of redemption will return for our Africa. But you can hear the wind. It is coming! One day, like a storm, we will have it here!).[139] Garvey's ideals of black pride are lauded, but Zapata makes him the voice of liberation on the American continent as well, a Changó lightning storm that would spin off into Malcolm's international liberation project as an adult. The latter is enlightened on the matter of the color line through his 1964 Hajj, or pilgrimage to Mecca, and proclaims, "Los días de desunión han pasado, ahora sólo vivo para congregar la dispersa familia del muntu. Sólo así se construirá la sociedad anunciada por Changó donde los vivos activen el nudo que los ata a los muertos, donde los ekobios de todas las razas puedan llamarse hermanos" (The days of disunity have passed; now I only live to gather the disperse Muntu family. Only that way will the society announced by Changó continue, one where the living activate the knot that ties them to the dead, where the ekobios of all races can call themselves brothers).[140] The spirits of the text transcend race, nation, and religion, proposing an alternative to previous notions of imagined community. The slave rebellions that began on the African continent, continued on the *Nova Índia*, and erupted throughout the Americas have by then reached a global scale, encompassing Malcolm's sermons against South African Apartheid.[141] It is with Malcolm's international and anticolonial vision that the historical diaspora is as all-encompassing as the spiritual one that, in the text, begins before slavery.

Whereas the historical events in the Latin American sections of the novel have an overall northward trajectory, Du Bois and the two prophets have a west-east route.[142] All three have the goal of a return to what they interpret as "Africa." Garvey has the goal of repatriating the African diaspora in what he thought was their former homeland. These three thinkers return to Africa, or attempt to return as in Garvey's case, as primarily Western subjects whose double consciousness is in struggle with the colonial projects of the United States, one of the latest manifestations of the White Wolf of imperialism in the Americas. Africa inspires them to rise up against oppression, but they can never return to a stable Africa as it was before slavery. There is no "pure" Africa to which to return, the mistake Garvey and Asante made. Continuing the poetic use of blasphemy and "sympathy for the devil" in the text, which is sympathetic to virtually all the black movements it depicts, these prophets are impure "false" prophets, iconoclasts, like the one of the biblical Armageddon.[143] The novel's Jubilee is not "pure" in a traditional interpretation of the Bible, but "impure" in its cultural and religious mixture.

The African Diaspora Is Part of a New World History beyond the Nation

If the history of the New World is shared by all of its inhabitants, then its traumas must be inherited and worked through by all. This can be further seen as an imagined return to a metaphorical, not literal, Mother Africa for all of humanity. Gilroy also argues that "the history of blacks in the West and the social movements that have affirmed and rewritten that history can provide a lesson which is not restricted to blacks."[144] The muntu is not a race in the physiological sense inherited from eugenics but a seething sea of tempests leading to a possible future redemption for humanity. Like the Black Atlantic, its global scope and lack of racial purism allow for an understanding of world history that includes the intersecting histories of all people, including those excluded by the limitations of previous historians and philosophers of history.

Gilroy notes the root of the international diaspora model in Jewish thought.[145] Zapata's text acknowledges its debt to Africanist and Jewish exile Herskovits, but is not limited by his view of history of Africans as the losing half of the master-slave dialectic.[146] There is a moment when the text seems to say both "thank you" and "no thank you" to one of the early scholars of the diaspora. "Ancestors" opens with a theatrical dialogue between its protagonist, Agne Brown, and her professor at Columbia University. Originally, this section was titled "Herskovits," dubbed "Harrington" in the final version.[147] He was among the first white scholars to form a vision of the African diaspora that spans the Americas, and Asante based his Afrocentrism, in part, on his works.[148]

Agne notes the limitations of Herskovits's idea of blacks as "Atlas," the muscle holding up the progress of whites throughout history:

> Nos afirmamos en la hermandad del muntu preconizada por los Orichas africanos y en las luchas de nuestros Ancestros en las plantaciones, en los slums, en las fábricas, donde quiera que Changó enciende su rebeldía. Será una nueva religión para todos los oprimidos cualesquiera que sean sus sangres.[149]
>
> (We claim to be the brotherhood of the Muntu foretold by the African Orishas and in the struggles of our Ancestors in the plantations, the slums, the factories, wherever Changó lights his rebellion. It will be a new religion for all the oppressed, no matter what their bloodlines are.)

Shocked, Harrington replies, "Se trata entonces de africanizar la actitud religiosa del Blanco americano?" (You mean, then, to Africanize the White Man's religious character?).[150] Agne is dramatizing Zapata's vision of the diaspora as being united by African oral traditions of the Orishas and the Ancestors and the liberation projects they inspire in art, philosophy, and politics.

Harrington's reaction does two things: it summarizes a common assumption regarding Herskovits's theory of one-way (European over African) acculturation and transfers it to the United States.[151] Cuban anthropologist Fernando Ortiz rejected Herskovits's use of the term "acculturation" in reference to the cultural contact between Europeans and Africans from colonial times to the present.[152] In his *Contrapunteo cubano del tabaco y el azúcar* (*Cuban Counterpoint of Tobacco and Sugar*, 1940), Ortiz replaces it with "transculturation," claiming that both cultures influenced one another, forming hybrid identities. Ortiz can be viewed as an intellectual ancestor of Agne because he unites the magical, oral world of Afro-Cubans with the lettered world of the Hispanic and, eventually, Anglophone academies. Agne's project, like Ortiz's and Zapata's, is a transculturation of the Americas. The Orishas and the Ancestors transcend the limits of race and nation and unite everyone in a quest for justice. The spirit of Africa is still visible on this stage, but it is an ideal, not a plan to return to a pure, material space.

DuBoisian "second sight," which Gilroy revisits as a counterculture to modernity, has parallels with another anthropologist's notion of cultural negotiation, Roger Bastide's "principle of compartmentalization."[153] Those who practice syncretic faiths like Candomblé or Santería interpret the world through "logics or categories that are supposedly otherwise incompatible and irreducible." One can thus live in two worlds, one Catholic and one African. They are both what anthropologist Stefania Capone might call "re-Africanization" through religious practices. For Capone, "This tendency to retain ancestral knowledge and to compensate for ritual loss is what fuels African American religions."[154] It is a desire to unite Africa and the Americas.

Agne's Worship of Life and Ancestors is an example of compartmentalization and double consciousness, and she has another historical precursor. In 1962 Oba Ofuntola Oseijeman Adelabu Adefunmi founded the Yoruba Temple in Harlem and in 1970 founded the Oyotunji Village in South Carolina.[155] He was born Walter Eugene King in Detroit in 1928. Both Adefunmi and Agne put into practice a performance of culture that turns double consciousness into cultural activism that displays a bifurcated African American consciousness.

The Americas have been imagined as a community of three races (white, black, and Amerindian) since the Conquest. Zapata is clearly aware of this, but he presents an alternative, hybrid narrative for the evolution of the Americas from colonies to republics. This is still a double consciousness because of the limits of language itself. The novel follows the diaspora as it comes in contact with other languages and traditions. Therefore, if one were to choose a colonial term to describe the content of the novel, it could be called a history of *negros*, though Zapata uses the more encompassing terms *ekobio* (brother) and *muntu* (humanity) to subvert colonial language. This usage reflects Zapata's interest in language as the root of politics and its role in the amelioration of psychic colonization. The content of the novel, even when it narrates interactions with the myriad and diverse groups colonized as *indios*, places *negros* center stage, even as they evolve through conflict and creativity into different communities. In the documentary *Abridor de caminos* (*Trailblazer*) he says he wishes he had time to finish his history of the indigenous, *La maraca encantada* (*La maraca encantada*), now at Vanderbilt, so it is his goal to give an overview not of indigenous but of black history in the Americas in *Changó*.[156] This focus on people of African descent alters the representation of the indigenous in the novel, whose importance to the narrative is dependent on their interactions with the African diaspora. Even depictions of the Olmecs in Mexico are Africanized by the inclusion of the theory that they were descended from African explorers who discovered the Americas before the Europeans.[157] In the essay "Los problemas de identidad de los escritores afro-latinoamericanos" (Identity Problems of Afro–Latin American Writers), he claims the Olmecs were descended from African explorers, a narrative that has been excluded from those that construct the Mexican nation, an exclusion of African influences that is paralleled in many Latin American nations.[158] He describes the pre-Colombian African exploration of Mesoamerica proposed by Ivan van Sertima in his *They Came before Columbus* ([1976] 2003).[159] Here he falls into the trap of Asante of transposing twentieth- and nineteenth-century notions of race onto the pre-Colombian past. As Bernard Ortiz et al. show, this is mostly a dream without sufficient historical evidence.[160] Nevertheless, this origin myth shows that Afro-Mexicans come from heroic explorers like Nagó the Navigator as well as survivors like the Chingada, a synthesis of cultures that incorporates and empowers blacks as mestizos and sees their pain.[161]

In *Changó* all indigenous, mulato, zambo, and mestizo people of Mexico are children of Yemayá, the great mother of humanity.[162] Therefore, the story of the indigenous is part of the history of the African diaspora. Since the Conquest began in Africa, since the indigenous occupy an oppressed position in regards to Europe and its descendants in the New World, and since they share a common origin myth with the African diaspora in the novel, they are all muntu.

At the narrative level of form, double consciousness continues in Zapata's attempt to use European language to fight off European imperialism. He knew that language was the instrument of oppression, as he shows in the dialectological study *Nuestra Voz* and "El substrato negro en el español de América" ("The Black Substrate in Latin American Spanish"), which focus on how black and popular speech have enriched the Spanish language.[163] Despite the Babel of languages present in the novel (Yoruba, Taíno, Kikongo, Portuguese, etc.), it must remain in Spanish (or English, in the translation) for the reader to understand, and many of the non-Spanish terms are defined in the glossary. This comprehension is what allows the reader to have his or her consciousness altered by contact with non-Western terms. Therefore, the novel creates a new consciousness because the reader is presumed to speak Spanish, which uses terms that bear the weight of colonialism, like those for "white," "Amerindian," and "slave," and therefore able to communicate with the reader through the novel for him or her to begin the process of decolonization through language. This process is a struggle analogous to the master-slave dialectic because the European language remains dominant but dependent on the Other, be that contact with other languages or the creativity inherent in language to re-create itself as it becomes a new community, a Nuevo Muntu.

Zapata makes the combination of double consciousness with the three "races" of América explicit in "Los problemas de identidad de los escritores afro-latinoamericanos" ("Identity Problems of Afro–Latin American Writers").[164] He laments that "la alienación del escritor de ascendencia africana en Latino América se expresa fundamentalmente en el uso de una lengua prestada" (the Afro-descendant writer in Latin America expresses himself by using a borrowed language). The double consciousness of black history as a counterdiscourse to national history is paralleled by literary language itself in Latin America, which is of European origin and originally imposed through colonialism. Language continues oppressive structures, such as the *castas* he lists that imply that nonwhite races are inferior, alienating these groups. As he puts it in "El mestizaje en la novela hispanoamericana,"

> El fenómeno más trascendente en la evolución de nuestros pueblos es el mestizaje operado entre el colonizador europeo y las etnias indígena y africana. Dicha antinomia que ha sido caracterizada como el cruce de miradas entre el "yo" del conquistador y el "otro" del indígena, en lo social se revelaba entre la "pureza étnica" del europeo y las "razas infames" con las que indefectiblemente debió fundirse.[165]
>
> (The most transcendental phenomenon in the evolution of our peoples is the hybridity that has operated between the European colonizer and African and Amerindian ethnicities. This antinomy has been characterized as crossed gazes between the "self" of the conquistador and the "other" of the Amerindian; in the social aspect it was revealed in the "ethnic purity" of the European and the "infamous races" with whom he had to meld without exception.)

This quote reaffirms double consciousness (master/slave, self/other) and takes aim at cultural and racial purity projects. The "black soul" he describes in the first essay, while it seems essentialist, is not so stable in his novel. There are commonalities between blacks in Colombia, Haiti, and the United States, and there are heroes and spirits that reappear in different contexts, but the other side of double consciousness in the novel is the non-European terms, concepts, and histories that alter the novel's language. This polyphony shows the cultural diversity of marvelous realism, which can be traced back to the origins of the Americas, when the conquistadors were the minority among a Babel of peoples they knew as blacks and Indians. They marveled at the unknown magic of the Other. Double consciousness begins with Africa and the Americas for Zapata, and his novel seeks to create a new language for this community using the multiple influences that make it up.

The reader, as indicated in the preface "Al compañero de viaje" (To the Fellow Traveler), begins as the opposite of what Zapata asks him (or her) to become.[166] The author calls him or her to enter a new kind of double consciousness unknown before the novel. He or she is of the Americas, a wo/man who must become like a child. He or she finds some words strange like ghosts, and must take them as a "desafío a tu imaginación" (challenge to your imagination).[167] He or she is locked in a struggle that is similar to Zapata's, who is simultaneously the "prisoner" and "liberator" of language, the "discoverer" and "founder" of new communities in it, as these terms from the preface indicate. The implicit author writes the "Cuaderno de bitácora" (Notebook), then he tells the reader to resist it, I would add, like a slave in conflict with his master. The preface ends with a reminder: "Tarde o temprano tenías que enfrentarte a esta verdad: la historia del hombre negro en América es tan tuya como la del indio o la del blanco que lo acompañarán a la conquista de la libertad para todos" (Sooner or later you had to confront this reality: the history of the black man in America is as much yours as that of the Amerindian and the white man that will accompany him to the conquest of freedom for all).[168] He presumes that the reader is ignorant of the black history that the work will reveal and that his or her notions of history will be in conflict with the counternarrative of the novel. His new historiography places the *negro* at its center, even while it uses poetic language to reimagine the *negro* as muntu, and muntu as everything and everyone with which it has come in contact. This includes a revised history of the nations of the Americas.

The Haitian Revolution is the first time black liberation aligned itself with national liberation, and the novel presents it as an expansion of the liberty for which the slave rebels in San Basilio, Colombia, had begun fighting in the seventeenth century. Zapata shows that the nation is incomplete in its nineteenth-century form, a curse inherited by the contemporary reader. Before the muntu betrayed the nation, the nation betrayed the muntu. While the U.S. muntu continues to evolve after emancipation, Latin America remains stilted in the 1800s. Brazil remains a colony, the presence of which becomes only a ghost in the twentieth-century section.[169] Where is Vasconcelos's cosmic race? By what betrayal were these dreams lost? In a word, Bolívar. His life and the nations he founded exemplify, in the novel, Du Bois's claim that African Americans' strivings to be both "Negro and American" are constantly in tension, though Latin America's history differs significantly from that of the United States.

"The Liberator" Bolívar's final judgment in the novel comes from his admiral, Padilla, the Haitian Revolution, the African spirits he ignored, and his own wet nurses. It is striking how short the chapter on Bolívar is, especially when compared to the one on his zambo friend and comrade in arms. In the novel Admiral Padilla's monument stands taller than the man whose image is synonymous with Spanish American freedom. Padilla's military victories are told in painstaking detail, while Bolívar is literally put on trial by those he failed. Padilla was tried and executed for treason, but his life and death speak to the heart of Latin America and the road to freedom it has not yet traveled. Both Bolívar and Padilla have black ancestry in the novel.[170] The theory of Bolívar's African ancestry is still marginal among historians, though it was promoted by Venezuelan president Hugo Chávez.[171] In the novel Padilla never forgets his African and indigenous heritage. To show this their childhoods are juxtaposed, as if they were brothers. José Prudencio is the spiritual son of the personified Atlantic, Yemayá, and Nagó the Navigator, the slave rebel and sailor that shares so much with the slaves and black sailors Gilroy studies. Luis considers him the beginning of a "black," diasporic consciousness in the novel.[172] José Prudencio remembers his origins to the extreme of recalling his life in the womb and suckling at his mother's breasts, the waters that would protect and fortify him throughout his life. This is his DuBoisian "second sight" beyond Western Reason. On the other hand, "Simoncito" forgets the black "ayas," such as Hipólita, who care for and nourish him even when his own mother has no milk, as if he forgot his own Ancestors.[173] Hipólita's daughter, his *hermana de leche* (one to share the same breast), dies at birth. There is an absence in Simoncito's (little Simon's) life that is identified with the feminine and the African, syncretized with the indigenous in this context, which comes back to haunt and judge him in death "ante el tribunal de los Ancestros" (before the Ancestors' court). Nana Taita, his black Ancestor revealed by the speaking Orinoco and who shares a name with Taita Facundo in Nicolás Guillén's "Balada de los abuelos" (Ballad of the Grandfathers), joins his *ayas* in asking why he sided with the slave owners when he "freed" five nations from Spain.[174] This is foreshadowed by the Dog Shadow in Simón, a continuation of the White Wolf, the race/spirit that seeks to dominate the other two. Already in this chapter the notion of "mácula" (stain) is challenged since the white "race" considered immaculate in the nineteenth century is the "la parte impura que tiraniza a los hermanos indios" (impure part that tyrannizes his indigenous brothers).[175]

Bolívar's trial in death makes him a foil for Padilla, who is tried while alive. While Simón's mother sees five flags for five nations when he is born, Padilla's vision of nation is different: "En Trafalgar, padre [Nagó], perdí mi capitán, mi barco y mi Rey, pero gano otra bandera: mi raza" (At Trafalgar, father [Nagó], I lost my captain, my ship, and my King, but I won another flag: my race).[176] This is not a eugenic determinism but a hope for a future cultural mixture that will lead to true and universal freedom. It is also the flag of a diaspora between nations. As Padilla's battles wear on, he finds himself caught between Britain and Spain at the Battle of Trafalgar, then between these two and Napoleon's France as he is treated like a slave in Cartagena, and between France, Spain, and the Independence fighters during the Bolivarian Wars. He is continuing the Afro-descendant tradition of Caribbean blacks who sometimes allied with invaders and at others defended Spain.[177] Amid these nations sails the enslaver/pirate Aury, who shows that racism and exploitation transcend nation as well.[178] Padilla is a man without a country who is simultaneously fighting to create a new, democratic one. The admiral's valor and skill lead to the strategic victory at the Battle of Maracaibo that sealed the Bolivarians' hold on the Americas.[179] However, his vision for American liberty is greater and more trustworthy than Bolívar's. Along with the Cuban Romero, he wants a free nation for all, not just landowning whites. Padilla fights alongside Haitian ships, granted to the rebels by Pétion under the condition that Bolívar abolish slavery in the new republics. However, when the smoke clears, Bolívar betrays Pétion. The aristocratic Conventionists treat him as if he were a threat to the republic, and they accuse Padilla: "Has sublevado el Batallón de los Pardos en Cartagena" (You have made the Mulatto Batallion rise up in Cartagena).[180] He is executed by a firing squad, then hanged. His bloody wounds, his "condecoraciones" (awards), ally him with the nation, but his hanging body allies him with the African diaspora, such as those lynched in the United States later in the novel, and with Changó, who died by hanging in a version of his myth.[181]

If Bolívar and Padilla are like brothers, then we should also note that Padilla has an important but barely mentioned blood brother in Guyana,

Piar, in the novel.[182] Historically, he and Padilla were executed by Bolívar for fear of them leading a *pardo* (mulatto) uprising, though they were not relatives.[183] This decision haunts the Libertador beyond his death in the novel.[184] Piar is the leader of an army of maroon slaves, like the Colombian Bioho and Zumbi de Palmares, who appears in the Brazil chapter.[185] Piar tells Padilla that the maroons were free well before the French and their imitators began to chant "liberté" (freedom) in the Americas. Maroons like these were the armies of the Loas that began the rebellion in Saint-Domingue before the Haitian Revolution knew what it was, and they were the fighters who sought community beyond an eighteenth- and nineteenth-century notion of nation. These maroons, across Latin America, never forgot the oral traditions of the African Spirits. This forgetting is the root of the nation's betrayal of the African diaspora and the indigenous because it allows Bolívar to establish Catholic nations led only by whites. This forgetting allows Pétion and Christophe to betray their nation by persecuting the Vodou that founded it and imitate the French emperor they died fighting. This forgetting allowed Latin American politicians and historians to overlook the contributions of the African diaspora to their respective nations in language, art, culture, love, war, and anything else that makes a subject human and makes a community great.

In *Changó* cultural hybridity defines Latin America in a way that it did not in the United States at the time the novel was written. There is a rupture between the Americas that begins with "Ancestros combatientes" (Ancestors in Combat).[186] More space is dedicated to the United States than any other country in the novel. This is because of the singular importance the nation played in racial politics in the twentieth century, as the inspirational figures of diasporic thinkers Garvey and Malcolm's presence in the novel indicates.[187] Zapata traveled the United States from the 1940s to the end of his life in 2004. His *He visto la noche* (*I Have Seen the Night*) depicts his clear understanding of what W. E. B. Du Bois considered the defining element of the twentieth century: the color line.[188] Zapata felt Jim Crow in the flesh as a dark-skinned mestizo who was aware that there were other concepts of race, diaspora, and oppression that Du Bois could not have known in the United States in 1903 when he wrote *The Souls*.

While Du Bois's relative ignorance of race in Latin America is forgivable given his context, his intellectual progeny, Gilroy, does not attempt a synthesis of Anglo and Latin America at the end of the twentieth century. This oversight highlights the importance of Zapata's novel. *Changó* shows that the elements that should transcend time and space in Latin American history in the form of memory are the African spirits themselves outlined in "Los orígenes" (Origins), which have been marginalized and demonized from the Conquest to this day. "American Muntu" and "Vodou Rebellion" show slave rebellions that do not come solely from national liberation projects and enlightenment ideals, though the French Revolution and its declarations of equality influenced the Haitian Revolution alongside the Saints and, in the novel, Taíno deities. These three elements (magic, maroons, and mestizaje) are minimized in Gilroy's work because these practices and beliefs were much more tightly controlled in the Protestant-dominant United States. There were not large maroon communities in the post-independence United States like those of Haiti, Cuba, and Brazil, though there were numerous escape stories of those headed to the abolitionist North or Canada. The U.S. government's genocide of the indigenous population was more extensive than in the Latin American mainland, where exploitation and oppression were the norm, and Washington corralled those who remained in the United States onto reservations.

As "Ancestors in Combat" opens, the griot Ngafúa calls out to the protagonist, Agne Brown.[189] This inverts the opening of "Origins" in which Ngafúa cries to the muntu, the reading/listening public, and he invokes the spirits Elegba and Changó.[190] Ngafúa's call to her implies that she and the African Americans she represents do not have the same memory of the diaspora that Latin American practitioners of Afro-Catholic faiths do.[191] This opening scene presents the departure between the binary, segregated world that Agne is born into in the U.S. South. Agne's life begins with strong parallels to those of Du Bois and Zapata, who lived through these harsh conditions. But Zapata shows that the two Americas in the novel, Anglo and Latin America, can and should be synthesized into a sum that is greater than its parts along the lines of Vasconcelos's cosmic race.

Most of the United States in the 1960s, when Agne comes of age, did not recognize the *zambo* (Afro-Amerindian) elements of its national identity, and much of this aspect of the U.S. fabric is still ignored. Agne's enslaved Ancestor Zaka revises her understanding of her own history and ancestry. He notes that his father was Seminole and that the indigenous helped him escape the plantation.[192] He tells Agne of pre-Colombian (Afro-Olmecs) and Conquest-era (Estebanico of *Naufragios*) Afro-indigenous alliances and Indian reservations where blacks work to build a life in the Old West alongside their Native American brethren.[193] These zambo alliances are not a whitening project like Vasconcelos's but a revision of U.S. history that includes black, indigenous, and Latin American elements in the greater narrative of the rise and fall of racial segregation from slavery to the novel's end. Du Bois, a product of his time, did not include these alliances in his double consciousness, and Gilroy's focus also overlooks them.

Raised by a white Protestant minister, Reverend Robert, in the Midwest, Agne is not in contact with oral Afro-Catholic traditions like the Latin American muntu.[194] As these two groups (Latin muntu and U.S. muntu) come together in the twentieth century, not all of their elements are repeated. Agne is a well-cared-for individual who has many of the privileges of what was then considered a "white" world, such as financial stability, "white" schooling from elementary school to college, and the more limited racist violence of Kansas and, later, New York.[195] Raised in Lawrence, birthplace of Langston Hughes, she dramatizes the *Brown v. Board of Education* case of 1954, which integrated public schools. She has more options than her enslaved Ancestors to express her identity and be recognized. The violence of the past, such as the slave revolts in Palenque de San Basilio and Saint-Domingue and even the revolutions of Bolívar, Tiradentes, and Morelos are no longer the most effective modes of resistance and recognition by the dominant culture. She has even more access to education and written culture than Aleijadinho had in his time, so she can look back at history with distance and determine what elements of that past can be applied to her present. She looks to African American thinkers from Zaka to Sojourner Truth, from Booker T. Washington to Du Bois, but she also communicates with Latin American and Native American elements and the Orishas to evolve in her consciousness into something new. Agne's coming of age allows her to reconnect with the silenced traumas of her past, such as the lynching of her father in the U.S. South as well as an awareness of the Americas' trauma bond, which is slavery.[196]

Double consciousness, if understood as a binary, biologically determined notion of race, is not big enough for the muntu. In the novel double consciousness is a synthesis of the best of the Americas, including the mestizo and zambo cultural elements that flourished in the Latin America that Gilroy ignores. Zapata maps out the diaspora through the lens of a more extensive DuBoisian double consciousness that synthesizes the best of African diaspora thought with other American traditions with the goal of opening the possibility for universal liberation, recognition, and self-understanding.

Zapata, Precursor of Today's Latin Americanist Critics of Gilroy

Zapata's trailblazing in avoiding Gilroy's blind spots is continued today by Latin Americanist critics. He anticipates key aspects of theorist Walter Mignolo's postcolonial theory. He argues for "border thinking" that challenges the Western worldview, philosophy, and history.[197] He rejects the tendency for the "First World" to export science and philosophy and the tendency of marginal nations and cultures to export "culture" to nations at the center of a globalized world. He advocates "bilanguaging" (making new combinations of languages possible) of knowledge, or border thinking, to bypass epistemological grounding in national and imperial languages. He means a "way of life between languages: a dialogical, ethic, aesthetic, and political process of social transformation rather than energeia emanating from an isolated speaker." Examples of this thought, as the name "border thinking" implies, are in Gloria Anzaldúa's "new mestiza consciousness" from *Borderlands/La Frontera: The New Mestiza* (1987)—more than a combination of marginal and colonial/modern forms of thought, but also one that disrupts the dominant narratives that support Eurocentricity, racism, and ethnocentrism.[198] Alongside Anzaldúa, he mentions Du Bois's double consciousness and the work of Paul Gilroy as examples of "border thinking."[199] Likewise, he advocates philosophical and cultural "creolization," which means to feel that one is "of" the Americas (as opposed to Europe) and culturally mixed in a colonial context. This thinking subverts hegemonic local histories by altering the global systems that form knowledge. Subversive mestizaje is central to *Changó*, as is the coloniality of power and the revision of history. The Nuevo Muntu, which will come about through the overcoming of racism and coloniality, is rooted in a combination of African, indigenous, and European elements that anticipates border thinking.

Other scholars have made important developments to the Black Atlantic. Colonial Hispanists are revisiting Gilroy. I echo Herman Bennett's observation that Gilroy is too focused on the former British Empire.[200] To counter this, Bennett analyzes the Inquisition records of Luisa de Abrego, a Christianized African in Mexico. Nicholas Jones claims Sor Juana Inés de la Cruz should be seen as a Black Atlantic writer in the tradition of Gilroy, since she is the first writer to imitate the speech of blacks, one of whom she owned, in her poetry.[201] David Wheat's transatlantic study even shows that nearly forty thousand of the so-called settlers of the Hispanic Caribbean in the sixteenth and seventeenth centuries were African captives and their descendants.[202] In the fall 2017 *Afro-Hispanic Review* issue on marronage, Graciela Maglia and John Maddox employ his use of the Bakhtinian chronotope, applying it not to the ship as metaphor, as Gilroy does, but to the maroon figure, who unites Latin America (Spanish America, Brazil) with Anglo-America (Jamaica, the United States).[203]

Chris Schmidt-Nowara corrects a blind spot on Wright in *The Black Atlantic*: the U.S. writer's perception of the "Black Legend" of Spain's backwardness and thus marginality to modernity.[204] He claims Gilroy replicates the Protestant world's emphasis on individual and innovation and the Catholic world as synonymous with archaism and backwardness.[205] Schmidt-Nowara counters that "Spain and Portugal were at the vanguard of the modernity theorized in the Black Atlantic," and horrifyingly, they did so by creating the slave trade in the fifteenth and sixteenth centuries that Britain would dominate in the eighteenth. These historical novels redress the marginalization of the Ibero-Atlantic in the Black Atlantic.

Schmidt-Nowara is not alone. José Jorge de Carvalho notes that Gilroy ignores syncretic religious traditions, the rich Afro-Latin music tradition, and the power differences between the British Atlantic and the diaspora in Africa, the Caribbean, and Latin America.[206] Cultural critic Eduard Arriaga relies heavily on Paul Gilroy's transnational Black Atlantic to draw links between Colombia, Canada, and Equatorial Guinea.[207] Like me, he notes that the majority of the African diaspora have always lived in the Spanish- and Portuguese-speaking Americas.[208] Writing after Gilroy, he also notes the centrality of digital cultural production to the diaspora today.[209]

Argentine ethnomusicologist Norberto Pablo Cirio departs from Gilroy because of the population he studies, Afroargentines "del tronco colonial" (of the colonial trunk).[210] This group does not identify with the African diaspora, he says, and their interests do not lie beyond the nation, Gilroy's focus. They should be viewed as diasporic and rhizomatic, and Zapata made a mistake in leaving them out of his masterpiece because it reaffirms the notion of a Southern Cone without blacks.

Mônica Prates Conrado and Alan Augusto Moraes Ribeiro continue to rely on Gilroy as a sociological model of black hybridity, but they go farther in developing a feminist theory of the intersectionality of black masculinity black experience:

> Construindo o que Paul Gilroy (2001) identifica como "epistemologias do ponto de vista" (p. 121), os escritos feministas negros de autoras negras como Lélia Gonzales (1988), Sueli Carneiro (2003; 2013), Luiza Bairros (1988), Angela Davis (1983), bell hooks, Patricia Collins . . . fortaleceram um olhar analítico para as maneiras pelas quais experiências sociais de mulheres negras se tornaram visíveis em diferentes escritos, elaborando linguagens e narrativas em que essas experiências foram explicadas e usadas para pensar sobre outras experiências de outros grupos sociais.[211]
>
> (Building what Paul Gilroy identifies as "epistemologies of point of view," black feminist writers like Lélia Gonzalez (1988), Sueli Carneiro (2003; 2013), Luiza Bairros (1988), Angela Davis (1983), bell hooks, Patricia Collins . . . strengthened a critical gaze for the ways through which the social experiences of black women became visible in different writings, elaborating languages and narratives in which these experiences were explained and used to think about other experiences and other social groups.)

Their dialogue with González, Carneiro, and Barros results in an adaptation of Gilroy's Eurocentric approach to a uniquely Brazilian reality of "cordial" (romantic, falsely harmonious) representations of exaggerated black sexuality, masculine and feminine, on the plantation.[212] Artist Marsha Pearce does well to include Gilroy's notion of hybridity in her artwork and essay, which interprets the triangular Middle Passage, and black identity, through the Pythagorean Theorem.[213]

Brazilian Eduardo de Assis Duarte notes that the emerging self-conscious black literature in Brazil is not limited to Black Atlantic influences, though *Defeito*'s transatlantic voyage and protagonist, Kehinde, share the worldview and "values" of the Black Atlantic.[214] Anne Garland Mahler's 2018 theorization of the Tricontinental and the Global South continues to use the term "Black Atlantic" as a synonym for "black internationalist" and "black transnational."[215] However, she calls it insufficient since the Marxists she studies go to Russia and Asia.

Anthropologist Miguel Vale de Almeida used Gilroy to do just that in his *Um mar da cor da terra* (*A Sea the Color of Earth*, 2006), which goes beyond the Anglophone Atlantic and adapts diaspora studies to the *mes-*

tizo reality of an "Atlântico Pardo" (Mixed-race Atlantic), which defines the Luso-Atlantic.[216] Almeida's insights, inspired partly by Gilroy, attempt to adapt and combine the paradigm with his fieldwork with Afro-Brazilians in Bahia and his frequent recourse to Brazilian literature. Some Afro-Brazilian activists reject "ethnic" identity, which they associate with nonblacks (Amerindians, immigrants); others reject "race," in favor of multiculturalism.[217] Blacks often are not seen as an "ethnicity" there, but Amerindians are, which has some parallels with the Colombian cases studied by Peter Wade, to which Almeida refers.[218] Almeida sees Gilroy's paradoxical "anti-anti-essentialism" and protean, transatlantic identities as a way out of the conundrum. Another issue is the three "knots" of hegemonic narratives of race in Brazil: "mestiçagem" (miscegenation), "branqueamento" (whitening), and "democracia racial" (racial democracy), which form the bases of arguments that racism is not a problem in Brazil and thus no action must be taken.[219] Afro-Brazilians' Black Atlantic identity, however, is also tripartite: the imagination of an "African" origin, the ethnic diversity of African homelands, and different European colonizers. Portugal, for example, occupied a "subalterno" (subaltern) status on the continent—but was not an exceptionally "harmonious" colonizer.[220] One must overcome the dualism Brazil–United States (one being more or less "racist") and the folklorization (and thus rendering innocuous) of black culture as well as being simultaneously "African" and "Brazilian." Blacks are not a minority in Bahia. Almeida develops his own model of diaspora for Brazil, a sort of Atlântico Pardo (Mixed Atlantic), inspired by Gilroy's sailors and ships:

> . . . o aparente paradoxo entre o fluxo e o ancoramento, a busca—sobretudo pelos afro-descendentes—de um lugar na terra do novo mundo sem esquecer o culto da terra de "origem" do outro lado do mar, de onde portugueses e luso-brasileiros arrancaram os seus antepassados. Este mar é, por fim, navegado pelo personagem do Marinheiro, personagem (ou entidade) da religião afro-brasileira, figura de Mercúrio comunicante e abridor de passagens, cuja simbologia é abordada no último capítulo.[221]
>
> (. . . the apparent paradox between flux and anchorage, the search—above all by Afro-descendants—for a place in the land of the New World without forgetting the cult of the land of "origin" on the other side of the sea, from which Portuguese and Luso-Brazilians tore their ancestors. This sea is, in the end, navigated by the character of the Sailor, a character (or entity) from

> Afro-Brazilian religion, a communicating figure of Mercury and one who opens paths, whose semiology is broached in the final chapter.)

The Marinheiro (Sailor) comes not only from the modernist tradition of the Black Atlantic but also from the syncretic African religions of Bahian origin.[222] He is a multifaceted, paradoxical figure who has much in common with the indigenous *caboclos* in that he is an "ancestor" and "dono da terra": he has a right to the land like the indigenous, but he also has the experience and open-mindedness of the sea's discoveries. He is thus like Exu (Elegua, Legba) in that he opens new paths to the future beyond those offered by Brazilian and black nationalisms. Zapata already imagined a Nagó the Navigator based on Portugal's Henry the Navigator in 1983, and like Almeida, he hybridizes the Western canon with syncretic New World traditions. He even invites the reader to become a "Compañero de Viaje," a Malungo or shipmate, an association with slavery and seafaring, and a term used between enslaved Africans during colonial times. The Marinheiro/Martim/Malungo is imagined as white by black subjects, reaffirming the paradoxes and hybridity of the Black Atlantic. If the reader is understandably not satisfied with a white symbol of the African diaspora, then he or she need look no further than Kehinde, who is hybrid, contradictory, maritime, and immersed in Brazil, Africa, and the Black Atlantic in between. In addition, given that the person who told Almeida of the Marinheiro was an Afro-Brazilian woman, it is not contradictory to see Kehinde herself as the Marinheiro.

"Double consciousness" defines the Black Atlantic. Cuban intellectual Roberto Zurbano argues that contemporary Afro-Cuban painters exhibit a "third consciousness" that is different from Du Bois's "double consciousness." Unlike Gilroy, he believes Du Bois was not aware of his "diasporic condition."[223] Much of this consciousness, which I maintain is still dual in nature, is already present in Zapata's novel (self/other, Western/non-Western). Zurbano advocates liberating racial consciousness, emancipation of "ciudadanos del futuro" (citizens of the future), coalition building, and the righting of violent cycles of history and political amnesia.[224] He sees the dialogue with cultural memory as linked to African spirituality like the muntu, even considering the artist akin to an Afro-Cuban medium like Zapata does.[225] Like Zapata's novel, this diasporic unity transcends religion, nation, and color in battle with oppression.

Zapata anticipates sociologist Agustín Laó-Montes's articulation of *afro-latinidades* in 2007. He notes that the use of the term "African diaspora" dates only to the 1950s.[226] He charts a genealogy of diaspora models, placing Gilroy's among "pan-African" movements that are not "Afrocentric."[227] Like Zapata, he sees the African diaspora as central to the revision of history and a central component to any discussion of the modern world.[228] He notes the importance of Third World feminism in adding gender to the theorization of diaspora, just as Zapata does in *Changó* through Agne.[229] He cites Puerto Rican Arturo Alfonso Schomburg as a precursor to Afro-Latinidad, tying the Harlem Renaissance to it as Zapata does between the Harlem Renaissance and the various settings of his novel.[230] Laó-Montes also sees the U.S. Afro-Latinos Zapata does not, but he is otherwise in line with the Colombian's thought. He sees the Black Atlantic as a composition of "diasporas entrelazadas" (intertwined diasporas) in which Afro-Latinxs have been fundamental.[231] He believes "Afroamérica" should be a heterogeneous, polyphonic, creolized crossroads, just like Zapata's mestizo diaspora.[232]

Despite precursors of Afro-Latinidad dating back to intellectuals like Arturo Schomburg and political precursors like the fighters of the Haitian Revolution, Laó-Montes considers the beginning of today's Afro-Latinx politics the turn of the 1980s.[233] In Latin America, neoliberal policies encouraged communication between African Americans and black intellectuals in Latin America like Zapata already did from the 1940s to 2004. He notes the coalition between the indigenous in Latin America and blacks, just like Zapata. Afro-American and Latino studies converge for him in transnational anti-imperialist and frequently anticapitalist liberation politics. Zapata's Marxist New World is the Nuevo Muntu.

Lioba Rossbach de Olmos believes the Black Atlantic is the antithesis of the legal and lived realities of Afro-Colombians in the Chocó, the Pacific region Zapata treats in his *El fusilamiento del diablo* (*Devil's Execution*), which began as part of *Changó*. I disagree with her belief that his "cultural hybridity" could become dogma, as long as it remains a becoming, as Gilroy notes.[234] Like Zapata, she bases her essay largely on empirical anthropological study of Afro-Colombian communities.[235] She notes that anthropologists Richard Price and Sidney Mintz were already writing in the 1970s about cultural creolization, the centrality of orality to black cultures, and corporality, and Zapata surely knew their work.[236] She does not see a counterculture in the Chocó, since there were few slave rebellions or *palenques* there, and auto-sufficiency always trumped community. The closest *chocoano* analogue to Du Bois that she finds is the politician and lawyer Diego Luis Córdoba, who is seen not as a black nationalist but as an advocate for regional autonomy and education.[237] While there is little memory of slavery in the Chocó, they continue to call themselves *libres* (freedmen), referring to the days of manumission, not to Africa or slavery itself.[238]

So where does the compulsion to call themselves "black" or "afro" come from? The late 1980s brought with them two movements that would change this community's identity: indigenous movements for sovereignty and liberation theology Catholics.[239] The Law 70 (1993) of the 1991 Constitution recognized Pacific blacks' collective rights to their lands, even if they continue not viewing themselves as a collective.[240] Black leaders, church leaders, state leaders, and anthropologists have sought to create "black consciousness" among the libres, going so far as to educate them on their African origins, and lawyers are scouring frustrated appeals from Afro-Colombians for land rights.[241] Union activists have complained that this treatment ghettoizes blacks. This lack of communication with the rest of the black diaspora and the imposition of identity from without virtually stands not only Gilroy's but also Zapata's diasporas on their heads: the "white" church and virtually every other hegemonic structure are "teaching" people how to be "black like Amerindians," to the chagrin of the left. Rossbach fears it is a way for the nation-state to wash its hands of its responsibilities to provide services to these communities under a neoliberal mask.[242]

Zapata's unique double consciousness precedes not only Gilroy but also his critics in proposing a way to link the Americas and both sides of the Atlantic through the African diaspora. Jossianna Arroyo and Elizabeth Marchant guest edited a special issue of *Comparative Literature Studies* that addresses the "surprising gap in research on the cultures of the African diaspora, since more than ten times as many Africans were forcibly taken to the Spanish and Portuguese colonies in the Americas than to the United States."[243] They gathered essays on double consciousness in the Iberian world. In the issue, Guillermina de Ferrari puts Gilroy into dialogue with Édouard Glissant; Luiza Franco Morreira writes on Cuba, the United States, and Brazil; Rodrigo Lopes de Barros writes on modernismo in Brazil and the Cuban avant-garde; and Brady Smith writes on double consciousness and *mestiçagem* (miscegenation) in Cabo Verde.[244]

The Black Atlantic is the basis for Daiana Nascimento dos Santos's 2017 article on how the enslaved interpreted the ocean and the slave ship in their testimonies.[245] In addition to Equiano and Baquaqua, she mentions Zapata's novel and analyzes Gonçalves's.[246] She extends the Black Atlantic to the Black Pacific in Ecuador, Perú and Chile.[247]

Jerome Branche's *The Poetics and Politics of Diaspora* (2015) bears the marks of Gilroy and Zapata. Regarding Gilroy, he sees double consciousness and *The Black Atlantic* as an important part of the African diaspora, in Colombia, Brazil, Europe, and Africa. Regarding the foundational myth of Changó's curse, he claims that it bears an "overemphasis on myth" that renders the novel's representation of diaspora "more romantic than radical."[248] Perhaps it is ironic, then, that he structures his own "malungaje" (camaraderie) theorization of diaspora along virtually the same lines as *Changó*. The *malungo* is, as he admits, a *compañero de viaje* (fellow traveler) on the slave ship who recognizes black solidarity but also welcomes "transracial" alliances and cultural hybridity.[249] He bases the term on the Salamaka Bush people of contemporary Surinam. They have a mythical "First Time," which is the eighteenth century before their people were enslaved. Today, they build on this myth as they struggle for their land against the government. Branche structures his appropriation of their thought as a foundational preslavery myth, a bond formed in shared suffering and rebellion during the Middle Passage, resistance on the mainland through maroon communities, the culmination of black national freedom in the Haitian Revolution, being "conscripted" into the white-dominant nation-states during independence, and drawing on Palenque traditions in contemporary "outer-national" struggles.[250] "Outer-national" comes from Gilroy, but the structure parallels the one Zapata started developing as early as 1963. Branche simply adds Equatorial Guinea.

Partly inspired by Gilroy, Phaf-Rheinberger's *Modern Slavery and Water Spirituality* (2017) keeps the sea as the chronotope of diaspora, but includes the Spanish- and Portuguese-speaking regions of the Americas and Africa.[251] She analyzes the sea not only as a geopolitical space but also as a metaphor for social change beginning with the slave trade's representation in literature.[252] Among other revisions to Gilroy's model of the sea, she adds the water deity Yemayá as a metaphor for the African diaspora, and she includes *Defeito*.[253]

Zapata and Gonçalves map the boundaries of presence and power from the margins of history, and they control the lives of hundreds of characters across a vast sea with their voices. In both works, ships and songs set this stage before and beyond Gilroy's *Black Atlantic*, historically and geographically speaking. In the next chapter I show that novelists before Gonçalves explored transatlantic history, yet her text weaves both sides of the Atlantic together with the plantations of Bahia and the villages of Africa in a unique way that incorporates the point of view of a woman who has lived on both sides of the master-slave dialectic and slavery itself.

4

Women, Gender, and the Nuevo Muntu

Whereas last chapter discussed the limits and benefits of Gilroy's text to our understanding of the African diaspora, this one focuses on the roles of women and sexuality in both texts. First, *Defeito* shows how a transatlantic woman's life builds a bigger Black Atlantic, drawing on the transnational canon on Afro-Brazilians who returned to Africa. Then, I discuss the role of women and queer characters in both her novel and Zapata's. Both novels present slavery as a foundational rape. In this way they can be seen as continuing the tradition Octavio Paz began with "the Chingada" (The One That Got Fucked Over).[1] I show that, using poetic language inspired by Paz, Zapata presents his final prophet, Agne Brown, as the Whore of the Apocalypse who brings about an earth-shattering gathering of black souls from slavery to the present. While Gilroy broached gender briefly by discussing Toni Morrison, no model of diaspora is complete without considering gender and sexuality, which intersect race and nation.

The Black Atlantic from an Afro-Brazilian Woman's Point of View

Ana Maria Gonçalves maps the common histories of Brazil, Benin, and Nigeria in a way that is similar yet supplementary to Gilroy's Black Atlantic. The master-slave dialectic is also at work in Kehinde/Luísa's perception, so she is an example of double consciousness. Her frequent shifts in geographic location and socioeconomic status alter this struggle. Therefore, double consciousness and hybridity are not "meaningless" in this Brazilian novel, as critic Melissa Schindler claims regarding Conceição Evaristo, whose work, for her, shows the sexism and cultural inappropriateness of the Black Atlantic for women writers of Brazil.[2] To better understand the context of Gonçalves's novel, let us turn to the history of slavery in the region where her novel begins. Kehinde and the character Agontimé represent the 61 percent of individuals embarked in the Bight of Benin as slaves destined for Bahia, which corresponds to the 91 percent of slaves disembarked in Bahia from Benin from 1770 to 1850.[3] Their stories are the stories of 337,000 lives. Examining one life can illuminate theirs.

Domingos Álvares and the Black Atlantic Kingdom of Dahomey

Though Brazil's only official slave narrative in the abolitionist tradition is Mahomah Gado Baquaqua's, today's historians have used colonial documents to reconstruct the lives of the enslaved. James Sweet's biography of Domingos Álvares describes not only an enslaved African in Brazil and Portugal but also the African wars that led to his captivity. Álvares was the son of two priests of the *vodun* (force, god) Sakpata, who controls the earth (burial) and disease (particularly smallpox).[4] He was heir to his family's practice of healing. Álvares shares this devotion with enslaved characters in *Changó*, who worship Chankpana, god of leprosy and other diseases.[5] Álvares also hailed from the same region of Africa as Luíza Mahin, called Mahi.[6] According to Sweet, "The layers could run concentrically from natal kin to meta-ethnic signifiers like 'Mahi,' or even broader still to regions of provenance like the 'Costa da Mina.' These identities operated like Russian dolls, one inside the other, the utility of each determined by context and circum stance."[7] For this reason, Kehinde is at once from Savalu, Mahi, and Mina. The Costa Mina corresponds to the Gold Coast, where she was shipped, like

Álvares, to the New World at Ouidah.[8] The Mahi region, which came to be her historical last name (Mahin), came into being due to the wars that stigmatized Álvares's religion and led to his journey. Under King Agaja of Dahomey, a scorched-earth campaign was launched to consolidate power under his absolute monarchy and to take control of the port at Ouidah, controlled by the Hueda people, the intermediaries who traded captives with the Portuguese.[9] Dahomey warred with the Yoruba kingdom based at Òyó, and the region between them was called Mahi (Mahin), meaning in Fon "the rebels" or "those who divide the market."[10] The multiethnic towns that made up this region formed the "Mahi confederacy," but slave raids on towns like Savalu fueled an important part of the trade.[11] Initially, the Dahomey religion worshiped only the king and his ancestors; hence, they massacred the snakes representing the serpent god Dan when they took Ouidah in 1727.[12] Nonetheless, the court noted that local areas were dedicated to different voduns, which they consolidated into a pantheon. Local legend puts it this way: "There were no voduns in Dahomey until Agaja demanded that they be brought into the kingdom. Until that time, women of Dahomey gave birth to goats, and goats gave birth to humans. In order to alleviate this imbalance in nature, eleven voduns were carried en masse from the Fon heartland in Adja to Abomey. Among these were Hevioso, Gu, Dã, Fa, and Legba."[13] The consolidation of religion was a tool to pacify conquered territories that had previously been devoted to individual gods. Nonetheless, the Sakpata priests resisted and subverted Agaja's authority, and their prophesies were seen as a direct threat to his authority, and so they were enslaved.[14] The priests told their followers to fight the Dahomean invaders that brought down the god's wrath as smallpox.

Mahin reportedly gave birth to Luís Gama 103 years after the fall of Ouidah to Dahomey, but she is part of Agaja's legacy. The most direct link to previous Dahomean generations in the novel is the African side of the story of Na Agontimé, whose life in Brazil Gonçalves imagines. She was wife of King Agonglo, who reigned from 1789 to 1797, and Queen Mother of King Guezo, who ruled 1818 to 1858.[15] Luísa's grandmother had served in her court.[16] King Adandozan seceded his father, Agonglo, and legend has it that the former sent Agontimé to Brazil as a slave.[17] In Brazil, she became known as Maria Mineira Naê, according to the novel.[18] Ana Lucia Araujo has reconstructed the life of this Afro-Brazilian icon. The well-known Casa das Minas was reportedly a temple she founded to house Dahomean Nesuhwe worship (as in members of the royal family, including one named Savalu) in São Luís do Maranhão after having lived in Bahia as a captive.[19] Agontimé was entitled to a role in choosing Agonglo's successor after his assassination, so she represented a political threat to Adandozan.[20] As a priestess, her supernatural powers were also a threat, and she had supported Adandozan's half-brother, her son Gezo ("Guezo" in the novel), to be coronated.

Gezo's propaganda may have invented some or all of Agontimé's biography. Guezo deposed Adandozan with support from slave merchant Francisco Félix da Souza, or Chachá da Souza.[21] Gezo's queen mother was not the only enslaved person to return to Dahomey and fuel the trade through empire—Joaquim Almeida achieved manumission, returned to Africa, and worked as a slave-merchant.[22] Reportedly, when Gezo assumed the throne, he sent Chachá to rescue Agontimé, he found her in Bahia, and returned to Dahomey, where he was named the viceroy of Ouidah, though he may have actually sent a man named Dosso-Yovo in his stead. It is said she was returned to serve as queen mother for Gezo.[23]

However, none of this can be verified, since there are virtually no written records of royal women in Dahomey from this time, so Gonçalves is imagining a voice for a silenced woman on the other side of the Atlantic. Even the name "Agontimé" is a symbol of transatlantic double consciousness. Upon being named Queen Mother, she assumed the name, which means "the monkey has come from the country of the whites and is now in a field of pineapples."[24] She is defined by both her slavery in Brazil and her royalty in (and joy upon return to) Dahomey. Gonçalves's novel makes her oral legend visible to a national and international audience, but she has the character remain in her new Brazilian homeland.

Gonçalves and Antônio Olinto's Black Atlantic

Gonçalves is not the first author to map the African diaspora in Brazil, and she readily admits that she is building on a long-standing tradition, as is evidenced by her novel's ample bibliography of literary, historiography, and anthropology texts.[25] The first novelist to follow the retornados, those who went back to Africa after being enslaved like Luísa Mahin (Kehinde), the mother of mulatto abolitionist lawyer Luís Gama, is Antônio Olinto. His *A casa d'água* (*The Water House*, 1969), the opening of his trilogy *A alma da África* (*The Soul of Africa*), treats a family's voyage from Brazil to what is now Nigeria roughly during the time in which Kehinde lives, as Eurídice Figueredo notes.[26] Gonçalves lists Olinto among her sources for the work, and he is a prime example of an African proverb, one of the novel's epigraphs: "uma chama não perde nada ao acender outra chama" (a flame loses nothing by starting another flame).[27] Ineke Phaf-Rheinberger briefly connects Gonçalves with Olinto, but the following discussion shows that her reception of Olinto supports my argument that Gonçalves's text is as transnational and philosophically hybrid as Gilroy's, yet it includes Africa and Brazil.[28] Hence, I agree only partially with Phaf-Rheinberger's claim, in her comparison between *Defeito* and Conceição Evaristo's *Ponciá Vicêncio* (2003), that in both "l'Atlantique noir de Gilroy se connote d'afro-brésilianité" (Gilroy's Black Atlantic relates to Afro-Brazilianness).[29] I now show the transnational aspects within and beyond the Black Atlantic in the novel.

One could say that Olinto himself is an example of a Black Atlantic intellectual. Nonetheless, purist followers of Asante might assert that Olinto is not black. Like Gonçalves, Olinto was from Minas Gerais, but he served as a diplomat in Nigeria.[30] His African experience made him interested in the African influences in Bahia and Rio de Janeiro.[31] While he was serving in Lagos in 1964, Lusophone African independence movements were starting to take military action, and the Portuguese Empire on the continent was beginning the downward spiral that would end in 1975. One could see his work as a ship sailing between the Brazilian literary tradition and the emerging Postcolonial Luso-African novelistic tradition, who have written on the colonial wars in Africa roughly during the time Olinto was living and writing in Nigeria.[32]

A casa d'água takes place between 1898 and 1968. The image of former slaves sailing back to Africa, to invoke Zapata and Gilroy's ships, is central to Olinto's depiction of the Santos family. They are retornados (returnees) in search of opportunities well after the abolition of slavery that granted them liberty, at least in the eyes of the law. Gonçalves depicts roughly the same retornados during the 1830s and 1840s. *A casa*'s geographical trajectory, like much of Gonçalves's novel, inverts the Middle Passage. Instead of a voyage west in chains, the characters sail eastward in search of self-determination. The geographical center of the novel is a historical, not mythical, Benin and Nigeria (Lagos and surrounding towns). The area is in transition from its past as various European colonies. The protagonist, Mariana, sells potable water from her home, which evokes the characters' fluidity of identity, of sea on land, and gives the novel its name.[33] In addition to associations with Atlantic slavery, water also evokes mother goddesses like Yemayá (the sea) and Oshún (rivers, fresh water). The fluidity of identity and cosmopolitanism of Zapata and Gilroy is evident on the African continent itself. It shows that a homogeneous "Africa" is a dream rooted in the scattering of diaspora, though the continent itself is scattered by slavery's colonial legacy. As in *Defeito*, Brazilian national identity is exported with the retornados to the Portuguese colony of Lagos, primarily to Bangboshe Street.[34] Here, a new colony emerged as blacks and mulattoes return to Africa only to find that they are very different from the locals. They bring Portuguese language and literacy (79, 94); religious ceremonies (82); music and dance (124–125); folktales like the *bumba-meu-boi* (79, 188); national literature like José de Alencar's *O guarani* (*The Guarany*, 1857) and Amado's *Gabriela, cravo e canela* (*Gabriela, Clove and Cinnamon*, 1958) (194, 323); and rituals of baptism (165), marriage (106), and death (90).[35] They continue a Brazilian national, ethnic, and even colonial identity in an African context. In the novel there is no solidarity or redemptive return, as Garvey might hope. In Africa, the over one hundred characters move among Portuguese (Lagos), Spanish (Fernando Poo), and German (Aduni) colonies and speak many languages. The trade networks clustered around the port of Lagos bring people of all races from all over Europe, the United States (including an African American), Beirut, and various regions of Brazil (Rio de Janeiro, Bahia, Minas Gerais).[36] Characters and political boundaries develop in constant change, constant fragmentation of identity and questioning of values, practices, and traditions. These in turn are taken back to various regions of Brazil, including the ports of Rio de Janeiro and Salvador da Bahia, as well as Brasília, shortly after its founding in 1960.[37] It is as if Nagô's ship sails between these nations, and a transnational consciousness marks the characters of this novel, which ends with the establishment of Zorei, a new, independent nation that Nigeria would eventually subsume.[38]

Because of literary trailblazers of the Nuevo Muntu like Olinto, Gonçalves can build an international, mobile, panoramic vision of the African diaspora that deepens and supplements the national history of Brazil. Her plot starts in Dahomey, which would become Benin after colonialism.[39] The course of the novel's voyage begins with movement within historical Africa at the end of the eighteenth century, depicting the continental wars between African kingdoms of which the international slave trade formed part through business deals and political manipulation.[40] Kehinde is taken from her village of Savalou to Ouidah, where she is shipped to Brazil with the other slaves.[41] Upon Kehinde's arrival in Bahia, Gonçalves draws on the work of scholars like Gilberto Freyre and recasts it from the perspective of a female slave.[42] His descriptions of the big house, the small (domestic) slave quarters, and the big (manual laborer) barracks provide the setting for the work. His portrait of customs, mores, and demographics of the plantation become Gonçalves's characters. Kehinde appears to be the only narrator for most of the novel, a strong "I" that belongs to a female slave, though the work has hundreds of characters. This allows her to show the diversity of the enslaved and how, unlike the chattel slavery of the Anglophone world that Gilroy treats, many central aspects of African identity (e.g., language, music, religion) are allowed to continue in many social settings. After the auction block, she is taken to be a house slave and lives in the small slave quarters, near the master's house.[43] Kehinde's mistress blames the girl when she miscarries, and the former house slave must live in the squalid big barracks.[44] She is rented out to a British family, revealing the hypocrisy and economic and political pragmatism of British abolitionism.[45]

Luís Gama's Brazil in the Black Atlantic

The course of Gonçalves's novel within Brazilian territory, particularly after she loses her son, roughly follows the biographies of Luís Gama by Elciene Azevedo (1992) and Sud Mennucci (1938) that Gonçalves cites in her bibliography.[46] This allows the implicit author to follow the development of the Brazilian nation through the eyes of a slave and a free person of color, not unlike Du Bois's double consciousness. Kehinde, whether on the plantation or selling goods in cities, is at times not considered "fully" Brazilian by those around her (most evident in her fear of being deported after the Revolta dos Malês in 1835 and her inability to own land).[47] At other times she considers herself "fully" part of a black community, whether among the enslaved (on the plantation; as a wage slave) or as a free person of color at the syncretic Washing of the Steps ceremony in Salvador.[48] These identities form around language, music, and oral storytelling, just like in Gilroy's essay and Zapata's novel, and they change constantly.

Kehinde's journey beyond Bahia begins with the Revolta. While she is exiled from Salvador due to the uprising, her lover Alberto sells Luís to settle gambling debts.[49] Luís was born in 1830 and sold in 1840. At this time, Bahia's bustling port benefitted not only from slave ships from Africa, many of which operated illegally, but also from the domestic slave trade. Azevedo shows that Gama was loaded onto the *Saraiva* and shipped south, where he was to be sold to work on a coffee plantation. Rio de Janeiro, the capital since

1763, was an important midpoint for such ships, and Gama was handed over to a Portuguese man, Vieira, who worked in the clandestine slave trade. This stop is important, because it revisits the capital as a space of ethically problematic figures like Vieira. It condemns Brazil for its continued exclusion of the vast majority of the African diaspora in its borders from the national project through slavery and the political structures that emerged from it. São Paulo's coffee industry, often imagined as a source of political progress beyond slavery through European and Japanese immigration, wage labor, and greater social mobility, is shown as part of the complex web of the slave trade.[50] The boy's trajectory to Santos, Campinas, and eventually the capital of the province is also revealing of Afro-Brazilians' role in national history. According to Azevedo, he was not purchased at auction because the Revolta dos Malês (1835) had struck fear into the hearts of those driving the slave trade, and Bahia was the primary source of captives after the British blocked the transatlantic trade. Slaveocrats likely saw him as a threat to order, even at ten years old, a widespread phobia that was an important factor in the Europeanization of São Paulo's labor force.[51]

Kehinde follows her son to Rio de Janeiro, where she becomes part of a black community, though her own black identity is gradually more conflicted. In her time, the city is up to 50 percent enslaved, and they predominate in the streets.[52] Most were of Central African ethnicities, not Mina like Kehinde.[53] She falls in love with one of these *angolas*.[54] Their union exemplifies James Sweet's argument that the influx of Mina slaves into the predominantly Central African-Brazilian slave communities was central to "Africanization" in Brazil. By this term he means the syncretization of two or more ethnicities and worldviews.[55] Piripiri, a *capueira*, is a practitioner of Brazilian dance fighting.[56] This martial art originated among rebel slaves not unlike Piripiri. Through oral history, it can be traced back to Central Africa, but today there are two types: *capoeira angola* and *capoeira regional*. Kehinde's exposure to *capoeira* occurs before it is codified, revealing an unknown side of a practice that has been appropriated as a "Brazilian" art and an understanding of it as part of her recollection of Africa in Brazil, something that is as of yet rebellious and untamed.

Piripiri takes her to a secret meeting on the Corcovado in 1840, though the iconic Christ the Redeemer would not be built until 1931.[57] At the time the novel is set, the Corcovado is topped by quilombos, escaped slave communities, though the same *capueiras* were used to protect the city as well.[58] Their performance is a previously unrecognized, Afro-Brazilian identity that lies in a past of struggle that is all too often cloaked by narratives of racial democracy that continue today.[59] James Sweet traces elements of capoeira to the *xinguilas*, or spirit mediums, of Central Africa who were possessed by ancestors.[60] They would walk on their hands and make high kicks designed to access the "inverted" world of the spirits and draw strength from it.[61] Capoeira can be used with deadly force, and it is a form of self-assertion and self-defense for its practitioners, all of whom are blacks in the novel.[62] Practitioners associate it frequently with the music of the African *berimbau* and dances of African spirits, such as São Bento/Oxumarê in which "players" flail as if they are *chicoteando*, becoming whips amid the cries of the music that can be associated with slavery and resistance.[63] It is another example of the bond between syncretism, music, and the body in the intellectual history of the enslaved. However, like other syncretic practices, it remained hidden from the eyes of the elite until the 1930s, a "game" to be "played," a seemingly harmless exercise. In a time before the statue of the Cristo, as the national icon is called, slaves and freedmen were creating their own community, within and beyond the boundaries of the nation.

Her appropriation of national and colonial symbols is repeated with Joaquim Manuel Macedo's *A rua do Ouvidor* (Ouvidor Street, 1878).[64] The novel imagines a black protagonist in the "Paris" of Brazil during its heyday, changing how a classic author's detailed description of Rio's geography and reminding the reader of Macedo's role in abolitionism.[65] Kehinde is actively involved in writing his novels, among the first in the nation, thus writing herself (and Gonçalves) into the Brazilian canon.[66] Something similar happens when she meets the freeborn Kuanza, in Bahia, who gives her the manuscript of José Saramago's *Memorial do convento* (*Memorial of the Convent*) (1982), which Kuanza claims was written by his father.[67] The latter was a slave at the monumental Palácio Nacional-Convento in Mafra, Portugal, who is able to move unnoticed through the labyrinthine social networks of the eighteenth century, as Kehinde is in Brazil. Kuanza is ninety years old, facing death like the Portuguese Empire in Brazil at the time, and he is relieved that his family's story will see the light of day. By fictitiously making Portuguese Nobel Laureate Saramago's work authored by a slave, Gonçalves is once again using the African diaspora to transcend national boundaries in the creation of her work. This is not a matter of abandoning the nation or even the colonial past as imagined communities. It is a clear desire for memories of flexible and mobile identities that she shares with Zapata and Gilroy. Her imagining of Kuanza in the novel also begs the same question as the novel's prologue: If an eighteenth century slave found a way to write a manuscript like Gonçalves's, would anyone then know or care? Would anyone today know? The fictitious author, whose manuscript is eventually lost in the Atlantic, speaks to a silence in Brazilian letters, an ignorance of certain kinds of history and literature.[68]

Kehinde follows her son from Rio de Janeiro, to Santos, and finally Campinas. After learning to read, Gama heads to São Paulo.[69] Entering the world of letters is what allows him to eventually become a lawyer and advocate for slaves, and Gonçalves's novel is a continuation of this emancipation project today, bringing his mother into the lettered world. It is also the point when Kehinde decides she cannot find Luís on her own. Once she loses her son's trail, Kehinde becomes directionless.[70] The guilt she feels for allowing his brother to die is added to her shame for letting Luís be sold, and to these is added the guilt of abandoning the search for him to others. She leaves the search to a lawyer, the husband of her former young mistress, Maria Clara, and heads for Africa as a *retornada*. This supplements what little Gama claimed to know of his mother after she was sold.

Defeito presents Luísa's decision to leave as impulsive and carried out with little explanation. Nonetheless, other moments in the text present ample evidence that this return to Africa was common for someone in her context. It is not done in the name of any sort of Brazilian benevolence, by slave owners or the Brazilian government. Nor is it done in the name of some glorious return to an African homeland like the one Garvey imagined. Kehinde goes because of political and economic pressures. It is impressive that she was able to travel as much of Brazil as she did as a black woman, a conspirator in a slave revolt, and a fugitive. She is separated from her son because of her precarious state, when she must flee to São Luís do Maranhão.[71]

To illuminate her decision's relationship to double consciousness, anthropologist Manuela Carneiro da Cunha's *Negros, estrangeiros* (*Blacks, Foreigners*, 1985) is useful.[72] It shows that *libertos*, manumitted slaves, were not entirely unlike U.S. segregation-era blacks in their social and legal restrictions, or as Du Bois put it, "the freedman has not found in freedom his promised land."[73] The white-dominant, slave-based Brazilian nation had built itself upon an ideology in which freed blacks were often barred access to political, economic, and religious power, and even their physical mobil ity was limited in many cases.[74] Carneiro argues that someone in Kehinde's situation is a foreigner in her own land, feared for how she looks.[75] The Brazilian scholar traces the fear of mass black revolt to documents from 1792, when concerns that a Haitian-style revolution could take place in Brazil.[76] Paranoia among slave owners intensified with the Bahian revolts of 1826, 1828, and 1830, led by Nagô (Yoruba) slaves.[77] Kehinde notes the greater legal restrictions placed on free and enslaved blacks during this time, which included arbitrary beatings, death sentences, and deportation.[78] Revolts were spurred, arguably, by the constant flux of African-born slaves like Kehinde from the Bight of Benin. They were exported to Bahia long after the British prohibition of the slave trade, most famously by the Brazilian-born warlord in Ouidah, Chachá Francisco Félix de Souza, along with several former slaves who rose to become slavers themselves in Africa.[79] The constant importation of those who knew a reality outside of slavery made them a threat to the Bahian status quo. It became apparent during the Revolta in Salvador da Bahia. The struggle led to mass deportations, which the novel also records.[80] Black people in this context, even when they were not slaves, were not "fully" Brazilian.[81] The empire was happy to ship them back to Africa to avoid further problems with the rebels or the abolitionist British.

On the ship, her diaspora identity is once again evident as she interacts with Afro-Brazilians and those from the British colony of freed slaves at Sierra Leon.[82] "Africa" is imagined by some to be a lost Paradise, though Kehinde quickly learns otherwise. Her experience in Africa parallels that of Olinto's characters.[83] The spaces of the Rua Bangboshe, Lagos, Ouidah, the Portuguese Fort D'Ajuda, the celebrations of Our Lord of the Bonfim return in her novel.[84] She has new twins, who have European names—unlike the Brazilian-born twins with African names—both of which go to Paris to study.[85] One returns to Africa while the other stays in Europe.[86] At no point is Africa a static, unified, or ideal entity. It is a place of human struggle with masters and slaves, just as Brazil was.

In Africa, Kehinde's diaspora identity slips away just as abruptly as it emerged when she was shoved onto a squalid ship headed west. As with Olinto's novel, this is most evident when she attempts to start anew. However, the seeds of transculturation are clearly being planted while Kehinde is still enslaved. These take root in a way that would be unfathomable to the slaves Du Bois and Gilroy describe. As a wage slave, she sells cookies to Amleto, a mulatto who is in charge of his absent master's estate, something she could not have done from the senzala grande.[87] Luísa models herself after the masters. She hires her friends as wage laborers, but she also buys slaves to carry her in an elegant *cadeirinha* (chair).[88] These were status symbols at the time used by virtually anyone who could afford them, and a white man takes off his hat in respect to this black woman whose friends playfully call her "sinhá" (mistress).[89] Elsewhere, I have written on how perceptions of race are altered by whether one is the slave at the bottom or the passenger atop the chair: this was the case of mulatto icons Chica da Silva and Aleijadinho (depicted in Zapata's work), and carriers' near invisibility for Kehinde is indicative of this reality. Economic demands often trumped racial solidarity in all sectors of Brazilian society, and the incentives of manumission and gaining better working conditions were often driving forces in Brazil, especially in urban environments. This is not to argue that Brazilian slavery was "better," but to invite the reader to consider how it operates on Kehinde's vision of diaspora in a way unlike Douglass's, for example.

Like in her perception of the Revolta dos Malês, Kehinde forms her identity around her relationships between family and friends in Africa. Daviken Studnicki-Gizbert has shown that the Portuguese Empire beyond its terrestrial boundaries was based entirely on family and friend relationships.[90] For the historian, the seafaring Portuguese nation, scattered across the globe not only in its own colonies but also in those of Spain, itself functioned much like a diaspora. Portuguese and Luso-Africans were frequently the most numerous non-Spanish Europeans in the Hispanic Caribbean during the sixteenth and seventeenth centuries.[91] In what could be interpreted as chaos, community bonds were centered on personal relationships, not a stable notion of national loyalty. This must be kept in mind in the case of the retornados, since they originally referred to themselves as "Portuguese" and formed colonial networks that were all Catholic (or Muslim, in some cases) and had a heterogeneous appearance that ranged from white to black and had the supposedly "easy, agreeable manners" of Southern Europe.[92] They ate Brazilian food and had Brazilian religious festivals. They were often involved in the slave trade. Ouidah was governed by the Brazilian viceroy, and all communication with Portugal went through him so Brazil had a direct role in the governance of the Slave Coast and its slave traders were highly influential.[93]

Transoceanic networks partially explain the hundreds of characters in Gonçalves's novel, many of which are flat. One lived in a world of flat characters to participate in the local economy was to make friendships or relationships that were functional enough to meet one's needs, and support networks, however ephemeral, were essential for survival as one traveled between cites. This is to say that the hundreds of characters in the novel reflect the narrator's historical reality. In addition, sailing the sea is not always the same in black and white cases. Phaf-Rheinberger notes the traumatic nature of Kehinde's transoceanic family relations, which create bonds in Africa and Brazil.[94] Slaves repeatedly sought to form new kinship bonds to replace those at the center of their social and spiritual lives in Africa.[95] One must not overlook Gonçalves's choice to include that reality in her writing. These ordinary lives are written back into history through Gonçalves's carefully constructed historical fiction. In fact, there were so many that the author had to cut out six hundred pages and entire lives, indicating her desire to include as large and diverse a group of Brazilians, particularly Afro-Brazilians, as her novel would allow.[96] Also, not all of her characters are flat: Kehinde's friendship with her white sinhazinha and her husband, her love for her mulatto children and her lover Alberto, and her bond with historical abolitionist and novelist Joaquim Manuel Macedo are steps in becoming more than having only a "black" identity in any purist sense of the word.[97]

The Return to Africa and the Gradual Inversion of the Master-Slave Dialectic

Language is at the heart of Kehinde's transculturation. As a child she finds pleasure on the plantation in learning new words, be they in Portuguese or in an African language. Upon learning to read, she finds more doors open to her, such as the bond with Macedo, formed in a bookstore through a conversation about João dos Passos's poetry, a conversation that would have been largely impossible for the Anglophone slave system. She learns the language of the Cleggs, her British "renters" in Bahia.[98] English is a colonial tongue that gives her more opportunities. In learning it she becomes less tied to her fellow slaves, be they on the plantation in Bahia or in Rio de Janeiro, though it also allows her to communicate with Anglophone former slave John.[99] He fathers her children in Africa.[100] By the time she reaches the capital of Brazil, she has contradictory feelings about her sense of community. She recalls a black porter's confusion at being asked to carry the Afro-Brazilian's weighty trunk of books and other possessions when she disembarks, again feeling different from him.[101] She witnesses the coronation of Brazil's self-proclaimed "Enlightened Monarch," Dom Pedro II, on July 18, 1841, and recalls that it corresponds to Yemayá's feast, A Festa da Kianda.[102]

This resignifying of national symbols through double consciousness (emperor/African goddess) stands in stark contrast to her statements moments later:

> Estava com vergonha de vender comida, pois já tinha feito coisas muito mais importantes e rentáveis . . . mas hoje até me envergonho de tal pensamento. Eu, que sempre quis ser justa, que não aceitei ser escrava porque sempre achei que um branco não podia me tratar como se fosse superior, estava me julgando melhor do que as pretas que trabalhavam de maneira humilde.[103]

> (I was ashamed to sell food, because I had already done much more important and profitable things . . . but today I'm even ashamed of such thoughts. I, who always tried to be fair, who never accepted being a slave because I always thought a white man couldn't treat me as if he were superior, I judged myself to be better than the black women that did humble work.)

Even as she is maintaining close relationships with Afro-Brazilians around her, the perception of elevated status that comes with economic advancement is altering her identity. While I agree with Phaf-Rheinberger that she is pragmatic, I also see that her identity is changing in power relations very similar to the master-slave dialectic.[104]

Kehinde, like the other brasileiros in Africa (what the retornados and their descendants are now called), builds a Brazil on the backs of the so-called *selvagens* (savages).[105] All of this is historically accurate.[106] In fact, her contact with a haughty *sarô* (freed person in Sierra Leone) would heighten her sense of superiority to the local population. Phaf-Rheinberger notes that the Brazilian retornados were more highly educated than local Nigerians when they returned and quickly formed part of the local elite.[107] They had crafts they could practice in large coastal cities.[108] If they left them for their villages of origin (provided they could still find them), they ran the risk of being captured once again.[109] She and other brasileiros build a colony that has more in common with the slaveocrats of Brazil than the Africans with whom they cohabit. According to Phaf-Rheinberger there were thousands of such returnees in Lagos and they were called *agudás* (the black whites), in the sense that the word *agudá* is said to come from the Portuguese *algodão*, which means cotton. In 1880 they were about 9 percent of the city's population of 27,500 people.[110] Gilroy briefly mentions the cultural exchange between Brazilian retornados with other Nigerians in the 1840s as an example of the transformation of African cultures by those of the diaspora, but he goes no further.[111]

This new Brazil in Africa must be recognized, just as Hegel's slave must recognize his or her master, by the selvagens who live in Nigeria and Dahomey. Kehinde starts a company named Casas da Bahia (Bahia Houses), which builds houses like those she remembers from the other side of the Atlantic.[112] In this sense she is continuing the feminine tradition of creating "home" according to critic Melissa Schindler, but she is doing so in a way that involves engaging in a capitalist and still slave-based system that has not overcome the master-slave dialectic.[113] She hires workers and collaborates with slave traders, combining two economic systems, but she is driven by profit, not a sense of community beyond that of a diasporic *brasileira*.[114] She is no more benevolent or violent than mainland Brazil's enslavers. As in Brazil, owning slaves was a means of social and financial advancement, even for slaves.[115] For example, she teaches her house slaves to read along with her children, and her daughter Maria Clara uses part of her family's profits to establish a school so that integrates selvagens and brasileiros, which was uncommon in Brazil.[116] This simultaneously empowers these students by giving them opportunities along the lines of those Kehinde herself enjoyed and makes them more brasileiro, which can be seen as a psychological form of colonization. The text, however, demonstrates that this is always a transculturation, since Geninha learns to read for the first time at the school.[117] She is the scribe to whom an old, blind Kehinde narrates the novel. There is no delineation in the text between who is creating its language, whether it is only Kehinde or Geninha.[118] Geninha and her narrative hybridity with Kehinde is another example of double consciousness.

Upon Kehinde's arrival in Africa, Gonçalves ceases to follow the path of Olinto's Mariana. Kehinde has no water house like Olinto's protagonist, but a series of businesses that contribute to a new Brazil in Africa, with all the problems of the historical Brazil. Kehinde's experience in Lagos overlaps with that of the characters in British author Bruce Chatwin's *The Viceroy of Ouidah* (1980), which also appears in Gonçalves's bibliography.[119] Here, the *retornada* depends on the protection of a viceroy, Chachá de Souza, like Chatwin's brasileiro patriarch in Dahomey.[120]

She abandons her African name, which she always uses in Brazil, and calls herself Luisa Andrade da Silva. This transformation occurs when she signs the contract on her new land, making her more like the slaveocrats of Brazil.[121] It is no coincidence that Chatwin's novel treats the Silva family, who descended from the nineteenth-century *chachás* who controlled the market in slaves and other exports between present-day Benin, Lagos, and

Bahia.[122] Adopting former masters' surnames for social advancement was common among Africans on both sides of the Atlantic.[123] Gonçalves and Chatwin both describe the Brazilification of African kings served by chachás. The former loved cigars and rum from the New World as much as powerful Brazilians and profited from selling the adversaries they defeated in war.[124] Chatwin's novel links these final African slave traders from the nineteenth century to the end of the twentieth, through the story of Mama Wéwé da Silva, who is over one hundred years old and whose last words, uttered in Lagos in 1953, are "remember, you are Brazilians!"[125] Though it may seem ironic at first glance, Chatwin's Africans actually mourn the days of slavery because it was the source of their family's riches, and they prize whiteness because they still associate it with status.[126]

On the other hand, the husband of Gonçalves's narrator-protagonist's husband, John, is guilt ridden for their profits from these wars: "Ele apenas tinha feito um negócio que não sabia se eu também teria feito. . . . Se ele garantia que era um bom negócio e que a venda estava garantida, por mim estava tudo bem. Ele me pareceu aliviado" (He had simply made a deal he didn't know if I would have made. . . . If he could guarantee it was good business and the purchase was guaranteed, it was fine by me. He seemed relieved).[127] Great Britain, the same country that was spreading abolitionism around the Atlantic, was simultaneously driving slavery economically on the continent, making it as ambiguous an actor as the characters. Like Kehinde, John was freed from slavery, in his case due to British intervention. However, he convinces her to sell weapons in addition to palm oil. The character's discomfort may say more about Gonçalves's own discomfort with this history and that of the contemporary reader. The characters are once again focused solely on profit and their family, which during this conversation is about to include their twins. However, Luisa has been a slave, and she is writing this story to her son, who has been sold into slavery, which would explain her and John's apologetic tone: "porque é assim que vejo tudo isso, como um grande mea-culpa" (because this is how I see all this, as one great mea culpa).[128] She is driven by profit and is emotionally conflicted about her participation in an economy she knows is brutal. The weapons in turn drive the wars that drive the slave trade, and Kehinde knows it:

> Ás vezes eu ficava um pouco constrangida por me relacionar com mercadores de escravos, mas logo esquecia, já que aquele não era problema meu. Eu não conseguiria resolvê-lo mesmo se quisesse, e também não poderia ficar com

> muitos escrúpulos depois de fornecer armas para o rei Guezo, sabendo que seriam usadas em guerras que fariam escravos.[129]
>
> (At times I found it a little strange to interact with slave traders, but then I would forget about it. It wasn't my problem. I couldn't fix it even if I wanted to, and I couldn't be very scrupulous after sending weapons to King Guezo, knowing they would be used in wars to make slaves.)

Once she is free and presented with the opportunity to dominate and differentiate, she does. Nevertheless, her indifference shows the importance of memory of and empathy with the enslaved that comes from her narrative. According to Strickrodt,

> From our point of view, this affinity between slave traders and former slaves may seem ironic and difficult to understand, just as the fact that many of the returned ex-slaves engaged in the slave trade. However, it was not ironic. As has been pointed out by historians, the ex-slaves were inherently pragmatic and tried to make a living and better their situation under very harsh conditions. For most, the return to Africa meant the arrival in a strange country, where they suffered abuse and extortion from the local African authorities and risked not only their property but often enough their freedom and even their lives.[130]

An inversion of master and slave for Kehinde is completed in Africa. If a nation in "Africa" starts as a far-off utopia beyond suffering for the retornados, "Brazil" assumes this role almost immediately upon arrival. Her vision of those she meets upon disembarking parallels those of Chatwin's characters, though the latter take it to the extreme of believing that one left the continent and returned to Brazil upon death, inverting the common slave belief of returning to Africa.[131] In Luísa's case, "Brazil" evokes national or ethnic pride among the Brazilian diaspora in Africa (once the African diaspora in Brazil).[132] However, they are the new elites and landowners, and like the Brazilian landowners, their part in this community is an entitlement. They do not have to fight their way into it, like many blacks who remained behind in Brazil during its first national (or imperial) political project, the Paraguayan War from 1864 to 1870.[133] When Gonçalves's retornados learn of the war's outbreak, none of them wants to return to fight.[134] In this sense, their "Brazil" in Africa has more in common with the South American slaveocrat elite. The war was fought primarily by Afro-Brazilians such as the

Zuavos sent by their masters or overlords to fight.[135] Many blacks viewed it as a new sense of national pride and a pathway to citizenship through dedication, sacrifice, and service. It was anathema to the slave system, as depicted in a drawing of a proud black soldier who returns to the plantation only to be horrified at the conditions of his enslaved black brothers, or in other horror stories of men returned to slavery after fighting for a country they thought was theirs.[136] While the diaspora was becoming part of a nation in Brazil through struggle, in Africa the retornados have become Brazilian when they disembark and fear losing their Brazilianness to the Africans or debasing themselves by fighting a war instead of reaping the profits of war in the transatlantic market. In both cases a free Brazil is as much a dream as a free Africa, though these protean desires are central to national and diaspora identities in Gonçalves's novel. This, in fact, reaffirms Schindler's assertion that Afro-Brazilian women writers break down the barrier between "nation" and "home."[137]

Luísa continues to exhibit a double consciousness because of her syncretic faith and her family ties. Nonetheless, her position in the master-slave dialectic has changed, since she has adopted the language and customs of her former owners along with analogous socioeconomic privileges. She may be a *brasileira* (Brazilian) among *selvagens* (savages), but the ceremonies she celebrates, such as the Washing of the Steps and her devotion to Changó, are syncretic and primarily African. Her Catholicism is not shared by those she views as inferior, but neither is it shared by the pope or even the purist missionaries of the Fort of Ajuda, the last Portuguese stronghold in Lagos, or the French missionaries there.[138] This is historically accurate.[139] Furthermore, while she is no longer enslaved, she is bound to slavery by her son. It is telling that she has two boys in Brazil, both born into slavery, and twins in Africa, both born into freedom. They are the personification of Kehinde's double consciousness. Both her Brazilian boys were sacrifices to the colonial system that made Kehinde black as well as Brazilian, often in contradictory ways. Banjokô's death severs her emotional ties with her mistress (who largely raises him), a bond with the plantation that temporarily solidified her black identity.[140] This rupture is not complete, however, since his death is explained as a curse for not performing Vodou rituals, a common belief.[141] His mother furiously scrubs his body, expressing mourning, not only for him but likely for all those who died under slavery. Historian James Sweet notes that voduns could curse as well as protect and imagines the horror of slaves beholding those who died upon arrival in slave ports with no

African death ceremony.[142] He notes their bodies were carelessly left in shallow graves or thrown in the sea.[143] Kehinde is ensuring no such thing happens to her son. On the other hand, it is the discovery of Luís's survival that severs her ties with Africa.[144] Though Kehinde imagines nations and diasporas, her strongest emotional and moral bond is to her family, not the community at large. Perhaps this makes her simultaneously the most Portuguese, Brazilian, and African diaspora character of all, the founder of nations upon the Ocean Sea.

The novel's resolution is the apex of double consciousness in the novel. In the final pages, she discovers that her search for Luís has been cursed by the voduns because she did not complete a necessary religious ritual.[145] While she expects to find a gift in a trunk for her African granddaughter's wedding, what she discovers is a horrific revelation about her Brazilian past. It contained letters from the lawyer she left in charge of the search, saying Gama had been found and that he was a well-known lawyer and poet. She had mistaken the letters for financial documents relating to her pursuit of wealth building homes in Lagos. Despite her modern, capitalist lifestyle and outlook, her non-Western, mythological past catches up to her:

> Não pensei que aquele homem que tinha tentado me assaltar na estrada para o sítio onde morávamos em São Salvador estivesse incluído nesse tipo de espírito. Isto é, nunca me vi como uma assassina, apenas como uma pessoa se defendendo de outra. Mesmo sem entender quase nada, a Geninha não me fez uma pergunta sequer, nem sobre o Piripiri, pois foi por causa dele que o Maboke conseguiu descobrir o que havia de errado na minha vida.[146]

> (I did not think that man who tried to rob me on the road to the farm where we lived in São Salvador was included in that kind of spirit. Rather, I never saw myself as a murderer; just as someone defending herself from another. Even without understanding anything, Geninha didn't even ask, nor poor Piripiri, since it was because of him that Maboke was able to discover what was wrong with my life.)

Kehinde's fear of the robber is like that of the plantation owners who feared the free movement of maroons and enslaved blacks at night.[147] Furthermore, she is wearing the borrowed dress of sinhazinha, her friend and former owner, when she kills him.[148] By this point she has divorced part of herself from the black community, but she is bound to Africa by the spirits. Interestingly, it is Piripiri, the capueira that taught her about black resistance and art by bringing her to a *roda* (gathering/fight) that notifies Maboke of her son's purloined letter, returning her to her African side. He is a *tata kisaba, curandeiro*, or healer.[149] Like the historical healer Álvares, he is a prophet who heals physical, political, and psychic wounds. He uses African myth to show her how to heal a deep trauma of slavery. It is because of the letter he reveals that she sets sail for Brazil, hoping to heal the tear in her double consciousness that is the loss of Luís Gama, the son that defines her identity to the point that, historically, and as I have shown, she exists only in his words. The novel does not resolve the tension between them, leaving her voyage as an open-ended quest, not a triumphant resolution between her two warring souls.

Rape in the Novels of Zapata and Gonçalves

As I have endeavored to show in a philosophical and historiographical breakdown of both texts, there are differences between *Changó* and *Defeito* that go beyond the fact that one was written by a man and the other was written by a woman. Let us not be essentialist or simplistic and overlook the contributions of both to the inclusion of silenced, enslaved Afro-descendant women into history. Their doubly marginalized role, encapsulated in Sojourner Truth's foundational question "Ain't I a Woman?," calls for special attention. There are no traditional slave narratives by women in the Latin American world.[150] Helene Carol Weldt-Basson has examined the importance of feminism and postcolonialism as approaches to the historical novel, including *Defeito*, noting how the subgenre, especially in the last few decades, includes women who are too often ignored.[151] Even Gilroy, in his ambitious attempt to theorize a literal and metaphorical ocean, limits himself to the Gardner case discussed last chapter and Toni Morrison, the writer who gave it a rebirth in *Beloved* (1987).[152] This has garnered him criticism from feminist critics Natasha Barnes and Melissa Schindler, the latter of whom sagely notes that Morrison is the only writer in *The Black Atlantic* whose travels are not discussed.[153] I now develop a comparison of female characters in *Changó* and *Defeito*. I also incorporate another marginalized gender group, nonheterosexual characters, to show their importance in the struggle for a Nuevo Muntu. Both aesthetics and politics are tied to gender in the novels.

Zapata has been scrutinized for his depictions of women and sex. Diana Catalina Zapata-Cortés shows that Delia and Manuel Zapata created an idealized, folklorized vision of Afro-Colombians as part of the Liberal Republic's impetus to create a culturally mestizo national identity.[154] Despite what she considers problematic representations of black libertinism regarding sexuality and violence, they created an image of black people as a source of rebellion and creativity beginning with the subversion of slavery.[155] Captain-Hidalgo argues that Zapata erases his feminine characters' quests to be self-determined "women as women."[156] She states that it is not until his final published novel, *Hemingway, el cazador de la muerte* (Hemingway, the Deathstalker, 1993), that Zapata shows feminist growth by treating feminine sexuality explicitly.[157] This concern for the role of women in Zapata's work is shared by Uchenna Vasser.[158] Madeleine Henry considers *Changó* "androcentric" aside from the character of Agne Brown.[159] Daiana Nascimento dos Santos repeats this opinion when she repeatedly emphasizes the female narrator in Gonçalves's text but rarely mentions the female presence in Zapata.[160]

One defense of Zapata's legacy for gender studies is the broad impact of *Changó* on female writers. Critic M'bare N'gom has written an article on the first anthology of Afro-Colombian poetry, *¡Negras somos!* (*We Are Black Women!*, 2008), edited by Alfredo Ocampo Zamorano and Guiomar Cuesta Escobar.[161] N'gom notes the silence that women of color have suffered in Colombian letters until this anthology and considers its treatment of the memory of slavery and African spirits.[162] Ocampo and Cuesta show that Zapata is among the writers who have most influenced *afrocolombiana* writers.[163] The novelist's influence came from his celebration of *lengua cimarrona* (maroon language), the alteration of Spanish by contact with other cultures, particularly African, as well as the importance of music.[164] Novelist Hazel Robinson Abrahams continues Zapata's project in her novel *No Give Up, Maan* (2002), a portrait of the nineteenth century in the Colombian archipelago of San Andrés.[165] Adelayda Fernández Ochoa's novel *La hoguera lame mi piel con cariño de perro* (*The Fire Licks My Skin with the Love of a Dog*, 2015), winner of the Casa de las Américas Award, is directly inspired by the work to narrate the history of slavery in Colombia from a woman's perspective.[166] Afro–Puerto Rican author Carmen Montáñez channels the muntu worldview, which she calls by its name, in the novella *Pelo bueno, pelo malo* (*Good Hair, Bad Hair*, 2012).[167] María Mercedes Jaramillo and Lucía Ortiz call their essay collection on Afro-Colombian women *Hijas del Muntu* (*Daughters of the Muntu*, 2011).[168] Afro-Colombian poet Ashanti Orozco has titled her work "Poética del muntú renaciente" (Poetics of the Reborn Muntu) at a reading in Uruguay and elsewhere.[169] Zapata had to inspire these writers not only because of his focus on black identity but also because of his empowering depictions of women of color. Elba Mercedes Palacios Córdoba explicitly cites his study of rebellious women or "cimarronas" in her epilogue to *Demando mi libertad* (2018) as part of an empowering history for black women that gives voice to the silenced.[170]

Changó is, in many ways, a palimpsest in which he superimposes slave history upon African myth, and both of these are reflected upon by twentieth-century youth. To put it another way, Yoruba mother goddess Yemayá is Sosa Illamba, who is also Agne Brown.[171] In an interview with Krakusin, when asked why Changó is central to the novel, Zapata replied that Yemayá is even more important because she is the universal mother.[172] Maternity, birth, child rearing, and denouncing sexual violence are all important to the representation of women in the novel.

Sons of God and the She-Devil

Tragically, rape is a part of enslaved motherhood. Zapata sought out previous myths to portray such a horrifying yet frequent phenomenon. A voracious reader who spent several years in Mexico, Zapata was clearly influenced by Octavio Paz, whose "Los hijos de la Malinche" (Sons of Bitches), from his landmark *El laberinto de la soledad* (*The Labyrinth of Solitude*, [1950] 1992), describes the psychological, political, and cultural implications that lie in the word family of the ubiquitous Mexican verb *chingar* (fuck).[173] Paz associates *chingar* with the mythical rape of the Mexican Eve, la Malinche, by Hernando Cortés. They are imagined to have produced a mestizo nation. This repressed Mother, however, is a silence that rejuvenates language: "Para todos los grandes poetas, la mujer no es solamente un instrumento de conocimiento, sino el conocimiento mismo. El conocimiento que no poseeremos nunca, la suma de nuestra definitiva ignorancia: el misterio supremo" (For all the great poets, woman is not only an instrument of knowledge, but knowledge itself. Knowledge that we will never possess, the sum of our definitive ignorance: supreme mystery).[174] He notes how the subaltern alters the Western intellectual, and for Paz the result is poetry, a new language. In the essay the poetic and the feminine are enigmas, and Paz extends these categories to include "the Oriental," "blacks," "woman," "the worker," and "Mexico" itself, as perceived by purist, bourgeois intellectuals.[175] Silviano Santiago notes that, for Paz, the unconscious and poetic language are potential saviors for humanity.[176] Santiago sees three superimposed *Paces* in the essay: the ethnographer who attempts to listen to the marginalized masses, the essayist who uses reason to organize and argue the implications of this language and history, and the poet who attempts to move beyond enlightened reason in search of a new language inspired by the masses.[177] Paz is testing the limits of Western knowledge by coming (almost) into contact with the subaltern. Nevertheless, like the Nuevo Muntu novelists, he is rejuvenating literature with oral traditions that are beyond the limits of the West.

According to Santiago, the search for enigmas led Paz to be the first Latin American critic who does not hide (from) the feminine in his treatment of Mexico.[178] His poetics is, for Santiago, founded on a "feminine opening" to outside influences. These include the study of women in history who commit what the essay treats as the mortal and original sin of *rajarse*: opening up body and mind instead of remaining closed to new meanings, new influences.[179] The poetics of his essay center on the conflicts between "closed" ideas and people (Cortés, machos, conservatives, xenophobes) versus "open" ideas and people (la Malinche, women, *chingados* [gays], cosmopolitans, poets, seekers of a new revolution) to revalue the "open," which had been previously marginalized by scholars.[180] When Paz attempts to understand the subaltern other, an intellectual crisis ensues, since he inherits not only their marginality (the dominant, Eurocentric, vision of history) but also the legacy of Cortés, the violence of colonialism that left behind its language. Paz considers facing this abject origin therapeutic since the archetypical "first mestizo" emerged in a mixture of Eden and Hell: the rape of "la Chingada."[181]

Beholding abject origins is not enough, however. These must be worked though if a new future, a *devenir*, is to unfold.[182] For Paz, the poet is the only hope.[183] For the essayist, religion no longer provides the answer to life's great questions unequivocally, and in Mexico, it is just as closed as revolution and liberalism.[184] Religion's language, and the resignification of words, can lead to new poetic possibilities. This reinvention of the past implies rupture with history by the poet (whose words transcend it) and a search for an unknown future. Poetry is a means for imagining a radical form of love, which Santiago reads as a profanation of Christian *agape* (love for community) and is based on *eros* (sexual love).[185] This healing mixture of bodies and ideas is the only way to overcome the Original Sin of la Malinche and Cortés by creating a new idiom.[186] All of Latin America is an *hijo de la Malinche* (Son of a Bitch), the product of a silenced rape that marks the language inherited from the conquistadors.

Paz's conflict of "open" and "closed" Latin Americas informs the title of Zapata's novel: *Changó, el Gran Putas*. Piquero explains that the epithet refers to a Colombian folk devil but implies "the best" or "most extreme," the *Gran Chingón* in Mexican vernacular: "en los negocios, en la política, con las mujeres" (in business, in politics, with women).[187] In Mexico *chingón* is always superlative and always taboo, related largely to its sexual overtones if not its sexual denotation. In Colombia the same can be said of *el Putas*.[188] Paz gives a critique of *machismo* at the heart of the Mexican's meditations on rape: "Lo chingado es lo pasivo, lo inerte y abierto, por oposición a lo que chinga, que es activo, agresivo y cerrado" (The fucked is what is passive, inert, and open, in opposition to what fucks, what is active, aggressive, and closed).[189] The *chingón* (badass), for Paz, is the personification of the conquistador who simultaneously destroyed and created Mexico by violating an abject mother, La Malinche. Zapata's title appears to be as strong and impenetrable as the fortresses of Cartagena and the Slave Coast. Nevertheless, *Changó el gran putas*'s signifier and signified are opened by its epithet: el Gran Putas is at once the impure devil himself and a harem of *putas* (whores).[190] He is paradoxically singular and plural, masculine and feminine, an abject origin (the curse of conquest and slavery) and a harbinger of the end (liberty, Jubilee), violator and violated. If, for Paz, the conquistador is the abusive father of Mexico, for Zapata, the Law of the Father in the psychoanalytic tradition, or written and spoken Spanish in the novel, must be altered if Mother Africa is to have a presence in the Americas.

Mother Africa

Building upon Paz's focus on maternity allows Zapata to shed light on women's contributions to the Americas from before the Conquest to the late twentieth century, even those who were unrepresented in the public sphere. It also allows the reading of Mother Africa as an all-too-forgotten, repressed origin of the New World. Zapata returns to the trauma of slavery like Gilroy. This is Mother Africa, an origin of the New World, "mi nación ultrajada" (my raped nation).[191] This trauma is the origin of the entire New World.

Zapata has ample historical basis to claim that rape and reproduction were tools of conquest. In addition to personal pleasure, and terrorization through violence, the conquistadors had every reason to create more blacks and mulattoes. In addition to their own illegitimate offspring, they brought the majority of *pobladores* (populators) to the Hispanic Caribbean from Africa in slave ships.[192] Édouard Glissant theorized the slave ship as "a womb abyss," "pregnant with as many dead as living under sentence of death."[193] In some cases the slave ship substituted the womb, since gender imbalances, malnutrition, and disease made it difficult and expensive to raise a slave from childhood to adulthood—and cheaper to import a substitute.[194]

In Zapata's section on José María Morelos, he uses myths, religious, literary, and "historical" to include the largely unexplored history of African influences in Mexico, particularly its past as a slave-owning society.[195] Morelos, like Colombian José Prudencio Padilla, does not forget Mother Africa, represented by Yemayá, or her children who no longer remember her. Cuervo Hewitt considers Yemayá an "American womb" in the novel that permeates its language and makes it resistant to colonial ideologies.[196] The novelist mixes Mother Africa's influence with the Aztec-Catholic icon La Virgen de Guadalupe / Tonantzin in Morelos's struggle to free himself from prison and his *mestizo* people from oppression.[197] She also appears syncretized with Tláloc, the Aztec rain god, returning her to an "open" goddess of fertility, not a Virgin.[198]

This initial rape reoccurs in the repeated violations at the foundations of the New World, which Paz himself explores in his horrifying portrait of the domination and exploitation of the indigenous and Zapata depicts in detail once the muntu arrives in the Americas.[199] Changó embodies the conquistador and the poet as Paz understood them. For the Mexican author, God the Father (personified by Cortés) is the "dueño del rayo y del látigo, el tirano y el ogro devorador de la vida" (owner of thunder and lighting, the tyrant, and the ogre who devours life).[200] The allusions to tyranny and lightning fit well with Changó, who is the god of lightning and the tyrant who brought the White Wolf to enslave the African diaspora. However, Paz's chingón archetype is tamed by the poetic muse because of his feminine side and the influence of his mother, personifying what Paz considers the poet, "a domadora do raio (tamer of lightening)," the one nourished by a return to the maternal and the one who imagines a new language of love.[201] This language can be imagined by men, women, or others because all poets use language. Unlike Paz's rape scene between Cortés and the Malinche, Zapata personifies the muntu as the child of the dead slave Sosa Illamba, who swims from Nagó's ship to the shore, where he is suckled by indigenous women, a tender scene that shows a bond between the African and the indigenous and a valorization of love and poetry over violence against the oppressed.[202] In "Cien años" (One Hundred Years), a note at Vanderbilt, Zapata plans to form the structure of the novel around cycles beginning with the gestation of the Muntu in Sosa Illamba, which culminates in the physical, cultural, and physical rebirth of the pregnant activist Agne Brown.[203] This child is given new love and attention, just as the illegitimate children of slaves were sometimes preferred to legitimate ones, since they were the product of desired unions instead of those arranged by the Church or enslavers.[204]

The Madonna-Whore binary is evident in "The Trade" in the form of the *Chingada* Sosa Illamba and the *puta* Ezili, the two-part representation of motherhood during the enslavement of Africans. This is fitting, given the colonial association of *marronage* and heresy.[205] As in the Bible, the earth in the novel is first destroyed by water, which for Zapata is the territory of Yoruba mother goddess of fertility, Yemayá, often syncretized with a Catholic Virgin. As in the Bible, the Apocalypse is a repetition of the Great Flood (destruction by the sea, or slavers), only in the form of fire, the domain of Changó/Santa Barbara in *santería*.[4] Likewise, the European invasion of Africa and the Americas was the end of a world and the beginning of another.

The promiscuous woman who represents the sinful nature of antediluvian humankind in the novel is Ezili, the mixed-blood harlot of Upper Guinea who deals with the Portuguese slave traders. She represents the female merchants called *nharas*, or in the Hispanic Caribbean context, *negras horras*, who sold captives alongside other merchandise.[206] Interestingly, the focus on black women in the origins of slavery is appropriate, since Herman Bennett notes that, in 1441, the first person taken slave by the Portuguese and designated "black" to justify it was a "black Mooress" in Sagres.[207] Their descriptions of her body tied its color to the justification of her enslavement.[208]

Ezili shares a name with the Dahomean-Haitian Loa who is the equivalent of the Yoruba spirit Yemayá. Ezili's face, breasts, and promiscuity, all specified in the narrative, are as "impure" as her body's mixture of white Berber and black Nigerian blood.[209] She is apparently greedy as well, selling Yoruba slaves not only for work but also for sexual pleasure to the Portuguese. She inflates the captives' price, saying that they are submissive and allowing the merchants to believe that the women are "virgins" ("closed," in Paz's language), that they have not yet been "opened" physically or culturally.[210] The Portuguese captain chingón, Muñís, attempts to rape and kill her.[211] However, his performance reveals a need for knowing a lost Mother: instead of penetrating her, he claims he will suck the salt from her (as if she were the sea, Yemayá) and proceeds to suckle at her bellybutton as if his mouth contained an invisible, forgotten umbilical cord. This interpretation subverts the colonial Christian Baptism of Africans, which involved giving them salt and splashing them with water.[212] It also aligns with many Africans' belief that their enslavers were taking them away to eat them.[213] Ezili's request "Llévame contigo" (Take me with you) is a foreshadowing of Muñís's end: she poisons him with a delicate earring before killing herself, a "turn toward death."[214] Unbeknownst to the conquistador, she penetrates him with something feminine. Ezili brings about the end of three world orders: medieval Europe, preslavery Africa, and the pre-Colombian Americas.[215]

If Ezili sold the world, yet created a new one, then Sosa Illamba, an archetype of enslaved women, is the *Chingada* whose fertility belies the force of the chingón enslaver. Sosa Illamba is invoked as a deified African Ancestor.[216] A slave, she is turned into merchandise when she is sold for a gun, a symbol of conquest.[217] Her story is a mixture of prose and poetry, written discourse and oral storytelling, as in the mythical story of her father, Katima Mololo, narrated by the storyteller Ngafúa to Nagó the Navigator so that he might care for her in the New World.[218] Mother Africa is inseparable from Changó's "son" Nagó the Navigator, and her avatar is Illamba, a repetition of Changó and Yemayá. Yemayá knows more than mortals perceive, and she is present in the sea, the rhythms of nature and song, as in Paz's interpretation of the *Chingada* as a poetic muse.

The climax of "The Trade" begins with the phrase "Las lobas están en celo" (the wolves are in heat).[219] The enslavers sexually assault the slaves. To the captives' surprise, Illamba's rapist has old, "nalgas arrugadas" (wrinkled buttocks) and his "bolsas están vacías" (sack is empty). Their macho attempts to use rape as a weapon, to use their masculine bodies to subject African mothers to pure pain at the expense of their pure pleasure, leads only to the colonizers' destruction. In fact, the conquistadors/enslavers' traditional role as rapist/father is subverted by Illamba's African fertility: she was with child before he attacked her. Furthermore, during the assault, the captive Malinké women literally "arrancan a dentelladas" (bite off) his genitals, not unlike the snakebite that kills Kehinde's master in *Defeito* and thus causes his plantation to collapse.[220] The ship burns with Changó's fire, and they all sink into the Atlantic, where they remain until the baby muntu is born again and suckled by indigenous mothers in the Americas.[221] This is the beginning of the New World on American soil. The three "races" (black, white, indigenous) are the three sister-concubines impregnated in one dark night, the Middle Passage, by Changó, aided by the sea of his mother, Yemayá.[222]

Ezili and Yemayá, the two faces of the Chingada in the text, set the stage for the long series of mothers and lovers that populate the text, which culminates in Agne Brown's life in the twentieth century. I will return to Brown shortly, but for now let it suffice to say that Zapata's women are foundational. They are fraught with the very real suffering of slavery. Nevertheless, they are strong women who maintain the African tradition of fertility alongside the American tradition of mestizaje. His women are virtually all mothers who face the various forms of oppression that come with living at the intersection of gender and race.

Gonçalves's Raw Realism of Rape

If rape is, for Zapata and Paz, represented by myth and poetry, for Gonçalves it is represented by plainspoken language. Both speak to the inseparability of politics and aesthetics that Gilroy sees in the Black Atlantic. Gonçalves opts for the nineteenth century realist-naturalist aesthetic. While space does not permit a deeper definition of naturalism in Brazil, one must keep in mind that it was informed by positivism, which focused on scrubbing novels' language of myth, unnecessary metaphor, and fantasy to provide all the details of human experience.[223] Gonçalves's novel evokes a common nineteenth century subgenre, the epistolary novel, which not only evokes the primary means of communication but also the desire for the novel to represent something "real" (a pragmatic text) and not a self-enclosed fantasy. In the wake of Darwin, nineteenth century novelists saw scientifically determined fate as impossible to overcome, which is evident in the many attempts to overcome her fate, which are inevitably crushed, such as last chapter's discussion of *abikus* (spirit children born to die [as children]). The obsession with detail, which contributes substantially to the novel's length, is also influenced by the nineteenth-century *costumbrista* aesthetic, which sought to record a local culture like ethnography, often to record unique practices of a nation in formation. An example of *realismo-naturalismo* influenced by *costumbrismo* in Brazilian letters is Aluízio de Azevedos's *O cortiço* (*The Slum*, 1890), which depicts the often brutal, grotesque life of prostitutes, pimps, and other marginal characters in the slums of Rio de Janeiro that are now known as *favelas*.[224] Regina Delcastagnè shows how the naturalist aesthetic continues to be employed by João Ubaldo Ribeiro, and I would say Gonçalves as well, to unflinchingly depict the violence carried out upon the oppressed.

Like Azevedo, Gonçalves does not look away from the horrific details of rape in Brazil's slave past. In fact, in a speech she stated that she sees rape as an appropriate metaphor for the violence and foundational nature of slavery in Brazil.[225] Her use of simple, transparent, realist language does not mask the horror of sexual assault on slaves with poetry. Zapata does this not only to dialogue with Paz, but also to elevate the lives and suffering of the enslaved to epic proportions and thus garner respect for them in the context of the highly philosophical and often graphic novels of the boom, such as Mario Vargas Llosas's *Los cachorros* (*The Bear Cubs*, 1967), a contemplation of castration.[226] Furthermore, he is arguing throughout the novel that "black is beautiful," so images that might be seen as denigrating or making black women look ugly do not fit his aesthetic. The metaphors of "open," "closed," "pure," and "impure" people in Zapata's text are not present in Kehinde's recollection of her mother's rape by invaders in Africa.[227] Her mother's vision of the *abikus* dancing around her is seen from the outside as the child Kehinde witnesses her rape and murder, and it is presented with the distance of an elderly woman who still remembers this foundational trauma in her life.[228] The first-person narrator-protagonist in Gonçalves's depiction of rape on the African coast is different from Zapata's first-person, which is the voice of Ngafúa, a captive, a witness, a griot, and a hanging victim, but not a rape survivor.

Let us dwell on the role of sexual violence in Kehinde's capture. While rape is a sex crime, it is ultimately an abuse of power. The depiction of forceful penetration, pivotal to Paz's and Zapata's description, results in pregnancy and leads to metaphors of "closed" and "open" individuals. On the other hand, Kehinde is a prepubescent child when she is assaulted, so pregnancy is not possible, but trauma is self-evident:

> O guerreiro forçava a minha mão contra o membro, que, de início, estava mole, e mexia o corpo para a frente e para trás, fazendo com que ficasse duro e quente. A minha avó chorava encobrindo o rosto, não sei se para esconder as lágrimas ou se para se esconder do que via. Um outro guerreiro se aproximou dela e, com a ponta da lança, sem se importar se estava machucando ou não, descobriu os seus olhos, mandando que ela olhasse o que estava acontecendo, dizendo que a feitiçaria dela nada adiantava contra a força deles.[229]

> (The warrior forced my hand against his member, which, at the beginning, was limp, and he moved his body forward and backward, making it hard and hot. My grandmother cried, covering her face, I don't know if to cover her

> tears or to hide from what she was seeing. Another warrior approached her and, with the tip of his spear, not caring if it hurt or not, uncovered her eyes, making her watch what was happening, saying that her sorcery could do nothing against their strength.)

The Chingada and Sosa Illamba are able to bear children like Kehinde's mother. The men rape the child and the elderly woman in the novel, and it focuses on the first-person experience and the trauma in clear language. Witnessing the event is central to the attack as well, as the grandmother's forcibly opened eyes attest. In this case the foundational trauma of slavery is altering African premodern beliefs, like Gilroy's African critic Piot attests, showing that the Black Atlantic, what I call Nuevo Muntu, encompasses the former Slave Coast.[230] "Sorcery," what becomes the Enlightenment's scorn for myth, is a term appropriated by an African kingdom radically disrupted by the Europeans' invasion century before. Once on the plantation in Brazil, the child would be called a "feiticeira" (sorceress) by the sinhá, who also views her as inferior due to her cultural difference and power.[231] The gratuitous nature of the rape is represented by the final juxtaposition of Adandozan's warrior's ejaculate and the blood of Kokumo, Kehinde's dying brother, in the ground. From this moment forward, the reader is forewarned that Brazilian slavery was anything but harmonious or benevolent, as some readers of Gilberto Freyre believe.

Gonçalves revisits Brazil's own primal scene, making it more violent and realistic in much the same way Paz and Zapata do with their respective foundations (Mexico and the Nuevo Muntu). Perhaps Freyre's most famous lines include sexual initiation by a young mulatto woman on the plantation:

> Trazemos quase todos as marcas da influência negra. Da escrava ou sinhama que nos embalou. . . . Da mulata que nos tirou o bicho-de-pé de uma coceira tão boa. Da que nos iniciou no amor físico e nos transmitiu ao ranger da cama-de-vento, a primeira sensação completa de homem.[232]
>
> (Almost all of us bear the marks of black influence. Of the slave woman or nurse that swaddled us. . . . Of the mulatto woman that pulled out the bugs biting us and scratched our itch. Of the one that initiated us in physical love and transmitted to us, on the creaking bed, our first feeling of being real men.)

This is among the most famous versions of the sensual mulatta trope that reappears, for example, in Jorge Amado, Gonçalves's guide through Bahia.

She accentuates that an enslaved woman, perhaps no women, in this context, could give consent to have sex, and so master-slave sex is rape by today's standards. She chooses the character Verenciana to represent sinhô José Carlos's concubine. In her first appearance, the foreman Cipriano forces her out of the senzala grande (field slaves' barracks) at night, dispelling any romantic notions of seduction.[233] While Freyre is often used to depict Brazilian hybridity as harmonious, his work is replete with violence, as Gonçalves states in an interview: "[Freyre] fala 'olha, a escravidão que aconteceu no Brasil, ela não foi tão violenta assim,' mas também havia casos de estupro, casos de fuga, de morte, de extrema violência" ([Freyre] says "hey, the slavery that happened in Brazil was not all that violent," but there were also cases of rape, cases of runaways, of death, of extreme violence).[234] In *Casa-Grande* he tells of mistresses' jealousy of their husbands' concubines and of a case of one having her eyes cut out.[235] While Freyre's text has an ethnographer's distance and purported objectivity, the child Kehinde's first-person testimony makes the scene visceral.

The assaults on Verenciana take multiple, gendered forms. Being kidnapped and raped and impregnated by one's captor is no doubt traumatizing. It is one of the torments the enslaved Margaret Garner flees in Kentucky and one of the reason she kills her favorite child.[236] Verenciana's beauty is also part of the crimes against her:

> A Verenciana estava de pé, altiva, presa pelos braços, não falava nada, mas também não desviava os olhos dos olhos da sinhá. Ela era linda, alta, um corpo que parecia ser cheio de curvas mesmo sob a roupa larga. Tinha pele lisa e castanha, os cabelos escuros e longos, pelo menos era o que mostravam os cachos que escapavam por baixo do lenço amarrado na cabeça. Muito mais jovem e bonita que a sinhá, e já dava para perceber que estava mesmo pejada, a barriga saliente sob a bata.[237]
>
> (Verenciana was standing, defiant, held by the arms, not saying anything but also not turning her eyes away from the sinhá. She was beautiful, tall, a body that seemed to be full of curves, even under the long clothing. She had smooth, chestnut skin, dark, long hair, or at least that is what the curls showed that escaped from under the cloth tied to her head. Much younger and prettier than the sinhá, and one could already tell that she was really pregnant, her body protruding below the cloth.)

The predictably seductive captive is actually dark-skinned and from the field slaves, Gonçalves's affirmation that, in Brazil, black is also beautiful, not just light-skinned mulattoes. Gonçalves's character Verenciana personifies the bellicose Ogun, as her green, unyielding eyes show.[238] However, beautiful is problematic when it ignores the violence of slavery and confines white women to the role of "frigid" women. Verenciana is not coquettish but "defiant," as her eyes communicate, reaffirming a strength that is more subtle than most of the slave rebels Zapata depicts. Her fertility, a special power in Zapata's novel, is the justification for the sinhá's victim blaming.

Her punishment combines the components of rape Kehinde and her grandmother suffer: physical violence, power, and witnessing. Adandozan's warriors attacked Kehinde with their bodies and their spears. Likewise, the sinhá attacks Verenciana with a knife she keeps under her skirt.[239] She assails her with verbal abuse, a related form of power. She forces male slaves to hold her, traumatizing them, Esméria, and Kehinde as they watch her stab her eyes and tear them out. While they fear the master, they are too terrified to overthrow the mistress, reaffirming a slave consciousness, as Gilroy might note. The role of slavery adds to the craven nature of the sinhá's vengeance, since she cannot only torture the woman, but she can separate her from her child, and intends to do so. She leaves her eyes in the sinhô's food to punish him.[240] It shows that the sinhô is powerful and violent, but that there are other forces in the hierarchy of the plantation. These include the patriarchal forces that drive the sinhá to torture her slave when she cannot produce an heir. It also shows that the power of the sinhô is limited, since he has to avoid his demented wife in order to promise his concubine secret manumission and lodging to escape.[241] Like Douglass, the slaves in Itaparica come to realize that they can escape and find their own solutions beyond the masters' influence.[242]

Later, Kehinde and Lourenço's rape also exemplify the multiple forms sexual violence took in slave societies. Kehinde's rape at age twelve is partly a twisted coming of age since sexual activity and exploitation of these women began soon after menarche, as in the novel.[243] It humiliates her, but it is also a humiliation of her first love, Lourenço.[244] His rape and castration at the hands of the same assailant bonds them and shows that rape affected not only women, as it does for Paz (beyond a brief mention of the *rajado*) and Zapata, but men as well. This practice was common. The enslaved Rosa Egipcíaca testified that she saw a fellow slave's testicles pulled down painfully by a weight as he was suspended by his arms.[245] A Bahian planter raped two male slaves repeatedly.[246] A *pardo* (mixed-race) soldier raped an enslaved boy in the street in Minas Gerais.[247] Priests molested male slaves.[248] Male slaves who were raped were punished with the galleys since their role was seen as more sinful, and their masters received no consequences.[249] The soldier was imprisoned for his flagrant crime. Could anyone imagine him in Padilla's *pardo* battalion in *Changó*? Even when these novels show the shocking reality of slavery, the historical record can be far worse, and gender and sexuality are parts of that.

Changó / Santa Bárbara and Queer Characters

Depicting a man raping another man is part of a greater political departure between Zapata and Gonçalves. While Zapata apparently strives to include all of the oppressed in his novel (black, poor, Amerindian), he leaves out the lesbian, gay, bisexual, transgender, and queer (LGBTQ) community, with a few key exceptions. The simplest observation is that, in both Yoruba and Dahomean faiths (syncretized as Santería and Vodou), male entities can inhabit female mediums and vice versa, as in the case of Verenciana, who has the personality of Ogum. Zapata choses, from the vast pantheon of Orishas, a male warrior god who is represented in the Hispanic Caribbean by a female, Santa Bárbara.[250] Changó's androgyny could have begun in preslavery accounts of his life, since the story of his escape from prison dressed as a woman is so widespread. This probably informed the slaves' logic in syncretizing him with Saint Bárbara in Cuba, which Cabrera recounts. Zapata tells of an almost identical syncretism in Colombia.[251] According to González-Wippler, while his most known syncretism is with the female saint, he is also imagined as male saints, so it seems this is an intentional choice on the author's part.[252] Zapata also notes that some interpret him as bisexual but that he never loses his virility.[253] In the novel it seems to be no coincidence that the scourge he allows to assail his followers, the Loba Blanca, is entirely male in the novel (the conquistadors), and yet the gender of their spirit is female. This gender bending complicates their highly gendered crimes like rape, since they are technically the embodiment of a female spirit.

His queer characters, like Gonçalves's, occupy a silence that Gilroy mentions but never fills: that of those who do not conform to traditional gender and sexuality roles. Gilroy claims that Afrocentric thinkers are mistaken in overemphasizing the reconstitution of male masculinity and the patriarchal family, which have been decimated by slavery: "These crises are most intensely lived in the area of gender relations where the symbolic reconstruction of community is projected onto an image of the ideal heterosexual couple. The patriarchal family is the preferred institution capable of reproducing the traditional roles, cultures, and sensibilities that can solve this state of affairs."[254] Yet none of the authors or characters he discusses are queer.

Zapata's syncretism of African and Mexican deities like Tlaloc and Tonantzin precedes Gloria Anzaldúa's *Borderlands/La Frontera: The New Mestiza* (1987).[255] He chooses deities that challenge gender norms in opposition to a conformist interpretation of Christianity before she does. Zapata's recognition of the importance of women and those descended from Africans in Mexico's past and their shared marginality and frequent invisibility precedes Anzaldúa's contributions, speaking as a *mestiza* with heritage from Africa, to *This Bridge Called My Back* (1983).[256] One can see the continuation of queer interpretations of the god in the short story "Changó" in *Transmutadxs* (2016).[257] In her work, an immigrant from the Dominican Republic to Puerto Rico undergoes a series of sexual and gender transformations, eventually becoming the deity Changó Almonte.[258]

Zapata also includes the "marimacho" (bull dyke) Olokún among the pantheon of the "Grandes Orishas," which, while based in the tradition, is his own selective use of it.

> ¡Olokún marimacho!
> Marido y mujer de Olosa
> tu hermana y esposa.
> En los abismos del mar
> mal repartís los sexos,
> barbas ponéis a las mujeres;
> a los hombres largos senos.[259]
>
> (Olokún the bull dyke!
> Husband and woman of Olosa
> Your sister and wife.
> In the abyss of the sea
> you distribute the sexes wrong;
> you put beards on the women;
> and on men long breasts.)

In addition to confusing secondary gender traits, Olokún is "enamorado de los machos" (in love with males).[260] He is presented as a trickster, not a representative of an oppressed subculture. While he appears only twice in the text, Henao Restrepo considers him/them both "hermafrodita" (intersex) and the god/dess of the matriarchy and the patriarchy that governs the ancestors.[261] This heteronormative outlook can be debated and the terms are out of date, but it is clear that Zapata's deities are not all envisioned as traditional Western heterosexuals. Even Changó's incestuous relationship with his mother/concubine Yemayá and his powerful concubine-sisters reaffirms his strength and influence while challenging conservative notions of family. While Olokún has no other explicit role in the text, she does one thing: he gives Kanuri Mai the power to determine what is beautiful.[262] After that, all aesthetics stem from Kanuri Mai in the work, including the creations of Aleijadinho and Du Bois. This is a very powerful contribution, and it reaffirms Gilroy's challenging the separation of politics (here, gender politics) and aesthetics (black beauty, black creativity).

However, in *Changó*, in the world of mortals, one is either heterosexual or described in negative terms. For example, Zapata includes the media rumors that the slave rebel Nat Turner was "torpe, vengativo, místico, depravado y hasta homosexual. No te incomodes [Agne Brown], los muertos somos tan vulnerables a las críticas como el cristal a la luz" (clumsy, vindictive, mystic, depraved, and even homosexual. Don't worry [Agne Brown]; the dead are as vulnerable to criticism as glass is to light).[263] While "mystic" is not an insult, the rest are, and he calls "homosexual" a criticism. While the historical Turner likely could have been only homophobic, Zapata chose to represent secular queer subjectivities as a defect.

The blues is liberating in the novel, but in a heteronormative way. In "Ancestros combatientes" (Ancestors in Combat), when Joe Stephens plays the banjo at a Harlem night club, Susan, Agne's sexually liberated white "sister," awaits his performance at the West End Blues Bar in Harlem.[264] As Kinitra Brooks shows, the blues is considered the "viscera that remains" of the patriarchal Black Church's quest for respectability after abolition.[265] It creates intimacy and speaks of the body, emotions, and individuality, all sacred aspects of life that were rejected by the church.[266] The blues is even associated with conjuring spirits, as in Robert Johnson's famous deal with the devil, so Agne's bond with sexually liberated Susan and her vagabond love interest is a challenge to gender roles, an example of her rejecting her "good girl" past, even in a heteronormative way.[267] It is no coincidence that the blues, then, is part of her journey to become a conjure woman.[268]

At the blues bar, an unexpected scene ensues: "Se apagaron las luces y solo chisporrotean las lentejuelas de los cigarrillos. Flotando en un rayo de luz apareció una cara infantil con cabellos rizados y las pestañas maquilladas. Los aplausos acogieron a aquella criatura híbrida con bigotes rasurados" (The lights go out and only the glasses sparkle from the cigarettes. Floating on a beam of light appeared a child-like face with curly hair and false eyelashes. Applause welcomed the hybrid creature with a shaved mustache).[269] While Zapata works to show the importance of both women (Sosa Illamba, Hipólita, Agne) and men (Benkos Bioho, Toussaint L'Ouverture, Simón Bolívar) in black history, if one does not fit rigid gender scripts in the terrestrial realm, one is described as "child-like" and a "hybrid creature."[270] Though most of the novel is set before Stonewall (1969) and other benchmarks of U.S. LGBTQ activism, it is still a valid criticism that this characterization of queer identities is distant from contemporary notions of progress.

For example, he presents black hero José Prudencio Padilla's bestiality with a "pollina" (mule) as perfectly normal, a stepping stone toward sex with women.[271] His seemingly proud father congratulates him and tells him, "La hembra no es para aporrearla sino para amarla y hacerla parir" (Females are not to be beaten but to be loved and made to bear children).[272] While this is not the sexual abuse depicted in the *bacanales* (Bacchanals) of the Colombian plantation setting (another elision of the messy details of rape), it is a heteronormative assumption and one that reduces women to uteri.[273]

Returning to the West End Blues Bar, one can read the "marica" (fag) as Olokun/Kanuri Mai, inspiring Joe to play music inspired by Africa on an instrument with African origins, the banjo.[274] Nevertheless, in the most forgiving interpretation, anything not defined by heteronormativity and a limited notion of fertility is confined to the spirit world, not the mundane. This reaffirms Gilroy's criticism that African diaspora studies all too often focuses on a stable, patriarchal family to the detriment of models of community that offer more options to men, women, and other genders.[275]

Zapata's limitations are thrown into relief by Kameelah Martin's comparison between the blues and the conjure woman.[276] After slavery, those with formal education adopted a secular outlook.[277] They excluded inconvenient elements of black culture, including syncretic religious practices and secular music. This cultural offal expressed vital elements of people's lived experience. Blues music popularized black conjure practices and created a welcoming environment for depictions of them in Zora Neale Hurston's work. *Changó*'s heterosexual love affair between Joe and Agne anticipates Arthur Flower's novel *Another Good Thing* (1992), a love story of a bluesman and a conjure woman, which Martin praises for its feminism.[278] Nevertheless, he could have taken a step further and depicted the blues *woman*. Brooks rescues the life story of Memphis Minnie, the blueswoman who sang about conjure (which she practiced) and bent numerous gender norms: cursing, drinking, and celebrating sex, including with women.[279]

On the other hand, Gonçalves's sprawling cast of characters includes at least two relatively developed representations of homosexual identities. Kehinde takes in some wanderers, Jongo and Adriano, who show up on the farm near Salvador.[280] They appear to be a gay couple, but their origins are unknown.[281] They make so much noise at night that the others who live with Kehinde find it strange. She asks her mentor Esméria, who quotes a Yoruba proverb that states "nas coisas entre marido e mulher ninguém dá palpate" (nobody should mess with things that are between husband and wife). She interprets it as needing no further explanation and lets them stay, unquestioned. In fact, since they are cooks, she shares recipes with them at her bakery.[282] This proverb may shed light on Zapata's Yoruba-influenced text: perhaps apparently heteronormative terms are interpreted in ways that, in the end, can apply to nonheterosexuals, but Gonçalves makes it explicit.

Even slave-era homophobia is depicted differently in Gonçalves's text. Once the Muslims move in with Kehinde and begin their plot to revolt in Bahia, they refuse to speak to Jongo and Adriano and the latter decide to leave.[283] "Disseram para não me importar porque já estavam acostumados com tratamentos como aquele, que acontecia mesmo entre os patrícios deles, ao lado de quem estavam indo morar" (They told me not to worry because they were already used to that kind of treatment, which even happened among their countrymen, with whom they were going to live).[284] Gonçalves's realism is not anachronistic, but there are identities the contemporary reader can recognize as homosexual, which is likely a more realistic representation of demographics in the area.

James Sweet notes two types of same-sex acts in colonial Brazil. Due to desperation stemming from a huge gender imbalance, some men "recast their sexual identities."[285] Of course, they also had the options of masturbation and bestiality. Jongo and Adriano, identifiable as a pair of ordinary individuals, seem much more secular and ordinary to the contemporary reader than the "third genders" Sweet discovered in Portuguese Inquisition sodomy cases: the Benin and Central African *jinbandaa*, *chibados*, and *quimbandas*.[286] These individuals were known for their healing powers and were a priestly caste.[287] They advised kings and were respected in Africa as leaders during burials. *Quimbandas* dressed as women, had a "buraco" (hole) like a woman—likely referring to being a receptor during sex—and lived in bands.[288] In Portugal, one of them lived as a prostitute. They, as in all the cases of passive gay partners, were sentenced to hard labor or even death by the Inquisition due to Portugal's patriarchal, heteronormative laws. These customs of slave colonies destroyed these third-gendered individuals' kinship structures.

In *Defeito*, the second queer individual Kehinde meets is in Africa. His (her?) name is Van-van, and he is a "*travesti liberto afrancesado* free, frenchified transvestite—or transgender person."[289] S/he is the family interior decorator and wedding planner.[290] While this dandified trans person seems quite modern, male priests dressed as women were prominent as a third gender in Central Africa and Lower Guinea, so they add to the historical realism of the novel.[291] These details, while they may not be central to the plot, show that Gonçalves's perspective is more in line with our times than Zapata, who seeks a Nuevo Muntu for all but does not have the vision or vocabulary to include sexuality in his liberation project when the book is published in 1983. This does not mean he does not present his own feminist intervention through his revolutionary Nuevo Muntu.

Agne Brown and the Apocalypse

As I have been arguing by comparing their novels, both Zapata and Gonçalves have made attempts at presenting black heroines that embody black feminist causes. Zapata is more idealist, while Gonçalves is more realist in her depictions. Zapata's palenques and quilombos are directly related to the Civil Rights and Black Power struggles in the late 1960s in the United States. They also bind the African diaspora in Latin America with African Americans.

Agne Brown is the culmination of the muntu's struggle for liberty under black feminist leadership. Her last name and her unique first name (Agne) evoke pride in her skin color, reaffirming the novel's philosophy that "black is beautiful."[292] Her name also is an allusion to Foxy Brown, the strong, sensual female protagonist of Jack Hill's eponymous 1974 film. She is the counterpart to Blaxploitation film character Shaft, the "Bad Mother . . . ," who inspired Zapata's title with his bravado.[293] While Agne is beautiful, sensual, and proud—like her spiritual father Changó—she is also a much more complex character whom the Ancestors instruct to learn from the women and men of black history so that she can overcome the White Wolf, the spirit of oppression.

Zapata begins her story when the griot Ngafúa calls out to her while she is in the shower. Like the baby muntu of Sosa Illamba, the reader discovers her in an enclosed space she must leave, like the slave ship. The scene evokes Alfred Hitchcock's *Psycho* (1960), in which a white woman is murdered in the shower.[294] Instead, in the novel, a culturally "whitened" black woman faces her own "monsters": the history of black oppression. The griot Ngafúa reunites her with her ancestors, in particular Zaka, a black maroon who is transculturated by the Seminole and Hopi people he joins.[295] On the other hand, as a priestess she is able to summon forth not only Zaka but also all the black rebels depicted in the novel. The work depicts the importance of women as mothers and objects of desire from the beginning of the work as part of a celebration of African fertility and *mestizaje* (cultural and familial mixing). This is intended to reverse the eugenicist notions that it was desirable to "breed out" black traits. While Yemayá is the spiritual archetype of the African Mother, it is the maroon Sosa Illamba who gives birth to the muntu. Malcolm X tells Agne she is Sosa Illamba, who gathers in her breast hundreds of millions of blacks murdered by the White Wolf.[296]

The novelist's choice of Yemayá/Iemanjá for a whitened character is appropriate since the divinity has been reinterpreted as a white, "pure," ethereal woman in Brazilian Umbanda.[297] This is partly due to Marianism and her association with Our Lady of Aparecida and Our Lady of Navigators, white apparitions of the Virgin. Her sexual and mundane characteristics are projected onto the holy streetwalker *pombagira*, a favorite of Brazil's marginalized.[298] Agne must learn to embrace her fertility, her African heritage, and her black beauty. She must fight the oppression she experiences alongside the prostitutes with whom she is jailed for her "cult" of the ancestors. Following the novels diabolical motif, Pombagira is an *Exu-mulher*, both a "devil-woman" and an opener of pathways and new beginnings.

Agne is a feminist character, and her shocking discovery of African ghosts in the shower ties her story to the works of horror that Kinitra Brooks analyzes in *Searching for Sycorax: Black Women's Hauntings of Contemporary Horror* (2018).[299] Agne transitions from being a repressed preacher's daughter to the leader of a fertility cult based on summoning ghosts (the Ancestors) and African deities. Depending on the reader's point of view, this could be a terrifying enterprise. Zapata does not exoticize her choices and powers, but Brooks's insights are still relevant. First, the choice to cast a black female as the protagonist in a shower scene is radical. There were virtually no black female protagonists in horror films. Exceptions are Blaxploitation works like *Blackula* (1972), whose characters Agne would likely resemble in dress and hairstyle.[300] Agne's discovery of her sexuality and her ability to raise the dead form a more dignified representation of a faith leader than *Blackula*'s Sugah, who can do this but is depicted as a black Jezebel.[301] Brooks analyzes African American novelist Nalo Hopkinson's *Sister Mine* (2013), in which a character, Daddy Wood, is based on the Vodou spirit Kouzin Zaka, whose name comes from Iwa Azaka.[302] He is a vagabond who works with his hands, so his name is well suited to the wandering maroon in *Changó*. Agne's growth in accepting her ancestors and her blackness is part of a greater project of making blackness no longer synonymous with monstrosity, as it was in the U.S. context in the 1960s.[303]

Agne learns that the societal role of women changes in history, starting with U.S. rebels. The muntu's destiny is to start a rebirth of humanity, which is tied to women's ability to give birth, both physiologically and metaphorically.[304] Executed maroon leader Nat Turner tells Agne of reaching his Jerusalem by resisting slavery and even saving poor whites, and he prophesies that women and children will lead the revolution after him.[305] African traditions of reincarnations like those that those Agne knows may have actually influenced Turner since his mother said he was an embodiment of a previous ancestor as a child.[306] Abolitionist Sojourner Truth takes the lead, arguing for her son to be returned from having been sold from New York to Alabama.[307] Her uncle Saudey fought off slave catchers with an axe, and she assumed her leadership at fifty years of age, recruiting blacks for the Union Army. Truth's struggle for justice shows that the Civil War was only the most partial of victories because blacks remained oppressed during and after it. Harriet Tubman tells her of Fort Pillow during the Civil War.[308] Blacks want to join the invading Union, but the whites often reject them. At Fort Pillow the black soldiers are massacred. Hence, Agne is, as a black woman, heir to these maroons' struggles for liberty in the United States. In addition, as Turner's vision attests, she is heir to the need for immediate, even violent, intervention against an unjust system. Like Turner, John Brown is the symbol of violent collective uprising, which gives even more nuance to

Agne's last name. As Malcolm dies, John Brown's spirit returns to hold his head alongside Du Bois as they sing that words divide while action unites.[309]

This violence is both collective and private, since Agne is the granddaughter of Margaret Gardner.[310] The woman who escaped Kentucky for Ohio only to kill her children when slave catchers arrive cries out to Tubman and claims death is a form of freedom. Gardner tells Agne that she is alive in her, so Agne is the grandchild of one of the children Margaret did not kill. The reader should note that Zapata presents Gardner's choice of infanticide over enslavement as a radical struggle for freedom four years before Morrison did so in *Beloved* (1987).[311] Agne's bloodline reaffirms that the maroon rebellions of the past are the historical precedent for the activism of Agne's time, and that she, though a woman and thus capable of bearing life, is as strong, just, and determined as anyone in black history as well as a leader in the public sphere. In fact, she embodies history's culmination.

In addition to the previous models for Agne (Foxy, Truth, Tubman, Brown), Angela Davis is clearly an inspiration. In an earlier version of the *Changó* manuscript, her name was still Angela.[312] Davis is a perfect basis for a strong black leader in the tradition of black revolts because she is the "big bad Communist enemy" of U.S. imperialism, which reaffirms Zapata's Marxist ideology.[313] She was arrested because she owned the guns used in the deadly Marin County Courthouse shootout on August 7, 1970.[314] She was a former assistant professor at the University of California, Los Angeles and a member of the Black Panther Party, so she was a black feminist intellectual. Her imprisonment, like Agne's, is the motive of strong youth protests, some of many during the heated times of racial integration and the Vietnam War.[315]

The character Joe Stephens, Agne's love interest, is likely based on Joseph Stevens, a communist activist from Harlem who spoke out against Davis's imprisonment.[316] This said, in a mythical interpretation of events loosely based on history, Zapata also seems to be syncretizing Joe with Exu Zé Pilintra, whose name is a popular Brazilian form for the name "Joseph."[317] He is a *malandro* (rascal) figure, a traditional Brazilian trickster who personifies the street life of the city. He usually is represented as mulatto or black. Exu is also Elegua/Legba, one who can open doors to a new realm or start a new beginning. Thus, he is the perfect partner for Exu pombagira / Yemayá, personified in Agne, his love interest.

Davis's autobiography illuminates the plot of "Ancestors in Combat." She left Birmingham, Alabama, to study at the all-white Brandeis University in Boston and did volunteer work in the Latin Quarter of New York.[318] She heard Malcolm speak.[319] Interestingly, though she traveled throughout Europe, Gilroy overlooks her.[320] She was a member of the Che-Lumumba Club, which supported Cuban and Kenyan liberation movements, and she went into exile in Cuba, so she unites the struggles of the United States with Africa and Latin America.[321] She is a founding figure of black feminism and the U.S. prison reform movement.

Agne's role in the novel is also that of a radical alteration of black history as it relates to struggles of the present. The traditional form of her name, "Agnes," means "pure," which indicates a repressed and whitened form of femininity. The novel states that unlike the mulatto women who whitened the skin of their children by sleeping with their captors, Agne is whitened by leaving the South and is granted a "white" education as the first black child to integrate her school in Lawrence.[322] Naturally, this is an allusion to the *Brown v. Board of Education* case, which integrated public schools and sparked the Civil Rights Movement in many ways. Zapata takes this moment not as an emancipation, just as he claims the Civil War only returned blacks to slavery, but as a chance to show how U.S. culture needs to become mestizo in that it should teach black history and have integrated schools. Agne's childhood friend Joe sees her as a whitened person due to her upbringing as a white preacher's adopted child and privileged education.[323]

Agne discovers her African past. She assists her professor, Dr. Harrington, at the Natural History Museum in New York, cleaning African artifacts.[324] Hoping to frighten her friend Dorothy, she puts on a Changó mask and his spirit fills her. She loses a "white mask" and begins to sleep "en el magara de [sus] ancestros" (in the magara of [her] ancestors).[325] Her visage parallels the metal muzzle placed on the Nagó el Navegante, the mutineer who brings Changó's spirit to the Atlantic.[326] While he is marred by a mask of slavery (and fighting it), she is liberated by a mask representing Africa. Liberation through symbolic clothing is not limited to masks though. As in the myth of Changó's escape from prison, she wears the god's sister-concubine's skirt that allows Zapata and the reader to attempt an escape from a vision of history that does not include black ideas and black struggles.[327]

Agne is not raped or prostituted like her female precursors in *Changó*. Nonetheless, she is culturally violated and suffers highly gendered violence. Recalling the prologue and Ezili's rape/rebellion, "¡Desnúdate!" (Strip!) is the first thing Agne Brown is told when she is jailed for prostitution and polygamy in part for serving Changó as a priestess and activist.[328] This humiliation is a symbolic rape at the hands of a female warden, a *chingona* who loves to hear helpless prostitutes cry as she shears off their locks. This is a retelling of Davis's imprisonment, when voyeuristic guards force her to wear unwashed prison-issued underwear.[329] Agne's cultural context determines this form of degradation because during the 1960s it was a form of rebellion for a black woman to let her hair grow into an afro, symbolizing a conscious cultural return of the repressed memories of centuries of denial and control of African bodies and culture in the United States. Her cold, naked scalp is like her cold, hard cell. Her "rape" is an example of how horrific "criminal justice" has seemed to overshadow the rape of black women in U.S. popular consciousness, namely the "punishment" of lynching.[330]

Agne has also been trapped in a seemingly impenetrable lettered world, ignorant of black history. When racists lynch her African American biological father, a white Protestant minister raises her. She calls him "padre" (father/priest).[331] She is taken from the South to Kansas, where she is raised in a primarily Caucasian, Christian world and educated at white schools from childhood to her anthropology studies at the New School. She is the only black student in her school. Her way out of this prison house is through the spiritual language of the Orishas, which she discovers as an adult.

She is imprisoned for her beliefs, but these give her a means of escape through a subversive interpretation of the events, beyond the comprehension of her jailers: "El número 999999. Supe al verlo que es la edad exacta de mi más remoto Ancestro. . . . En vez de palparme la cabeza rapada como lo espera mi carcelera, preferí aplacar las serpientes de Legba oprimiendo mis senos bajo el uniforme de carcelaria" (Number 999999. I knew when I saw it that it is the exact age of my most remote Ancestor. . . . Instead of touching my shaved head like my jailer expects, I prefer to placate the serpents of Legba by pressing my breasts beneath the prison uniform).[332] This *oprimiendo* is oppressing, indicative of the oppression of blacks she bears in her skin, but the act is simultaneously autoerotic. Mother Africa surges forth in the novel's language, opening it like the semigod of doorways into a source of creativity, sexualizing it, making it fertile like Yemayá and her son Changó. The serpents of Changó are called a "mácula" (stain) or "tattoo," which, to the warden, makes her more whorish, and it had such importance for the author that he originally called the first section of "Ancestors in Combat" "La macula" (The Stain).[333] One cannot ignore the association between her "macula" (stain) and the "*Immaculate* Conception" of the Virgin Mary (the one who is pure, or without blemish, as the term implies). In the jail other prisoners taunt the pregnant Agne, laughing that her children were not conceived by the Holy Spirit.[334] This, of course, is not true because the fertility of Yemayá and Changó is the source of all pregnancy in Agne's cult of the Ancestors, something beyond written language (represented by the carnet that the police request from the devotees), beyond Western reason.[335] Thus, she is an "impure" Agne, not a "pure" "Agnes" (Pure), as her name in Latin would be.

Agne's mark is gendered. While her chest bears the Serpents of Legba, the mark of Changó's chosen, this mark is also on King Benkos Bioho.[336] Cuervo Hewitt considers Agne the "twin" of Benkos.[337] The author mentions Bioho's serpents in five key moments of the maroon's life. First, he is born bearing them in a ceremony unbeknownst to the Church, which shows that his birth is divinely ordained by the Orishas.[338] Second, the snakes appear at his baptism-like yet Yoruba consecration at the hands of a babalawo, Domingo Falupo.[339] When he is taken to the seminary, his babalawo/priest senses them writhing on his body, a symbol of his rebellion against indoctrination.[340] They are visible to all of King Benkos's subjects at his coronation.[341] Nagó the Navigator touches his own serpents of Elegguá to revive Bioho.[342] His undead words cry "muera el amo" (death to the master) as he sets off a slave revolt against the Inquisition and the colonizers. Bioho is a chosen one like Agne, but his marks are on his shoulders like the lashes of a whip or the burden of a yoke.[343] They are the marks of pain and oppression; they fuel fire, destruction, and war, the side of Changó associated with masculinity. However, within all of these rebellions, there is a cultural mestizo born, like Agne and Bioho, a new entity that comes from the fertility of Changó's bond with Yemayá.

Agne is a feminist revision of the iconic black conjure woman and spirit work. "I contend that the conjure woman is often an autonomous persona who disrupts ideas of gender and femininity, exercises self-determination, and defies authority and Western ideologies of cultural supremacy as she sees fit, seldom forgetting that her otherness is often the source of her autonomy," says critic Kameelah Martin.[344] She argues that conjure, her blanket term for syncretic African beliefs, be they as simple and pragmatic as "root work" or as complex as the pantheons of New Orleans Voodoo and Santería, is a form of double consciousness that ties black women to their ancestors in culture and the arts. Christian black women will often turn to African traditions to reach pragmatic ends or simply to reconnect with their sexuality. African faiths often celebrate fertility and sexuality.[345] An example is Ismael Reed's *Mumbo Jumbo* (1972), which focuses on Vodou Loa Erzulie. Combining the sea imagery of Yemayá and the eroticism of Oshun, this deity has much in common with Agne. Though an African American raised by a white Protestant minister, she is a sensual, rebellious conjure woman who is in touch with her ancestors. As a rebel she continues the tradition of Zapata's Haitian Marie-Jeanne Lamartinière, a deified ancestor who died in the Haitian Revolution.[346]

Zapata represents the feminine through a Madonna-Whore binary like Paz. The Mexican critic juxtaposes the maternal Virgin of Guadalupe with the defiled Chingada, showing that both represent the Mother.[347] Agne, like Zapata and the Nuevo Muntu he recounts, is profane and impure, and this is the source of her creativity and her unity with a previously forgotten past. The serpents of Eleggu‡ mark Nagó the Navigator, Changó's first earthly messenger, a "macula" (stain) or "tatuaje" (tattoo), which evokes the ceremony to Elegguá and Changó in "Los orígenes":

Loba pelo rojo
tienes hocico de hiena
coagulada sangre en los ojos
. . . .
Tu huella ceniza
carimba
rencor que no se olvida
tatuado en mi piel
. . . .
Donde renazca tu chispa
. . . .
estará presente el llanto
memoria de la madre muerta,
hueso partido en cruz
por la espada de tus santos.[348]

(The cry will be present
the memory of the dead mother
a bone split into a cross
by the sword of your saints
Red-haired Wolf
you have the snout of a hyena
coagulated blood in your eyes
. . . .

Your trace ash
Branded
Unforgotten rage
. . . .
Where your spark is reborn
. . . .)

This explanation of the tattoo, the snakes, is repeated and reinterpreted throughout the novel in gendered terms. The serpents are both memory and urges that can be transformed into creativity. The double entendre of *mácula* is that of the stain as well as that of the eye, or macula. The rigidly divided Americas must thus be seen in a different, "impure" light that "stains" their symbols to create something new and transculturated. Dark skin, once viewed as a blight or curse, will be a source of creativity like the dark waters of Yemayá pouring forth into dry, hard cultural symbols.

In jail Agne meets a son of Changó, Malcolm, who seems to be trapped in a prison of anger, and she says, "Veo poco probable que puedan ayudarme. Tengo serias discrepancias sobre las ideas que predica la Nación de Islam porque soy enemiga de la segregación" (I do not think it likely that you all can help me. I have serious discrepancies about the ideas that the Nation of Islam preaches because I am an enemy of segregation).[349] To this, Malcolm replies, "Alá ha dado al Honorable Maestro una espada de dos filos para cortar el Diablo Blanco que se ha incrustado en nuestra mente" (Allah has given the Honorable Master a double-edged sword to cut down the White Devil that has been encrusted on our mind). He reads a newspaper report on Agne's arrest. He is infuriated by the paper's accusations that she is at once a preacher, a mystic, a prostitute, a practitioner of public polyandry (polygamy), and a perpetrator of *proxenetismo* (serving as a madame). While there is no reason for her to be imprisoned for these charges, she also feels no reason to deny them. She is a priestess of Changó who evokes the Ancestors as his Chosen One, creating most of the characters and narrative of the "Ancestors in Combat," as the title implies. Many sub-Saharan cultures practice polygamy, and her Cult of Shadows serves the prostitutes of Harlem, parallels of those in Minas. Prostitutes come to her white step-father's church in Harlem, pregnant from absent white fathers, many unknown, and her father tells them that even so the child is theirs.[350] At church, they are ashamed, but her cult gives her congregants pride. Agne is called a prostitute in prison.[351]

Malcolm cannot yet hear the waters of Yemayá in Agne's words or those of the press, but the goddess's melancholy marks the vision to which Elegguá opens Agne's imprisoned eyes. On Malcolm's masculine chest, instead of the writhing serpents of Elegguá, he has a gunshot wound. Malcolm, who, through Islam, is able to see the potential unity in humanity instead of a quest for purity and separation, is killed in New York's Audubon Ballroom.[352] His funeral is held at Agne's Temple of Shadows in Harlem. Places of death are simultaneously places of eternal life. In death, he sees beyond purity. He sees a vision of Illamba wrapping him in "blancas olas" (white waves) and calls out "eres tú, Agne Brown, la hija de Yemayá, madre que no necesitas del engendro del varón para parir heroes y mártires" (it is you, Agne Brown, daughter of Yemayá, mother who needs no man's seed to bear heroes and martyrs).[353] Because of faiths, Bantu, Yoruba, Dahomean, Christian, Muslim, humanist, and syncretic, Agne/Zapata can arrange knowledge into an illusion that gives meaning, love, and imagination to a horrifying history rooted in slavery and the Conquest. Religious discourse is, in fact, poetic discourse that opens language to what it cannot yet represent. This new world is the Nuevo Muntu.

Evoking the biblical Apocalypse, Agne is not only a whore but also "La Gran Puta," as the title indicates. *Puta* is translated several ways in the Bible, which depicts the end of the world in *Revelation* (*Apocalipsis* in Spanish). Saint John, the author, has a vision of a woman named "Secret, Babylon the Great, the Mother of the Whores and the Abominations of the Earth" who represents an earthly empire under what was in the saint's time the unthinkable reign of a woman.[354] Cuervo Hewitt considers this New World to be the continental realization of Benkos Bioho's palenque.[355] One must not forget that maroons' fractiousness was considered a biblical plague in the colonies, and the rebels were considered demonic, says the scholar.[356]

Changó rewrites not only the origins of the New World but also the end of history as it is known. Cuervo Hewitt considers this narrative of history to be "apocalyptic wind-words of the orisha Shango [*sic*]."[357] The end of the familiar is the only way out of the prison of language because the latter is tied to the past and cannot yet capture the future, so the unforeseen future can be imagined in language only as the Apocalypse. It is fitting that this Apocalypse comes from a feminine character, since "in the cultural imaginary of the Caribbean writer, *monte* and Palenque become signifiers for a (m)other space of refuge and difference, a space from where to summon the Windstorm force of the Word; from where to reiterate an ideological and cultural cimarronaje always already in the archival memories of the Caribbean."[358] This resignification must "replace traditional myths of difference and exclusion" like racism, thus creating a myth of a completely new world, an Apocalypse.

Agne's Temple of Shadows in Harlem is the summoning of all the spirits that will fight in a syncretic Armageddon between races, nations, and cultures around Malcolm's corpse. The gathering of the dead is the supernatural equivalent of the 1967 March on the Pentagon of the National Mobilization Committee to End the War in Vietnam.[359] The center of the march is a great stone phallus not unlike the colonial fortresses of old, the Washington Monument: "Parecíamos diminutas hormigas tratando de derribar un misil atómico. . . . Todos vienen a sembrar las semillas de sus hijos: la Negra, la Amarilla, la Blanca, la solidaridad del Muntu: '¡No hagas la guerra, practica el amor!'" (We seemed to be tiny ants trying to topple an atomic missile. . . . We all come to plant the seeds of their children: the Black, the Yellow, the white, the solidarity of the Muntu: "Make love, not war!").[360] Martin Luther King Jr. speaks against racial supremacy and violence of all kinds. The pure white phallus represents the "nuevo César" (new Caesar) of this Apocalyptic Rome, empire of the Loba Blanca, a political and cultural order dominated by white male America that sends the dark and the marginalized to die in the wars that support its empires. Grotesque birds, "Jim Crows" (in English in the original), descend upon the protesters and attempt to keep them from "sembrar el árbol de la justicia en América" (planting the tree of justice in America). In Gold Coast and Central Africa, crows were an omen of impending war, so the omen is syncretic.[361] Amid them are the Black Scorpions, militants who learned Changó's fire in Vietnam and Korea and who are willing to fight the "Octágono" (Pentagon). These marchers do not give in to the violence that burns within and around them; the end of this world is consumed not in fire but in water. As veterans, recruits, and idealists burn their uniforms and draft cards, symbols of war imploding, authorities descend upon them with a "látigo de água" (water whip).[362] Instead of destroying the Nuevo Muntu, they unite them as slavery once united a simultaneously scattered African diaspora. "A gatas frente a la pared, nos hincharon los vientres disparando chorros de agua contra nuestras nalgas desnudas" (On our hands and knees, against the wall, they filled our wombs gushing water against our naked buttocks).[363] Changó's power to make war and destroy, the same power of the conquistador, the *negrero*, and the chingón, is made fertile by the healing waters of Mother Yemayá.

The unknown future for the profane world is foreshadowed in the afterlife. At Malcolm's funeral a sacred, maternal baobab sprouts from his body and breaks the walls around it.[364] Elegguá opens the door to death as he closes the novel. The undead Malcolm wonders if he will be the gunpowder of an apocalyptic battle, when he pauses. Changó marches over the sea like a horseman of the Apocalypse. He and his warrior brothers are only held back by the waters of Yemayá: "Ochosí, arco iris, mantenía tensa la lanza que hiere la lluvia. . . . Ogún los [los truenos] ahoga entre sus manos. . . . Y cerrada la boca, rojos los ojos, el Oricha de la ira, Orún, contenía su furia" (Ochosí, rainbow, tensely held the spear that wounds the rain. . . . Ogun drowns the thunder between his hands. . . . And with mouth closed, eyes red, the Orisha of rage, Orún, contains his fury).[365] Elegguá tells the Ancestors and the Orishas to control themselves, lest the Armageddon between the oppressed and oppressor begin. However, he calls to the reader and cries "comparad vuestros insignificantes actos con las hazañas de nuestros Antepasados y encontraréis justificada la furia de los Orichas" (compare your insignificant acts to the feats of our Forebears and you will find that the fury of the Orishas is justified). If one merely invokes the rage and violence of Changó, one will see only a call to violence, Armageddon, destruction. The goal of the Apocalypse is justice for Christians, just as justice is the goal of history for Zapata. This justice has not yet arrived, but anger and destruction, the masculine side of Changó, cannot achieve this unknown justice. It must come from his feminine side, the fertile, fluid side that he shares with his Mother Yemayá and that seeps into the novel's poetic language.

Agne is central to this opening of possibilities. Like Illamba, she is pregnant with a child of unknown origin, the symbol of an equally unpredictable future. Agne is a fighter who does not fear death or imprisonment, just as Changó and Nagó el Navegante are, but her erotic side is just as important for revealing a new future for the Nuevo Muntu. Half of her is separated by segregation. She is courted by Joe Stephens, a black man of humble origins who graduates from a historically black college because he refuses to be a "nigger descolorido" (discolored nigger).[366] He plays the banjo, an instrument of West African origin that he learned from his father and generally represents an organic knowledge not found in the halls of (white, segregated) academia.[367] He does not know the syncretic oral traditions of Latin America, nor does he have the New School education that Agne does.

Joe clearly has something to add to this Nuevo Muntu as well. Whereas she is inmate number 999999, pure presence, he is pure absence, 0000000, just as the color black is pure absence (it absorbs all light) and white is pure presence of light (it reflects all light).[368] The prisoner Joe compares U.S. prisons to a stone cold womb where the blacks of the future are gestating as if they were part of the abject slum where many blacks live.[369] In prison, where he has no pen with which to write, he goes beyond letters and returns to the oral traditions to communicate with his brothers through songs and rhythm like his enslaved ancestors. However, he must translate his spoken words into writing for Agne to read his letter. No doubt overcome by the world crumbling around her, Agne never returns his letter during the novel, but it is clear that, although she and Joe are separated, there is a possibility for love and rebirth. It is no coincidence, then, that Zapata gives him the name of Mary's earthly husband in the Bible, despite his love for 999999, the "devil" with the Mark of the Beast from the Sea.[370] They learn from one another, since Joe's previous lover was a red-haired woman, a European ideal of beauty that he must challenge by considering black women an object of desire as well.[371]

Despite the prisons that confine them, Joe and Agne have the ability to create a new idiom through love. Here Paz's discourse on love is helpful. One cannot know what will become of this unity between Joe and Agne, but it will be something that removes the capital letters from the words "Black and White" that emerge only in the U.S. half of the novel, leading to a new language that itself is a form of Apocalypse: both revelation and rebirth. Unlike Saint John's vision, this is a "Kingdom of this World." It is a "New Jerusalem" where the "impure" yet creative live in peace and justice with one another.[372] Zapata's valuing of poetic language, silence, and faith is his own working through of lost Mother Africa. He is a Western subject trapped in the written world and the symbolic order. However, there is hope for a new mestizo world-family and thus a return of Mother Africa silenced by a purity based in violence. This implementation of the Nuevo Muntu is the narrative that unites the slave revolts of the past to the student activism of the "present" (1960s) and creates the possibility for the future.

Both Zapata's and Gonçalves's texts can be read as different forms of black feminism. Within these struggles, the intersectionality of race with gender is ever present. While Gonçalves's text is more nuanced and realist, Zapata idealizes his characters to show the way to a better future. Both are Nuevo Muntu texts because they unite the Americas in a history that gives visibility to the African diaspora without resorting to simplistic, essentialist ideologies. The diaspora changes according to its cultural context and is hybridized at every step.

Conclusion

The Nuevo Muntu Today and Tomorrow

The Nuevo Muntu model of diaspora, which links the Americas to understand the past of slavery and oppression toward black subjects, is highly relevant today. In the conclusion I discuss the legacy of Angela Davis as it relates to Manuel Zapata Olivella's novel and today's closest equivalent to slavery, mass incarceration and discriminatory policing. Ana Maria Gonçalves became an Afro-Brazilian activist because of her novel, and this role is evident in her monthly 2017 column for the liberal newspaper the *Intercept Brasil*. Finally, I invite the reader to look to the future as I relate the novels to Afrofuturism, an aesthetic closely tied to science fiction and fantasy that includes previously absent representations of the African diaspora in their futures, just as these novels represent these communities in the past.

El Putas, U.S.A.

Angela Davis, the only surviving character from *Changó* (though she is masked as Agne Brown), made her first visit to Colombia because of the violence the Pacific continues to suffer in 2010. In an *El Espectador* (*Spectator*) article, the reason for her being there becomes clear: "Her crusade today is for Afro-Colombians who have lived in the mines of northern Cauca since 1636. The state privatized ten thousand hectares since 2002 and now wants to evict them. The situation has turned violent: eight miners were killed in April and several community leaders have been threatened. There is an ongoing guardianship."[1] A large, enthusiastic crowd received her at the small mining town where she spoke, La Toma. Her discussant compared her current activism to her work as a young idealist in the mining town of Birmingham, Alabama. She criticizes international mining interests, and those are not all:

> But what interests me is not to bring the analysis of racism in the United States, but to study the relationship between the U.S. government and military and the Colombian government and military. For example, I am interested in seeing the ways that the United States is supporting the creation of a repressive apparatus in Colombia such as that of the U.S. prison-industrial complex. . . .
>
> What I call the prison-industrial complex allows us to see clearly how racism is used to generate profit. In fact, the relationship is evident here in this mining region, where the commercial mining interests promote a kind of racism that will produce huge profits. In the U.S., a good number of companies are involved in the development and continuous expansion of the prison system, in which 2.4 million people are confined. Of every 100 adults, one is behind bars.[2]

Her following quip sums up this reality's stark contrast to the fading euphoria of the first U.S. black president: "A black man in the White House does not compensate for a million blacks in the Big House." She also used the opportunity to criticize members of the Congressional Black Caucus that supported the radical expansion of the United States–Colombia Trade Agreement signed that year, which she feared would lead to further exploitations of Afro-Colombians. In response to questions about Colombian affirmative action, she challenged any form of affirmative action that did not bring substantial material and political change for minorities. In short, her Colombia visit can be seen as an example of how prophetic *Changó* was in its linking of black struggles in the United States with those of Latin America and emphasizing the role of prisons and capitalist expansion in the continuation of institutional racism.

Agne Brown / Angela Davis is still struggling to free blacks. In 2019, she condemned the assassination of Afro-Colombian activists in Cauca:

> Black social movements are being systematically targeted in Colombia in the aftermath of the 2016 Peace Accords. I have been informed that on May 4, four gunmen stormed into a building in Santander de Quilichao, in the Northern Cauca region of Colombia, opened fire, and tossed a grenade into a crowd of Afro-Colombian activists and two children. The gathering included leaders from several grassroots Afro-Colombian organizations, and they planned to discuss an upcoming meeting with the Colombian government. The attack occurred in a region of Colombia that I had the opportunity to visit in 2010. Among those targeted yesterday was activist Francia Marquez [*sic*], winner of the 2018 Goldman Prize, and someone with whom I have worked in solidarity for nearly a decade.[3]

Denouncing these brazen, unconscionable attacks is part of Davis's continued global struggle for justice.

It is not the only kind of violence the muntu is suffering. In the context of mass incarceration and state violence, legal scholar Michelle Alexander has argued that fighting for and celebrating affirmative action legislation could lead to distraction from urgent threats to African Americans. Prisons have expanded rapidly over the past fifty years, which disproportionately house Afro-descendants, particularly those from poor neighborhoods.[4] The Americas are witnessing the criminalization of poverty and the global expansion of the prison industry. For example, Brazil's prison population has exploded since 1993 as part of the U.S.-led expansion of neoliberalism and the war on drugs, as sociologist Loïc Wacquant has shown.[5] This coincided with the deindustrialization of Brazil, for example, and the evaporation of legal jobs for the urban poor. Following U.S. "get-tough" criminal policies, Brazil began implementing minimum sentencing for nonviolent offenders.

Alexander has directed the United States' attention to its prisons to show that it is a primary way of disenfranchising blacks. In the United States, many lose their right to vote, a primary victory of the Civil Rights struggle *Changó* depicts.[6] They lose the ability to attain legitimate employment. Even after release they lose the ability to legally live and work with others, which further diminishes the black solidarity the novel attributes to the muntu.[7] In these harsh conditions, recidivism is high and the cycle of poverty very difficult to overcome. Alexander argues that this is akin to Jim Crow policies designed to keep blacks under slave-like oppression.[8] If Jim Crow was "slavery by another name," then the "incarceration-industrialization complex," coined by Davis, is its latest moniker.[9] The complex generates huge amounts of money for a variety of entities, particularly large private corporations.[10] Often, one of the most basic elements of slavery, labor without pay, is part of this imprisonment as large international corporations receive cheap or free prison labor. Alexander argues that the expansion of prisons intensified with the war on drugs, begun by Richard Nixon.[11] Two of the political benefits of this war were the presentation of Nixon as "tough on crime" and appealing to anti-integrationists and other racists alienated by the Civil Rights Act of 1964.[12]

Alexander's most disturbing observation is that both political parties use this "tough on crime" rhetoric during campaigns and implement it through mandatory minimal sentencing.[13] Prosecutors often drive up prison sentences, the accused have no defense lawyers or very little contact with them, and they rarely see a judge or jury.[14] "Stop and frisk" policies and arrest quotas, applied disproportionately to black communities, constantly fuel this system with men, and increasingly women, to house.[15]

Few other texts have expressed this phenomenon's effects on the African diaspora in as broad a context as *Changó*. Agne Brown's imprisonment for prostitution is the contemporary manifestation of centuries of captivity. Her sentence allows her to meet Malcolm X, who discovered Islam in prison, a recruiting ground for black Muslims. Her sentence allows her a new commonality with working-class Joe.[16] Prison equalizes her with the prostitutes to whom she ministers through the Cult of Shadows.[17] Her unjust sentence inspires activists to challenge the system. For Joe, it is a badge of honor, since he is arrested for singing songs of protest during peaceful demonstrations against the war in Vietnam.[18] The imprisonment of the present carries echoes of the sentences of the past: José Prudencio Padilla's imprisonment by the treasonous Simón Bolívar, Toussaint L'Ouverture's imprisonment by the lying Napoleon, and the Inquisition's incarceration of Domingo Falupo.

Colombianist Fernando Esquivel-Suárez has shown that the war on drugs has created a "Global Color Line" that I believe parallels the one Du Bois feared at the beginning of the twentieth century.[19] Communities of color are being disproportionately policed, jailed, and killed throughout the Americas. He shows that Buenavista, a largely black Colombian city, epitomizes the deleterious effects of the military-prison-industrial complex on marginalized communities.[20] Despite generating 60 percent of the country's trade,

64 percent of the city is unemployed, which fuels drug syndicates (2 percent). The militarization and paramilitarization of the region since 2008 has produced a spike in murders but no decrease in drugs. Afro-Colombians have been displaced from their ancestral homes to develop port infrastructure. Like the leaders of *Changó*, some of their leaders' struggle against the expansion of capitalism, militarism, and imprisonment has ended in violent death.

Colombia's 1991 constitution and Law 70 (1993), which are designed to protect Afro-Colombian rights, seem to have done woefully little to improve the lives of blacks on the Pacific coast. They did not save the town of Bojayá from suffering a tragic massacre of innocent Afro-Colombians on May 2, 2002.[21] At the Church of Bellavista, an explosion of gas cylinders killed 79 people (48 of them minors), injured 167, and displaced 5,771.[22] The Revolutionary Armed Forces of Colombia (FARC) committed this mass murder in a war with the Bloque Elmer Cárdenas paramilitary. The Pacific coast of Colombia, where Bojayá is located, does not play a major role in *Changó*. However, it is the setting of Zapata's follow-up novel, *El fusilamiento del Diablo* (*Devil's Execution*, 1999).[23]

Gonçalves's novel treats arrest and imprisonment differently, but they are ever present. The most prominent prison in the novel that is alufá Licutan, a leader of the Malês. His incarceration threatens the conspiracy. Among the primary goals of the revolt is to free him.[24] The imprisonment of the low-level conspirators of the revolt is a primary reason Kehinde leaves Bahia after the uprising fails. She herself is arrested and jailed after the Cemiterada Revolt of 1836 in Salvador, but she escapes.[25] Stringent laws limiting the movement and activities of black Bahians implemented after the revolt.[26] In some ways these activities paralleled Jim Crow vagrancy regulations implemented after U.S. abolition. Naturally, the law and its application are central to manumission in the novel, making slavery part of the genealogy of the colonial and, implicitly, the contemporary prison. Alberto can sell Luís into slavery because the legal system is on his side. The sinhá can change the price and ignore requests for Kehinde and other slaves' manumission.

William Luis has asked, what would Manuel Zapata Olivella say had he lived past 2004 to see the election of the first U.S. black president, Barack Obama, in 2008?[27] What would he say about President Donald Trump? I would argue that he would continue *Changó* along the lines of Alexander's haunting arguments: despite the victories of the Civil Rights Act, including universal enfranchisement and affirmative action policies, blacks remain the target of an unjust social system that makes money by disenfranchising them.

Trump has proven to be a useful monstrosity that serves the rich, the racists, the militaristics, and certain Christians. His rhetoric has divided the United States into "Americans" (white Anglo citizens) and "sons of bitches," a term he used for professional football player Colin Kaepernick in a speech while Puerto Rico lay in ruins after Hurricane Maria. The football player was protesting police killings of unarmed blacks. Trump's intensification and celebration of Obama's incarceration and deportation infrastructure has shown that the White Wolf of imprisonment and destruction continues to assail the Americas, affecting the descendants of the Central American mothers who nourished the baby muntu in colonial times.

Trump's distorted orange mask embodies the ugliness of U.S. racism and coloniality, but Changó is beautiful. His curse is a challenge. The more oppressive the White Wolf gets, the more revolutionary and creative the muntu must become in order to implement a Nuevo Muntu, a united, just, and beautiful American continent that is deeply culturally tied to Africa.

Nuevo Muntu History and Gonçalves's Journalism

If *Changó*'s struggle for utopia pushes us onward in the daily struggle against the White Wolf, then Ana Maria Gonçalves and her novel show us how she is fighting it in the United States and Brazil. While her novel is not limited to a classic revolutionary project—her protagonist is both oppressed and oppressor—its publication is what made the author an Afro-Brazilian activist. Her most partisan political work is a play called *"Tchau, querida!"* (*"Bye, hon!"*), which depicts the impeachment of the liberal Workers Party candidate Dilma Rousseff.[28] She gained a new sense of black pride in New Orleans, where she lived for eight years.[29] She traveled the country educating audiences about Brazilian slavery and its echoes in today's racism. Her columns continue the activism her novel began.

On February 27, 2015, she wrote an open letter to Rui Costa, governor of Bahia, regarding continued racism in Brazil and drawing on the history of slavery to do so. She denounces police violence against blacks in Bahia by focusing on the governor's donning, during a photo op, of an Ilê Aiê shirt that honors Jamaican maroons. It displays heroes from the 1865 Morant Bay

Rebellion, which the British colonial government brutally suppressed. She uses black history to inform her activist stance:

> "Capital baiana onde vive o maior número de negros da América Latina." Palavras suas, governador, que só fazem sentido se vierem acompanhadas do respeito à NOSSA história. E se o senhor acha que a história do povo negro da Jamaica não lhe diz respeito, tomemos então a história dos negros da Bahia. . . . "A história se repete, a primeira vez como tragédia e a segunda como farsa." História que vai continuar se repetindo, se não prestarmos atenção a ela. E com maior intensidade a cada geração que a herda, porque ações e atitudes que tentam apenas mascará-la são construídas sobre escombros cada vez mais frágeis e contestáveis, exatamente porque ela, a História, se acumula e ganha peso.[30]
>
> ("Capital of Bahia where the largest number of blacks live in Latin America." Your words, governor, that only make sense when accompanied by OUR history. And if you think that the history of black people in Jamaica has nothing to do with it, let us take the history of blacks in Bahia. . . . "History repeats itself, first as a tragedy and again as a farce." History will continue repeating itself if we pay no attention to it. And with greater intensity with each generation that inherits it, because actions and attitudes that merely try to cover it up are built on the evermore fragile rubble, and questionable exactly because History accumulates and weighs heavier.)

Gonçalves sees Jamaican and Bahian struggles, nineteenth-century and twenty-first-century struggles as part of a whole. She also notes the need for a clear vision of black history that myths of racial harmony or national exceptionalism do not whitewash.

She associates Queen Nanny of the Maroons with the aforementioned Zeferina, leader of the Quilombo do Urubu (Buzzard Quilombo). Citing Silvia Maria Silva Barbosa, she claims that the queen was reborn from her own ashes, despite being executed in an 1826 revolt. She grants "subversive memory" to every act of protest in the poor black neighborhood of Cabula, as the site of Urubu is called today. Gonçalves believes that due to the criminalization of poverty in the region, the mere survival of Cabula is a rebellion akin to those of the quilombo. She links Cabula to Malês. The police in the region began with slave crackdowns and continue to oppress blacks. White fear of Black Power in a majority black area has always supported them. This context was missing from the discussion of the Military

Police's murder of twelve black residents of Cabula as vengeance for an officer being shot in the foot during a confrontation with drug traffickers. During the murder the police shot eighty-eight times at the victims, some of whom survived. She argues that the current war on drugs is just the latest justification for white elite fear and oppression of black people, dating back to the times of Zeferina and the Malês. Today the quilombos of the past are called *favelas* (slums). As in *Changó*, the law serves only some whites in Cabula, not blacks:

> Um dos produtos mais insidiosos da criminalização da pobreza é a desqualificação jurídica do pobre e do negro (ele não precisa ser tratado como inocente até que se prove o contrário, porque sua cor e sua condição social são tidas como justificativas suficientes para sua condenação), fazendo com que sua palavra não tenha o mesmo peso da palavra que, sem provas, muitas vezes o condena.[31]
>
> (One of the most insidious results of the criminalization of poverty is the legal disqualification of the poor and the black (they do not need to be treated as innocent until proven guilty, because their color and their socioeconomic status are considered justification enough for their sentencing), making their word not have the same weight as the word that, often without proof, condemns them.)

She shows that this not only discredits the law and the state but also dehumanizes blacks to quell the fears of the elite, the "right humans," instead of "human rights." She notes that white children are frequently apprehended with drugs and turned over to their families, while black children enter the criminal justices system. She is describing the New Jim Crow in Brazil. She compares it to the use of black soldiers in the Paraguay War (1864) as cannon fodder by the state. Likewise, the Military Police continue to kill and incarcerate arbitrarily and with impunity. She proposes as an alternative the end of the Military Police, the decriminalization of drugs, the dismantling of the prison-industrial complex, and the revitalization of police training to end the police's role as twenty-first-century slave catchers and the poor's role as twenty-first-century maroons. In fact, she argues for retraining modeled on Colombia's Cultura Ciudadana y Policía Ciudadana programs, which integrate police, former criminals, and the rest of the citizenry. Her concerns are national but her solutions are transnational. A step in this direction is Bahia's Reaja ou será morta! Reaja ou será morto! (React or You Will Be

Killed!), begun in 2005 to combat black genocide carried out by the police. The U.S. reader will note parallels with Black Lives Matter.

Gonçalves became a columnist for the *Intercept Brasil* during 2017. Famed editor Glenn Greenwald welcomed her with the following statement regarding her bilingual columns: "What makes Gonçalves's journalism particularly valuable for *The Intercept* is that it simultaneously examines the unique political and cultural manifestations of race in Brazil while also illuminating the most relevant debates that are unfolding today in the U.S."[32] She links the Americas like the Nuevo Muntu. She shows how white Brazilians do not want to accept their racism (not unlike white "Americans").

Her December 2, 2016, article on the "bem intencionados" (well-intentioned white people) begins with the contemporary case of a U.S. black mother and daughter listening to Tupac Shakur while parked at a grocery store.[33] A white woman asked them to move their car so that she could unload her groceries, but the mother refused since she felt the woman had plenty of space. The white woman's response was "I marched for you people!" This contemporary fragmentation and even reversal of the muntu that marched on Washington in *Changó* leads Gonçalves to reflect on the history of well-intentioned but unrelentingly racist whites. The columnist notes that the unfortunately named Alma White (Alma means "soul" in Portuguese) was a U.S. feminist pioneer born in 1862, the first female bishop in the United States. On the other hand, she was also a Ku Klux Klan supporter. Both White and the woman of the parking lot are presented as individuals who expect eternal gratitude for their progress while remaining contradictory and racist.

"Falta empatia para entender a revolta dos negros" (You Need More Empathy to Understand Black Revolt)" analyzes the film on the 1831 Nat Turner Rebellion by Nate Parker, *The Birth of a Nation* (2017), and ties it to the #MeToo Movement with a unique perspective.[34] Allegations that Parker, who plays Turner in the film, was accused of rape in 1999, scandalized audiences. Gonçalves points out that like the victims of rape and sexual assault whose pain and stories are not heard, there are black pain and stories that have gone unheard. Furthermore, movie reviews that criticize the film as too violent do not provide enough historical context. They merely display white privilege and ignorance of black history in her view. Evoking Luís Gama, she considers Turner's bloody uprising "legítima defesa" (self-defense) and that, had the critic in question read the historical account of the abuses Turner suffered, he would not criticize the film as "novelesco" (exaggerated).

The historical record is itself bloody, a violence implicit in the title, which alludes to David Griffith's Ku Klux Klan propaganda film of 1915. She continues Zapata's chronicling of Turner's uprising.

On February 8, 2017, Gonçalves reported on the Brazilian navy's sieges on the twenty-first-century Quilombo Rio dos Macacos (Monkey River Quilombo), part of centuries of similar oppressive acts by the country's military.[35] Descended from captives, they remained on the land after abolition, including after the navy's illegal appropriation of the land in the 1950s and 1960s. That force is now denying them access to the river. The *quilombolas* (quilombo dwellers) cannot access the school, and they must wear a badge that states "invasor" (invader/squatter) in order to access the Military Village on the land where their families lived for generations. The navy responded to Gonçalves with a letter stating that their actions were legal and amply documented. The military's defense is that it has a right to remove the quilombolas since the land is theirs, but they have allowed them to stay. They claim the military will provide the community running water, but Gonçalves's report from the quilombolas relays suspicion. The struggle for land rights continues in Brazil in terms that recall preabolition times.

Her March 22 installment dialogues with sociologist Vera Malaguti Batista on negrophobia in Brazil.[36] Batista argues that black people, since before their enslavement, embody white fear. Immediately after independence in 1822, elites feared slave uprising, which led directly to the formation of the military police. Like Zapata, she ties these battles to contemporary protests: "Estava, oficialmente, instaurada a despolitização das manifestações contra o regime escravocrata e a criminalização dos rebeldes, da mesma maneira que acontece hoje com os movimentos sociais" (Protests against the slaveocrat regime were officially depoliticized and the rebels criminalized, in the same way that occurs today with social movements.) She notes that liberated and enslaved Africans were denied free movement. Today she sees the suspension of due process regarding poor black people as a Lombrosian extreme of "guilty until proven innocent" due to fear and binary logic. Like Lombroso, Osmar Serraglio, minister of justice, claims he cannot allow unchanging (poor, black) "bandidos" to roam the streets. Thus, she ties slavery to today's racism and judicial systems like Zapata and Alexander.

In her April 5 article she reports on the representation of black suffering and black death. In a polemic simulacrum, the body of fourteen-year-old black lynching victim Emmett Till in Mississippi became the subject of numerous representations. His mother had his deformed body photographed and the images sent to *Jet* magazine, which then had an all-black readership. Painter Dana Schutz re-created the image as an abstract work on canvas, which was displayed in the Whitney Museum in New York. Its audience is majority white. In response, artist Parker Bright created a performance by standing in front of the painting, using his live black body, brandishing a shirt that says "black death spectacle—no lynching." Gonçalves notes that some whites cannot handle the suffering of black bodies due to slavery and its aftermath. For her, abstract art by a white painter for a mostly white audience masks Till's mutilated corpse. The columnist ties it to the smiling, apparently "pain-free," as a television journalist commented, representation of slavery by the Vila Isabel during the 2017 Carnival competition of *samba enredos* in Rio de Janeiro.

The April 20 issue expresses discontent with Luislinda Valois's public declaration that the conservative president Michel Temer of Brazil is the "padrinho das mulheres negras" (godfather of black women or advocate of black women). History serves to vindicate Valois as an individual but to condemn the system that was founded on systematic racism. Public education in Brazil was founded by eugenicists. They followed Cesare Lombroso in seeing blacks as incapable of learning, and so an educational environment was invented to prove these theories. Among those professors who saw black women as good only to be cooks was one that infuriated the young Valois to the point that she became a lawyer and actually argued the first successful case against racial discrimination in Brazil in 1993. She rose to be minister of human rights, but as part of the political system, it seems the educational "vengeance" of this self-proclaimed granddaughter of slaves has come to naught. By praising Temer, she is commending the state structures that continue to oppress black women. Like her treatment of Kehinde, the slave who enslaved, Gonçalves seems fair but unsparing.

The May 3 issue criticizes a meeting of intellectuals and activists of the establishment left of Brazil attended by 217 representatives, all but 2 white. The overwhelming majority were white men. The meeting was held in a room at the University of São Paulo. There, journalist Eleonora de Lucena claimed, Brazilians of "all colors" wrote into law the abolition of slavery. Gonçalves counters that the USP barred abolitionist Luís Gama from admission for being black. She also notes that slave revolts, like the ones described in her book, were a source of black self-liberation that did not even cross the mind of the speaker. Gama's absence is part of a generalized absence of black awareness in Brazilian academia.

The May 31 installment connected what she and other Afro-Brazilian thinkers perceived as a need for a break with the Western Canon, which they call "cânone branco" (white canon), and black art inspired by black lived experience.[37] She found a model for this in the Netflix series *Dear White People* (2017–2018), which is about black students at an elite U.S. university. The U.S. youths' trivia game, won by a black man who brags that he knows his own culture and what is considered "general knowledge," reminds her of Brazil's 2003 law that requires teaching black history. The need for such a law reaffirms the ignorance of Afro-Brazilian culture. She agrees with the students' assessment of Quentin Tarantino's polemic spaghetti western *Django Unchained* (2012), in which a black outlaw ousts a plantation owner and his thugs to save his enslaved lover. One of the students complains that Tarantino apparently thinks that just because he has the black protagonist kill racists, he himself can use racist stereotypes. She compares the "white savior" played by Brad Pitt in the film *Twelve Years a Slave* (2013) to today's well-intentioned, paternalistic "allies" of black people, a complaint she shares with characters from *Dear White People*. Thus, her column sheds light on how she interprets filmic historical fiction about slavery with many parallels to her own work. Finally, she laments Brazil's creation of an all-white screenwriter's union, which she doubts is capable of representing Afro-Brazilians in as nuanced a manner as *Netflix*.

In "Longe de Charlottesville, São Paulo também celebra 'o lado errado da história'" (Far from Charlottesville, São Paulo also celebrates the "wrong side of history"), Gonçalves explains who Robert E. Lee was to a Brazilian public.[38] She explains that the slaughter of nine black churchgoers in the name of white supremacy led to the removal of some Confederate monuments in 2015. She notes that the state of São Paulo, for the past thirty years, has sponsored the annual "Festa Confederada" (Confederate Festival) in Santa Bárbara D'Oeste, founded by slaveocrat clergyman Ballard S. Dunn. It is organized by the descendants of Confederates who fled the United States to run slave-based plantations in Brazil between the Civil War and its aftermath in the 1860s and the South American nation's ultimate abolition of slavery in 1888. She argues that Brazilian immigration law was, from before that time until 1945, an overt whitening project. Emperor Dom Primeiro II encouraged Dunn's mission to establish cities like Santa Bárbara D'Oeste and Americana, which brandished a Confederate battle flag on its city seal until 1998. Unlike the Charlottesville racists, however, Americana condemned the murders in Charleston and the murder of a protester in

Charlottesville. They also argue that, since arriving in Brazil, they have integrated. However, they wrongly claim Lee did not own slaves and thus should not be associated with white hate groups. Gonçalves cites correspondence from Lee stating that God condemned blacks to slavery in order for them to be civilized by whites. She further argues that the 2017 protestors fighting to keep the statue in place hold the same views as Trump. Gonçalves respects honoring one's ancestors, but she refutes misinformation that only supports racism.

She reviewed the Brazilian film on slavery *Vazante* (2017) by Daniela Thomas. The critic argues that—unlike in her own novel—"no filme, a escravidão vira mera moldura, plano de fundo, com personagens negros sem voz, sem nome, sem profundidade, sem desenvolvimento, servindo de escadas para os personagens brancos" (in the film, slavery becomes a mere frame, a background, with voiceless black characters, nameless, with no depth, no development, serving as ladders for white characters).[39] Gonçalves's 2020 miniseries of *Um defeito de cor* will likely contribute to undoing these symbolic injustices.[40]

Defeito marks the beginning of her work as a commentator on the memory of slavery. She blames the director's mistakes, or at least her limited point of view on what Robin DiAngelo calls "white fragility":

> Nesse estado, a mínima quantidade de estresse se torna intolerável, provocando uma série de atitudes defensivas, que incluem demonstrações de raiva, medo e culpa, e comportamentos como silenciamento e afastamento da situação que causou o estresse. Isto funciona para restabelecer o equilíbrio racial branco que, por sua vez, pode levar a um isolamento e uma proteção ainda maiores, que voltam a provocar o estresse quando acontece um novo confronto com o tema. Ou seja, um ciclo vicioso que impossibilita o diálogo aberto e honesto e mantém o status quo.[41]
>
> (In this state, the least cause of stress becomes intolerable, provoking a variety of defense mechanisms, which include demonstrations of anger, fear, and guilt, and behavior like the silencing and avoidance of the situation that caused the stress. This functions to reestablish the white racial equilibrium that, in turn, can lead to even greater isolation and protection, which once again cause stress when another confrontation with the issue occurs. In other words, a vicious cycle that makes open and honest dialogue impossible and maintains the status quo.)

She ties the film's emphasis on white characters' agency and point of view to today's politics in Brazil and the United States. Much like the United States, which the Trump presidency has forced to confront its racism (though many deny racism had anything to do with Trump, confirming their white fragility), Brazil is facing down its own denied racism because of the discourse surrounding Afro-descent. Today, "Tropical Trump" Bolsonaro has made racism more open.

Gonçalves published a poem by Afrocentric thinker, novelist, and musician Nei Lopes in her column defending the use of African-inspired turbans in Brazil. The work is dedicated to the playwright and senator Abdias Nascimento. It is called "Brechtiana," alluding to the world-famous radical playwright. While it repeats Asante's mistake of homogenizing Egyptians with Yoruba peoples, it continues the project begun with *Defeito*'s dialogue with other texts:

> E escreveram a História ao seu modo.
> Chamando nações de "tribos"
> Reis de "régulos"
> Línguas de "dialetos."[42]
>
> (And they wrote history in their way.
> Calling nations "tribes"
> Kings "kinglets"
> Languages "dialects.")

Gonçalves and Lopes continue to criticize representations of history that demean blacks and reinforce Eurocentrism.[43]

Gonçalves added a note of suspicion to the January 2017 Women's March on Washington to protest the U.S. president recorded bragging about being able to "grab 'em by the pussy," referring to any woman he wants.[44] Thousands of white women marched, but one marcher, a man, wore not a pink "pussy hat" but a Brazilian African-inspired turban. On it was written, "I will see all you cool women at the next #BlackLivesMatter march, right?" Again, Gonçalves perceives U.S. and Latin American struggles for justice as intimately linked.

Writer Eliane Brum quoted the article extensively in the Spanish newspaper *El Pais* (*The Nation*).[45] The Twitter War inspired Gonçalves's reflections on black history as a way to decide if white women should wear

African-inspired turbans in Brazil. Brum is white. She argues that Gonçalves's account of the symbol of black womanhood and centuries of struggle, threatened by the commercialization of anything considered exotic in Brazil, is the reason a white woman dressed as a black woman is offensive.

Again in 2017 Gonçalves takes on identity and literature. She criticizes the recent conservative appropriation of the term "meritocracy," which originated in 1958 Britain to criticize the tracking of rich and poor children in schools into privileged education and low-skilled labor, respectively. She sees a similar tracking at Brazil's largest and most prestigious annual literary festival, the Festa Literária Internacional de Paraty (FLIP):

> A *FLIP 2017* nos trouxe muito a pensar nesse sentido. Pela primeira vez em suas 15 edições, o número de mulheres convidadas se equiparou ao dos homens. Nestes quinze anos, mulheres compuseram apenas 1/4 do elenco de convidados principais. . . . Também pela primeira vez, escritoras e escritores negras/os representaram 30% dos convidados, provavelmente atingindo um número que não deve ficar muito longe do que representaram em todos os outros anos juntos. Será que, com esta composição, foi a FLIP da falta de mérito?[46]

> (*FLIP 2017* gave us a lot to think about in that sense. For the first time in its fifteen years, the number of women invited was equal to men. In these fifteen years, women composed one in four of the main guests. . . . Also for the first time, black writers represent 30 percent of the guests, likely attaining a number not far from all the previous years combined. Could it be that, with this composition, did FLIP lack merit?)

Her answer is that, if otherwise marginalized groups have the opportunity to present their work, their merit will be noticed. She praised professor Diva Guimarães's keynote on black mothers. Gonçalves has begun work with Maria Valéria Resende on a women's literature festival called the Mulherio das Letras, designed to diversify Brazilian literature.

Finally, in "A aula de racismo e machismo" (The Class on Racism and Sexism), Gonçalves debates the secretary of education of Rio de Janeiro César Benjamin, who mocked a black actress, Taís Araújo, for claiming that people avoid her and her seven-year-old son on the street due to the color of their skin.[47] He responds that the claim of racism is an "idiocie racial" (racial stupidity) in Brazil. He has the audacity to say the internet would leave him "linchado" (lynched) for his opinion. He blames the Ford Foundation, which he considers an arm of the U.S. Department of State, for "implanting" claims of racism in the 1990s. But Gonçalves, due to her inter-American approach to diaspora studies, notes that U.S. scholars often denied that racism could exist in the racially hybrid Brazil until African American and Afro-Brazilian writers challenged this hegemony, as exemplified in David Hellwig's *African-American Reflections on Brazil's Racial Paradise* (1992). It took precursors to Araújo, such as Brazilian Afonso Arinos and African American Katherine Dunham, to challenge racism in Brazil through the law—decades before the time he describes. Unfortunately, white men who consider speaking out against racism to be unpatriotic still govern. Gonçalves's novel, journalism, and activism fight the myth of racial democracy and use history to inform the debates regarding racism in her country and the United States.

If *Defeito* uses a realist aesthetic that presents a protagonist that sometimes challenges the status quo, the novelist's career afterward has presented a more radical turn. Her column criticizes racism and sexism in Brazil and the United States. Clearly, Gonçalves's novel on Brazil's past marks a major turning point in her turn to discussing current issues regarding racism and the African diaspora in her country, the United States, and other areas of the America. Now let us turn from current affairs to the future to see how Nuevo Muntu novels fit into the recent tradition of Afrofuturism.

Afrofuturism

While many thinkers in Latin America have newly focused on defining the Afro-descendants of the present, scholars in the United States have focused on the future of the diaspora in what has been called "Afrofuturism." Paul Gilroy, who inspired me to challenge his diaspora model, is considered by critics David DeIuliis and Jeff Lohr to be a "proto-Afrofuturist."[48] This aesthetic has grown to become an inter-American phenomenon, like the Nuevo Muntu itself, which can be seen as a less U.S.-focused variant. Afrofuturism has spawned other minority "futurisms," which I also discuss, since Zapata and Gonçalves have had ample contact with the United States, giving them commonalities with "Latin@futurisms."

The most reductive definition of Afrofuturism is "black science fiction and its critics." The best-known example worldwide is Marvel's film *Black Panther* (2018), based on the first mainstream black comic book character, who debuted in 1966.[49] While the aesthetic is focused on technology and the future, its critics often look back to its patriarchs, musicians Sun Ra and George Clinton, and today to its queens Grace Jones and Janelle Monáe. The term came about in 1993 when Mark Dery, Greg Tate, Tricia Rose, and Samuel Delaney sought to answer why there appeared to be no black-written science fiction, and disturbingly, most speculative fiction presented all-white or nearly all-white futures.[50] Dery developed the interview into an edited volume, *Flame Wars*, the following year.[51] Already in the 1950s Sun Ra was performing jazz during the space race. He adopted the persona of an extraterrestrial Egyptian god.[52] He performed under this persona until his death in 1993. Clinton's science-fiction persona, Dr. Funkenstein often emerged from the Mother Ship during performances from the 1970s to 2019. The most influential literary author of this aesthetic is Octavia Butler, whose novel *Kindred* (1979) reimagines the slave narrative genre through time travel.[53] Her African American protagonist Dana travels from her present in 1976 California to an antebellum plantation in Maryland where she sees how her ancestors lived under slavery. Nonetheless, the genre exists avant la lettre in William Edward Burghardt Du Bois's story "The Comet" (1920), in which a black man and a white woman appear at first to be the only people on earth, a shocking tale for the time.[54] It is understudied in Spanish America, a gap in scholarship that Reynaldo Anderson and Yajaira de la Espada address in a forthcoming edited volume.[55] The style has enjoyed more popularity in Brazil, as exemplified by the 2006 issue of *Rizoma* dedicated to the topic, as I will show. Latinx critics have noticed "Latin@futurism" or, more often, "Chicanafuturism" since Catherine S. Ramírez used the term in 2004, based on Afrofuturism.[56]

Afrofuturism's focus on technology has led to theorizations of Afrofuturism 2.0 and even 3.0. In their volume *Afrofuturism 2.0: The Rise of Astro-Blackness* (2016), Anderson and Charles Jones define the 2.0 version as the interdisciplinary, multimedia reaction to the rise of social media in the mid-2000s, gender fluidity, and pan-Africanism (what I would call inter-Americanism).[57] It includes African religious beliefs like the Nigerian Ifa as well as Western science, though I notice it less than in Latin American works.[58] Nettrice Gaskins even argues that there is an Afrofuturism 3.0 through augmented space, in which virtual reality alters how one sees the surrounding area.[59] Gaskins compares this to the conductors on the Underground Railroad who used symbols on quilts as maps to guide fugitives to safety in the abolitionist North. His description of how black people have imagined space uniquely (vernacular cartography) since slavery has parallels with Nuevo Muntu cosmopolitan cartography.

Changó is not science fiction, but it has Afrofuturist elements. Zapata called his aesthetic "mythological realism" because it relies so heavily on African myths.[60] Sun Ra speaks of a "Myth Science" with parallels to Zapata's thinking, which is not based in a positivistic search for truth.[61] It is, however, an aesthetic that reveals the narrative construction of writing both history and future utopias. The reader sees something similar to Ra's heliocentric (and narcissistic) imagining of himself as a sun god in a heliocentric universe in the novel's repeated allusions to "Changó-Sol."[62] The Yoruba king is the governing deity of the epopee and the archetype of the first of many great black people, but he is not traditionally god of the sun. He is the center of a new universe in the novel—the Nuevo Muntu.

As in *Kindred*, there is time travel in Changó, but it is not technology that permits it but the Ancestors themselves. Agne has the ability to summon them and communicate with them. That is how she meets Zaka, her forebear who rejects slavery and joins the indigenous.[63] Aleijadinho recalls his lost mother, and Ngafúa is the narrator who opens the novel by telling the reader of his African ancestors.[64] For this reason, the novel has a preface that tells the readers they are climbing aboard a slave ship—the narrative itself is a unique kind of time travel that was previously unknown for most.

One of the injustices Afrofuturism symbolically corrects is the exclusion of black people from access to technology. In addition to a dearth of Afro-descendant characters in the space ships of science fiction, there continues to be a racialized digital divide regarding access to the latest technology. This lack of access can be traced back to slavery. Throughout the Americas, to be enslaved was to be illiterate. Writing was an extremely difficult power to attain, as Juan Francisco Manzano's biography shows.[65] Slavery is a prime example of Walter Ong's assertion that writing is a form of technology that radically alters how one thinks and communicates.[66] In *Changó*, when heretic priest Domingo Falupo is imprisoned by the Inquisition, he uses his Catholic education to rebel against the Church, writing a letter to the pope in defense of African religions.[67] Ultimately, Agne Brown, with her higher education, uses that technology alongside the knowledge of her ancestors to bring forth the beginnings of the Nuevo Muntu.[68] Her working-class lover, Joe, recalls the oral tradition. He communicates with her using field hollers and earns a living playing the banjo, an instrument with African roots and displaying the alternative technologies the enslaved used in the absence of literacy.[69] As historian James Sweet shows in his analysis of Brazilian *bolsas de mandinga*—a curiously absent practice in *Defeito*—illiterate non-Muslim and even non-Christian blacks would keep bags as talismans with hair, teeth, and slips of sacred writing from these faiths.[70] The paper was seen as being able literally "to speak," and the magic voices surely came from either the powerful gods of the enslavers or, more likely, their own powerful deceased ancestors.[71] Writing history in a way that puts Africans and their myths at the center and looks forward to a racially integrated future in the Americas is a use of technology that was long denied to the enslaved and often coveted.

Scholar tobias c. van Veen considers Afrofuturism a form of "chronopolitics," or politics of reimagining the past, present, and future. It uses the past and present as a means to alter how the future is imagined. "Chronopolitics is the temporal production of countermemories and counterrealities to combat corporate, whitewashed, or technocapitalist futures of dystopia."[72] The oppressive forces of our time shape not only how history is recorded but also how the future is imagined. *Changó* intervenes in this process in a time when black history as a field of study was almost nonexistent in Colombia and inchoate in the United States. What is more, he reimagines the cosmic race in a way that places black people at the center. Hence, he rejects what Ra calls the "manufactured history" that confines black people to passive entities in history.

Zapata reflects on his vision for the future in *Changó* and *¡Levántate!* in a 2001 interview with Margarita Krakusin. He admits he was inspired by Vasconcelos but notes that the Mexican's "cosmic race" of the future excluded blacks and Amerindians as "savages."[73] He traces the human drive for discovery from the first inhabitants of the Americas to the conquistadors to those exploring space and the origins of the universe.[74] He views revising and writing black history as part of this exploration, since humanity emerged in Africa.[75] He believes the United States will be a leader both in exploration and in peace due to its technology, which must be turned from economic exploitation to the public good.[76] He foresees the overcoming of racism and warfare:

> Después de estos periodos sangrientos y dolorosos [of oppression] siempre han venido periodos de nuevas auroras, de reconciliación humana, criterios humanísticos, criterios de renacimiento, de bienestar, de compartir el planeta

> amigablemente; y esos son los ideales, y son los sueños que a mí me impulsan a escribir y a mirar siempre adelante.[77]
>
> (After these bloody, painful periods [of oppression] there have always been times of new dawns, human reconciliation, humanistic criteria, criteria of rebirth, of well-being, of sharing the planet amicably; and these are the ideals, and they are the dreams that drive me to write and always look forward.)

He believes humanity must work together to avoid a nuclear holocaust, expressing his realist perspicaciousness as well as his deep optimism for a future determined by Afro-descendants alongside the rest of humanity.[78] His concern for sharing resources may help stave off even worse destruction at the hands of global warming. Zapata includes African Americans and the diaspora in his vision of struggle for an egalitarian future. His idealism and eloquence reflect his U.S. college audience in the interview, but there are also popular voices that would come after Zapata.

Partly inspired by Gilroy, van Veen builds his theory on 1980s and 1990s socially conscious rappers Public Enemy's assertion that "Armageddon been in effect."[79] As I showed in chapter 4, the Apocalypse is a biblical construct that Zapata refashions through Yoruba and Bantu myth to call for a radical overthrow of the systems that oppress blacks and others today. However, for van Veen, "Armageddon commences with Africans abducted by aliens to a strange land; everything that follows is played out in a post-apocalyptic dystopia."[80] This interpretation of history begs the question: were there two apocalypses? If Agne Brown is the whore of the Apocalypse who unites the ancestors and the Orishas to fight off the White Devil in the 1960s and 1970s, is she not simply personifying Ezili, the sensual slaver from Mali who sells her African brethren into servitude? It would explain their names: while Agne is the personification of mother goddess Yemayá, Ezili is the loose Dahomean equivalent. Both of these mothers herald a new world order.

Afrofuturist Jimi Hendrix said it better: "I won't see you no more in this world. / I'll catch you on the next one / now, don't be late."[81] Blacks have been in battle since their enslavement—one must not forget that Armageddon is the struggle at the end of the world, and blacks struggle throughout the novel for their freedom. Hence, Agne heralds a new struggle that is only beginning as the ancestors and orishas appear and implore the reader to action.

Hendrix, whom van Veen considers an "Afronaught," combines the tradition of blues music with the technology of psychedelia.[82] His call for a new world could be one based on a Christian notion of Jubilee as well as a trip to another planet by space travel, acid trip, or music. While Zapata did well to recover the African roots of the banjo, he was mistaken to overlook Hendrix's experiments, which pushed the technology of the electric guitar to its limits. Gilroy considered him an example of the Black Atlantic in Europe, but he confines him to the role of modern-day minstrel.[83] He, and likely Zapata, sees him as a whitened performer, which pushed him away from the black community. Does not his avant-garde music and mixed-race, cosmopolitan persona embody the ideals of a Nuevo Muntu? Was his death in 1970 not also a great loss to the creative future of a new humanity that simultaneously placed him among the ancestors? His wild stage presence and hypersexualized persona, Gilroy notes, is Changó in the flesh.[84] He is even famous for having an androgynous aesthetic, what with his scarves and bright colors, so Zapata should have memorialized him.[85] His flaming guitar could easily be seen as Changó's fire. It is likely that Zapata is alluding to Harlem Renaissance author Claude McKay's novel *The Banjo* (1957, first published 1929) about blacks in Paris, but the contemporary reader is unlikely to know that information. The banjo, despite its African origins, has become a whitened instrument. Prior to the Civil War, it was associated only with the enslaved and minstrels; afterward it became a parlor instrument for women.[86] What Hendrix did with the guitar, as in "Machine Gun" and his Woodstock rendition of the national anthem, much better embodied the antiwar spirit and generalized crisis of the United States in the late 1960s. Zapata may have also been drawing on the U.S. protest music of Pete Seeger, who played the banjo and popularized "We Shall Overcome," the anthem of the Civil Rights Movement.[87] However, he ignores the ubiquitous great black music of the late 1960s, including the obvious counterpoint. James Brown, a veteran of the segregated Chitlin' Circuit and common soundbite in early hip-hop, could have been the popular, unapologetically black equivalent to the more "whitened" and alienated Hendrix. The latter played to "his people" in Harlem, the mecca of *Changó*, and was jeered by an all-black audience immediately after playing Woodstock.[88] At the Temple of Shadows, Agne Brown could have united Hendrix with James Brown—and John Brown—to create a truly revolutionary, futuristic aesthetic for the Nuevo Muntu. Nonetheless, Zapata was prescient regarding music's role in social movements.

African American music would change after *Changó*'s final setting, but fighting racism would remain a constant. In Public Enemy's "Fight the

Power" (1989), there is a sentiment that is absent from most Afrofuturist aesthetics: a collective drive to overthrow authority.[89] Zapata wanted to foment revolution. In "Fight the Power," in addition to the title verse, there is an attempt to "revolutionize" and instill black pride. For van Veen, the video of the song asks "what would revolt look like today?"[90] Zapata likely would have supported a violent uprising against oppressive forces like those that imprison his protagonists. He opposed U.S. imperialism. He considers the riots in Watts, Newark, New York, Cleveland, and Detroit to be the "Noches de Damballa," nights of the powerful Dahomean snake god.[91] While the still unawakened Agne continues to preach resignation in Harlem, the walls burn down around her before she discovers the ancestors. Public Enemy's aggressive anthems call for action against injustice. Moreover, they would be the soundtrack for the Rodney King Riots of 1992.[92] While it is debatable if Public Enemy are calling for anarchy or justice or simply do not know what will come, their call for future change can be seen as part of a greater understanding of Afrofuturism. Author van Veen sees the "Powers" music video as proof that the new revolutions must be televised, that media must be a part of revolution, which has proven prescient in our Web 2.0 and 3.0 age. Zapata wrote at a time when collective action still brought a sense of optimism, but not all that idealism is gone, in the United States or in Latin America.

While William Mina Aragón argues that Zapata is a humanist, he is a certain kind of humanist. The muntu includes the subject, those around them, nature, and the spirits of the dead.[93] In this way, the Nuevo Muntu is "becoming-other-than-human," a trademark of Afrofuturism for van Veen, if that "human" is synonymous with the Cartesian subject Gilroy challenges.[94]

To revisit Gilroy's focus on black theology, I must mention that theologian Andrew Rollins is also looking to Afrofuturist theology as a way to confront the challenges of postmodernity.[95] Like Zapata, he alludes to Alain Locke's New Negro to denote a black man who never knew slavery and had black pride and a cosmopolitan outlook.[96] Nonetheless, the Black Church must change to address the radical changes in technology as well as the New Jim Crow, which perpetuates racialized oppression through imprisonment.[97] Hence, Rollins calls for a black liberation theology based on neo-Pentecostalism.[98] Zapata already developed a black liberation theology, one based on African deities, the Nuevo Muntu.

Brazil

Due to a direct dialogue with the United States, Brazil has a well-developed community of Afrofuturist critics and artists. That said, the Afrofuturism of Brazil is different from the Afrofuturism of the United States. I juxtapose a prime example of African American Afrofuturism with examples of works from Brazil that share much with Zapata: particularly, Latin American setting, African diaspora religious beliefs, and a heavier influence of Marxism.

In African American Martine Syms's "Mundane Afrofuturist Manifesto" (2013), she scoffs at the "hackneyed tropes" of Afrofuturism, taking aim at Ra and Clinton, among other artists.[99] She creates a list or "bonfire of Stupidities" on which to cast what she sees as "harmless" and ineffectual. Among these are "magical negroes," "obvious, heavy-handed allusions to double consciousness," "no flying Africans to whisk us off to the Promised Land."[100] Further prohibitions include magic or supernatural elements, mulattoes, time travel, teleportation, Mammies, and revisionist history. In their stead, she expects Afrofuturists to create futures "in which we only have ourselves and this planet." They are to focus "worldbuilding outside of imperialist, capitalist, white patriarchy," but she sees this happening via "our science, technology, culture, politics, religions, individuality, needs, dreams, hopes, and failings" and the rituals of daily life. There is no *Changó* without magic. It is the African element that destabilizes the Western-imperial structures she criticizes. The spirits of African Diasporic faiths have supernatural powers, and people sincerely believe in them. In addition, what would she make of the *ayas* (maids) that cared for Bolívar?[101] Would she dismiss them as Mammies? By what purism does she dismiss all mulattoes? Hybridity, genetic and cultural, is central to *Changó* and the Latin American reality it depicts. Its magic is not escapism; it is a telling of historical events through religion that creates a radical, empowering future for blacks and the Americas.

Zapata was a direct influence on one novelist and musician that I consider Afrofuturist, Nei Lopes. Lopes's *Oiobomé: A epopeia de uma nação* (*Oiobomé: Epic of a Nation*, 2010) reimagines the past, present, and future of Brazil.[102] Lopes knows the work of Zapata Olivella.[103] Much like in Zapata's novel, there is a focus on alternative foundations rooted in slave resistance. In *Oiobomé*, Afro-Brazilian Domingos dos Santos abandons the Minas Conspiracy of 1789 to form a quilombo in the Amazonian archipelago of Marajó.[104] This nation is majority black with an Amerindian minority. The evolution of the nation parallels outside events, such as Brazilian independence, the world wars, and the Cuban Revolution.[105] Entrepreneurs in the black nation discover diamonds in their soil.[106] With these as the basis of their economy and a communist-inspired government, they are led by a just lesbian queen and prime minister.[107] They move the capital city to a new, high-tech capital called Dominga in honor of their founder.[108] The national religion is a *vitalismo* (worship of lifeforce) that is rooted in Afro-Brazilian religions.[109] Media produce only healthy images for youth.[110] There is no crime but universal access to health care and education. Lopes's text is another Nuevo Muntu novel that tells the history of the diaspora to imagine a more just future.

In addition to fiction, music is central to U.S. Afrofuturism. In Brazil this is also the case, but the Latin American nation draws on its more explicit African roots in Salvador.[111] Russo Passapusso leads BaianaSystem, which has led the movement since 2009. He sees the future in the past: "Ancestrality is the future." Their precursors A Bronkka, Fantasmão, and Psirico popularized Pagodão, a style associated with the favelas of Salvador. Afrocidade is a rap-rock protest band opposed to Brazilian president Jair Bolsonaro. ÀTTØØXXÁÁ uses futuristic sampling and the influence of Ra, Janelle Monáe and Buraka Som Sistema. Female performers include Xênia França, Luedji Luna, and Larissa Luz. They combine electronic technology with ancient rhythms unique to Salvador and previously unknown in the southeastern metropolises where music is usually popularized. They often oppose the superficial tourist-friendly image of an ever-joyous "Black Rome," which too often ignores the poverty and discrimination black Bahians face. Their challenge to this stereotype parallels Gonçalves's painful chronicle.

Syms's snark and African American perspective is quite different from Brazilian Afrofuturists' outlook. *Carioca* Fábio Kabral is gaining recognition for his Afrofuturist science fiction through graphic novels, blogs, and narrative prose, such as his graphic novel *O caçador cibernético da Rua 13* (*The Cyber-Hunter of Thirteenth Street*, 2017).[112] His narrative universe is the flying metropolis Ketu Três. In the short story "A diretora analista de mídias oníricas" (The Head Analyst of Oneiric Media), he describes the patrons of the fine dining restaurant Ikoko Amo on the station:

> *Black powers*, tranças e *dreadlocks*, saias, batas, turbantes, barretes e ternos coloridos, peles melaninadas do marrom mais claro aos tons mais escuros da realeza: todo mundo ali possuía dons psíquicos, lógico, uma vez que eram da alta linhagem ẹmí ẹjẹ—os que haviam despertado os poderes do sangue dos espíritos.[113]

> (Afros, braids, and dreadlocks, skirts, robes, turbans, barrettes, and colorful suits, melaninful skins from the lightest brown to the darkest tones of the royalty: everyone there had psychic gifts, of course, since they were of the high ẹmí ẹjẹ bloodline, those who had awakened the powers of the blood of the spirits.)

This panorama stands in contrast to Sym's reasonable realism. Mulattoes are welcome in Ketu, although the royalty have the most African features. They are proud of their blackness and do not use the Brazilian "mulatto escape hatch" to deny their blackness, as Carl Degler theorized.[114] This is evident in their proud display of black hair, which is often straightened to seem less African. Yoruba words are common in the description, since Kabral is a practitioner of Candomblé who clearly is aware of the language and of Yoruba history.[115] Ketu Três is named for the ancient Yoruba capital that is now in Benin, and the restaurant and bloodline names are Yoruba. The matter of "alien" elements in science fiction is exemplified by recasting a language associated with primitivism (Candomblé, preindustrialized African cultures) as powerful, refined, and futuristic. Their supernatural powers come from Candomblé, not Western technology. Vital spirit forces give their bloodline its strength. The most important character of this family for Kabral is mercenary João Arolê. He has not only powers from the ancestors, like teleportation, but also cybernetic implants. One arm is made of techno-organic snakes that assume different forms. One side of his face is a titanium computer system. He occupies a gray zone between good and evil like the Yoruba deities. Like Zapata's Agne Brown, Kabral's protagonist has the best of both worlds: Western technology and education (computers) and a deep-rooted bond with syncretic African traditions. The hybrid bond to the past is so similar that the universe of his stories is called not Nuevo Muntu but Mundo Novo (New World), appropriating the utopia of the Americas from the colonizers. This new vision of history adds nuance to the author's pen name: if Brazil was discovered by Pedro Ávares Cabral and based on African slavery in the past, then *Kabral* is imagining a parallel Brazil in the future where blacks assume leadership through a hybrid Afro-Brazilian utopia. As in colonial Brazil, deified ancestors are central to predicting the future of Afro-Brazilians.[116]

Afrofuturism is the topic of the Brazilian TED talk by Afro-Brazilian activist Nátaly Neri.[117] For her, it is the "ideia radical" (radical idea) that black people exist in the future, an idea that does not limit blacks to "primitive" or "archaic" roles. She notes that, in Butler's *Kindred*, black women have no space in which they do not suffer in U.S. history. Neri embraces Ra's escapist idea that only "space is the place" for black people to live free as an inspiration to create a just future for black people. She touts the importance of Kabral's racial integration of science fiction. She ends her speech with a crescendo of impassioned apologies for including Afro-Brazilians in visions of the future, fictional or otherwise. It imagines that black people are alive. It puts forth that they will no longer die violent deaths like young men do or women of all ages. It imagines that mass incarceration and the cultural genocide of slavery will end: "Ele é a certeza de que nós as minhas gerações, as presentes e as futuras não serão a morte na praia do nado de anos e anos dos nossos ancestrais . . . pessoas negras precisam de utopias" (It is the certainty that we, my generation and future ones will not mean death on the beach after our ancestors swam here . . . black people need utopias). The brutal reality she depicts of Rio de Janeiro and other urban spaces in Brazil and historical consciousness is not unlike Zapata's portrait of Harlem. Neither she nor the Colombian embraces simplistic escapism, but they do embrace African diaspora religions that include deified ancestors or *ancestrais*.

Kabral appears alongside Mário Bentes and Felipe Damiani in the anthology *2084: Mundos Cyberpunks* (*Cyberpunk Worlds*), anthologized by Lídia Zuin. Bentes combines magic with futuristic technology and questions of gender. In his "O Pajemancer" ("The Pajemancer"), an agender person is thrown from a building in Manaus.[118] This, despite the fact that the opera house is covered with cameras. The mechanism was inexplicably deactivated. The narrator-protagonist is a Pajemancer or "mancer," which means that he has the powers of a *pajé*, or Amerindian shaman, but that he helps police find criminals. It seems the killer is too. As in Zapata, there are links between the Amerindian and the African. In Kabral's story black women with similar powers fight each other, as is the case with Bente's futuristic noir.

In Damiani's "Loucura Artificial" (Artificial Madness), racism is clearly a problem that continues in the future. The narrator-protagonist is horrified to see on the news that a Caucasian man killed his wife and child because they are black.[119] He did not know his wife was born black since she underwent a medical procedure to lighten her skin and assume a different identity. Since the narrator undergoes the same process and cannot recall his past, it is implied that he is the murderer.[120] This crime is the extreme of whitening discourse, which, while present in the United States, does not manifest in the same way as in more prominently mestizo Latin American nations.

Neri, Bentes, Lopes, and Kabral are not alone in their interest in combining African magic with Western technology. A counterpoint to Syms is a Brazilian periodical that shares a name with the one in which she published her manifesto, *Rhizome/Rizoma*. Alongside translations of well-known Anglo Afrofuturists like Paul D. Miller, Mark Sinker, and Mark Dery, one finds contemplations of texts closer to Afro–Latin American reality yet simultaneously more cosmopolitan.[121] Dirk van Weelden analyzes the complex world of white American-Canadian novelist William Gibson in the trilogy *Neuromancer* (1984), *Count Zero* (1986), and *Mona Lisa Overdrive* (1988).[122] Like Kabral's heady blend of technology and spirits, Gibson imagines a dystopia in which street gangs in service of Vodou spirits (*Loas*) vie for power.[123] The spirits are a means for accessing the all-powerful matrix by summoning Legba and other divine beings through magic rituals. The juxtaposition of African ritual and urban modernity is like *Changó*, and Gibson may have influenced the Brazilian "pajemancer," as the name implies.

Critic Erik Davis builds on the Black Atlantic to imagine a Black Electronica marked by the polyrhythms of Africa.[124] For example, he notes that "science" means a mixture of natural medicine and magic or obeah in Jamaica.[125] He cites Robert Pelton's study of similarities between modern science and Yoruba folk medicine as another example of the multiple Afro-enlightenment connections and ties them to Jamaican dub musicians who combine African rhythms with technological innovations. *Changó* was already doing these things by referencing the *tambor brujo* (bewitched drum) of the Hispanic Caribbean and the Rastafarian Zion that Davis considers "virtual reality."[126] *Rizoma* writer Hermano Vianna's laudatory essay on Gilroy laments that he overlooked the Black South Atlantic, namely Brazil.[127] Cristiano Henrique Ribeiro dos Santos clearly embraces Candomblé by comparing the tree archetype in the religion to the internet. The tree links the concrete and mundane to the abstract, divine, and limitless. He compares consulting the Ifá poems via Exu (Legba), a means of divining the future, to consulting the internet.[128] While the Orishas precede the internet, today the latter permits communication between babalawos and the spiritually initiated. In this way the technology that defines the new millennium is contributing to the construction of a Nuevo Muntu in a way that Zapata's novel predicted in some ways, given its emphasis on the Ifá.

Ivana Bentes ties white communist filmmaker Glauber Rocha to Afrofuturism by analyzing his film shot in the Congo, *Der Leone Have Sept Cabeças* (1970).[129] He ties postcolonial resistance to the Palmares quilombo, naming one character Zumbi and the other Che. Livio Sansone ties Afro-Brazil, particularly Salvador, to Gilroy's Black Atlantic and states that, alongside "black globalization" in communication with other nations, it has its own landmarks and rituals on which to draw.[130] However, racism is also an extending transnational force that proves to be equally influential in the years to come, in Brazil, in the United States, and throughout the Americas.

Latinx Futurism

The Nuevo Muntu that Zapata's novel develops is a precursor to Latin@ futurism and its variants. While Spanish America has been slow to adopt the term "Afrofuturism," the aesthetic has flourished in Latinx literature under different guises. The closest terminology to "Nuevo Muntu" that has been used in this criticism appears in Isabel Millán's "Engineering Afro-Latina and Mexican Immigrant Heroines," part of a 2015 dossier in *Aztlán: A Journal of Chicano Studies* guest edited by Catheryn Josephina Merla-Watson and B. V. Olguín.[131] While "Afro-Latina" is the closest term to the black protagonists of *Changó*, the concept was actually first theorized as "Chicanafuturism" by Catherine Ramírez in "Deus ex Machina" for its 2004 issue.[132] The evolving terminology reflects the evolving parameters of an ethnic minority or minorities that are working to redefine their currently marginal place/s in U.S. politics and academic circles. I refer to them as "Latinxs," the genderless term some prefer today, but others have been used and I will repeat them according to those the authors use. While the aesthetics create a vision of the future, the tendency is to focus on technology and limits of the human.

In "Afrofuturism / Chicanafuturism: Fictive Kin," Ramírez reflects on her creation: "The concept of Chicanafuturism, which I introduced in *Aztlán* in 2004, borrows from theories of Afrofuturism. Chicanafuturism explores the ways that new and everyday technologies, including their detritus, transform Mexican American life and culture. It questions the promises of science, technology, and humanism for Chicanas, Chicanos, and other people of color. And like Afrofuturism, which reflects diasporic experience, Chicanafuturism articulates colonial and postcolonial histories of *indigenismo, mestizaje*, hegemony, and survival."[133] Whereas Zapata remedies the lack of black presence in novels of the Latin American boom tradition, Ramírez also brings to light the absence of nonwhite/non-Anglo characters in speculative fiction (science fiction, fantasy), partly inspired by black novelist

Octavia Butler. As Zapata does with Agne, Ramírez creates strong female role models. Ramírez praises Martinez's visual art, Cherríe Moraga's play *The Hungry Woman* (1987), and Gloria Anzaldúa's writings, both in her *Borderlands/La Frontera* (1987) and in her science fiction.[134] They all associate Chicana women with progress and technology. For example, Martínez creates an "Az-techna" brooch and a "Mixed-Techna" wall hanging of multiple media. Zapata's solidarity between blacks and the indigenous of Mexico and the United States anticipates the concepts in her work. These mestizo futures are not superficial in nature, says Ramírez. They challenge the status quo by depicting alternative worlds for the future, present, and past, exposing history's "constructedness."[135] They make science fiction "a rich, exciting, and politically charged medium for the interrogation of ideology, identity, historiography, and epistemology." What Zapata did for historical fiction, these young authors are doing for the speculative genres.

In "Engineering Afro-Latina and Mexican Immigrant Heroines," Millán merges Afrofuturism and Chicanafuturism to analyze and compare Afro-Latina and Chicana protagonists in the works of novelist Jacqueline Carcy's Haitian-Chicana protagonist Loup Garron and María Isabel "Isa" Reyes in the films of José Néstor Márquez.[136] Both protagonists are treated as disposable and subhuman by government and business forces, thus reflecting the bio/border politics of the United States in the new millennium.[137] Loup has the powers of strength and fearlessness.[138] Isa's brain has a chip implanted that communicates with a powerful corporate computer that exploits her dreams, which she cannot distinguish from reality.[139] Their connection of the African with the Latinx and the American, along with their supernatural feminine strength is a continuation of Agne Brown's syncretic *zamba* (Afro-Amerindian) identity and spiritual powers.

The guest editors claim the genealogy of Chicanafuturism goes back to the "Plan Espiritual de Aztlán" (Aztlán Spiritual Plan, 1969), the manifesto of Rodolfo "Corky" Gonzales and the First National Chicano Liberation Youth Conference held that year.[140] Like the Nuevo Muntu, Gonzales's (and Alberto Urista's) Chicano-led utopia Aztlán, inspired by the ancient Aztec homeland in what is now the United States, is inspired by Marxist projects, not an infatuation with technology:

> Those institutions which are fattened by our brothers to provide employment and political pork barrels for the gringo will do so only as acts of liberation

> and for La Causa. For the very young there will no longer be acts of juvenile delinquency, but revolutionary acts.
>
> 6. CULTURAL values of our people strengthen our identity and the moral backbone of the movement. Our culture unites and educates the family of La Raza towards liberation with one heart and one mind.[141]

With this revolutionary Chicano nationalism in mind, the co-editors see elements of Chican@futurism in Gonzales's epic "I Am Joaquín" (1967), which claims the Chicano "WILL ENDURE" through the struggle for a better future. These calls from a previous era show that Marxism was a part of Latin@futurist "utopian yearnings," as the co-editors call them. Zapata's text would have done well to mention them as a continuation of Morelos's post-colonial battle in the United States, but he focuses on the African diaspora.

The journal is limited to the parameters of its title, *Aztlán: A Journal of Chicano Studies*, which simultaneously allows it to give focus to an under-served group, Mexican Americans. Nonetheless, the co-editors note that the most successful cultivator of the aesthetic has been Dominican American Junot Diaz.[142] His *Brief, Wondrous Life of Oscar Wao* (2008) rhetorically asks, "What more sci-fi than Santo Domingo?"[143] I explain that the novel combines science fiction, U.S. nerd culture, and a fascination with Japan with African American Vernacular English, the history of slavery, and syncretic beliefs to create a new idiom for the island and New Jersey.[144] Hence, magical realist tropes, rooted in African diaspora and Caribbean realities, continue after McOndo writers reject magical realism. While the work is (post) apocalyptic (postslavery, post-Trujillo) and expresses a fascination with futuristic idioms, the work does not chart a plan for the future or depict a futuristic society, so it has elements of Afrofuturism without having an Afro- or Latinx-futurist setting. It does show how including the history of slavery in the New World sheds new light on the marginalization of minorities and immigrants.

The "Latinx" elements of Latinx-futurism are often of indigenous or African origin, depending on the substrate of the authors' origin. If the work is Chicanx, indigenous elements tend to predominate; if the work is Caribbean, African heritage will shine to the fore. Thus, we come full circle to Latinx-futurism's Afrofuturist roots.

There are black authors who adopt an aesthetic that is more "Latin" than the "Mundane Afro-Futurist Manifesto" allows. Kinitra Brooks challenges

Afrofuturism in the genre fiction by blacks that she studies.[145] She sees its focus on the future as myopic; it ignores the preslavery sub-Saharan African past and gives prominence to science fiction.[146] Alternatively, she considers "folkloric horror" more appropriate for the specific texts she analyzes, which share some aspects of Afrofuturism.[147] Novels like Erna Brodber's *Louisiana* (1997), Gloria Naylor's *Momma Day* (1988), and Nilo Hopkinson's *Sister Mine* (2013), folkloric horror novels, exhibit Santería and Vodou traditions and elements of science fiction.[148] They include women's oral storytelling, spirit possession, living-dead, spiritual growth, and honoring female spiritual leaders.[149] While neither *Changó* nor *Defeito* is a horror novel, they exhibit the same aspects that show the limits of an African American focus on a life lived without African spirits. These entities and the spiritual leaders, often women, who keep them relevant in people's lives are the "Latin" elements of spaces like New Orleans. They also link the United States with Latin America.

Ana Maria Gonçalves

Where does Gonçalves fit in the trajectory of Afrofuturism in Brazilian literature? *Defeito* is not an Afrofuturist text, but it does contain Afrofuturist elements. First, as historical fiction, it denaturalizes history and historiography. Like the aesthetic, it notes the exclusion of racial minorities from visions of the nation. Like Zapata's text, it notes the struggle for the enslaved to have access to one of the most powerful technologies of their time: writing. Kehinde's remarkable privilege as an enslaved woman who learns to read and speak multiple languages (Portuguese and English) grants her impressive power in her context. Furthermore, knowing Brazilian construction and business allows her to start an enterprise upon returning to Africa. Another element it shares with Afrofuturism is the relationship between the future and the present, as her prologue indicates.[150]

In "Serendipidades!" (Serendipities!) we read that she leaves the ultramodern city of São Paulo for Brazil's colonial capital of Bahia, specifically the island of Itaparica in the Bahia de Todos os Santos. She seems pulled into the past, not the future. She happens upon a guide to Bahia that Jorge Amado published in 1938. Upon arrival, she marvels at street addresses that do not even have numbers, only small-town directions like "seventh house, after the pharmacy."[151] A modern outsider, she knows what to do with the ersatz colonial manuscripts that a cleaning woman rescues from a modern-day church:

> Ela então contou que tinha pegado os papéis, junto com algumas revistas, na Igreja do Sacramento, na vila de Itaparica, onde também fazia limpeza. Uma troca de padres levou o padre antigo a pedir que ela se desfizesse de tudo que estava guardado em um quartinho nos fundos da casa paroquial, e com dó de jogar fora, principalmente as revistas cheias de figuras, ela pediu permissão para levar para casa. Quase tinha posto fogo nos papéis, mas se lembrou de que o Gérson vivia procurando papel para desenhar e que, quando não encontrava, desenhava até nas paredes.[152]
>
> (Then she said she had picked up the pages, together with some magazines, from the Igreja do Sacramento, in Itaparica Island, where she also was a cleaning lady. When they changed priests, the old priest asked her to do away with everything that was stored in a little room at the back of the parsonage, and feeling bad about throwing them out, mainly the magazines with all the pictures, she asked permission to take them home. She almost burned the papers, but she recalled Gérson was always looking for drawing paper and that, when he could not find any, he would even draw on the walls.)

Like Ramírez, Gonçalves values the detritus of technology—texts that were considered unwanted, people excluded from reading them. In some ways, the journey to Bahia that Gonçalves makes to recover the lives of those cast aside by traditional Brazilian historiography is a domestic version of what Patrícia de Santana Pinho calls "African American roots tourism."[153] Since the 1970s U.S. black tourists have made a "detour" to Bahia to discover "tradition," roots, or its role as Brazil's (and the diaspora's) past, from the powerful point of view of "modern" middle-class positions. Gonçalves does more justice to this potentially superficial gaze by the nuanced portrait she leaves of Bahia, though her perspective as a privileged outsider should not be ignored. The Afro-Brazilian cleaning woman Dona Clara appreciated images only because she was unable to read the colonial Portuguese. Gérson, a child and thus a symbol of the future, can create, but he is limited by his lack of access to reading. Gonçalves's novel uses the technology of writing and publishing to end the exclusion of first-person black female narrator-protagonists from the Brazilian canon in the context in which they were most marginalized: slavery. This opening to the novel, which presents the text as a time machine, is not unlike the time travel of Octavia Butler's *Kindred*.[154] The ending also looks forward to a future in which the reader is able to combine Kehinde's life story with her son's, presumably after reading the novel. This would be the last chance for the narrator to *abençoar* (bless/greet) her son.[155] The reader also looks for a future in which the secret narrator of the text, the scribe Geninha, can write her own story independently of Kehinde.[156] Nevertheless, these readings merely show how the concerns Afrofuturism raises allow a new appreciation of black historiography, technology, and utopianism.

Gonçalves's following novel, which has been released only as a blog preview, is an Afrofuturist text. It is called *Quem é Jocenildo?*[157] Journalist André Cáceres considers it part of a recent rebirth of Brazilian fantasy fiction along with the thirty authors Nelso de Oliveira gathers in *Fractais tropicais* (*Tropical Fractals*, 2018).[158] Gonçalves describes it as a *policial de ficção científica* (science fiction crime novel) set in 2064 São Paulo. The state has seceded from Brazil, and the white, female narrator is an émigré from the Outra Cidade (Other City). The protagonist, thirteen-year-old Jocenildo, disappears. His parents think he has been kidnapped, the police think he ran away from home, and his friends think he killed himself. His disappearance calls attention to the all-too-frequent absence of blacks in futuristic fiction. The year calls attention to the continued relevance of the 1964 coup d'état that led to a regime that reigned for over twenty years in the country and that President Jair Bolsonaro has praised as a golden age. In the future, Jucenildo's uncommon and racialized name and skin color are targets of derision by his classmates, who opt to call him "Black Pack." Additionally, he is a nerd who studies hard and speaks a little too correctly, evoking Oscar Wao. He is the only Afro-descendant in his class, indicating that racism is no weaker in the future. Jair remains resilient but passive until the students suspect they have driven him to kill himself. Then they fear he will suicide-bomb them, perhaps with his book bag. He leaves it with the narrator as she sees him running from the police. While the blog does not answer the questions this exposition asks, it does indicate that this young adult novel is an example of Brazilian Afrofuturism, in which radical utopian-dystopian change is accompanied by the same racial problems of the present. When the novel is released, it will be interesting to note if, like Kabral, it includes a fascination with both Afro-diasporic religions and technology and, like Lopes and Zapata, includes a call for revolution.

A Past and a Future Bigger Than the Black Atlantic

As I have shown in this book, Manuel Zapata Olivella is a groundbreaking theorist of diaspora in *Changó*. His model of diaspora predates Gilroy and includes Latin America, where the majority of captives were taken during the slave trade. His work shows the origins of slavery, not just the form that began in 1619 in the British colonies. He presents Bantu philosophy as a means of approaching diaspora, not just U.S.-European approaches like Gilroy. He makes gender a part of the struggle for black consciousness, black liberation, and the creation of a just mestizo society throughout the Americas. His presentation of history sets out to chart this Nuevo Muntu through a history of struggles. Unlike Gilroy, Gonçalves grants the black retornados much more deserved attention. She shows that double consciousness also existed in Brazil, but that the complex system of oppression there allowed subjects to evolve and become contradictory in their legacy as both oppressed and oppressor. She provides a different gendered perspective than *Changó*, and they both treat more religious traditions than just a monolithic, Protestant Black Church like Gilroy does. She represents the survival instinct of a mother charged with caring for her children. *Changó* was begun around 1963 and published twenty years later.[159] His forward-looking philosophy anticipates Afrofuturism as a theory by over ten years. He is a precursor to Afrofuturist and Latinx-futurist authors in Brazil and the United States.

Latin America is catching up to Zapata; we need to continue to understand him better. As for Gonçalves, her novel deserved its Casa de las Américas award and is a return to the simultaneous struggles of slave revolts and abolitionists to create a just, egalitarian hemisphere. Through serendipity, a favorite concept of the author, she was born later than Zapata. At no point have I endeavored to claim Zapata was better or more important than Gonçalves, though to date he has published more and had a greater impact. Gonçalves has created a groundbreaking diasporic portrait in *Defeito*. In 2020 it will come to an even greater audience via Brazilian television on Rede Globo through Maria Camargo's adaptation.[160] Her career as a writer has just begun. She has lived to see and combat the racism of today, emboldened by a wave of reactionary conservatism and the elections of Donald Trump and Jair Bolsonaro. She continues to intervene in ways that advocate for the understanding and inclusion of the African diaspora in politics and culture. Her work as a writer and columnist is still an evolving struggle to create a more just, understanding world. Like her, the reader must heed the call of the enslaved ancestors for justice, knowing that a Greater White Wolf may still come when we least expect it. Nevertheless, once it is vanquished, a Nuevo Muntu awaits in the Americas. We must fight for, create for, study for, and question for it until it arrives. We will not know it without the context and vision these monumental novels provide.

Acknowledgments

I am very fortunate to have had the support and privilege that enabled me to complete this book. My father, the Reverend J. Thomas Maddox III, raised me to value education deeply. My wife, Luciana Silva, made Brazil a central part of my life and made many sacrifices so that I could write this book. My professors at the University of Georgia prepared me well, particularly Susan Quinlan, Lesley Feracho, and Betina Kaplan. I am grateful to Ana Maria Gonçalves for our interview and her input regarding this book. At Vanderbilt University, my dissertation's co-director Earl Fitz affirmed and fostered my belief that the Americas should not be divided by language and literature but united by them. My co-director William Luis introduced me to *Changó*, and the *Afro-Hispanic Review* showed me the expanding frontiers of the African diaspora. Cathy Jrade watered the seeds of this book, and Luciano Tosta and Emanuelle Oliveira-Monte helped it flourish. Jane Landers was an encouraging professor, and it is because of her and librarian Paula Covington that I worked with the then-still-unfiled Manuel Zapata Olivella Collection at the Heard Library. Thank you to the Robert Penn Warren Center, particularly Mona Frederick and Edward Friedman, for the time to write and share my work with colleagues. Thank you to Maria Helena Lima, Joan Anim-Addo, Ineke Phaf-Rheinberger, and Nicholas Jones for their input.

Notes

Introduction

All translations are mine unless otherwise noted.

1. I use the Henao edition throughout unless otherwise noted.
2. Antonio Tillis, *Manuel Zapata Olivella and the "Darkening" of Latin American Literature* (Columbia: University of Missouri Press, 2005), 77.
3. Manuel Zapata Olivella, *Changó el gran putas* (Bogota: Ministerio de Cultura, 2010), http://babel.banrepcultural.org/cdm/ref/collection/p17054coll7/id/2.
4. Ibid., 647.
5. Jonathan Tittler, "Translator's Note and Acknowledgments," in *Changó, the Biggest Badass*, by Manuel Zapata Olivella (Lubbock: Texas Tech University Press, 2010), ix–xii.
6. Manuel Zapata Olivella, *Manuel Zapata Olivella: Por los senderos de sus ancestros: Textos escogidos. 1940–2000* (Bogota: Ministerio de Cultura, 2010), http://babel.banrepcultural.org/cdm/ref/collection/p17054coll7/id/17.
7. "Olivella Acquisition Boosts Library's Latin American Collection," *Acorn Chronicle*, January 13, 2010, www.vanderbilt.edu/acorn-chronicle/2010/01/olivella/; Pablo Gómez, "La colección de Manuel Zapata Olivella," *Revista de Estudios Colombianos* 37–38 (2011): 117–118. "Manuel Zapata Olivella," Vanderbilt University Heard Library, digital projects "La Voz de los Abuelos," "Correspondence," and "Grupo Etnográfico," http://mzo.library.vanderbilt.edu/.
8. Gustavo Tatis Guerra, "Bajo el árbol brujo de Zapata Olivella," *El Universal*, May 27, 2018, http://m.eluniversal.com.co/suplementos/facetas/bajo-el-arbol-brujo-de-zapata-olivella-279361.
9. "Cátedra Manuel Zapata Olivella," Universidad de Antioquia, www.udea.edu.co.
10. "El año Manuel Zapata Olivella," *La Palabra*, May 27, 2019, Universidad del Valle, http://lapalabra.univalle.edu.co.
11. Eugênio Nascimento, "Nobel," in Ineke Phaf-Rheinberger, *Modern Slavery and Water Spirituality: A Critical Debate in Africa and Latin America* (New York: Peter

Lang, 2017), 53; Luciano Oliveira, "Um Prêmio Nobel para Ana Maria Gonçalves—Luciano Oliveira," *Revista Será*, December 3, 2014, http://revistasera.ne10.uol.com.br/um-premio-nobel-para-ana-maria-goncalves-luciano-oliveira/.

12. Agência EFE, "Ana Maria Gonçalves ganha Prêmio Casa de Las Américas 2007," *Jornal do Brasil*, July 31, 2007, www.jb.com.br/cultura/noticias/2007/01/25/ana-maria-goncalves-ganha-premio-casa-de-las-americas-2007/.
13. "Ana Maria Gonçalves—Flip (2016)—Parte 1/4," Ministério da Cultura / Ancine / Itaú Cultural, July 18, 2016, www.youtube.com/watch?v=cfkNH5RtoZs; Glenn Greenwald, "Ana Maria Gonçalves—New Columnist for The Intercept," December 2, 2016, https://theintercept.com/2016/12/02/the-intercept-brasil-welcomes-ana-maria-goncalves-as-a-columnist-on-race-politics-and-culture/.
14. "Globo fará minissérie baseada em livro sobre ex-escrava; saiba mais," *RD1*, August 13, 2017, https://rd1.com.br/globo-fara-minisserie-baseada-em-livro-sobre-ex-escrava-saiba-mais/.
15. Redação, "'Um defeito de cor' será a nova supersérie da Globo," O Planeta TV, May 18, 2019, https://oplanetatv.clickgratis.com.br/noticias/bastidores/um-defeito-de-cor-sera-a-nova-superserie-da-globo.html.
16. Greenwald, "Ana Maria Gonçalves."
17. François Bogliolo, *Manuel Zapata Olivella (Négritude et problèmes du noir)* (Dakar: Nouvelles Éditions Africaines, 1979); Yvonne Captain-Hidalgo, *The Culture of Fiction in the Works of Manuel Zapata Olivella* (Columbia: University of Missouri Press, 1993); Ciro Alfonso Quintero, *Filosofía antropológica y cultural en el pensamiento de Manuel Zapata Olivella* (Quito: Ediciones Abya-Yala, 1998); José Luis Garcés González, *Manuel Zapata Olivella, Caminante de la literatura y de la historia* (Bogota: Ministerio de Cultura, 2002); Tillis, *"Darkening"*; William Mina Aragón, *Manuel Zapata Olivella: Pensador humanista* (Cali: Artes Gráficas del Valle Editores 2014); William Mina Aragón, ed., *Manuel Zapata Olivella: Un legado intercultural* (Popayán: Universidad del Cauca 2017).
18. Placide Tempels, *Bantu Philosophy*, trans. A. Rubbens and Collin King (Centre Aequatoria, November 2006), www.congoforum.be/upldocs/Tempels%20BantuPhil%20English%201959.pdf.
19. Paul Gilroy, *The Black Atlantic: Modernity and Double Consciousness* (New York: Verso, 1993).
20. Octavio Paz, *El laberinto de la soledad* (Mexico: Fondo de Cultura Económica, 1992).
21. Yvonne Captain, "Hacia su habitación propia: La mujer en Manuel Zapata Olivella," in *Literatura colombiana del siglo XX*, vol. 3, no. 2, ed. Maria M. Jaramillo et al. (Bogota: Ministerio de Cultura, 2000), 147–167.
22. Manuel Zapata Olivella, "Changó. Revisiones S.F." (unpublished manuscript, n.d.), Vanderbilt Manuel Zapata Olivella Papers, Nashville, TN.
23. Antonio Olliz Boyd, "Manuel Zapata Olivella," in *Dictionary of Literary Biography: Modern Latin-American Fiction Writers*, vol. 113, ed. William Luis and Ann González (Detroit: Gale Research, 1992), 314.
24. Manuel Zapata Olivella, *¡Levántate mulato! Por mi raza hablará el espíritu* (Bogota: REI Andes, 1990), 40.
25. Garcés, *Caminante*, 16; Zapata, *¡Levántate!*, 41, 315.
26. Garcés, *Caminante*, 18.
27. Olliz, "Zapata," 314.

28. Ibid., 315.
29. Zapata, *¡Levántate!*, 33.
30. Garcés, *Caminante*, 19; Olliz, "Zapata," 314.
31. Zapata, *¡Levántate!*, 41.
32. Dario Henao Restrepo, introduction to *Changó, el gran putas*, by Manuel Zapata Olivella, in *Biblioteca de Literatura Afrocolombiana*, vol. 3, ed. Darío Henao Restrepo (Bogota: Ministerio de Cultura, 2010), 12, http://babel.banrepcultural.org/cdm/ref/collection/p17054coll7/id/2.
33. Olliz, "Zapata," 315.
34. Ibid.
35. Garcés, *Caminante*, 26; Zapata, *¡Levántate!*, 216, 247.
36. Olliz, "Zapata," 313.
37. François Bogliolo, *La négritude et les problèmes du Noir dans l'oeuvre de Zapata Olivella* (Dakar: Nouvelles Éditions Africaines, 1978), 242.
38. *Manuel Zapata Olivella: Abridor de caminos*, directed by María Adelaida López (Colombia: Azul y Naranja Producciones, 2007), YouTube video, 28:21, posted by "Johan Jaramillo Burgos," February 23, 2012, www.youtube.com/watch?v=3Dpc4w2Kp6I.
39. Germán Espinosa, "Realidad y pararrealidad de Manuel Zapata Olivella," in *Ensayos completos*, vol. 1 (Medellín: Fondo Editorial Universidad de Escuela de Administración, Finanzas e Instituto Tecnológico, 2002), 242.
40. Manuel Zapata Olivella, *Hotel de vagabundos: Teatro* (Bogota: Ediciones Espiral, 1955); "Los pasos del indio" (unpublished manuscript, n.d.), Vanderbilt Manuel Zapata Olivella Papers, Nashville, TN; "Caronte Liberado," in *Teatro*, by Juan Zapata Olivella and Manuel Zapata Olivella (Bogota: Intituto Colombiano de Cultura, 1972), 1–30; Manuel Zapata Olivella, *Cuentos de muerte y libertad* (Bogota: Iqueima, 1961); Zapata, *¿Quién le dio el fusil a Oswald? y otros cuentos* (Bogota: Editorial Revista Colombiana, 1967).
41. Zapata, *¡Levántate!*, 349.
42. Olliz, "Zapata," 320.
43. Manuel Zapata Olivella, *Manuel Zapata Olivella: Por los senderos de sus ancestros: Textos escogidos. 1940–2000*, ed. Alfonso Múnera (2010), 159, http://babel.banrepcultural.org/cdm/ref/collection/p17054coll7/id/17.
44. Tittler, "Note," x.
45. Andrés Pastrana Arango, "Palabras del señor presidente de la república, Andrés Pastrana Arango, con motivo de la imposición de la Orden de Bocayá a ocho ilustres colombianos por su aporte a la cultura," *Afro-Hispanic Review* 20, no. 1 (Spring 2001): 3–5; Dorita Piquero Nouhad, introduction to *Changó el gran putas* by Manuel Zapata Olivella (Bogota: Grupo Editorial Educar, 2007), cover; Zapata, *¡Levántate!*, cover.
46. Tittler, "Note," ix–x.
47. Jonathan Tittler, "Catching the Spirit: "Changó, el gran putas" in English Translation," *Afro-Hispanic Review* 20, no. 1 (Spring 2001): 78.
48. Jonathan Tittler, "Mi Manuel," *Guaraguao* 9, no. 20 (Summer 2005): 129, www.revistaguaraguao.org/archivo/sumario/20.htm.
49. Piquero, introduction, 9.
50. William Luis, introduction to *Changó the Biggest Baddass* by Manuel Zapata Olivella, trans. Jonathan Tittler (Lubbock: Texas Tech University Press, 2009), xii–iv.

51. Ian Smart, "Introduction: *The Afro-Hispanic Review*," *Afro-Hispanic Review* 21, nos. 1–2 (2002): i.
52. Ibid., iii.
53. Manuel Zapata Olivella, "El código guerrero," *Afro-Hispanic Review* 1, no. 1 (Spring 1982): 16; "Navego," *Afro-Hispanic Review* 1, no. 1 (Spring 1982): 16; "Visión: La travesía," *Afro-Hispanic Review* 1, no. 1 (Spring 1982): 16.
54. Zapata, "Código," 16; "Navego," 16; "Visión," 16.
55. Sandra Alzate, "La relatividad de la verdad: Testimonio, narración y memoria en la obra de Manuel Zapata Olivella," *Afro-Hispanic Review* 30, no. 1 (Spring 2011): 31.
56. Manuel Zapata Olivella, "El Muntu en América," *Afro-Hispanic Review* 20, no. 1 (Spring 2001): 13–14; José Luis Díaz-Granados, "Premio Aplauso," *Afro-Hispanic Review* 20, no. 1 (Spring 2001): 10; Manuel Zapata Olivella, "Conversación informal con Manuel Zapata Olivella," by Margarita Krakusin, *Afro-Hispanic Review* 20, no. 1 (Spring 2001): 15; James Davis, "Afterword: A Personal Perspective on the Humanism of Manuel Zapata Olivella," *Afro-Hispanic Review* 20, no. 1 (Spring 2001): 115; Andrés Pastrana Arango, "Palabras del Señor Presidente de la República, Andrés Pastrana Arango, con motivo de la imposición de la Orden de Boyacá a ocho ilustres colombianos por su aporte a la cultura," *Afro-Hispanic Review* 20, no. 1 (Spring 2001): 5.
57. William Luis, "Editor's Note," *Afro-Hispanic Review* 25, no. 1 (Spring 2006): 5.
58. Manuel Zapata Olivella, "Artel, el maestro," *Afro-Hispanic Review* 25, no. 1 (Spring 2006): 147–161; "El mestizaje en la nueva novela hispanoamericana," *Afro-Hispanic Review* 25, no. 1 (Spring 2006): 163–170; "Los problemas de identidad de los escritores afro-latinoamericanos," *Afro-Hispanic Review* 25, no. 1 (Spring 2006): 171–173.
59. Luis, "Note," 5.
60. Lawrence Prescott and Antonio Tillis, introduction to *Afro-Hispanic Review* 25, no. 1 (Spring 2006): 10.
61. Antonio Tillis, "*Changó, el gran putas*: A Postmodern Historiographic Metafictional Text," *Afro-Hispanic Review* 20, no. 1 (2000): 15–28.
62. Marvin Lewis, "*En Chimá nace un santo*: Myth and Violence," *Kentucky Foreign Language Quarterly* 25 (1978): 145.
63. Manuel Zapata Olivella, "Hemingway, el cazador de la muerte: Kenya en la novela de un afrocolombiano," *Publication of the Afro-Latin American Research Association* 2 (1998): 28.
64. Lawrence Prescott, "Liberating Blackness: The Theme of Whitening in Two Colombian Short Stories," *Callaloo* 35, no. 2 (2012): 475.
65. Ian Smart, "*Chango, el gran putas* as Liberation Literature," *CLA Journal* 35, no. 1 (January 1991): 15.
66. Cristina Rodríguez-Cabral, "Postmodernismo y postcolonialismo en *El fusilamiento del diablo* de Manuel Zapata Olivella," *CLA Journal* 50, no. 2 (June 2006): 239–240.
67. Edward Waters Hood. "Manuel Zapata Olivella y Gabriel García Márquez," *Ciberayllu*, January 16, 2004, www.andes.missouri.edu/andes/Cronicas/EWH_Zapata.html.
68. Lawrence Prescott, "Journeying through Jim Crow: Spanish American Travelers in the United States during the Age of Segregation," *Latin American Research Review* 42, no. 1 (2007): 3–28. *Informe Académico*, http://lasa-4.univ.pitt.edu/LARR/prot/fulltext/Vol42no1/prescott.pdf.

69. Khalma Dhouti Martínez, "Rewriting the Other: Manuel Zapata Olivella's *¡Levántate Mulato!*," *Letras Hispanas* 4, no. 2 (Fall 2007): 130.
70. Margarita Krakusin, "Estructura y técnica en Changó, el gran putas de Manuel Zapata Olivella," *Caribe* 4, nos. 2–5 (2001–2002): 69.
71. Richard Jackson, "Myth, History, and Narrative Structure in Manuel Zapata Olivella's *Changó el Gran Putas*," *Revista/Review Interamericana* 13, nos. 1–4 (1983): 109.
72. John Barry, "Abriendo el canon para Manuel Zapata Olivella: 'Santa Bárbara, Bendita, ayúdanos a vivir,'" *Confluencia* 8, no. 2/9, no. 1 (Spring and Fall 1993): 254.
73. Gertrude James González de Allen, "Enrique Dussel and Manuel Zapata Olivella: An Exploration of De-colonial, Diasporic, and Trans-modern Selves and the Politics of Recognition," *World Knowledges Otherwise* 2, no. 1 (2006): 1, https://pdfs.semanticscholar.org/4f02/c35de86f84221c670d7d03c5a24de33e6ff5.pdf.
74. Captain-Hidalgo, *Culture of Fiction*, ix.
75. Earl Fitz, *Rediscovering the New World: Inter-American Literature in a Comparative Context*, Iowa City: University of Iowa Press, 1991.
76. Tillis, *"Darkening,"* 93.
77. Ibid., 70.
78. Ian Smart, *Amazing Connections: Kemet to Hispanophone Africana Literatures* (Washington: Original World Press, 1996), 116.
79. Ibid., 127, 134.
80. Timothy Cox, *Postmodern Tales of Slavery in the Americas: From Alejo Carpentier to Charles Johnson* (Shrewsbury: Garland, 2001), 136.
81. Haakayoo Zoggyie, *In Search of the Fathers: The poetics of Disalienation in the Narrative of Two Contemporary Afro-Hispanic Writers* (New Orleans: University Press of the South, 2003), 70.
82. William Megenney, "Time and Space: Africa and America in Manuel Zapata Olivella's *Changó, el gran putas*," in *Studies in Honor of Myron Lichtblau*, ed. Fernando Burgos (Statesboro, GA: Juan de la Cuesta, 2000), 229–230.
83. Richard Jackson, *Black Literature and Humanism in Latin America* (Athens: University of Georgia Press, 1997), 64.
84. Lawrence Prescott, "Race, Ethnicity, and Nation in Manuel Zapata Olivella's *¡Levántate mulato!*," in *Race, Colonialism, and Social Transformation in Latin America and the Caribbean*, ed. Jerome Branche (Gainesville: University Press of Florida, 2008), 236.
85. Cristina Cabral, "Myth, Legend, and Reality: Redesigning the Narrative Style in Manuel Zapata Olivella's Hemingway, the Death Stalker," in *Critical Perspectives on Afro-Latin American Literature*, ed. Antonio Tillis (New York: Routledge, 2012), 99.
86. Patricia Fox, *Being and Blackness in Latin America: Uprootedness and Improvisation* (Gainesville: University Press of Florida, 2008), 4.
87. Julia Cuervo Hewitt, *Voices Out of Africa in Twentieth-Century Spanish Caribbean Literature* (Lewisburg, PA: Bucknell University Press, 2009), 255.
88. Jerome Branche, *The Poetics and Politics of Diaspora: Transatlantic Musings* (New York: Routledge, 2015), 161.
89. Ibid., 8.
90. Manuel Zapata Olivella, "El Muntu en América," in *Bridging Scholarship and Activism: Reflections from the Frontlines of Collaborative Research*, ed. Bernd Reiter

and Ulrich Oslender (East Lansing: Michigan State University Press, 2014), 99–104.

91. Ciro Alfonso Quintero, *Filosofía antropológica y cultural en el pensamiento de Manuel Zapata Olivella* (Quito: Ediciones Abya-Yala, 1998).
92. Ibid., 119.
93. Ibid., 134.
94. William Mina Aragón, *Manuel Zapata Olivella: Pensador Humanista* (Cali: Artes Gráficas del Valle Editores, 2014), 8.
95. Ibid., 26.
96. Ibid., 96.
97. Ibid., 89.
98. Ibid., 104.
99. Ibid., 101.
100. Mina Aragón,. *Manuel Zapata Olivella: Un legado intercultural.*
101. Quince Duncan, "El afrorealismo: Una dimensión nueva de la literatura latinoamericana," *Istmo* 10 (January 25, 2005), http://istmo.denison.edu/n10/articulos/afrorealismo.html.
102. Manuel Zapata Olivella, "Manuel Zapata Olivella—South America's Voice of African Consciousness," interview by Ja Johannes, *In Motion Magazine*, August 1993, www.inmotionmagazine.com/ac10/jj_mz.html.
103. Manuel Zapata Olivella, *Changó el gran putas*, ed. Darío Henao Restrepo (Bogota: Ministerio de Cultura, 2010), 646, http://babel.banrepcultural.org/cdm/ref/collection/p17054coll7/id/2.
104. Silvia Valero, "La construcción del 'sujeto afrodiaspórico' como sujeto político en *Un mensaje de Rosa* (2004) y *El pueblo afrodescendiente* (2012) de Quince Duncan," *Revista de Crítica Literaria Latinoamericana* 41, no. 81 (January 2015): 83.
105. Ibid., 93.
106. Ibid.
107. Ibid., 94.
108. Ibid., 104.
109. Silvia Valero, "¿De qué hablamos cuando hablamos de 'literatura afrocolombiana'? o los riesgos de las categorizaciones," *Estudios de Literatura Colombiana* 32 (2013): 35.
110. Ibid., 37.
111. Roland Forgues, *Palabra en el viento: Ensayos sobre creación e identidad en América Latina* (Paris: Editions Mare et Martin, 2008), 302.
112. Ibid., 302.
113. Ibid., 304.
114. Ibid., 310.
115. Ibid., 315.
116. Ibid., 318.
117. Samuel Mate-Kojo, "Identity, Solidarity, and Autonomy: African Agency in Manuel Zapata Olivella's *Changó, el Gran Putas*," in *Diasporic Identities within Afro-Hispanic and African Contexts*, ed. Yaw Agawu-Kakraba and Komla Aggor (Newcastle upon Tyne: Cambridge Scholars, 2015), 51.
118. Víctor Figueroa, *Prophetic Visions of the Past: Pan-Caribbean Representations of the Haitian Revolution* (Columbus: Ohio State University Press, 2015).

119. Lucía Ortiz, "Nacionalismo y transnacionalismo en Manuel Zapata Olivella," *Boletín Hispánica Helvética* 29 (Spring 2017): 130.
120. Haakayoo Zoggyie, "Lengua e identidad en *Changó, el gran putas*, de Manuel Zapata Olivella," *Estudios de Literatura Colombiana* 7 (2000): 9.
121. Mario Aguiar, "*Changó, el gran putas* o la tormentosa espiral del *Muntu* en América," *Estudios de Literatura Colombiana* 14 (January–June 2004): 11, 13.
122. Ibid., 23.
123. Lucía Ortiz, "Chambacú corral de negros de Manuel Zapata Olivella, un capítulo en la lucha por la libertad. In memoriam," *Inti* 63–64 (Spring–Fall 2006): 99.
124. Raymond Williams, introduction to *Ensayos de literatura colombiana* (Bogota: Editorial Plaza y Janés, 1985), 12–13.
125. Marvin Lewis, "La trayectoria novelística de Manuel Zapata Olivella: De la opresión a la liberación," in *Ensayos de literatura colombiana*, ed. Raymond Williams (Bogota: Plaza y Janés, 1985), 144.
126. Yvonne Captain-Hidalgo, "El espacio del tiempo en *Changó, el gran putas*," in *Ensayos de literatura colombiana*, ed. Raymond Williams (Bogota: Editorial Plaza y Janés, 1985), 158.
127. Ibid., 157.
128. Ibid., 150.
129. John Brushwood, "La novela colombiana en la perspectiva hispanoamericana," in *Ensayos de literatura colombiana*, ed. Raymond Williams (Bogota: Editorial Plaza y Janés, 1985), 172.
130. María Mercedes Jaramillo, "*Hotel de vagabundos*: Crisol racial de las Américas," *Revista de Estudios Colombianos* 44 (2014): 14, 17.
131. Yvonne Captain-Hidalgo, "The Legacy of Manuel Zapata Olivella," *Revista de Estudios Colombianos* 37/38 (2011): 30.
132. Ibid., 33.
133. Pablo Gómez, "La colección de Manuel Zapata Olivella," *Revista de Estudios Colombianos* 37–38 (2011): 117–118.
134. Ibid., 117.
135. Lucía Ortiz, *"Chambacú, la historia la escribes tú": Ensayos sobre cultura afrocolombiana* (Frankfurt: Vervuert, 2007), 15.
136. Liliana Ramírez, "Chambacú: heterogeneidad y representación," in *"Chambacú, la historia la escribes tú": Ensayos sobre cultura afrocolombiana* (Frankfurt: Vervuert, 2007), 171.
137. Raymond Williams, *Novela y poder en Colombia, 1844–1987* (Bogota: Tercer Mundo Editores, 1992), 151–152.
138. Liliana Ramírez, *Entre fronteras: Latinoamericanos y literaturas.* Balún Canán, Dreaming in Cuban *y* Chambacú (Bogota: Pontífica Universidad Javeriana, 2006).
139. Stefan Hofer, "Entre la contingencia y la predeterminación: Ritualidad en *Changó el gran putas* de Manuel Zapata Olivella," in *Ritualidades latinoamericanas: Un acercamiento interdisciplinario /* Ritualidades Latino-Americanas: Uma Aproximação Interdisciplinar (Frankfurt; Madrid: Vervuert; Iberoamericana, 2003), 402.
140. Daiana Nascimento dos Santos, *El océano de fronteras invisibles: Relecturas históricas sobre (¿el fin? de) la esclavitud en la novela contemporánea* (Madrid: Verbum, 2016).
141. Ibid., 52.
142. Ibid., 52.

143. Ibid., 138.
144. Ibid., 148.
145. Ibid., 151.
146. Ibid., 152.
147. Ibid., 156.
148. Ibid., 161.
149. Ineke Phaf-Rheinberger, *Historias enredadas: Representaciones asimétricas con vista al Atlántico* (Berlin: Tranvía-Verlag Walter Frey, 2011), 21.
150. Daiana Nascimento dos Santos, "La nueva novela histórica y sus insuficiencias teóricas: El emplazamiento negro africano," *Estudios Africanos* 27 (June 2017): 57.
151. Ibid., 59.
152. Ibid., 60.
153. Daiana Nascimento dos Santos, "Los tambores suenan, la voz del pueblo resuena: La representación del negro en la novela contemporánea," *Revista Alpha* 40 (2015): 168.
154. Ibid., 170.
155. Ibid., 172.
156. Daiana Nascimento dos Santos, "Atlántico negro: El océano en la narrativa de esclavizados," *Acta Literaria* 54 (2017): 37.
157. Henao, introduction, 18.
158. Piquero, introduction, 9–55.
159. Ibid., 10, 19, 33, 39.
160. Quintero, *Filosofía*, 158.
161. Manuel Zapata Olivella, "*Lève-toi, mulâtre! L'epirit parlera à travers ma race*," trans. Claude Couffon and Claude Bourguignon (Paris: Payot, 1987), cover.
162. François Bogliolo, *La négritude et les problèmes du Noir dans l'oeuvre de Zapata Olivella* (Dakar: Nouvelles Éditions Africaines, 1978).
163. Ibid., 250.
164. Luciana da Trindade Prestes and Emília Maria da Trindade Prestes, "A literatura como mecanismo de luta pelo reconhecimento social de mulheres negras na obra *Um defeito de cor*," *Afro-Ásia* 56 (2017): 131.
165. "Ana Maria Gonçalves," Internationales Literaturfestival, September 11–21, 2019, Berlin, http://literaturfestival.com/autoren-en/autoren-2013-en/ana-maria-goncalves. Her contribution to *As segundas palavras da tribo* (2002) is out of print.
166. Ana Maria Gonçalves, *Ao lado e à margem do que sentes por mim*, August 1, 2006, http://anamariagoncalves.blogspot.com/.
167. Ana Maria Gonçalves, *100 meias confissões de Aninha*, August 1, 2006, http://anamariagoncalves.blogspot.com/.
168. Ana Maria Gonçalves, *Um defeito de cor* (Rio de Janeiro: Editora Record, 2006).
169. Ana Maria Gonçalves, preface to *Do outro lado*, by Maurício Barros de Castro and César Fraga (São Paulo: Olhares, 2014); Maurício Barros de Castro and César Fraga, *Do outro lado* (São Paulo: Olhares, 2014), 18–19.
170. Ana Maria Gonçalves, email correspondence, December 30, 2016.
171. Agência EFE, "Ana Maria Gonçalves ganha Prêmio Casa de Las Américas 2007," *Jornal do Brasil*, July 31, 2007, www.jb.com.br/cultura/noticias/2007/01/25/ana-maria-goncalves-ganha-premio-casa-de-las-americas-2007/.
172. Cláudio de Sá Capuano, "História e africanidade em *Um defeito de cor* de Ana Maria Gonçalves," in *Alguma prosa: Ensaios sobre a literatura brasileira contemporânea*, ed. Giovanna Dealtry et al. (Rio de Janeiro: Editora Sete Letras, 2007), 87.

173. Ibid., 89.
174. Ibid., 92, 94.
175. Idelber Avelar, "Biblioteca Latino-Americana: Xangô, o grande fodão [Changó, el gran putas] de Manuel Zapata Olivella." *Forum*, March 16, 2012, www.revistaforum.com.br/idelberavelar/2012/03/16/biblioteca-latino-americana-xango-o-grande-fodao-chango-el-gran-putas-de-manuel-zapata-olivella/.
176. Adélcio de Sousa Cruz, "Ana Maria Gonçalves," in *Literatura e afrodescendência no Brasil: Antologia crítica*. vol. 3: *Contemporâneidade*, ed. Eduardo de Assis Duarte and Maria Nazareth Soares Fonseca (Belo Horizonte: Editora da Universidade Federal de Minas Gerais, 2011), 477–492.
177. Ibid., 479.
178. Ibid., 479.
179. Eduardo de Assis Duarte, "Na cartografia do romance brasileiro, *Um defeito de cor*, de Ana Maria Gonçalves," *Literafro*, www.letras.ufmg.br/literafro/arquivos/autoras/anamariacritica03.pdf.
180. Ibid.
181. Ibid..
182. Cristiane Felipe Ribeiro de Araújo Côrtes, "*Um defeito de cor*: O entre e o duplo da diáspora," *Literafro*, http://150.164.100.248/literafro/data1/autores/23/anamariacritica01.pdf.
183. Ibid., 3.
184. Ibid., 6.
185. Regina Dalcastagnè, "A cor de uma ausência: Representações do negro no romance brasileiro contemporâneo," *Afro-Hispanic Review* 29, no. 2 (Fall 2010): 97.
186. Ibid., 97.
187. Ibid., 106.
188. Ana Beatriz Gonçalves and Clara Alencar Pimentel, "A mulher e a maternidade: Breve leitura do romance *Um defeito de cor* de Ana Maria Gonçalves," *Terra Roxa e Outras Terras: Revista de Estudos Literários* 17, no. 2 (2009): 120, www.uel.br/revistas/uel/index.php/terraroxa/article/view/25011.
189. Ibid., 123.
190. Marcelo Cruz Dalcom Junior and Lícia Soares de Souza, "Nas entrelinhas de Um defeito de Cor: Desvio, discursos históricos e literários" (XI Congresso Internacional da Associação Brasileira de Estudos Canadenses, October 24–26, 2011, Universidade Federal da Bahia, Salvador, BA), 2, 8, www.anaisabecan2011.ufba.br/Arquivos/Dalcom-Souza.pdf.
191. Aline Najara da Silva Gonçalves, "A saga de Kehinde: Uma representação do protagonismo negro no romance histórico *Um defeito de cor*," *Historien—Revista de História* 4 (June 2011): 143, http://revistahistorien.blogspot.com/2011/06/4-edicao-da-revista-historien.html.
192. Ibid., 143, 145, 151.
193. Marcos Roberto Teixeira de Andrade, "A visão periférica da História em *Um defeito de cor*, de Ana Maria Gonçalves," *Darandina Revisteletrônica* 1 (2010): 1, 3–4, www.ufjf.br/darandina/files/2010/01/Marcos-Roberto-Teixeira-de-Andrade.pdf.
194. Ibid., 3.
195. Ibid., 3, 11.
196. Ibid., 13.
197. Ibid., 14.

198. Zilá Bernd, "Em busca dos rastros perdidos da memória ancestral: Um estudo de *Um defeito de cor* de Ana Maria Gonçalves," *Estudos da Literatura Brasileira Contemporânea* 40 (July–December 2012): 30.
199. Ibid., 38.
200. Ibid., 30.
201. Ibid., 30, 32, 34.
202. Ibid., 31.
203. Ibid., 32.
204. Ibid., 35–37.
205. Ibid., 32.
206. Ibid., 39.
207. Ibid., 40.
208. Ibid., 40.
209. Maria Josele Bucco Coelho, "(In)submissive Imaginaries in the Contemporary Brazilian Historical Novel: A Reading of *Um defeito de cor* by Ana Maria Gonçalves," in *Redefining Latin American Historical Fiction: The Impact of Feminism and Postcolonialism*, ed. Helene Carol Weldt-Basson (New York: Palgrave Macmillan, 2013), 209–210.
210. Ibid., 212.
211. Ibid., 216–217.
212. Ibid., 218, 227.
213. Ibid., 224.
214. Nascimento dos Santos, *Océano*, 164–165, 177.
215. Ibid., 166.
216. Ibid., 172.
217. Ibid., 173.
218. Ibid., 175.
219. Ibid., 177.
220. Ibid., 181.
221. Ibid., 184–185.
222. Ibid., 188.
223. Ibid., 199.
224. Ibid., 211.
225. Daiana Nascimento dos Santos, "Memoria y representación del barco y del mar en la travesía y la migración forzada," *Afro-Hispanic Review* 32, no. 1 (Spring 2013): 115–128. She argues that representing the slave ships humanizes the people who were forced onto them and that these were a foundational trauma (116).
226. Daiana Nascimento dos Santos, "História e memoria no romance *Um defeito de cor*," *Izquierdas* 31 (2016): 162.
227. Ibid., 166.
228. Ibid., 166.
229. Ibid., 166.
230. Ibid., 167.
231. Ibid., 169.
232. Annie Gibson, "Vencendo confins: A voz resistente na narrativa de Kehinde em *Um defeito de cor*," *Pterodáctilo*, no. 7 (Fall 2009): 2.

233. Antônio Luciano de Andrade Tosta, *Confluence Narratives: Ethnicity, History, and Nation-Making in the Americas* (Lewisburg, PA: Bucknell University Press, 2016).
234. Ibid., 100.
235. Ibid., 110, 113.
236. Ibid., 123, 125.
237. Ibid., 128.
238. Ibid., 181.
239. Paulo Thomaz, "Des-Reterritorialização: percursos possíveis do romance afro-brasileiro recente," *Estudos da Literatura Brasileira Contemporânea* 45 (2015): 25.
240. Ibid., 27.
241. Ibid., 28.
242. Ibid., 29.
243. Ibid., 32.
244. Ibid., 32–33.
245. Ineke Phaf-Rheinberger, "Myths of Early Modernity: Historical and Contemporary Narratives on Brazil and Angola," in *AfricAmericas: Itineraries, Dialogues, and Sounds*, ed. Ineke Phaf-Rheinberger and Tiago de Oliveira Pinto (Frankfurt: Vervuert, 2008), 148.
246. Ineke Phaf-Rheinberger, *Modern Slavery and Water Spirituality: A Critical Debate in Africa and Latin America* (New York: Peter Lang, 2017), 220.
247. Ibid., 220.
248. Ibid., 545–546.
249. Leila Lehnen, "Growing Up to Human Rights: The Bildungsroman and the Discourse of Human Rights in *Um defeito de cor*," in *Literature and Ethics in Contemporary Brazil*, ed. Vinicius Mariano de Carvalho and Nicola Gavioli (New York: Routledge, 2017), 101.
250. Ibid., 110.
251. Fabiana Carneiro da Silva, "Quando o que se discute é a realidade: *Um defeito de cor* como provocação à História," *Afro-Ásia* 55 (2017): 86.
252. Ibid., 100.
253. Ibid., 101.
254. Luciana da Trindade Prestes and Emília Maria da Trindade Prestes, "A literatura como mecanismo de luta pelo reconhecimento social de mulheres negras na obra *Um defeito de cor*," *Afro-Ásia* 56 (2017): 130–131.
255. "Ana Maria Gonçalves—New Columnist for the Intercept Brasil," YouTube, 2:04, Posted by "The Intercept Brasil," December 2, 2016, www.youtube.com/watch?v=FPFj5ToQ9xc.
256. Prestes and Prestes, "Mecanismo," 141.
257. Ibid., 141–142.
258. Ibid., 133.
259. John Maddox, "The Black Atlantic Revised: Ana Maria Gonçalves's *Um defeito de cor*," *Callaloo* 40, no. 4 (Fall 2017): 155.
260. Claire Williams, "Tracing Back Trauma: The Legacy of Slavery in Afro-Brazilian Literature by Women," *Angelaki: Journal of the Theoretical Humanities* 22, no 1 (March 2017): 103.
261. Ana Maria Gonçalves, "Inspiração e viagens através da diáspora: Uma entrevista com Ana Maria Gonçalves," interview by John Maddox, *Afro-Hispanic Review*

30, no. 2 (Fall 2011): 167–180; John Maddox, "Ana Maria Gonçalves," in *Oxford Dictionary of Caribbean and Afro-Latin American Biography*, ed. Franklin Knight and Henry Louis Gates (Oxford: Oxford University Press, 2016), 115–117.

262. Elciene Azevedo, *Orfeu de Caparinha: A trajetória de Luiz Gama na imperial cidade de São Paulo* (Campinas: Universidade de Campinas, 1999); Nelson Câmara, *Escravidão, nunca mais!: Um tributo a Luiz Gama* (São Paulo: Editora Via Lettera, 2009); Câmara, *Luiz Gama, o advogado dos escravos* (São Paulo: Editora Via Lettera, 2010); Maria Consuelo Cunha Campos, "Luiz Gama," in *Literatura e afrodescendência no Brasil: Antologia crítica*, vol. 1, ed. Eduardo de Assis Duarte (Belo Horizonte: Editora da Universidade Federal de Minas Gerais, 2011), 127–134; Luís Carlos dos Santos, *Luiz Gama* (São Paulo: Selo Negro), 2010; Lígia Fonseca Ferreira, *Com a palavra, Luiz Gama: Poemas, artigos, cartas, máximas* (São Paulo: Imprensa Oficial, 2011); Ferreira, ed., *Primeiras trovas burlescas de Getulino* (São Paulo: Martins Fontes, 2000). Ferreira is the only literary critic with a book on Gama.
263. Duarte, "Cartografia," *Literafro*, www.letras.ufmg.br/literafro/arquivos/autoras/anamariacritica03.pdf.
264. Ana Lucia Araujo, "Dandara e Luisa Mahin são consideradas heroínas do Brasil—O problema é que elas nunca existiram," *Intercept Brasil*, June 3, 2019, https://theintercept.com/2019/06/03/dandara-luisa-mahin-panteao-patria/.
265. Gilroy, *Atlantic*, 13; Aline Helg, "Oralidad y escritura en la historiografía de los esclavos afrodescendientes," in *Palenque Colombia: Oralidad, identidad y resistencia*, ed. Graciela Maglia and Armin Schwegler (Bogota: Editorial Pontífica Universidad Javeriana, 2012), 85.
266. James Sweet, *Recreating Africa: Culture, Kinship, and Religion in the African-Portuguese World, 1441–1770* (Chapel Hill: University of North Carolina Press, 2004), 8.
267. Ibid., 8.
268. Juan Francisco Manzano, *Autobiografía del esclavo poeta y otros escritos*, ed. William Luis (Frankfurt: Vervuert, 2007); Bruno Véras, "Projeto Baquaqua" (May 2016, Harriet Tubman Institute, York University; Universidade Federal de Pernambuco; Ministério de Cultura do Brasil), www.baquaqua.com.br/fontes-historicas/.
269. Deborah Plant, "Afterword and Additional Materials," in *Barracoon*, by Zora Neale Hurston (New York: Amistad, 2018), 131.
270. Miguel Barnet [and Esteban Montejo], *Biografía de un cimarrón* (Mexico: Siglo Veintiuno, 1968).
271. Plant, "Afterward," 124.
272. Zapata, *Changó*, 35. Hereafter, references to this edition are given parenthetically.
273. Tomás Antonio Gonzaga, "Cartas chilenas," Dominio Público, Ministério de Cultura, Universidade da Amazônia, Belém, Brazil, 2, www.dominiopublico.gov.br/download/texto/ua000293.pdf. Chilean governor *Fanfarrón* Minesio, a stand-in for Luís da Cunha Meneses, governor of Minas, according to Gonzaga, a Minas conspirator.
274. Gonçalves, *Defeito*, 949. Hereafter, references to this edition are given parenthetically.
275. Both terms refer to enslavers or whites in general—*senhora* and *senhorita*—and are paralleled by the masculine *sinhô/senhor*.

Chapter 1 Myth, Literature, and History in Zapata

1. Manuel Zapata, *¡Levántate mulato! Por mi raza hablará el espíritu* (Bogota: Rei Andes, 1990), 283.
2. Manuel Zapata Olivella, *Changó el gran putas* (Bogota: Ministerio de Cultura, 2010), 407, http://babel.banrepcultural.org/cdm/ref/collection/p17054coll7/id/2.
3. Zapata, *Changó*, 44–45.
4. Ibid., 94.
5. Manuel Zapata Olivella, "Tambores de América para despertar al Viejo Mundo," (unpublished manuscript, n.d.), Vanderbilt Manuel Zapata Olivella Papers, Nashville, TN.
6. Zapata, *¡Levántate!*, 348.
7. Zapata, *¡Levántate!*, 348.
8. Langston Hughes, "Letter to Manuel Zapata Olivella" (unpublished letter, n.d.), Vanderbilt Manuel Zapata Olivella Papers, Nashville, TN; Lawrence Prescott, "Brother to Brother: The Friendship and Literary Correspondence of Manuel Zapata Olivella and Langston Hughes," *Afro-Hispanic Review* 25, no. 1 (Spring 2006): 87.
9. María Adelaida López, dir., *Manuel Zapata Olivella: Abridor de caminos* (Colombia: Azul y Naranja Producciones, 2007), YouTube, February 23, 2012, www.youtube.com/watch?v=3Dpc4w2Kp6I.
10. Lucía Ortiz, "Nacionalismo y transnacionalismo en Manuel Zapata Olivella," *Boletín Hispánica Helvética* 29 (Spring 2017): 138, 1941.
11. Alain Locke, "Enter the New Negro," *Survey Graphic*, March 1925, National Humanities Center Toolbox: The Making of African American Identity, vol. 3, 1917–1968, 3, http://nationalhumanitiescenter.org/pds/maai3/migrations/text8/lockenewnegro.pdf.
12. Ibid., 4.
13. Ibid., 2; Langston Hughes, "Youth," *Crisis*, January/February 2002, 40, https://books.google.com.
14. George Palacios, "Apuntes sobre la música, el folclor, lo nacional-popular y la literatura en algunos de los escritos tempranos de Manuel Zapata Olivella," *Escritos* 23, no. 51 (2015): 468.
15. Zapata, *Changó*, 611.
16. Ibid., 611.
17. Ibid., 629.
18. Carla Kaplan, ed., *Zora Neale Hurston: A Life in Letters* (New York: Doubleday, 2002), 315.
19. Zora Neale Hurston, "Characteristics of Negro Expression," in *Negro: An Anthology*, ed. Nancy Cunard (New York: Frederick Ungar, 1970), 24.
20. Zapata, *Changó*, 51.
21. Hurston, "Characteristics," 25.
22. Ibid., 26.
23. Ibid., 27.
24. Ibid., 28.
25. Ibid., 29; Zapata, *Changó*, 638.
26. Alice Walker, "Foreword," in *Barracoon*, by Zora Neale Hurston (New York: Amistad, 2018), xi.

27. Daphne Mary Lamothe, *Inventing the New Negro: Narrative, Culture, and Ethnography* (Philadelphia: University of Pennsylvania Press, 2008), 231.
28. Ibid., 258.
29. Jorge Artel, *Tambores en la noche*, in *Si yo fuera tambó: Poesía selecta de Candelario Obeso y Jorge Artel, edición crítica*, ed. Graciela Maglia (Bogota: Editorial de la Pontífica Universidad Javeriana, 2010), 199–236.
30. Lawrence Prescott, *Without Hatred or Fears: Jorge Artel and the Struggle for Black Literary Expression in Colombia* (Detroit: Wayne State University Press, 2000), 221.
31. Lucía Ortiz, "La representación del mestizaje cultural en la literatura afrocolombiana," *Actas XIV Congreso Asociación Internacional de Hispanistas* 4 (July 16–21, 2001): 495–503.
32. Maglia, *Tambó*, 178.
33. Luisa García-Conde, "Jorge Artel: Versos y prosa de un poeta indomulato," in Maglia, *Tambó*, 189.
34. Zapata, "Artel, el maestro," *Afro-Hispanic Review* 25, no. 1 (Spring 2006): 149–150.
35. Ibid., 148.
36. Zapata, *Changó*, 340, 368.
37. Zapata, "Artel," 150–151.
38. Artel in ibid., 151.
39. Ibid., 151.
40. Prescott, *Hatred*, 89.
41. Ibid., 211.
42. Ibid., 153.
43. Zapata, "Artel," 153.
44. Ibid., 154.
45. Ernesto [Che] Guevara, *El socialismo y el hombre en Cuba*, Marxists.org, www.marxists.org/espanol/guevara/65-socyh.htm.
46. "Manuel Zapata Olivella," Catálogo Fondo Editorial Casa de las Américas, www.casa.co.cu/catalogoeditorial/fichaautor.php?cod=717.
47. Zapata, *¡Levántate!*, 21.
48. Ibid., 17.
49. Guevara, *Socialismo*.
50. Ibid.
51. Odette Casamayor, "Imagining the New Black (Subject): Ethical Transformations of Raciality in the Post-Revolutionary Cuban Nation," in *Black Writing and the State in Latin America*, ed. Jerome Branche (Nashville, TN: Vanderbilt University Press, 2015), 61, 72.
52. Ibid., 62.
53. Ibid., 65.
54. Ibid., 78.
55. Darío Henao Restrepo, introduction to *Changó, el gran putas*, by Manuel Zapata Olivella, in *Biblioteca de Literatura Afrocolombiana*, vol. 3, ed. Darío Henao (Bogota: Ministerio de Cultura, 2010), 12 http://babel.banrepcultural.org/cdm/ref/collection/p17054coll7/id/2.
56. Manuel Zapata Olivella, "Manuel Zapata Olivella—South America's Voice of African Consciousness," interview by Ja Johannes, *In Motion Magazine*, August 1993, www.inmotionmagazine.com/ac10/jj_mz.html.
57. Ortiz, "Nacionalismo," 137.

58. Ibid., 137; Manuel Zapata Olivella, "Conversación informal con Manuel Zapata Olivella," by Margarita Krakusin, *Afro-Hispanic Review* 20, no. 1 (2001): 15–28.
59. Manuel Zapata Olivella, *El árbol brujo de la libertad*, ed. William Mina Aragón (Cali: Universidad del Valle; Cartagena: Universidad de Cartagena, 2009), 25, 57.
60. Ibid., 25.
61. Zapata, *Changó*, 78; Zapata, *Árbol*, 57.
62. Henao, introduction, 13.
63. Anne Garland Mahler, *From the Tricontinental to the Global South: Race, Radicalism, and Transnational Solidarity* (Durham, NC: Duke University Press, 2018), 837.
64. Ibid., 569.
65. Ibid., 582.
66. Ibid., 918.
67. Ibid., 943.
68. Ibid., 1105.
69. Ibid., 1077.
70. Ibid., 1077.
71. Ibid., 1077.
72. Ibid., 1077.
73. Ibid., 1215; Richard Jackson, *Black Literature and Humanism in Latin America* (Athens: University of Georgia Press, 1997), xi.
74. Garland Mahler, *Tricontinental*, 1215.
75. Ibid., 626.
76. Ibid., 1753.
77. Placide Tempels, *Bantu Philosophy*, trans. A. Rubbens and Collin King, edited by Honoré Vinck (Centre Aequatoria, November 2006), www.congoforum.be/upldocs/Tempels%20BantuPhil%20English%201959.pdf.
78. James Sweet, *Recreating Africa: Culture, Kinship, and Religion in the African-Portuguese World, 1441–1770* (Chapel Hill: University of North Carolina Press, 2004), 192.
79. Ibid., 110.
80. Ibid., 199.
81. Ibid., 193.
82. Ibid., 193.
83. Ibid., 107, 207.
84. Ibid., 107, 207.
85. Ibid., 108.
86. Ibid., 19.
87. Ibid., 103.
88. Zapata, *Changó*, 660.
89. Ibid., 648.
90. Ibid., 648.
91. Ibid., 648.
92. Manuel Zapata Olivella, *La rebelión de los genes: El mestizaje americano en la sociedad futura* (Bogota: Altamir, 1997), 362.
93. Ibid., 361.
94. Ibid., 361.
95. Ibid., 361.
96. Ibid., 362.

97. Zapata, *Árbol*, 67–68.
98. Ibid., 322.
99. Ibid., 9.
100. Zapata, *Changó*, 87.
101. Sweet, *Recreating*, 2, 16.
102. Ibid., 16–17.
103. Ibid., 3, 16.
104. Ibid., 7.
105. Ibid., 113.
106. Ibid., 162.
107. Ibid., 161–162.
108. Ibid., 162.
109. Ibid., 217.
110. Henao, introduction, 16.
111. Lydia Cabrera, *El Monte: Notas sobre las religiones, la magia, las supersticiones y el folklore de los negros criollos y el pueblo de Cuba* (Havana: Letras Cubanas, 1993), 225.
112. Jerome Branche, *The Poetics and Politics of Diaspora: Transatlantic Musings* (New York: Routledge, 2015), 162; Víctor Figueroa, *Prophetic Visions of the Past: Pan-Caribbean Representations of the Haitian Revolution* (Columbus: Ohio State University Press, 2015), 196.
113. Daiana Nascimento dos Santos, *El océano de fronteras invisibles: Relecturas históricas sobre (¿el fin? de) la esclavitud en la novela contemporánea* (Madrid: Verbum, 2016), 144.
114. Ibid., 143.
115. Figueroa, *Prophetic*, 223.
116. Ibid., 224.
117. Yvonne Captain-Hidalgo, *The Culture of Fiction in the Works of Manuel Zapata Olivella* (Columbia: University of Missouri Press, 1993), 148; Figueroa, *Prophetic*, 225.
118. Figueroa, *Prophetic*, 227.
119. Ibid., 228; Anthony Pinn, *Why Lord? Suffering and Evil in Black Theology* (New York: Continuum, 1999).
120. Samuel Johnson, *The History of the Yorubas: From the Earliest Times to the Beginning of the British Protectorate* (London: Lowe and Brydone, 1921), 223.
121. Figueroa, *Prophetic*, 207.
122. Johnson, *History*, 150.
123. Ibid., 143; Zapata, *Changó*, 58.
124. Zapata, *Changó*, 58.
125. Cabrera, *El monte*, 224; Zapata, *Changó*, 58.
126. Zapata, *¡Levántate!*, 342.
127. Zapata, *Changó*, 586.
128. Ibid., 59.
129. Johnson, History, 157. Zapata departs from Johnson, who claims that some think Timi served under Changó, but that it was really the anonymous king of Ido.
130. Johnson, *History*, 157.
131. Ibid., 157.
132. Ibid., 159.
133. Zapata, *Changó*., 58.

134. Zapata, *Changó*, 58, 60.
135. Ibid., 61.
136. Ibid., 63.
137. Ibid., 637.
138. Johnson, *History*, 152.
139. Ibid.
140. Ibid., 154.
141. Ibid., 35.
142. Ibid.
143. Ibid., 36.
144. Ibid., 37.
145. Ibid., 37.
146. Zapata, *Changó*, 62.
147. Ibid., 73.
148. Ibid., 72.
149. Johnson, *History*, 650.
150. Antonio Tillis, *Manuel Zapata Olivella and the "Darkening" of Latin American Literature* (Columbia: University of Missouri Press, 2005), 98.
151. Zapata, *Changó*, 68–69.
152. Ibid., 70.
153. Samuel Mate-Kojo, "Identity, Solidarity, and Autonomy: African Agency in Manuel Zapata Olivella's *Changó, el Gran Putas*," in *Diasporic Identities within Afro-Hispanic and African Contexts*, ed. Yaw Agawu-Kakraba and Komla Aggor (Newcastle upon Tyne: Cambridge Scholars, 2015), 57.
154. Ibid., 635.
155. Sweet, *Recreating*, 119.
156. Manuel Zapata Olivella, *Las claves mágicas de América* (Bogota: Plazas y Janés, 1989), 96–97.
157. Ibid., 97.
158. Ibid., 98–103, 108.
159. Ibid., 98.
160. Zapata, *Claves*, 99.
161. Ibid., 99–101.
162. Zapata, *Claves*, 110.
163. Branche, *Poetics*, 158.
164. Tillis, *"Darkening,"* 98; José Vasconcelos, *La raza cósmica: Misión de la raza iberoamericana, Argentina y Brasil* (Mexico: Trillas, 2012), 179.
165. Zapata, *Claves*, 180.
166. Tempels, *Bantu Philosophy*, 73–74.
167. Ibid., 76.
168. Ibid., 76.
169. Zapata, *Changó*, 102, 166, 240, 483.
170. Tempels, *Bantu Philosophy*, 63.
171. Ibid., 18.
172. Ibid., 10.
173. Ibid., 10.
174. Ibid., 10.
175. Ibid., 22.

176. Ibid., 50.
177. Ibid., 53.
178. Ibid., 23.
179. Ibid., 23.
180. Frantz Fanon, *Black Skin, White Masks*, trans. Richard Philcox (New York: Grove Press, 2008).
181. Zapata, *Changó*, 493.
182. Tempels, *Bantu Philosophy*, 24.
183. Ibid., 24.
184. Ibid., 29.
185. Ibid., 25.
186. Janheinz Jahn, *Muntu: African Culture and the Western World*, trans. Marjorie Greene (New York: Grove, 1961); Diana Carolina Sierra Díaz, "El Muntu: La diáspora del pensamiento filosófico africano en Changó, el gran putas de Manuel Zapata Olivella," *La Palabra* 29 (July–December 2016): 26–27; Tempels, *Bantu Philosophy*, 27. Drawing on Janheinz Jahn, Diana Carolina Sierra Díaz claims the *muntu* can be further divided into Kinto (plants/animals/objects), Hantu (space/time), and Kuntu (lifestyle/aesthetics).
187. Tempels, *Bantu Philosophy*, 27.
188. Ibid., 30.
189. Ibid., 28.
190. Ibid., 31.
191. Ibid., 645.
192. Frantz Fanon, *The Wretched of the Earth*, trans. Constance Farrington (New York: Grove, 1963), 8.
193. Zapata, *Changó*, 73.
194. Tempels, *Bantu Philosophy*., 33–34.
195. Ibid., 48.
196. Ibid., 36, 45.
197. Ibid., 46–47.
198. Ibid., 47–48.
199. Zapata, *¡Levántate!*, 342.
200. Tempels, *Bantu Philosophy*, 57.
201. Ibid., 568.
202. Ibid., 59.
203. Ibid., 62.
204. Ibid., 68.
205. Ibid., 62–63.
206. Ibid., 58.
207. Ibid., 69.
208. Ibid., 70.
209. Ibid., 71.
210. Zora Neale Hurston, *Dust Tracks on a Road: An Autobiography*, 2nd ed. (Urbana: University of Illinois Press, 1984), 200.
211. Brian Palmer, "The 'Very Particular' History Being Presented at Confederate Sites," *Fresh Air*, National Public Radio, January 21, 2019, www.npr.org/2019/01/21/686547376/the-very-particular-history-being-presented-at-confederate-sites.

212. Herman Bennett, *African Kings and Black Slaves: Sovereignty and Dispossession in the Early Modern Atlantic* (Philadelphia: University of Pennsylvania Press, 2019), 247.
213. Ibid., 10.
214. Ibid., 247.
215. Ibid., 16, 30, 192.
216. Ibid., 21, 256.
217. Ibid., 97.
218. Ibid., 14, 36.
219. Ibid., 26.
220. Ibid., 38.
221. Júnia Ferreira Furtado, *Chica da Silva: A Brazilian Slave of the Eighteenth Century* (Cambridge: Cambridge University Press, 2009), 12.
222. Ibid., 13.
223. David Wheat, *Atlantic Africa and the Spanish Caribbean, 1570–1640* (Chapel Hill: University of North Carolina Press, 2016).
224. Ibid., 391.
225. Ibid., 394.
226. Armin Schwegler, "Sobre el origen africano de la lengua criolla de Palenque (Colombia)," in *Palenque Colombia: Oralidad, identidad y resistencia*, ed. Graciela Maglia and Armin Schwegler (Bogota: Editorial Pontífica Universidad Javeriana, 2012), 115.
227. Víctor Simarra, "Palenque de San Basilio hoy," by John Maddox, *Publication of the Afro-Latin American Research Association* 18 (2014): 87.
228. Zapata, *Changó*, 156; Manuel Zapata Olivella, *El árbol brujo de la libertad*, ed. William Mina Aragón (Cali: Universidad del Valle, 2009), 104.
229. María Cristina Navarrete, "Palenques: Cimarrones y castas en el Caribe colombiano—sus relaciones sociales (siglo XVII)," in *Palenque Colombia: Oralidad, identidad y resistencia*, ed. Graciela Maglia and Armin Schwegler (Bogota: Editorial Pontífica Universidad Javeriana, 2012); Navarrete, *San Basilio de Palenque: Memoria y tradición* (Cali: Universidad del Valle, 2008); Schwegler, "Origen," 118.
230. Navarrete, *San Basilio*, 45.
231. Camilo Delgado, *Historias, leyendas y tradiciones de Cartagena* (Cartagena: Colombia Mogollón, 1914).
232. Schwegler, "Origen," 117.
233. Ibid., 115.
234. Ibid., 117.
235. Aline Helg, "Oralidad y escritura en la historiografía de los esclavos afrodescendientes," in *Palenque Colombia: Oralidad, identidad y resistencia*, ed. Graciela Maglia and Armin Schwegler (Bogota: Editorial Pontífica Universidad Javeriana, 2012), 95.
236. Wheat, *Atlantic Africa*, 389.
237. Henao, introduction, 20.
238. Helg, "Oralidad," 101.
239. Branche, *Poetics*, 158.
240. Wheat, *Atlantic Africa*, 40.
241. Ibid., 33, 40.

242. Ibid., 228.
243. Ibid., 39–40.

Chapter 2 Afro-Brazil in Gonçalves and Zapata

1. Ana Lucia Araujo, "Dandara e Luisa Mahin são consideradas heroínas do Brasil—O problema é que elas nunca existiram," *Intercept Brasil*, June 3, 2019, https://theintercept.com/2019/06/03/dandara-luisa-mahin-panteao-patria/.
2. Lígia Fonseca Ferreira, ed., *Primeiras trovas burlescas de Getulino* (São Paulo: Martins Fontes, 2000).
3. Ricardo Henriques, *Desigualdade racial no Brasil: Evolução das condições de vida na década de 90* (Rio de Janeiro: IPEA, 1999), 807.
4. Lígia Fonseca Ferreira, *Com a palavra, Luiz Gama: Poemas, artigos, cartas, máximas* (São Paulo: Imprensa Oficial, 2011), 21–22.
5. Ana Lucia Araujo, "Dandara e Luisa Mahin são consideradas heroínas do Brasil—O problema é que elas nunca existiram," *Intercept Brasil*, June 3, 2019, https://theintercept.com/2019/06/03/dandara-luisa-mahin-panteao-patria/.
6. Sud Mennucci, *O precursor do abolicionismo no Brasil. Luiz Gama* (São Paulo: Companhia Editora Nacional, 1938), 19.
7. Ibid., 20.
8. Ferreira, *Palavra*, 22.
9. Mennucci, *Precursor*, 21–23.
10. Ferreira, *Palavra*, 22.
11. Ibid., 24.
12. Ibid., 30–31.
13. Ibid., 32.
14. Ibid., 81.
15. Ibid., 32.
16. Ibid., 18.
17. César Braga-Pinto, "The Honor of the Abolitionist and the Shamefulness of Slavery: Raul Pompéia, Luiz Gama, and Joaquim Nabuco," *Luso-Brazilian Review* 51, no. 22 (2014): 170.
18. Ibid., 172–174.
19. Maria Consuelo Cunha Campos, "Luiz Gama," in *Literatura e afrodescendência no Brasil: Antologia crítica,* ed. Eduardo de Assis Duarte, vol. 1 (Belo Horizonte: Editora da Universidade Federal de Minas Gerais, 2011), 127–34.
20. Ibid., 128–130.
21. Ibid., 142.
22. Emanuelle Oliveira, *Writing Identity: The Politics of Contemporary Afro-Brazilian Literature* (West Lafayette: Purdue University Press, 2008), 77.
23. Mennucci, *Precursor*, 20.
24. David Wheat, *Atlantic Africa and the Spanish Caribbean, 1570–1640* (Chapel Hill: University of North Carolina Press, 2016), 384.
25. Mennucci, *Precursor*, 20.
26. Dulcilei da Conceição Lima, "Desvendando Luíza Mahin: Um mito libertário no cerne do feminismo negro" (Master's thesis, Universidade Presbiteriana MacKenzie, 2011), 71.

27. Ana Maria Gonçalves, *Um defeito de cor* (Rio de Janeiro: Editora Record, 2006), 296; Lima, "Desvendando," 71.
28. Luís Gama, *Primerias trovas burlescas de Getulino*, ed. Lígia Fonseca Ferreira (São Paulo: Martins Fontes, 2000), 183.
29. Ibid., 183.
30. Ibid., 185.
31. Ibid., 185.
32. Ibid., 184.
33. Gonçalves, *Defeito*, 173.
34. Gama, *Trovas*, 184.
35. Ibid., 184.
36. Lima, "Desvendando," 37.
37. João José Reis, *Rebelião escrava no Brasil: A história do Levante dos Malês em 1835* (São Paulo: Companhia das Letras, 2004), 303.
38. Lima, "Desvendando," 47.
39. Ibid., 52.
40. Ibid., 48.
41. Ibid., 63; Arthur Ramos, *O negro na civilização brasileira* (Rio de Janeiro: Guanabara, 1971), 50–53.
42. Lima, "Desvendando," 63–64.
43. Ibid., 68–69.
44. Ibid., 19.
45. Ibid., 68–69.
46. Reis, *Rebelião*, 10.
47. Lima, "Desvendando," 74.
48. Ibid., 75.
49. Miriam Alves, "Mahin amanã," *Cadernos Negros* 9 (1986): 46.
50. Ibid., 46.
51. Alzira Rufino, "Luiza Mahin," in *Eu, mulher negra, resisto* (Self-published, 2010), 2.
52. Lima, "Desvendando," 101.
53. Ibid., 98.
54. Ibid., 104–105.
55. Sueli Carneiro, "Estrelas com luz própria," *Revista História Viva* 3 (2006): 48–49.
56. Gonçalves, *Defeito*, 16.
57. Ibid., 505.
58. James Sweet, *Recreating Africa: Culture, Kinship, and Religion in the African-Portuguese World, 1441–1770* (Chapel Hill: University of North Carolina Press, 2004), 16.
59. María Cristina Navarrete, "Palenques: Cimarrones y castas en el Caribe colombiano—sus relaciones sociales (siglo XVII)," in *Palenque Colombia: Oralidad, identidad y resistencia*, ed. Graciela Maglia and Armin Schwegler (Bogota: Editorial Pontífica Universidad Javeriana, 2012), 272.
60. Gonçalves, *Defeito*, 509.
61. Sweet, *Recreating*, 89.
62. Paul Gilroy, *The Black Atlantic: Modernity and Double Consciousness* (New York: Verso, 1993), 56.
63. Gonçalves, *Defeito*, 510.

64. Ibid., 524.
65. Ibid., 524.
66. Ibid., 528.
67. Gilroy, *Atlantic*, 63; Zapata, *Changó*, 284.
68. Gonçalves, *Defeito*, 529.
69. Ibid., 534.
70. Ibid., 535.
71. Ibid., 536.
72. Manuel Zapata Olivella, *¡Levántate mulato! Por mi raza hablará el espíritu* (Bogota: REI Andes, 1990), 259.
73. John Maddox, "Aleijadinho at Home and Abroad: 'Discovering' Race and Nation in Brazil," *CR: The New Centennial Review* 12, no. 2 (Fall 2012): 213.
74. Gilroy, *Atlantic*, 59.
75. Abdias Nascimento, *Quilombismo: Documentos de uma miltância pan-africanista* (Rio de Janeiro: Vozes, 1980), 260.
76. Ibid., 261.
77. Ibid., 256–257.
78. Ibid., 280.
79. Michael George Hanchard, *Orpheus and Power: The Movimento Negro of Rio de Janeiro and São Paulo, 1945–1988* (Princeton, NJ: Princeton University Press, 1994), 181.
80. Zapata, *Changó*, 385–388.
81. Sweet, *Recreating*, 61–62.
82. Zapata, *Changó*, 377.
83. Sweet, *Recreating*, 204.
84. Zapata, *Changó*, 377.
85. Wheat, *Atlantic Africa*, 265.
86. Zapata, *Changó*, 378.
87. Ibid., 379.
88. Ibid., 386.
89. Ibid., 384.
90. Ibid., 385.
91. Sweet, *Recreating*, 162.
92. Zapata, *Changó*, 377–378.
93. Ibid., 383.
94. Sweet, *Recreating*, 37.
95. Ibid., 61.
96. Ibid., 61, 69.
97. Ibid., 69–70.
98. Zapata, *Changó*, 405.
99. Ibid., 379.
100. Ibid., 387.
101. Ibid., 378.
102. Ibid., 380.
103. Ibid., 392.
104. Sweet, *Recreating* 35.
105. Martin Dreher, *A Igreja Latino-Americana no contexto colonial* (São Leopoldo: Sinodal, 2007), 116.

106. Zapata, *Changó*, 401.
107. Manuel Zapata Olivella, "Changó. Revisiones S.F." (unpublished manuscript, n.d.), 449, Vanderbilt Manuel Zapata Olivella Papers, Nashville, TN.
108. Zapata, *Changó*, 403.
109. Ibid., 444.
110. Ibid., 392.
111. Ibid., 403.
112. Ibid., 384.
113. Ibid., 388.
114. Ibid., 387.
115. Sweet, *Recreating*, 49–50.
116. Ibid., 82.
117. Maria Luisa Araújo dos Anjos, "A escolarização da peça Sortilégio II—mistério negro de Zumbi redivivo" (Master's thesis, Universidade de Brasília, Brasília, Brazil, 2007), 36; Abdias Nascimento, *Sortilégio: Mistério negro* (Rio de Janeiro: Teatro Experimental do Negro, 1959); Nascimento, *Sortilégio II: Mistério negro de Zumbi redivivo* (Rio de Janeiro: Paz e Terra, 1979).
118. Nascimento, *Sortilégio II*, 67.
119. Abdias Nascimento, *O genocídio do negro brasileiro* (São Paulo: Editora Perspectiva, 1978).
120. Niyi Afolabi. "A visão mítico-trágica na dramaturgia abdisiana," *Hispania* 81, no. 3 (Spring 1998): 531.
121. Ibid., 533.
122. Nascimento, *Quilombismo*, 255.
123. Denilson Lima Santos, "Abdias do Nascimento y Manuel Zapata Olivella: Intelectuales del siglo XX en el sendero de la discursividad ancestral yoruba y bantú," *Estudos de Literatura Brasileira Contemporânea* 44 (October/December 2004): 238.
124. Manuel Zapata Olivella, *El árbol brujo de la libertad*, ed. William Mina Aragón (Cali: Universidad del Valle, 2009), 98.
125. Gonçalves, *Defeito*, 90, 108, 135.
126. Ana Lucia Araujo, "History, Memory, and Imagination: Na Agontimé, a Dahomean Queen in Brazil," in *Beyond Tradition: African Women in Cultural and Political Spaces*, ed. Toyin Falola and S. U. Fwatshak (Trenton, NJ: Africa World Press, 2011), 46; Gonçalves, *Defeito*, 108, 135, 343.
127. Gonçalves, *Defeito*, 282, 578, 596, 612.
128. James Sweet, *Domingos Álvares, African Healing, and the Intellectual History of the Atlantic World* (Chapel Hill: University of North Carolina Press, 2011), 57.
129. Ibid., 68.
130. Ibid., 83.
131. Gonçalves, *Defeito*, 106, 171, 467.
132. Ibid., 447.
133. Ibid., 206.
134. Sweet, *Domingos*, 202.
135. Ibid., 202–204.
136. Ibid., 132.
137. Sweet, *Recreating*, 230.
138. Gonçalves, *Defeito*, 596.

139. Ibid., 592.
140. Ibid., 535.
141. Sweet, *Domingos*, 52.
142. Sweet, *Domingos*, 231.
143. Ibid., 230.
144. Ibid., 198.
145. Ibid., 230, 233.
146. Gonçalves, *Defeito*, 282.
147. Ibid., 200.
148. Ibid., 282.
149. Ibid., 200.
150. Gonçalves, *Defeito*, 281–282.
151. Sweet, *Domingos*, 284.
152. Ibid., 282–283.
153. Ibid., 284.
154. Ibid., 571.
155. Ibid., 580.
156. "31 anos," Geledés Instituto da Mulher Negra, www.geledes.org.br/.
157. Gonçalves, *Defeito*, 573.
158. Ibid., 582.
159. Ibid., 530, 573.
160. Ibid., 629.
161. Ibid., 583.
162. Ibid., 243.
163. Ibid., 595.
164. Ibid., 591.
165. Ibid., 186.
166. Ineke Phaf-Rheinberger, *Modern Slavery and Water Spirituality: A Critical Debate in Africa and Latin America* (New York: Peter Lang, 2017), 59–60.
167. Ibid., 130–131.
168. Ibid., 133.
169. Ibid., 134.
170. Ibid., 85.
171. Ibid., 146.
172. Sweet, *Domingos*, 228.
173. Gonçalves, *Defeito*, 133.
174. Ibid., 597, 600.
175. Ibid., 598.
176. Ibid., 612–613.
177. Ibid., 672.
178. Sweet, *Recreating*, 207.
179. Gonçalves, *Defeito*, 363.
180. Ibid., 629.
181. Sweet, *Recreating*, 207.
182. Gonçalves, *Defeito*, 630.
183. Sweet, *Recreating*, 57.
184. Ibid., 37–40.
185. Gonçalves, *Defeito*, 596.

186. Ibid., 630.
187. Ibid., 631.
188. Roberto González Echevarría, *Myth and Archive: A Theory of Latin American Narrative* (Cambridge: Cambridge University Press, 1990), 173.
189. Dorita Piquero Nouhad, introduction to *Changó, el gran putas*, by Manuel Zapata Olivella (Bogota: Grupo Editorial Educar, 2007), 25.

Chapter 3 Double Consciousness and Nation in Gilroy and Zapata

1. Benedict Anderson, *Imagined Communities: Reflections on the Origin and Spread of Nationalism* (New York: Verso, 1991), 2.
2. Paul Gilroy, *The Black Atlantic: Modernity and Double Consciousness* (New York: Verso, 1993).
3. Judith Newman, "Globalizing Gilroy," *Journal of Commonwealth and Postcolonial Studies* 17, no. 1 (Spring 2011): 99.
4. Elizabeth Maddock Dillon, "Atlantic Practices: Minding the Gap between Literature and History," *William and Mary Quarterly* 65, no. 1 (January 2008): 181–186; Newman, "Globalizing Gilroy," 94.
5. Newman, "Globalizing Gilroy," 94.
6. Eric Slauter, "History, Literature, and the Atlantic World," *William and Mary Quarterly* 65, no. 1 (2008): 135–166.
7. Christine Chivallon and Karen E. Fields, "Beyond Gilroy's Black Atlantic: The Experience of the African Diaspora," *Diaspora: A Journal of Transnational Studies* 11, no. 3 (Winter 2002): 359.
8. Bénédicte Ledent and Pilar Cuder-Domínguez, eds., *New Perspectives on the Black Atlantic* (New York: Peter Lang, 2012), 9.
9. Newman, "Globalizing Gilroy," 94.
10. Ibid.
11. Simone Pereira Schmidt, "Navegando no Atlântico Pardo ou a lusofonia reinventada," *Crítica Cultural* 1, no. 2 (July–December 2006): 1, www.portaldeperiodicos.unisul.br/index.php/Critica_Cultural/article/view/94/104.
12. Newman, "Globalizing Gilroy," 100.
13. Peter Erickson, "The Black Atlantic in the Twenty-First Century: Artistic Passages, Circulations, Revisions," *Nka: Journal of Contemporary African Art* 24 (2009): 69.
14. Kimberly Juanita Brown, *The Repeating Body: Slavery's Visual Resonance in the Contemporary* (Durham, NC: Duke University Press, 2015).
15. Ibid., 1.
16. Ibid., 4.
17. "JBHE's Annual Citation Rankings of Black Scholars in the Social Sciences and the Humanities," *Journal of Blacks in Higher Education* (2009), www.jbhe.com/news_views/63_citationrankings.html.
18. Senayon Olaoluwa, "African Diaspora beyond the Black Atlantic: Dynamics and Significance in the Latin American World and Elsewhere," *H-Net*, April 22, 2017, https://networks.h-net.org/node/20292/discussions/176852/african-diaspora-beyond-black-atlantic-dynamics-and-significance.
19. Gilroy, *Atlantic*, 4.
20. Ibid., xi.
21. Ibid., 4.

22. Ibid., 54.
23. Ibid., 189.
24. Ibid., 66.
25. Ibid., 72, 78, 84.
26. Paul Gilroy, *Darker Than Blue: On the Moral Economies of Black Atlantic Culture* (Cambridge, MA: Harvard University Press, 2011).
27. Paul Gilroy, *Small Acts* (London: Serpent's Tail, 1993), 173–237.
28. Paul Gilroy, *Against Race: Imagining Political Culture across the Color Line* (Cambridge, MA: Belknap, 2002), 15.
29. Paul Gilroy, *Postcolonial Melancholia* (New York: Columbia University Press, 2006).
30. Gilroy, *Darker*, 130.
31. Paul Gilroy, "Del Atlántico Negro a la melancolía poscolonial," interviewed by Jim Cohen and Jade Lindgaard, *Revista Iberoamericana* 82, no. 255–56 (April-September 2016): 301–321.
32. Ibid., 304.
33. Ibid., 303–304.
34. Ibid., 305.
35. Institute of Advanced Studies, "Professor Paul Gilroy Appointed Founding Director of Centre for the Study of Race & Racism" (University College London, May 21, 2019), www.ucl.ac.uk/institute-of-advanced-studies/news/2019/may/professor-paul-gilroy-appointed-founding-director-centre-study-race-racism.
36. Paul Gilroy, "Holberg Laureate Paul Gilroy's Acceptance Speech," *Holberg Prize*, May 31, 2019, www.holbergprisen.no/en/news/holberg-prize/holberg-laureate-paul-gilroys-acceptance-speech.
37. Natasha Barnes, "Black Atlantic–Black America," *Research in African Literatures* 27, no. 4 (Winter 1996): 106.
38. James Clifford, "Diasporas," *Cultural Anthropology* 9 (1994): 302.
39. William Boelhower, "The Rise of the New Atlantic Studies Matrix," *American Literary Theory* 20, nos. 1–2 (Spring–Summer 2008): 91, 94.
40. Daria Tunca, "Away from a Definition of African Literature(s)," in Ledent and Cuder-Domínguez, *New Perspectives*, 108.
41. Richard Follett, "The Spirit of Brazil: Football and Politics of Afro-Brazilian Cultural Identity," in *Recharting the Black Atlantic: Modern Cultures, Local Communities, Global Connections*, ed. Annalisa Oboe and Anna Scacchi (New York: Routledge, 2008), 95–96.
42. Ledent and Cuder-Domínguez, *New Perspectives*, 10–11.
43. James Sweet, *Recreating Africa: Culture, Kinship, and Religion in the African-Portuguese World, 1441–1770* (Chapel Hill: University of North Carolina Press, 2004), 2.
44. Laura Chrisman, "Journeying to Death: Gilroy's *Black Atlantic*," *Race & Class* 39, no. 2 (1997): 54–55.
45. Ibid., 57.
46. Ibid., 63.
47. Sweet, *Recreating*, 67.
48. Ibid., 62.
49. Lucía Ortiz, "Nacionalismo y transnacionalismo en Manuel Zapata Olivella," *Boletín Hispánica Helvética* 29 (Spring 2017): 130.

50. Alfonso Múnera, "Manuel Zapata Olivella y la nación inclusive," in *Por los senderos de sus ancestros*, by Manuel Zapata Olivella (Bogota: Ministerio de Cultura, 2011), 28.
51. Stephen Best, "On Failing to Make the Past Present," *Modern Language Quarterly* 73, no. 3 (2012): 453.
52. Chivallon and Fields, "Beyond Gilroy's Black Atlantic," 362.
53. Ibid., 371–373.
54. A. L. Reed Jr., *W. E. B. Du Bois and American Political Thought* (Oxford: Oxford University Press, 1997), 366.
55. David Scott, "An Obscure Miracle of Connection: Discursive Tradition and Black Diaspora Criticism," *Small Axe* 1 (1997): 19.
56. Ibid., 36.
57. Chivallon and Fields, "Beyond Gilroy's Black Atlantic," 377.
58. Ineke Phaf-Rheinberger, "Myths of Early Modernity: Historical and Contemporary Narratives on Brazil and Angola," in *AfricAmericas: Itineraries, Dialogues, and Sounds*, ed. Ineke Phaf-Rheinberger and Tiago de Oliveira Pinto (Frankfurt: Vervuert, 2008), 125–150; Phaf-Rheinberger and Pinto, *AfricAmericas*.
59. Phaf-Rheinberger, "Myths," 125.
60. Ibid., 145.
61. Tiago Oliveira de Pinto, "Crossed Rhythms: African Structures, Brazilian Practices, and Afro-Brazilian Meanings," in Phaf-Rheinberger and Pinto, *AfricAmericas*, 166.
62. Paul Tiyambe Zeleza, "Rewriting the African Diaspora: Beyond the Black Atlantic," *African Affairs* 104, no. 414 (January 2005): 37.
63. Ibid., 62–63.
64. Ibid., 37.
65. Ibid., 63.
66. Kim Butler, "Brazilian Abolition in Afro-Atlantic Context," *African Studies Review* 43, no. 1 (2000): 127; Zeleza, "Rewriting," 40.
67. Charles Piot, "Atlantic Aporias: Africa and Gilroy's Black Atlantic," *South Atlantic Quarterly* 100, no. 1 (2001): 156.
68. Ibid., 169.
69. Yogita Goyal, "Africa and the Black Atlantic," *Research in African Literatures* 45, no. 3 (Fall 2014): x.
70. Ibid., vi–vii.
71. Marlon Ross, "Trans-Atlantic Parochialism," *Callaloo* 39, no. 4 (Fall 2016): 887.
72. Ibid., 894.
73. Manuel Zapata Olivella, *¡Levántate mulato! Por mi raza hablará el espíritu* (Bogota: REI Andes, 1990), 348.
74. Ibid., 348.
75. Manuel Zapata Olivella, *Changó el gran putas*, introduction by Darío Henao Restrepo (Bogota: Ministerio de Cultura, 2010), http://babel.banrepcultural.org/cdm/ref/collection/p17054coll7/id/2, 535.
76. Ibid., 536.
77. Ibid., 536.
78. W. E. B. Du Bois, *The Souls of Black Folk* (Toronto: Dover, 1994), 65.
79. Zapata, *Changó*, 571.
80. Ibid., 537; Gilroy, *Atlantic*, 91.
81. Zapata, *Changó*, 443.

82. Ibid., 537.
83. Ibid., 569.
84. Ibid., 443, 569.
85. Ibid., 569.
86. Ibid., 560–570.
87. Ibid., 584–586.
88. Ibid., 614.
89. Du Bois, *Souls*, 155; Gilroy, *Atlantic*, 91; Zapata, *Changó*, 518, 532, 543.
90. Du Bois, *Souls*, 9.
91. Gilroy, *Atlantic*, 42.
92. Ibid., 19.
93. Ibid., 188.
94. Ibid., 144.
95. Zapata, *Changó*, 107, 110, 121, 128.
96. Ibid., 98.
97. Ibid., 90.
98. Ibid., 150.
99. Ibid., 177.
100. Armin Schwegler, "Sobre el origen africano de la lengua criolla de Palenque (Colombia)," in *Palenque Colombia: Oralidad, identidad y resistencia*, ed. Graciela Maglia and Armin Schwegler (Bogota: Editorial Pontífica Universidad Javeriana, 2012), 107.
101. Zapata, *Changó*, 277.
102. William Luis, "Introduction," in *Changó, the Biggest Badass*, by Manuel Zapata Olivella, trans. Jonathan Tittler (Lubbock: Texas Tech University Press, 2009), xiv.
103. Zapata, *Changó*, 9.
104. Luis, "Introduction," xxvi.
105. Zapata, *Changó*, 443–645.
106. Zapata, *¡Levántate!*, 106.
107. Gilroy, *Atlantic*, 189.
108. Zapata, *Changó*, 175, 473.
109. Antonio Tillis, *Manuel Zapata Olivella and the "Darkening" of Latin American Literature* (Columbia: University of Missouri Press, 2005), 98.
110. Ortiz, "Nacionalismo," 137–138.
111. José Vasconcelos, *La raza cósmica: Misión de la raza iberoamericana, Argentina y Brasil* (Mexico: Trillas, 2012), 9.
112. Ibid., 14.
113. Ibid., 10; Zapata, *Changó*, 243.
114. Gilroy, *Atlantic*, 197.
115. Zapata, *Changó*, 41–81.
116. David Wheat, *Atlantic Africa and the Spanish Caribbean, 1570–1640* (Chapel Hill: University of North Carolina Press, 2016), 450.
117. Gilroy, *Atlantic*, 208.
118. Ibid., 62.
119. Ibid., 200.
120. Ibid., 41.
121. Luis, "Introduction," xix.

122. Zapata, "Genealogía de los orichas yorubas" (paper, Ciclo de religiosidad afro-colombiana, Museo de Arte Religioso, Banco de la República, Bogota, Colombia, n.d.), Vanderbilt Manuel Zapata Olivella Papers, Nashville, TN.
123. Zapata, *Changó*, 511.
124. Kameelah Martin, *Conjuring Moments in African American Literature: Women, Spirit Work, and Other Such Hoodoo* (New York: Palgrave, 2012), 12.
125. Ibid., 9.
126. Gilroy, *Atlantic*, 102.
127. Nicolás Guillén, "Balada de los abuelos" (Centro Virtual Cervantes, 2018), https://cvc.cervantes.es/literatura/escritores/guillen/poemas/poema_11.htm.
128. Gilroy, *Atlantic*, 74.
129. Ibid., 36.
130. Ibid., 56.
131. Ortiz, "Nacionalismo," 131.
132. George Palacios Palacios, "Apuntes sobre la música, el folclor, lo nacional-popular y la literatura en algunos de los escritos tempranos de Manuel Zapata Olivella," *Escritos* 23, no. 51 (2015): 439.
133. Zapata, *Changó*, 452.
134. Gilroy, *Atlantic*, 50.
135. Zapata, *Changó*, 572, 582.
136. Ibid., 485.
137. Ibid., 485.
138. Ibid., 514.
139. Ibid., 517.
140. Ibid., 635.
141. Ibid., 622.
142. Luis, "Introduction," xxix.
143. Revelation 16:13–16.
144. Gilroy, *Atlantic*, 223.
145. Ibid., 205.
146. P. F. de Moraes Farias, "Africentrism: Between Cross-cultural Grand Narrative and Relativism," *Journal of African History* 44 (2003): 328.
147. Zapata, *Changó*, 450; Zapata, "Changó. Revisiones S.F." (unpublished manuscript, n.d.), Vanderbilt Manuel Zapata Olivella Papers, Nashville, TN.
148. Farias, "Africentrism," 328.
149. Zapata, *Changó*, 451.
150. Ibid., 451.
151. Stefania Capone, "Transatlantic Dialogue: Roger Bastide and the African American Religions," in *Africas of the Americas: Beyond the Search for Origins in the Study of Afro-Atlantic Religions*, ed. Stephan Palmié (Boston: Brill, 2008), 267.
152. Enrico Mario Santí, "Introducción," in *Contrapunteo cubano del tabaco y del azúcar*, by Fernando Ortiz (Madrid: Cátedra, 2002), 85.
153. Capone, "Transatlantic Dialogue," 266.
154. Ibid., 289.
155. Ibid., 287.
156. María Adelaida López, dir., *Manuel Zapata Olivella: Abridor de caminos* (Colombia: Azul y Naranja Producciones, 2007), www.youtube.com/watch?v

=3Dpc4w2Kp6I; Manuel Zapata Olivella, "La maraca encantada" (unpublished manuscript, n.d.), Vanderbilt Manuel Zapata Olivella Papers, Nashville, TN.
157. Zapata, *Changó*, 576.
158. Manuel Zapata Olivella, "Los problemas de identidad de los escritores afro-latinoamericanos," *Afro-Hispanic Review* 25, no. 1 (Spring 2006): 172.
159. Ivan van Sertima, *They Came before Columbus: The African Presence in Ancient America* (New York: Random House, 2003); Zapata, *Changó*, 437.
160. Bernard Ortiz de Montellano, Gabriel Haslip-Viera, and Warren Barbour, "They Were NOT Here before Columbus: Afrocentric Hyperdiffusionism in the 1990s," *Ethnohistory* 44, no. 2 (Spring 1997): 199.
161. Zapata, *Changó*, 415.
162. Ibid., 437.
163. Manuel Zapata Olivella, *Nuestra Voz: Aportes del habla popular latinoamericana al idioma español* (Bogota: Ecoe, 1987); Zapata, "El substrato negro en el español de América," Zapata, "La maraca encantada"; Zapata, *Manuel Zapata Olivella: Por los senderos de sus ancestros: Textos escogidos. 1940–2000*, ed. Alfonso Múnera (2010), 355, http://babel.banrepcultural.org/cdm/ref/collection/p17054coll7/id/17.
164. Zapata, "Problemas," 175.
165. Zapata, "El mestizaje en la nueva novela hispanoamericana," *Afro-Hispanic Review* 25, no. 1 (Spring 2006): 163.
166. Zapata, *Changó*, 35.
167. Ibid., 35.
168. Ibid., 36.
169. Ibid., 301.
170. Ibid., 320, 367.
171. John Lynch, *Simón Bolívar: A Life* (New Haven, CT: Yale University Press, 2006); Luis Esteban Manrique, "Vida de Libertador: La poliédrica figura de Simón Bolívar by John Lynch," *Política Exterior* 21, no. 118 (July–August 2007): 205–209.
172. Luis, "Introduction," xxv.
173. Zapata, *Changó*, 318–321.
174. Guillén, "Balada."
175. Zapata, *Changó*, 320.
176. Ibid., 319, 333.
177. Wheat, *Atlantic Africa*, 40.
178. Zapata, *Changó*, 337.
179. Ibid., 355.
180. Ibid., 370.
181. Ibid., 371.
182. Ibid.
183. Aline Helg, "Simón Bolívar and the Spectre of 'Pardocracia': José Padilla in Post-Independence Cartagena," *Journal of Latin American Studies* 35, no. 3 (August 2003): 470.
184. Zapata, *Changó*, 322.
185. Ibid., 363, 387.
186. Ibid., 443.
187. Ibid., 485–486.
188. John Maddox, "Una falla geológica de fallas raciales: El Sur norteamericano en Piri Thomas y Manuel Zapata Olivella," *Visitas al Patio* 10 (2017): 13.

189. Zapata, *Changó*, 443.
190. Ibid., 73.
191. Ibid., 444.
192. Ibid., 454.
193. Ibid., 598.
194. Ibid., 461.
195. Ibid., 467.
196. Ibid., 477.
197. Walter Mignolo, *Local Histories / Global Designs: Coloniality, Subaltern Knowledges, and Border Thinking* (Princeton, NJ: Princeton University Press, 2000), 263–265.
198. Gloria Anzaldúa, *Borderlands/La Frontera: The New Mestiza* (San Francisco: Spinsters, 1987).
199. Mignolo, *Local Histories*, 84, 87.
200. Herman Bennett, "The Subject in the Plot: National Boundaries and the 'History' of the Black Atlantic," *African Studies Review* 43, no. 1 (April 2000): 113.
201. Nicholas Jones, "Sor Juana's Black Atlantic: Colonial Blackness and the Poetic Subversions of *Habla de negros*," *Hispanic Review* 86, no. 3 (Summer 2018): 265.
202. Wheat, *Atlantic Africa*, 32.
203. Graciela Maglia and John Maddox, "Introduction," *Afro-Hispanic Review* 36, no. 1 (Spring 2017): 11.
204. Chris Schmidt-Nowara, "'This Rotting Corpse': Spain between the Black Atlantic and the Black Legend," *Arizona Journal of Hispanic Cultural Studies* 5 (2001): 149.
205. Ibid., 157–158.
206. José Jorge de Carvalho, *Las culturas afroamericanas en Iberoamérica: Lo negociable y lo innegociable* (Bogota: Universidad Nacional de Colombia, 2005), 13–15.
207. Eduard Arriaga, "La red de representaciones artísticas de lo afrodescendiente: Tejiendo imaginarios en la era digital. Colombia, Canadá y Guinea Ecuatorial," in *Identidades políticas en tiempos de la afrodescendencia: Autoidentificación, ancestralidad, visibilidad y derechos*, ed. Silvia Valero and Alejandro Campos García (Buenos Aires: Corregidor, 2015), 294.
208. Ibid.
209. Ibid., 297.
210. Norberto Pablo Cirio, "Construyendo una identificación desde la historia local: La categoría afroargentino del tronco colonial como experiencia etnogénica," in Valero and Campos García, *Identidades políticas*, 361.
211. Mônica Prates Conrado and Alan Augusto Moraes Ribeiro, "Homem negro, negro homem: Masculinidades e feminismo em debate," *Revista de Estudos Feministas* 25, no. 1 (January–April 2017): 74–75, https://periodicos.ufsc.br/index.php/ref/article/view/40165/33662.
212. Ibid., 88–89.
213. Marsha Pearce, "Transnational / Transcultural Identities: The Black Atlantic and Pythagoras's Theorem," *Callaloo* 30, no 2 (Spring 2007): 549.
214. Eduardo de Assis Duarte, "Na cartografia do romance brasileiro, *Um defeito de cor*, de Ana Maria Gonçalves," in *Leituras da resistência: Corpo, violência e poder*, ed. C. S. Tornquist et al. (Florianópolis: Editora Mulheres, 2009), 347.
215. Anne Garland Mahler, *From the Tricontinental to the Global South: Race, Radicalism, and Transnational Solidarity* (Durham, NC: Duke University Press, 2018), 6569.

216. Miguel Vale de Almeida, *Um mar da cor da terra* (Oeiras: Celta, 2006), 238.
217. Ibid., 63.
218. Ibid., 45, 237.
219. Ibid., 156–157.
220. Ibid., 238–239.
221. Ibid., xi.
222. Ibid., 242–243.
223. Roberto Zurbano, "Entramos en la pos-resistencia: Del álbum de los muertos al ciudadano del futuro," *AfroCubaWeb.com* (Lecture at Connecticut College, October 10, 2013), 1–8, www.afrocubaweb.com/zurbano/entramos-en-la-post.pdf, 5.
224. Ibid., 2.
225. Ibid., 5–6.
226. Agustín Laó-Montes, "Hilos descoloniales: Trans-localizando los espacios de la diáspora Africana," *Tabula Rasa* 7 (July–December 2007): 50, www.scielo.org.co/pdf/tara/n7/n7a03.pdf.
227. Ibid., 52.
228. Ibid., 55.
229. Ibid., 60.
230. Ibid., 61.
231. Ibid., 64.
232. Ibid., 68.
233. Ibid., 72–73.
234. Lioba Rossbach de Olmos, "¿Qué pasa con el Pacífico Negro en el Atlántico Negro? El Atlántico Negro de Paul Gilroy frente a los acontecimientos (afro)colombianos," *Memorias: Revista Digital de Historia y Arqueología desde El Caribe* 11 (July–December 2009): 199–219.
235. Ibid., 202.
236. Ibid., 204–206.
237. Ibid., 207.
238. Ibid., 208.
239. Ibid., 209.
240. Ibid., 211.
241. Ibid., 213.
242. Ibid., 214.
243. Jossianna Arroyo and Elizabeth Marchant, "Introduction," *Comparative Literature Studies* 49, no. 2 (2012): 163–164.
244. Ibid., 164–165.
245. Daiana Nascimento dos Santos, "Atlántico negro: El océano en la narrativa de esclavizados," *Acta Literaria* 54 (2017): 30.
246. Ibid., 31, 39–40.
247. Ibid., 31.
248. Jerome Branche, *The Poetics and Politics of Diaspora: Transatlantic Musings* (New York: Routledge, 2015), 158.
249. Ibid., 4, 153.
250. Ibid., 3, 8.
251. Ineke Phaf-Rheinberger, *Modern Slavery and Water Spirituality: A Critical Debate in Africa and Latin America* (New York: Peter Lang, 2017), 14.

252. Ibid., 21.
253. Ibid., 96.

Chapter 4 Women, Gender, and the Nuevo Muntu

1. Octavio Paz, *El laberinto de la soledad* (Mexico: Fondo de Cultura Económica, 1992), 35.
2. Melissa Schindler, "Home, or the Limits of the Black Atlantic," *Research in African Cultures* 45, no. 3 (Fall 2014): 76.
3. James Sweet, *Recreating Africa: Culture, Kinship, and Religion in the African-Portuguese World, 1441–1770* (Chapel Hill: University of North Carolina Press, 2004), 46.
4. James Sweet, *Domingos Álvares, African Healing, and the Intellectual History of the Atlantic World* (Chapel Hill: University of North Carolina Press, 2011), 49, 54–55.
5. Ibid., 54.
6. Ibid., 43.
7. Ibid., 42.
8. Ana Maria Gonçalves, *Um defeito de cor* (Rio de Janeiro: Editora Record, 2006), 12; Sweet, *Domingos*, 37.
9. Sweet, *Domingos*, 45.
10. Ibid., 41.
11. Ibid., 40.
12. Ibid., 44.
13. Ibid., 45.
14. Ibid., 50.
15. Ana Lucia Araujo, "History, Memory, and Imagination: Na Agontimé, a Dahomean Queen in Brazil," in *Beyond Tradition: African Women in Cultural and Political Spaces*, ed. Toyin Falola and S. U. Fwatshak (Trenton, NJ: Africa World Press, 2011), 46.
16. Ibid., 20.
17. Ibid., 46.
18. Gonçalves, *Defeito*, 81.
19. Araujo, "History," 46, 51.
20. Ibid., 48.
21. Ibid., 53.
22. Ibid., 54–55.
23. Ibid., 57.
24. Ibid., 56.
25. Gonçalves, *Defeito*, 949–951.
26. Eurídice Figueredo, "Os brasileiros retornados à África," *Caderno de Letras da UFF* 38 (2009): 52. www.uff.br/cadernosdeletrasuff/38/artigo3.pdf.
27. Ibid., 5, 950.
28. Ineke Phaf-Rheinberger, *Modern Slavery and Water Spirituality: A Critical Debate in Africa and Latin America* (New York: Peter Lang, 2017), 46.
29. Phaf-Rheinberger, "Deux romancièrs afro-brésiliennes: Conceição Evaristo et Ana Maria Gonçalves," *Afrique–Brésil* 43 (2017): 59.
30. Adonias Filho, "Introduction," in *A casa da água*, by Antônio Olinto, 4th ed. (São Paulo: Difusão Editorial, 1983), 2.

31. Ibid., 5.
32. Ibid., 2.
33. Olinto, *Casa da água*, 173.
34. Ibid., 73.
35. Ibid., 79, 82, 90, 94, 106, 124–125, 165, 188, 194, 323.
36. Ibid., 100, 114, 163, 201–202, 209, 333, 358.
37. Ibid., 351.
38. Ibid., 338.
39. Gonçalves, *Defeito*, 19.
40. Ibid., 844–848.
41. Ibid., 26.
42. Ana Maria Gonçalves, "Inspiração e viagens através da diáspora: Uma entrevista com Ana Maria Gonçalves," interview by John Maddox, *Afro-Hispanic Review* 30, no. 2 (Fall 2011): 170.
43. Gonçalves, *Defeito*, 72, 74.
44. Ibid., 104.
45. Ibid., 212.
46. Ibid., 949.
47. Ibid., 548–549.
48. Ibid., 108, 243, 486.
49. Elciene Azevedo, *Orfeu de Caparinha: A trajetória de Luiz Gama na imperial cidade de São Paulo* (Campinas: Universidade de Campinas, 1999), 35–36.
50. Daniel Masterson and Sayaka Funada-Classen, *The Japanese in Latin America* (Urbana: University of Illinois Press, 2004), 73.
51. Azevedo, *Orfeu*, 37.
52. Sweet, *Domingos*, 136, 164.
53. Ibid., 17.
54. Gonçalves, *Defeito*, 691.
55. Sweet, *Recreating*,18, 20.
56. Gonçalves, *Defeito*, 691.
57. Ibid., 691.
58. Ibid., 663, 672.
59. Michael George Hanchard, *Orpheus and Power: The Movimento Negro of Rio de Janeiro and São Paulo, 1945–1988* (Princeton, NJ: Princeton University Press, 1994), 44, 47.
60. Sweet, *Recreating*, 139.
61. Ibid., 142.
62. Gonçalves, *Defeito*, 666–667.
63. Ibid., 668.
64. Joaquim Manuel Macedo, *Memórias da Rua do Ouvidor*, ed. M. Cavalcanti Proença (Rio de Janeiro: Editora Tecnoprint, 1966).
65. Gonçalves, *Defeito*, 699.
66. Ibid., 656.
67. Gonçalves, *Defeito*, 615; José Saramago, *Memorial do convento* (Alfragide: Editorial Caminho, 1982).
68. Gonçalves, *Defeito*, 777.
69. Ibid., 721–722.
70. Ibid., 727.

71. Ibid., 593.
72. Manuela Carneiro da Cunha, *Negros, estrangeiros: Os libertos e sua volta à África* (São Paulo: Brasiliense, 1985).
73. W. E. B. Du Bois, *The Souls of Black Folk* (Toronto: Dover, 1994), 2.
74. Cunha, *Negros*, 68–69.
75. Ibid., 74.
76. Ibid., 72.
77. Ibid., 72.
78. Gonçalves, *Defeito*, 538.
79. Alberto da Costa Silva, "Introduction," in *Agudás—Os brasileiros do Benim*, by Milton Guran (Rio de Janeiro: Gama Filho, 1999), ix.
80. Gonçalves, *Defeito*, 538.
81. Cunha, *Negros*, 12.
82. Gonçalves, *Defeito*, 731, 735.
83. Ibid., 731.
84. Ibid., 769, 834.
85. Phaf-Rheinberger, *Modern Slavery*, 59.
86. Gonçalves, *Defeito*, 923–925.
87. Ibid., 269.
88. Ibid., 243, 311; "Aleijadinho at Home and Abroad: 'Discovering' Race and Nation in Brazil," *CR: The New Centennial Review* 12, no. 2 (Fall 2012): 183–216.
89. Gonçalves, *Defeito*, 311.
90. Daviken Studnicki-Gizbert, *A Nation upon the Ocean Sea: Portugal's Atlantic Diaspora and the Crisis of the Spanish Empire, 1492–1640* (Oxford: Oxford University Press, 2007), 67.
91. David Wheat, *Atlantic Africa and the Spanish Caribbean, 1570–1640* (Chapel Hill: University of North Carolina Press, 2016), 200.
92. Silke Strickrodt, "The Brazilian Diaspora to West Africa in the Nineteenth Century," in *Africaméricas: Itineraries, Dialogues, and Sounds*, ed. Ineke Phaf-Rheinberger and Tiago de Oliveira Pinto (Frankfurt: Vervuert, 2008), 37–38.
93. Ibid., 46–47.
94. Phaf-Rhenberger, *Modern Slavery*, 218.
95. Sweet, *Domingos*, 32.
96. Gonçalves, "Viagens," 175.
97. Gonçalves, *Defeito*, 699.
98. Ibid., 212.
99. Ibid., 735.
100. Ibid., 767.
101. Ibid., 637.
102. Ibid., 675–677.
103. Ibid., 680–681.
104. Phaf-Rheinberger, *Modern Slavery*, 57.
105. Gonçalves, *Defeito*, 757.
106. Cunha, *Negros*, 106–216.
107. Phaf-Rheinberger, *Modern Slavery*, 56.
108. Strickrodt, "Brazilian Diaspora," 54.
109. Ibid.
110. Ibid., 56.

111. Paul Gilroy, *The Black Atlantic: Modernity and Double Consciousness* (New York: Verso, 1993), 199.
112. Gonçalves, *Defeito*, 853–854, 862.
113. Schindler, "Home," 73.
114. Gonçalves, *Defeito*, 771, 867.
115. Sweet, *Domingos*, 153.
116. Gonçalves, *Defeito*, 921; Mara Loveman, "The Race to Progress: Census Taking and Nation Making in Brazil (1870–1920)," *Hispanic American Historical Review* 89, no. 3 (August 2009): 443.
117. Gonçalves, *Defeito*, 467.
118. Ibid., 888.
119. Ibid., 949.
120. Bruce Chatwin, *The Viceroy of Ouidah* (Manila: Summit Books, 1980), 8.
121. Gonçalves, *Defeito*, 789.
122. Chatwin, *Viceroy*, 8.
123. Wheat, *Atlantic Africa*, 456.
124. Chatwin, *Viceroy*, 8.
125. Ibid., 28.
126. Ibid., 9.
127. Gonçalves, *Defeito*, 759.
128. Ibid., 945.
129. Ibid., 771.
130. Strickrodt, "Brazilian Diaspora," 54.
131. Chatwin, *Viceroy*, 44; Miguel Barnet [and Esteban Montejo], *Biografía de un cimarrón* (Mexico: Siglo Veintiuno, 1968), 53.
132. Gonçalves, "Viagens," 169.
133. Hendrick Kraay, "Patriotic Mobilization in Brazil: The Zuavos and Other Black Companies," in *I Die with My Country: Perspectives on the Paraguayan War 1864–1870*, ed. Hendrick Kraay and Thomas Wigham (Lincoln: University of Nebraska Press, 2004), 61.
134. Gonçalves, *Defeito*, 905.
135. Kraay, "Patriotic Mobilization," 61.
136. Ricardo Salles, *A Guerra do Paraguai: Memórias e imagens* (Rio de Janeiro: Biblioteca Nacional, 2003), 102.
137. Schindler, "Home," 75.
138. Gonçalves, *Defeito*, 768, 824–826, 831–834, 879.
139. Strickrodt, "Brazilian Diaspora," 59.
140. Gonçalves, *Defeito*, 221.
141. Ibid., 466.
142. Sweet, *Domingos*, 141.
143. Sweet, *Recreating*, 177.
144. Gonçalves, *Defeito*, 946.
145. Ibid., 945–947.
146. Ibid., 945.
147. Sweet, *Domingos*, 121.
148. Gonçalves, *Defeito*, 445.
149. Ibid., 691.

150. Sojourner Truth, "Ain't I a Woman?," in *Internet Modern History Sourcebook*, ed. Paul Halsall (Fordham University, 1997), https://sourcebooks.fordham.edu/mod/sojtruth-woman.asp.
151. Helene Carol Weldt-Basson, ed., *Redefining Latin American Historical Fiction: The Impact of Feminism and Postcolonialism* (New York: Palgrave Macmillan, 2013), 9.
152. Toni Morrison, *Beloved* (New York: Knopf), 1987.
153. Natasha Barnes, "Black Atlantic–Black America," *Research in African Literatures* 27, no. 4 (Winter 1996): 106; Schindler, "Home," 175.
154. Diana Catalina Zapata-Cortés, "Mestizaje nacional: Una historia 'negra' por contar," *Memoria y Sociedad* 14, no. 29 (July–December 2010): 91–105, 92, www.scielo.org.co/scielo.php?script=sci_arttext&pid=S0122-51972010000200006.
155. Ibid., 103.
156. Yvonne Captain-Hidalgo, "Hacia su habitación propia: La mujer en Manuel Zapata Olivella," in *Literatura y Cultura: Narrativa Colombiana del Siglo XX*, vol. 3, no. 2, ed. María M. Jaramillo et al. (Bogota: Ministerio de Cultura, 2000), 152–153.
157. Manuel Zapata Olivella, *Hemingway, el cazador de la muerte* (Bogota: Arango Editores, 1993).
158. Uchenna Vasser, "Africanidad and the Representation of Female Characters in Manuel Zapata Olivella," *Revista Convivencia* 1, no. 1 (November 2014): 77–98, www.up.ac.pa/ftp/2010/v_postgrado/publicaciones/Convivencia/Convivencia-Vol1-No1.pdf.
159. Madeleine Henry, "Greece and Africa in *Changó, el gran Putas*" (paper, Classical Association of the Midwest and South, Southern Section, Tallahassee, FL, November 2, 2012), 3.
160. Daiana Nascimento dos Santos, *El océano de fronteras invisibles: Relecturas históricas sobre (¿el fin? de) la esclavitud en la novela contemporánea* (Madrid: Verbum, 2016), 175.
161. M'bare N'gom, "Representaciones de la otredad: experiencia femenina e identidad en ¡Negras somos!," *Cuadernos de Literatura* 19, no. 38 (2015): 119.
162. Ibid., 121, 129.
163. Guiomar Cuesta Escobar and Alfredo Ocampo Zamorano, eds. *¡Negras somos! Antología de mujeres poetas afrocolombianas* (Bogota: Ministerio de Cultura Colombiana, 2008), 26.
164. Ibid., 26.
165. Hazel Robinson Abrahams, *No Give Up, Maan* (Bogota: Ministerio de Cultura, 2010).
166. Ricardo Moncada Esquivel, "La escritora vallecaucana Adelaida Fernández ganó el premio Casa de las Américas," *El País*, February 12, 2015, www.elpais.com.co/entretenimiento/cultura/la-escritora-vallecaucana-adelaida-fernandez-gano-el-premio-casa-de-las-americas.html.
167. Thomas Wayne Edison, "Restored Roots: *Muntu* as a Healing Agent in *Pelo bueno, pelo malo* by Carmen Montáñez," *Hispania* 100, no. 4 (December 2017): 624.
168. María Mercedes Jaramillo and Lucía Ortiz, *Hijas del Muntu: Biografías críticas de mujeres afrodescendientes de América Latina* (Bogota: Panamericana, 2011).
169. Ashanti Orozco, "Poética del muntú renaciente," Facebook, June 23, 2019, www.facebook.com/dinahorozco/posts/10156890057737631.
170. Elba Mercedes Palacios Córdoba, "Epilogue," in *Demando mi libertad: Mujeres negras y sus estrategias de supervivencia en la Nueva Granada, Venezuela y Cuba*, ed.

Aurora Vergara Figueroa and Carmen Luz Cosme (Puntiel, Cali: Universidad Instituto Colombiano de Estudios Superiores de Incolda, 2018), 255–257.

171. Zapata, *Changó*, 443.
172. Margarita Krakusin, "Conversación informal con Manuel Zapata Olivella," by Margarita Krakusin, *Afro-Hispanic Review* 20, no. 1 (2001): 20.
173. Paz, *El laberinto de la soledad*, 35.
174. Ibid., 31.
175. Ibid.
176. Silviano Santiago, *As raízes e o laberinto da América Latina* (Rio de Janeiro: Rocco, 2006), 132.
177. Ibid., 182.
178. Ibid., 137–138.
179. Ibid., 145.
180. Ibid., 179.
181. Paz, *Laberinto*, 35.
182. Santiago, *As raízes*, 145, 194.
183. Ibid., 132.
184. Ibid., 194.
185. Ibid., 152.
186. Ibid., 212.
187. Paz, *Laberinto*, 31–32; Dorita Piquero Nouhad, "Introduction," in *Changó, el gran putas*, by Manuel Zapata Olivella (Bogota: Grupo Editorial Educar, 2007), 11.
188. Piquero, "Introduction," 11.
189. Paz, *Laberinto*, 36.
190. Manuel Zapata Olivella, *¡Levántate mulato! Por mi raza hablará el espíritu* (Bogota: REI Andes, 1990), 346.
191. Zapata, *Changó*, 77.
192. Wheat, *Atlantic Africa*, 33.
193. Édouard Glissant, *Poetics of Relation*, translated by Betsy Wing (Ann Arbor: University of Michigan Press, 1997), 6.
194. Sweet, *Recreating*, 37, 40.
195. Zapata, *Changó*, 407.
196. Julia Cuervo Hewitt, *Voices Out of Africa in Twentieth-Century Spanish Caribbean Literature* (Lewisburg, PA: Bucknell University Press, 2009), 256.
197. Zapata, *Changó*, 406–407.
198. Ibid., 407.
199. Ibid., 68.
200. Paz, *Laberinto*, 37.
201. Santiago, *As raízes*, 126.
202. Zapata, *Changó*, 145.
203. Ibid., 127.
204. Sweet, *Recreating*, 37.
205. Cuervo Hewitt, *Voices*, 207.
206. Wheat, *Atlantic Africa*, 44.
207. Herman Bennett, *African Kings and Black Slaves: Sovereignty and Dispossession in the Early Modern Atlantic*, (Philadelphia: University of Pennsylvania Press, 2019), 105.
208. Ibid.

209. Ibid., 87.
210. Ibid., 166.
211. Ibid., 105.
212. Sweet, *Recreating*, 195.
213. Ibid., 162.
214. Zapata, *Changó*, 107.
215. Ibid., 106.
216. Ibid., 476.
217. Ibid., 120.
218. Ibid., 121–123.
219. Ibid., 140.
220. Ibid., 142.
221. Ibid., 91.
222. Ibid., 58, 62.
223. Flora Süssekind, *Tal Brasil, qual romance? Uma ideologia estética e sua história: O naturalismo* (Rio de Janeiro: Achiamé, 1984).
224. Regina Dalcastagnè, "Da senzala ao cortiço—história e literatura em Aluísio Azevedo e João Ubaldo Ribeiro," *Revista Brasileira de História* 21, no. 42 (2001): 483.
225. Ana Maria Gonçalves, "Slavery and Human Rights in Brazil" (paper, University of Georgia, Athens, May 13, 2013).
226. Mario Vargas Llosa, *Los cachorros* (Barcelona: Lumen, 1937).
227. Gonçalves, *Defeito*, 24.
228. Ibid., 24.
229. Ibid., 23.
230. Charles Piot, "Atlantic Aporias: Africa and Gilroy's Black Atlantic," *South Atlantic Quarterly* 100, no. 1 (2001): 156.
231. Gonçalves, *Defeito*, 104.
232. Gilberto Freyre, *Casa-grande e senzala: Formação da família brasileira sob o regime de economia patriarchal*, 48th ed. (Recife: Fundação Gilberto Freyre, 2003), 367.
233. Ibid., 105.
234. Gonçalves, "Viagens," 170.
235. Freyre, *Senzala*, 217.
236. Gilroy, *Atlantic*, 66.
237. Gonçalves, *Defeito*, 105–106.
238. Ibid., 106.
239. Ibid., 105–106.
240. Ibid., 110.
241. Ibid., 115.
242. Gilroy, *Atlantic*, 233.
243. Gonçalves, *Defeito*, 171.
244. Phaf-Rheinberger, *Modern Slavery*, 54.
245. Sweet, *Recreating*, 60.
246. Ibid., 4–15.
247. Ibid., 70.
248. Ibid., 71.
249. Ibid., 73.
250. Lydia Cabrera, *El Monte: Notas sobre las religiones, la magia, las supersticiones y el folklore de los negros criollos y el pueblo de Cuba* (Havana: Letras Cubanas 1993), 233.

251. Zapata, *¡Levántate!*, 141–142.
252. Migene González-Wippler, *Powers of the Orishas: Santería and the Worship of Saints* (New York: Original Publications, 1992), 67.
253. Zapata, *¡Levántate!*, 142.
254. Gilroy, *Atlantic*, 194.
255. Gloria Anzaldúa, *Borderlands/La Frontera: The New Mestiza* (San Francisco: Spinsters, 1987).
256. Gloria Anzaldúa and Cherríe Moraga, eds, *This Bridge Called My Back: Writings by Radical Women of Color* (New York: Kitchen Table; Women of Color Press, 1983).
257. Yolanda Arroyo Pizarro, "Changó," in *Transmutadxs* (San Juan: Boreales, 2016).
258. Ibid., 13.
259. Zapata, *Changó*, 53.
260. Ibid., 57.
261. Darío Henao Restrepo, introduction to *Changó, el gran putas*, by Manuel Zapata Olivella, in *Biblioteca de Literatura Afrocolombiana*, vol. 3, ed. Darío Henao Restrepo (Bogota: Ministerio de Cultura, 2010), 17, http://babel.banrepcultural.org/cdm/ref/collection/p17054coll7/id/2.
262. Zapata, *Changó*, 130.
263. Ibid., 502.
264. Ibid., 542.
265. Kinitra Brooks, *Searching for Sycorax: Black Women's Hauntings of Contemporary Horror* (New Brunswick, NJ: Rutgers University Press, 2018), 116.
266. Ibid.
267. Ibid., 114.
268. Ibid., 119.
269. Zapata, *Changó*, 542.
270. Ibid.
271. Ibid., 372.
272. Ibid., 326.
273. Ibid., 186.
274. Ibid., 542.
275. Ibid., 139.
276. Kameelah Martin, *Conjuring Moments in African American Literature: Women, Spirit Work, and Other Such Hoodoo* (New York: Palgrave, 2012), 128.
277. Ibid., 132–133.
278. Ibid., 140.
279. Brooks, *Searching for Sycorax*, 121.
280. Gonçalves, *Defeito*, 375.
281. Ibid., 375–376.
282. Ibid., 376–377.
283. Ibid., 405.
284. Ibid., 486.
285. Sweet, *Recreating*, 51.
286. Ibid., 53.
287. Ibid., 57.
288. Ibid., 53.
289. Gonçalves, *Defeito*, 866.

290. Ibid., 866, 925.
291. Sweet, *Recreating*, 55.
292. Gonçalves, *Defeito*, 586.
293. Yvonne Captain-Hidalgo, *The Culture of Fiction in the Works of Manuel Zapata Olivella* (Columbia: University of Missouri Press, 1993), 148; Manuel Zapata Olivella, "Changó, the Holy Mother . . ." (unpublished television script, n.d.), Vanderbilt Manuel Zapata Olivella Papers, Nashville, TN. The critic compares Changó to Shaft and the Devil.
294. Alfred Hitchcock, *Psycho* (Shamley Productions, 1960).
295. Zapata, *Changó*, 452.
296. Ibid., 640.
297. Malgorzata Oleszkiewicz-Peralba, *Fierce Feminine Divinities of Eurasia and Latin America* (New York: Palgrave, 2015), 84.
298. Ibid., 100.
299. Brooks, *Searching for Sycorax*
300. Ibid., 139.
301. Ibid., 26.
302. Ibid., 87.
303. Ibid., 23.
304. Zapata, *Changó*, 537.
305. Ibid., 539.
306. Martin, *Conjuring*, 56. Turner later rejected such claims.
307. Zapata, *Changó*, 538–539.
308. Ibid., 565–567.
309. Ibid., 641.
310. Ibid., 553–555.
311. Toni Morrison, *Beloved* (New York: Knopf, 1987).
312. Manuel Zapata Olivella, "Changó. Revisiones S.F." (unpublished manuscript, n.d.), Vanderbilt Manuel Zapata Olivella Papers, Nashville, TN.
313. Angela Davis, *Angela Davis—An Autobiography* (New York: Random House, 1996), 16.
314. Ibid., 11.
315. Ibid., 46.
316. Ibid.
317. Oleszkiewicz-Peralba, *Fierce Feminine Divinities*, 91.
318. Davis, *Autobiography*, 118, 121.
319. Ibid., 126.
320. Ibid., 149.
321. Ibid., 203.
322. Zapata, *Changó*, 457–458.
323. Ibid., 498.
324. Ibid., 493.
325. Ibid., 493.
326. Ibid., 96.
327. Zapata, *¡Levántate!*, 141–142.
328. Ibid., 466.
329. Ibid., 324.
330. Brooks, *Searching for Sycorax*, 35.

331. Zapata, *Changó*, 444.
332. Ibid., 466.
333. Zapata, "Revisiones"; Zapata, *Changó*, 466.
334. Zapata, *Changó*, 466.
335. Ibid., 464.
336. Ibid., 452.
337. Cuervo Hewitt, *Voices*, 256.
338. Zapata, *Changó*, 155.
339. Ibid., 123.
340. Ibid., 163.
341. Ibid., 173.
342. Ibid., 228.
343. Ibid., 228.
344. Martin, *Conjuring*, 9.
345. Ibid., 12.
346. Zapata, *Changó*, 259.
347. Paz, *Laberinto*, 39.
348. Zapata, *Changó*, 73.
349. Ibid., 467–468.
350. Ibid., 494.
351. Ibid., 465.
352. Ibid., 633, 635.
353. Ibid., 642.
354. *Young's Literal Translation of the Holy Bible*, trans. Robert Young (Grand Rapids: Baker Book House, 1953), Rev. 17:5.
355. Cuervo Hewitt, *Voices*, 257.
356. Ibid., 207.
357. Ibid., 252.
358. Ibid., 252.
359. Zapata, *Changó*, 637.
360. Ibid., 635–636.
361. Sweet, *Recreating* 131.
362. Zapata, *Changó*, 638.
363. Ibid., 638.
364. Ibid., 644.
365. Ibid., 644–645.
366. Ibid., 499.
367. Ibid., 508.
368. Ibid., 467, 638.
369. Ibid., 638.
370. Rev. 13:1.
371. Zapata, *Changó*, 535.
372. Rev. 21:9.

Conclusion

1. Angela Davis, "Racism in Colombia Resembles the One in the United States," interview by César Rodríguez-G, trans. Yukyan Lam and Roberto Hernández,

Decolonial Translation, September 18, 2010, www.decolonialtranslation.com/english/itwangeladaviscolombiaEng.html.

2. Ibid.
3. Angela Davis, "Angela Davis Denounces Attacks on Afro-Colombian Social Movements," *Afro-Colombian Solidarity Network*, June 5, 2019, https://afrocolombian.org/2019/05/06/angela-davis-denounces-attacks-on-afro-colombian-social-movements/?fbclid=IwARoqaioAtTx_qdQ9tqs9QMMT-HVxslwrznIJVXbV40COCwhgiBrSdIa6YMw.
4. Michelle Alexander, *The New Jim Crow: Mass Incarceration in the Age of Colorblindness* (New York: New Press, 2011), 55.
5. Loïc Wacquant, "The Militarization of Urban Marginality: Lessons from the Brazilian Metropolis," *International Political Sociology* 2 (2008): 58.
6. Alexander, *New Jim Crow*, 158.
7. Ibid., 199.
8. Ibid., 195.
9. Ibid., 31.
10. Michael Cohen, "How For-Profit Prisons Have Become the Biggest Lobby No One Is Talking About," *Washington Post*, April 28, 2015, www.washingtonpost.com/posteverything/wp/2015/04/28/how-for-profit-prisons-have-become-the-biggest-lobby-no-one-is-talking-about/?noredirect=on&utm_term=.972abaf7e23a.
11. Alexander, *New Jim Crow*, 41.
12. Ibid., 44.
13. Ibid., 56.
14. Ibid., 59.
15. Ibid., 134.
16. Zapata, *Changó*, 508.
17. Ibid., 466.
18. Ibid., 637.
19. Fernando Esquivel-Suárez, "The Global War on Drugs," *Global South Studies: A Collective Publication with the Global South*, August 23, 2018, https://globalsouthstudies.as.virginia.edu/key-issues/global-war-drugs, 2.
20. Ibid., 2.
21. María Mercedes Jaramillo, "Bojayá in Colombian Theater: Kilele: A Drama of Memory and Resistance," in *Black Writing and the State in Latin America*, ed. Jerome Branche, trans. Emma Freeman (Nashville, TN: Vanderbilt University Press, 2015), 103.
22. Ibid., 103.
23. Manuel Zapata Olivella, *El fusilamiento del diablo* (Bogota: Plaza y Janés, 1999), 7.
24. Ana Maria Gonçalves, *Um defeito de cor* (Rio de Janeiro: Editora Record, 2006), 509.
25. Ibid., 566–568.
26. Manuela Carneiro da Cunha, *Negros, estrangeiros: Os libertos e sua volta à África* (São Paulo: Brasiliense, 1985), 74.
27. William Luis, "Introduction," in *Changó, the Biggest Badass*, by Manuel Zapata Olivella, trans. Jonathan Tittler (Lubbock: Texas Tech University Press, 2009), xxxv.
28. Livre Opinião, "'Tchau, querida!,' texto inédito de Ana Maria Gonçalves, tem leitura dramática no Auditório Ibirapuera com direção de Wagner Moura," *Livre Opinião*, November 22, 2016, https://livreopiniao.com/2016/11/22/tchau-querida-texto-inedito-de-ana-maria-goncalves-tem-leitura-dramatica-no-auditorio-ibirapuera-com-direcao-de-wagner-moura/.

29. Ana Maria Gonçalves, "Inspiração e viagens através da diáspora: Uma entrevista com Ana Maria Gonçalves," interview by John Maddox, *Afro-Hispanic Review* 30, no. 2 (Fall 2011): 170.
30. Ana Maria Gonçalves, "Carta aberta ao Governador Rui Costa, da Bahia," *Blogueiras negras*, February 27, 2015, http://blogueirasnegras.org/2015/02/27/carta-aberta-ao-governador-da-bahia/.
31. Ibid.
32. Glenn Greenwald, "The Intercept Brasil Welcomes Ana Maria Gonçalves as a Columnist on Race, Politics, and Culture," *Intercept Brasil*, December 2, 2016, https://theintercept.com/2016/12/02/the-intercept-brasil-welcomes-ana-maria-goncalves-as-a-columnist-on-race-politics-and-culture/.
33. Ana Maria Gonçalves, "É difícil fazer com que os 'bem intencionados' entendam o racismo," *Intercept Brasil*, December 2, 2016, https://theintercept.com/staff/ana-maria-goncalves/.
34. Ana Maria Gonçalves, "Falta empatia para entender a revolta dos negros," *Intercept Brasil*, January 11, 2017, https://theintercept.com/staff/ana-maria-goncalves/.
35. Ana Maria Gonçalves, "Marinha agride, intimida e ameaça comunidade quilombola na Bahia," *Intercept Brasil*, February 8, 2017, https://theintercept.com/staff/ana-maria-goncalves/.
36. Ana Maria Gonçalves, "O medo sempre nos traz algo de familiar, que é o nosso preconceito," *Intercept Brasil*, March 22, 2017, https://theintercept.com/staff/ana-maria-goncalves/.
37. Ana Maria Gonçalves, "Dear White People liberta a arte negra de referências brancas," *Intercept Brasil*, May 31, 2017, https://theintercept.com/staff/ana-maria-goncalves/.
38. Ana Maria Gonçalves, "Longe de Charlottesville, São Paulo também celebra 'o lado errado da história,'" *Intercept Brasil*, August 15, 2017, https://theintercept.com/staff/ana-maria-goncalves/.
39. Ana Maria Gonçalves, "O que a polêimica sobre o filme 'Vazante' nos ensina sobre fragilidade branca," *Intercept Brasil*, November 16, 2017, https://theintercept.com/staff/ana-maria-goncalves/.
40. Ana Maria Gonçalves, "'Um defeito de cor,' de Ana Maria Gonçalves, vai virar minissérie da Rede Globo," *Revistaórum*, March 26, 2019, https://revistaforum.com.br/um-defeito-de-cor-de-ana-maria-goncalves-vai-virar-minisserie-da-rede-globo/.
41. Gonçalves, "Polêimica."
42. Ana Maria Gonçalves, "Na polêmica sobre turbantes, é a branquitude que não quer assumir seu racismo," *Intercept Brasil*, February 15, 2017, https://theintercept.com/staff/ana-maria-goncalves/.
43. The November 11, 2017, installment criticized a "hot mic moment" in which a Brazilian newscaster, in front of a White House occupied by a black president, made racist remarks about a noisy black motorist. His interlocutor, the head of the Brazil Institute at the Woodrow Wilson Center, laughed at the comments. Gonçalves argues that he was complicit in the comment and that both should be held responsible.
44. Ana Maria Gonçalves, "Na polêmica sobre turbantes, é a branquitude que não quer assumir seu racismo," *Intercept Brasil*, February 15, 2017, https://theintercept.com/staff/ana-maria-goncalves/.

45. Eliane Brum, "De uma branca para outra: O turbante e o preconceito de existir violentamente," *El País*, February 20, 2017, https://brasil.elpais.com/brasil/2017/02/20/opinion/1487597060_574691.html.
46. Ana Maria Gonçalves, "Depois de 15 anos e muita pressão, o FLIP finalmente abre espaço para Mulheres e negros na programação," *Intercept Brasil*, July 26, 2017, https://theintercept.com/staff/ana-maria-goncalves/.
47. Ana Maria Gonçalves, "A aula de racismo e machismo à brasileira do secretário de Educação do Rio," *Intercept Brasil*, December 1, 2017, https://theintercept.com/staff/ana-maria-goncalves/.
48. David DeIuliis and Jeff Lohr, "Rewriting the Narrative: Communicology and the Speculative Discourse of Afrofuturism," in *Afrofuturism 2.0*, ed. Reynaldo Anderson and Charles Jones (Lanham, MD: Lexington Books, 2016), 178.
49. Miguel Juan Payán. "Black Panther," *Revista Acción*, November 1, 2018, Scribd.com, www.scribd.com/article/393009454/Black-Panther.
50. Mark Dery, "Black to the Future: Interviews with Samuel R. Delany, Greg Tate, and Tricia Rose," *South Atlantic Quarterly* 92, no. 4 (1993): 735.
51. Mark Dery, ed., *Flame Wars: The Discourse of Cyberculture* (Durham, NC: Duke University Press, 1994).
52. Ibid., 182.
53. Octavia Butler, *Kindred* (London: Headline, 2018); Dery, *Flame*, 188.
54. Kinitra Brooks, *Searching for Sycorax: Black Women's Hauntings of Contemporary Horror* (New Brunswick, NJ: Rutgers University Press, 2018), 69.
55. Reynaldo Anderson and Yajaira de la Espada, "Call for Papers: Afrofuturismo Project," Association for the Study of the Worldwide African Diaspora, April 8, 2019, http://aswadiaspora.org/call-for-papers-afrofuturismo-project/.
56. Catherine Ramírez, "Deus ex machina: Tradition, Technology, and the Chicanafuturist Art of Marion C. Martinez," *Aztlán: A Journal of Chicano Studies* 29, no. 2 (October 2005): 55.
57. Anderson and Jones, *Afrofuturism 2.0*, ix.
58. Ibid., x.
59. Nettrice Gaskins, "Afrofuturisms on Web 3.0: Vernacular Cartography and Augmented Space," in Anderson and Jones, *Afrofuturism 2.0*, 27.
60. Darío Henao Restrepo, introduction to *Changó, el gran putas*, by Manuel Zapata Olivella, in *Biblioteca de Literatura Afrocolombiana*, vol. 3, ed. Darío Henao Restrepo (Bogota: Ministerio de Cultura, 2010), 23, http://babel.banrepcultural.org/cdm/ref/collection/p17054coll7/id/2.
61. Tobias van Veen, "The Armageddon Effect: Afrofuturism and the Chronopolitics of Alien Nation," in Anderson and Jones, *Afrofuturism 2.0*, 83.
62. Zapata, *Changó*, 43, 138, 244, 622.
63. Butler, *Kindred*; Zapata, *Changó*, 452.
64. Zapata, *Changó*, 41, 381.
65. Juan Francisco Manzano, *Autobiografía del esclavo poeta y otros escritos*, ed. William Luis (Frankfurt: Vervuert, 2007), 301.
66. Walter Ong, *Orality and Literacy: The Technologizing of the Word* (New York: Routledge, 2012), 10.
67. Zapata, *Changó*, 216.
68. Ibid., 484.

69. Ibid., 508, 640.
70. James Sweet, *Recreating Africa: Culture, Kinship, and Religion in the African-Portuguese World, 1441–1770* (Chapel Hill: University of North Carolina Press, 2004), 179–180.
71. Ibid., 186.
72. van Veen, "Armageddon Effect," 79–80.
73. Manuel Zapata Olivella, "Conversación informal con Manuel Zapata Olivella," by Margarita Krakusin, *Afro-Hispanic Review* 20, no. 1 (2001): 15.
74. Ibid., 16.
75. Ibid.
76. Ibid., 17.
77. Ibid., 16–17.
78. Ibid., 19.
79. van Veen, "Armageddon Effect," 68.
80. Ibid., 69.
81. Jimi Hendrix, "Voodoo Child (Slight Return)," *Electric Ladyland* (Reprise, 1968).
82. van Veen, "Armageddon Effect," 75.
83. Paul Gilroy, *The Black Atlantic: Modernity and Double Consciousness* (New York: Verso, 1993), 94.
84. van Veen, "Armageddon Effect," 93.
85. Ibid., 75.
86. Sarah Meredith, "With a Banjo on Her Knee: Gender, Race, Class, and the American Classical Banjo Tradition, 1880–1915" (PhD diss., Florida State University, 2003), 13.
87. Noah Adams, "The Inspiring Force of 'We Shall Overcome,'" *All Things Considered*, National Public Radio, August 28, 2013, www.npr.org/2013/08/28/216482943/the-inspiring-force-of-we-shall-overcome.
88. Charles Cross, *Room Full of Mirrors: A Biography of Jimi Hendrix* (New York: Hyperion, 2005), 277.
89. Public Enemy, "Fight the Power" (Motown, 1989).
90. van Veen, "Armageddon Effect," 77.
91. Zapata, *Changó*, 620.
92. van Veen, "Armageddon Effect," 71.
93. Zapata, *Changó*, 649, 660.
94. Gilroy, *Atlantic*, 53; van Veen, "Armageddon Effect," 77.
95. Andrew Rollins, "Afrofuturism and Our Old Ship of Zion: The Black Church in Post-Modernity," in Anderson and Jones, *Afrofuturism 2.0*, 127–148.
96. Ibid., 133.
97. Ibid., 137.
98. Ibid., 142.
99. Martine Syms, "The Mundane Afrofuturist Manifesto," *Rhizome*, December 17, 2013, http://rhizome.org/editorial/2013/dec/17/mundane-afrofuturist-manifesto/.
100. Ibid.
101. Zapata, *Changó*, 655.
102. Nei Lopes, *Oiobomé: A epopéia de uma nação* (Rio de Janeiro: Agir, 2010).
103. Nei Lopes, *Enciclopédia brasileira da diáspora africana* (São Paulo: Selo Negro, 2011).
104. Lopes, *Oiobomé*, 49.

105. Ibid., 160, 207.
106. Ibid., 148.
107. Ibid., 198.
108. Ibid., 213.
109. Ibid., 92.
110. Ibid., 223.
111. Felipe Maia, "Meet the Brazilian Musicians Leading Bahia's Afrofuturism Movement," *Remezcla*, May 16, 2019, https://remezcla.com/features/music/artists-bahia-afrofuturism/.
112. Fábio Kabral, *O caçador cibernético da Rua 13* (Rio de Janeiro: Editora Malês, 2017).
113. Fábio Kabral, "A diretora analista de mídias oníricas," in *2084: Mundos Cyberpunks*, ed. Lídia Zuin (Manaus: Lendare, 2018), 31.
114. Carl Degler, *Neither Black nor White: Slavery and Race Relations in Brazil and the United States* (Madison: University of Wisconsin Press, 1971), 224.
115. Fábio Kabral, "Categoria: O caçador cibernético da Rua 13," June 2019, https://fabiokabral.wordpress.com/category/literatura/o-cacador-cibernetico-da-rua-13/.
116. Sweet, *Recreating*, 104.
117. Nátaly Neri, "Afrofuturismo: A necessidade de novas utopías" (lecture, TEDx-Petrópolis, Petropolis, RJ, January 21, 2018), www.youtube.com/watch?v=_D1y9yZRpis.
118. Mário Bentes, "O pajemancer," in *2084: Mundos Cyberpunks*, ed. Lídia Zuin (Manaus: Lendare, 2018), 132.
119. Felipe Damiani, "Loucura artificial," in Zuin, *2084*, 274.
120. Ibid., 279.
121. Mark Dery, "Negro para o futuro," *Rizoma.net*, 132–137, 2006, https://issuu.com/rizoma.net/docs/afrofuturismo; Paul D. Miller, "Afro-Futurismo: Uma declaração de intenções—De ponta cabeça, de cabeça para baixo," *Rizoma.net*, 16–17, 2006, https://issuu.com/rizoma.net/docs/afrofuturismo; Mark Sinker, "Amando o alien," *Rizoma.net*, 2006, 110–113, https://issuu.com/rizoma.net/docs/afrofuturismo.
122. Dirk van Weelden, "Religião de rua e magia da matrix," *Rizoma.net*, 2006, 67, https://issuu.com/rizoma.net/docs/afrofuturismo.
123. Ibid., 68.
124. Erik Davis, "Raízes e fios: Ciberespaço polirrítmico e eletrônica negra," *Rizoma.net*, 2006, 80, https://issuu.com/rizoma.net/docs/afrofuturismo.
125. Ibid., 82.
126. Ibid., 76.
127. Hermano Vianna, "Atlântico Negro," *Rizoma.net*, 2006, https://issuu.com/rizoma.net/docs/afrofuturismo, 99.
128. Cristiano Henrique Ribeiro dos Santos, "O simbolismo da árvore-mundo no candomblé: Conexão entre o mundo dos homens e o mundo dos deuses," *Rizoma.net*, 2006, 145–146, https://issuu.com/rizoma.net/docs/afrofuturismo.
129. Ivana Bentes, "Afryka teórica," *Rizoma.net*, 2006, 7, https://issuu.com/rizoma.net/docs/afrofuturismo.
130. Ibid., 42.
131. Isabel Millán, "Engineering Afro-Latina and Mexican Immigrant Heroines: Bio-politics in Borderlands Speculative Literature and Film," *Aztlán: A Journal of Chicano Studies* 40, no. 2 (Fall 2015): 167–185.

132. Catherine Ramírez, "Deus ex machina: Tradition, Technology, and the Chicanafuturist Art of Marion C. Martinez," *Aztlán: A Journal of Chicano Studies* 29, no. 2 (October 2004): 55.
133. Catherine Ramírez, "Afrofuturism/Chicanafuturism: Fictive Kin," *Aztlán: A Journal of Chicano Studies* 33, no. 1 (2008): 187.
134. Ibid., 187–190.
135. Ibid., 185–186.
136. Millán, "Engineering," 170.
137. Ibid., 168.
138. Ibid., 172.
139. Ibid., 175.
140. Rodolfo "Corky" Gonzales and Alberto Urista (Alaurista), "El plan espiritual de Aztlán," *El Grito del Norte* 2, no. 9 (July 6, 1969): 5, https://icaadocs.mfah.org/icaadocs/THEARCHIVE/FullRecord/tabid/88/doc/803398/language/en-US/Default.aspx; Cathryna Josefina Merla-Watson and B. V. Olguín, "Introduction: ¡Latin@futurism Ahora! Recovering, Remapping, and Recentering the Chican@ and Latin@ Speculative Arts," *Aztlán: A Journal of Chicano Studies* 40, no. 2 (Fall 2015): 138–139.
141. Gonzales and Urista, "Plan espiritual," 5.
142. Merla-Watson and Olguín, "Introduction," 138.
143. Junot Diaz, *The Brief, Wondrous Life of Oscar Wao* (New York: Riverhead Books, 2008), 6.
144. John Maddox, "Afro-McOndo en *The Brief, Wondrous Life of Oscar Wao*," *Caribe* 14, no. 2 (2011–2012): 27.
145. Brooks, *Searching for Sycorax*.
146. Ibid., 69.
147. Ibid., 89.
148. Ibid., 83–85.
149. Ibid., 102–103.
150. Ana Maria Gonçalves, *Um defeito de cor* (Rio de Janeiro: Editora Record, 2006), 5.
151. Ibid., 5.
152. Ibid., 14.
153. Patrícia de Santana Pinho, *Mapping Diaspora: African American Roots Tourism in Brazil* (Chapel Hill: University of North Carolina Press, 2018), 19.
154. Butler, *Kindred*.
155. Gonçalves, *Defeito*, 947.
156. Ibid., 888.
157. Ana Maria Gonçalves, "Quem é Jocenildo? Em processo," Blog do IMS, Instituto Moreira Salles, July 26, 2017, https://blogdoims.com.br/quem-e-josenildo/.
158. André Cáceres, "Literatura fantástica brasileira é redescoberta em dois livros," *O Estado de São Paulo*, January 5, 2018, https://alias.estadao.com.br/noticias/geral,literatura-fantastica-brasileira-e-redescoberta-em-dois-livros,70002667135.
159. Manuel Zapata Olivella, *¡Levántate mulato! Por mi raza hablará el espíritu* (Bogota: REI Andes, 1990), 349.
160. "'Um defeito de cor,' de Ana Maria Gonçalves, vai virar minissérie da Rede Globo," *Revista Fórum*, March 26, 2019, https://revistaforum.com.br/um-defeito-de-cor-de-ana-maria-goncalves-vai-virar-minisserie-da-rede-globo/.

Bibliography

Adams, Noah. "The Inspiring Force of 'We Shall Overcome.'" *All Things Considered*, National Public Radio, August 28, 2013. www.npr.org/2013/08/28/216482943/the-inspiring-force-of-we-shall-overcome.

Afolabi, Niyi. "A visão mítico-trágica na dramaturgia abdisiana." *Hispania* 81, no. 3 (Spring 1998): 530–540.

Agência EFE. "Ana Maria Gonçalves ganha Prêmio Casa de Las Américas 2007." *Jornal do Brasil*, July 31, 2007. www.jb.com.br/cultura/noticias/2007/01/25/ana-maria-goncalves-ganha-premio-casa-de-las-americas-2007/.

Aguiar, Mario. "*Changó, el gran putas* o la tormentosa espiral del *Muntu* en América." *Estudios de Literatura Colombiana* 14 (January–June 2004): 11–23.

Alexander, Michelle. *The New Jim Crow: Mass Incarceration in the Age of Colorblindness*. New York: New Press, 2011.

Almeida, Miguel Vale de. *Um mar da cor da terra*. Oeiras: Celta, 2006.

Alves, Miriam. "Mahin amanã." *Cadernos Negros* 9 (1986): 46.

Alzate, Sandra. "La relatividad de la verdad: Testimonio, narración y memoria en la obra de Manuel Zapata Olivella." *Afro-Hispanic Review* 30, no. 1 (Spring 2011): 31–46.

"Ana Maria Gonçalves." Internationales Literaturfestival, Berlin, September 11–21, 2019. http://literaturfestival.com/autoren-en/autoren-2013-en/ana-maria-goncalves.

"Ana Maria Gonçalves—Flip (2016)—Parte 1/4." Ministério da Cultura, Ancine, Itaú Cultural. July 18, 2016. www.youtube.com/watch?v=cfkNH5RtoZs.

Anderson, Benedict. *Imagined Communities: Reflections on the Origin and Spread of Nationalism*. New York: Verso, 1991.

Anderson, Reynaldo, and Charles Jones, eds. *Afrofuturism 2.0: The Rise of Astro-Blackness*. Lanham, MD: Lexington Books, 2016.

Anderson, Reynaldo, and Yajaira de la Espada. "Call for Papers: Afrofuturismo Project." Association for the Study of the Worldwide African Diaspora, April 8, 2019. http://aswadiaspora.org/call-for-papers-afrofuturismo-project/.

Anzaldúa, Gloria. *Borderlands/La Frontera: The New Mestiza*. San Francisco: Spinsters, 1987.

Anzaldúa, Gloria, and Cherríe Moraga, eds. *This Bridge Called My Back: Writings by Radical Women of Color*. New York: Kitchen Table; Women of Color Press, 1983.

Araujo, Ana Lucia. "Dandara e Luisa Mahin são consideradas heroínas do Brasil—O problema é que elas nunca existiram." *Intercept Brasil*, June 3, 2019. https://theintercept.com/2019/06/03/dandara-luisa-mahin-panteao-patria/.

———. "History, Memory, and Imagination: Na Agontimé, a Dahomean Queen in Brazil." In *Beyond Tradition: African Women in Cultural and Political Spaces*, edited by Toyin Falola and S. U. Fwatshak, 45–65. Trenton, NJ: Africa World Press, 2011.

Araújo dos Anjos, Maria Luisa. "A escolarização da peça Sortilégio II—mistério negro de Zumbi redivivo." Master's thesis, Universidade de Brasília, Brasília, Brazil, 2007.

Arriaga, Eduard. "La red de representaciones artísticas de lo afrodescendiente: Tejiendo imaginarios en la era digital. Colombia, Canadá y Guinea Ecuatorial." In *Identidades políticas en tiempos de la afrodescendencia: Autoidentificación, ancestralidad, visibilidad y derechos*, edited by Silvia Valero and Alejandro Campos García, 289–332. Buenos Aires: Corregidor, 2015.

Arroyo, Jossianna, and Elizabeth Marchant. "Introduction." *Comparative Literature Studies* 49, no. 2 (2012): 163–166.

Arroyo Pizarro, Yolanda. "Changó." In *Transmutadxs*, 13–33. San Juan: Boreales, 2016.

Artel, Jorge. *Tambores en la noche*. In *Si yo fuera tambó: Poesía selecta de Candelario Obeso y Jorge Artel, edición crítica*, edited by Graciela Maglia, 199–236. Bogota: Editorial de la Pontífica Universidad Javeriana, 2010.

Asante, Molefi Kete. *The Afrocentric Idea*. Philadelphia: Temple University Press, 1998.

Avelar, Idelber. "Biblioteca Latino-Americana: Xangô, o grande fodão [Changó, el gran putas] de Manuel Zapata Olivella." *Forum*, March 16, 2012. www.revistaforum.com.br/idelberavelar/2012/03/16/biblioteca-latino-americana-xango-o-grande-fodao-chango-el-gran-putas-de-manuel-zapata-olivella/.

Azevedo, Elciene. *Orfeu de Caparinha: A trajetória de Luiz Gama na imperial cidade de São Paulo.* Campinas: Universidade de Campinas, 1999.

Barnes, Natasha. "Black Atlantic–Black America." *Research in African Literatures* 27, no. 4 (Winter 1996): 106–107.

Barnet, Miguel [and Esteban Montejo]. *Biografía de un cimarrón.* Mexico: Siglo Veintiuno, 1968.

Barry, John. "Abriendo el canon para Manuel Zapata Olivella: 'Santa Bárbara, Bendita, ayúdanos a vivir.'" *Confluencia* 8, no. 2 / 9, no. 1 (Spring and Fall 1993): 249–255.

Belém, Euler da França. "Ana Maria Gonçalves, autora de 'Um defeito de cor' vai lançar novo romance pela Editora Record." *Geledes*, September 7, 2017. www.geledes.org.br/ana-maria-goncalves-autora-de-um-defeito-de-cor-vai-lancar-novo-romance-pela-editora-record/.

Bennett, Herman. *African Kings and Black Slaves: Sovereignty and Dispossession in the Early Modern Atlantic*. Philadelphia: University of Pennsylvania Press, 2019.

———. "The Subject in the Plot: National Boundaries and the 'History' of the Black Atlantic." *African Studies Review* 43, no. 1 (April 2000): 101–124.

Bentes, Ivana. "Afryka teórica." *Rizoma.net*, 2006, 6–10. https://issuu.com/rizoma.net/docs/afrofuturismo.

Bentes, Mário. "O pajemancer." In *2084: Mundos Cyberpunks*, edited by Lídia Zuin, 142–147. Manaus: Lendare, 2018.

Bernd, Zilá. "Em busca dos rastros perdidos da memória ancestral: Um estudo de *Um defeito de cor* de Ana Maria Gonçalves." *Estudos da Literatura Brasileira Contemporânea* 40 (July–December 2012): 29–42.

Best, Stephen. "On Failing to Make the Past Present." *Modern Language Quarterly* 73, no. 3 (2012): 453–474.

Biblioteca de Literatura Afrocolombiana. Bogota: Banco de la República / Ministerio de Cultura, 2010. http://babel.banrepcultural.org/cdm/landingpage/collection/p17054coll7.

Boelhower, William. "The Rise of the New Atlantic Studies Matrix." *American Literary Theory* 20, nos. 1–2 (Spring–Summer 2008): 83–101.

Bogliolo, François. *La négritude et les problèmes du Noir dans l'oeuvre de Zapata Olivella*. Dakar: Nouvelles Éditions Africaines, 1978.

Braga-Pinto, César. "The Honor of the Abolitionist and the Shamefulness of Slavery: Raúl Pompeia, Luiz Gama, and Joaquim Nabuco." *Luso-Brazilian Review* 51, no. 22 (2014): 170–198.

Branche, Jerome. *The Poetics and Politics of Diaspora: Transatlantic Musings*. New York: Routledge, 2015.

———, ed. *Race, Colonialism, and Social Transformation in Latin America and the Caribbean*. Gainesville: University Press of Florida, 2008.

Brooks, Kinitra. *Searching for Sycorax: Black Women's Hauntings of Contemporary Horror*. New Brunswick, NJ: Rutgers University Press, 2018.

Brown, Kimberly Juanita. *The Repeating Body: Slavery's Visual Resonance in the Contemporary*. Durham, NC: Duke University Press, 2015.

Brum, Eliane. "De uma branca para outra: O turbante e o preconceito de existir violentamente." *El País*, February 20, 2017. https://brasil.elpais.com/brasil/2017/02/20/opinion/1487597060_574691.html.

Brushwood, John. "La novela colombiana en la perspectiva hispanoamericana." In *Ensayos de literatura colombiana*, edited by Raymond Williams, 167–174. Bogota: Editorial Plaza y Janés, 1985.

Butler, Kim. "Brazilian Abolition in Afro-Atlantic Context." *African Studies Review* 43, no. 1 (2000): 125–139.

Butler, Octavia. *Kindred*. London: Headline, 2018.

Cabral, Cristina. "Myth, Legend, and Reality: Redesigning the Narrative Style in Manuel Zapata Olivella's Hemingway, the Death Stalker." In *Critical Perspectives on Afro–Latin American Literature*, edited by Antonio Tillis, 99–119. New York: Routledge, 2012.

Cabrera, Lydia. *El Monte: Notas sobre las religiones, la magia, las supersticiones y el folklore de los negros criollos y el pueblo de Cuba*. Havana: Letras Cubanas, 1993. First published 1954.

Cáceres, André. "Literatura fantástica brasileira é redescoberta em dois livros." *O Estado de São Paulo*, January 5, 2018. https://alias.estadao.com.br/noticias/geral,literatura-fantastica-brasileira-e-redescoberta-em-dois-livros,70002667135.

Cáceres Aguilar, Dagoberto. "*Changó el gran putas*: Reconfiguración de la historia. Reinventando caminos para no olvidar." *Poligramas* 28 (December 2007): 227–246. http://bibliotecadigital.univalle.edu.co/bitstream/10893/2990/1/Poligramas,%20No.28,p.227-246.pdf.

Camacho Buitrago, Dina. "Manuel Zapata Olivella, Letras Nacionales y la emergencia de un 'relato negro' en el campo intelectual colombiano." *Meridional: Revista*

Chilena de Estudios Literarios 4 (April 2015): 97–114. http://meridional.uchile.cl/index.php/MRD/article/viewFile/36532/38147.

Câmara, Nelson. *Escravidão, nunca mais!: Um tributo a Luiz Gama*. São Paulo: Editora Via Lettera, 2009.

———. *Luiz Gama, o advogado dos escravos*. São Paulo: Editora Via Lettera, 2010.

Camões, Luiz de. *Os Lusíadas*. Boston: Harvard University Press, 1946.

Campos, Maria Consuelo Cunha. "Luiz Gama." In *Literatura e afrodescendência no Brasil: Antologia crítica*, vol. 1, edited by Eduardo de Assis Duarte, 127–134. Belo Horizonte: Editora da Universidade Federal de Minas Gerais, 2011.

Capone, Stefania. "Transatlantic Dialogue: Roger Bastide and the African American Religions." In *Africas of the Americas: Beyond the Search for Origins in the Study of Afro-Atlantic Religions*, edited by Stephan Palmié, 255–292. Boston: Brill, 2008.

Captain-Hidalgo, Yvonne. *The Culture of Fiction in the Works of Manuel Zapata Olivella*. Columbia: University of Missouri Press, 1993.

———. "Entrevista con el doctor Manuel Zapata Olivella, Bogotá, 1980; 1983." *Afro-Hispanic Review* 4, no. 1 (Spring 1985): 26–32.

———. "El espacio del tiempo en *Changó, el gran putas*." In *Ensayos de literatura colombiana*, edited by Raymond Williams, 157–162. Bogota: Editorial Plaza y Janés, 1985.

———. "Hacia su habitación propia: La mujer en Manuel Zapata Olivella." In *Literatura y Cultura: Narrativa Colombiana del Siglo XX*, vol. 3, no. 2, edited by María M. Jaramillo et al., 147–167. Bogota: Ministerio de Cultura, 2000.

———. "The Legacy of Manuel Zapata Olivella." *Revista de Estudios Colombianos* 37/38 (2011): 30–34.

Capuano, Cláudio de Sá. "História e africanidade em *Um defeito de cor* de Ana Maria Gonçalves." In *Alguma prosa: Ensaios sobre a literatura brasileira contemporânea*, edited by Giovanna Dealtry et al., 85–98. Rio de Janeiro: Editora Sete Letras, 2007.

Carneiro, Sueli. "Estrelas com luz própria." *Revista História Viva* 3 (2006): 48–49.

Carpentier, Alejo. *El reino de este mundo*. New York: Rayo, 2009.

Carvalho, José Jorge de. *Las culturas afroamericanas en Iberoamérica: Lo negociable y lo innegociable*. Bogota: Universidad Nacional de Colombia, 2005.

Casamayor-Cisneros, Odette. "Imagining the New Black (Subject): Ethical Transformations of Raciality in the Post-revolutionary Cuban Nation." In *Black Writing and the State in Latin America*, edited by Jerome Branche, 61–82. Nashville: Vanderbilt University Press, 2015.

Castro, Maurício Barros de, and César Fraga. *Do outro lado*. São Paulo: Olhares, 2014.

"Cátedra Manuel Zapata Olivella." Universidad de Antioquia. www.udea.edu.co.

Ceballos, Diego, and Jorge Antonio Fortes, dir. *Afroargentinos*. Buenos Aires: Ancho Camino; Filmagem, 2005.

Chatwin, Bruce. *The Viceroy of Ouidah*. Manila: Summit Books, 1980.

Chivallon, Christine, and Karen Fields. "Beyond Gilroy's Black Atlantic: The Experience of the African Diaspora." *Diaspora: A Journal of Transnational Studies* 11, no. 3 (Winter 2002): 359–382.

Chrisman, Laura. "Journeying to Death: Gilroy's *Black Atlantic*." *Race & Class* 39, no. 2 (1997): 51–64.

Cirio, Norberto Pablo. "Construyendo una identificación desde la historia local: La categoría afroargentino del tronco colonial como experiencia etnogénica." In *Identidades políticas en tiempos de la afrodescendencia: Autoidentificación, ancestrali-*

dad, visibilidad y derechos, edited by Silvia Valero and Alejandro Campos García, 334–372. Buenos Aires: Corregidor, 2015.

Clifford, James. "Diasporas." *Cultural Anthropology* 9 (1994): 302–338.

Coelho, Maria Josele Bucco. "(In)submissive Imaginaries in the Contemporary Brazilian Historical Novel: A Reading of *Um defeito de cor* by Ana Maria Gonçalves." In *Redefining Latin American Historical Fiction: The Impact of Feminism and Postcolonialism*, edited by Helene Carol Weldt-Basson, 209–230. New York: Palgrave Macmillan, 2013.

Cohen, Michael. "How For-Profit Prisons Have Become the Biggest Lobby No One Is Talking About." *Washington Post,* April 28, 2015. www.washingtonpost.com/posteverything/wp/2015/04/28/how-for-profit-prisons-have-become-the-biggest-lobby-no-one-is-talking-about/?noredirect=on&utm_term=.972abaf7e23a.

Color de Colombia. "Manuel Zapata Olivella como clásico: Reflexiones potencialmente divergentes." *El Tiempo*, September 14, 2012. http://blogs.eltiempo.com/afrocolombianidad/2012/09/14/manuel-zapata-olivella-como-clasico-reflexiones-potencialmente-divergentes/.

Comparato, Fábio Konder. "Luiz Gama, contemptor de nossas falsas elites." In *Com a palavra, Luiz Gama: Poemas, artigos, cartas, máximas*, edited by Lígia Fonseca Ferreira, 11–14. São Paulo: Imprensa Oficial.

Conrado, Mônica Prates, and Alan Augusto Moraes Ribeiro. "Homem negro, negro homem: Masculinidades e feminismo em debate." *Revista de Estudos Feministas* 25, no. 1 (January–April 2017): 73–97. https://periodicos.ufsc.br/index.php/ref/article/view/40165/33662.

Côrtes, Cristiane Felipe Ribeiro de Araújo. "*Um defeito de cor*: O entre e o duplo da diáspora." *Literafro*. http://150.164.100.248/literafro/data1/autores/23/anamariacritica01.pdf.

Costa Contié, Fernanda Soares. "Motta Coqueiro: Entre a afro descendencia e a ideologia senhorial." *Literafro*, Universidade Federal de Minas Gerais, January 4, 2018. www.letras.ufmg.br/literafro/autores/28-critica-de-autores-masculinos/599-motta-coqueiro-entre-a-afro-descendencia-e-a-ideologia-senhorial-fernanda-soares-da-costa-contie.

Cox, Timothy. *Postmodern Tales of Slavery in the Americas: From Alejo Carpentier to Charles Johnson.* Shrewsbury: Garland, 2001.

Cross, Charles. *Room Full of Mirrors: A Biography of Jimi Hendrix*. New York: Hyperion, 2005.

Cruz, Adélcio da Souza. "Ana Maria Gonçalves." In *Literatura e afrodescendência no Brasil: Antologia crítica*, vol. 3, edited by Eduardo de Assis Duarte and Maria Nazareth Soares Fonseca, 477–492. Belo Horizonte: Editora da Universidade Federal de Minas Gerais, 2011.

Cuervo Hewitt, Julia. "Luis de Camoens en la tierra de Calibán: Las *Lusíadas* en *Changó el gran putas* de Manuel Zapata Olivella." *Afro-Hispanic Review* 22, no. 1 (Fall 2003): 13–23.

———. *Voices Out of Africa in Twentieth-Century Spanish Caribbean Literature.* Lewisburg, PA: Bucknell University Press, 2009.

Cuesta Escobar, Guiomar, and Alfredo Ocampo Zamorano. *¡Negras somos! Antología de 21 mujeres poetas afrocolombianas de la región pacífica*. Cali: Programa Editorial Universidad del Valle, 2008.

Cunha, Manuela Carneiro da. *Negros, estrangeiros: Os libertos e sua volta à África*. São Paulo: Brasiliense, 1985.

Dalcastagnè, Regina, "A cor de uma ausência: Representações do negro no romance brasileiro contemporâneo." *Afro-Hispanic Review* 29, no. 2 (Fall 2010): 97–108.

———. "Da senzala ao cortiço—história e literatura em Aluísio Azevedo e João Ubaldo Ribeiro." *Revista Brasileira de História* 21, no. 42 (2001): 483–494.

Dalcom Junior, Marcelo Cruz, and Lícia Soares de Souza, "Nas entrelinhas de Um defeito de Cor: Desvio, discursos históricos e literários." XI Congresso Internacional da Associação Brasileira de Estudos Canadenses, Universidade Federal da Bahia, Salvador, BA, October 24–26, 2011, 1–10. www.anaisabecan2011.ufba.br/Arquivos/Dalcom-Souza.pdf.

Damiani, Felipe. "Loucura artificial." In *2084: Mundos Cyberpunks*, edited by Lídia Zuin, 274–281. Manaus: Lendare, 2018.

Dantas, Mariana. *Black Townsmen: Slavery and Freedom in Eighteenth-Century Baltimore, Maryland, and Sabará, Minas Gerais*. New York: Palgrave Macmillan, 2008.

Davis, Angela. *Angela Davis—An Autobiography*. New York: Random House, 1996.

———. "Angela Davis Denounces Attacks on Afro-Colombian Social Movements." *Afro-Colombian Solidarity Network*, June 5, 2019. https://afrocolombian.org/2019/05/06/angela-davis-denounces-attacks-on-afro-colombian-social-movements/?fbclid=IwARoqaioAtTx_qdQ9tqs9QMMT-HVxslwrznIJVXbV40COCwhgiBrSdIa6YMw.

———. *Are Prisons Obsolete?* New York: Seven Stories Press, 2003.

———. "Racism in Colombia Resembles the One in the United States." Interview by César Rodríguez-G, translated by Yukyan Lam and Roberto Hernández. *Decolonial Translation*, September 18, 2010. www.decolonialtranslation.com/english/itwangeladaviscolombiaEng.html.

Davis, Erik. "Raízes e fios: Ciberespaço polirrítmico e eletrônica negra." *Rizoma.net*, 2006, 76–87. https://issuu.com/rizoma.net/docs/afrofuturismo.

Davis, James. "Afterword: A Personal Perspective on the Humanism of Manuel Zapata Olivella." *Afro-Hispanic Review* 20, no. 1 (Spring 2001): 115–116.

"'Um defeito de cor,' de Ana Maria Gonçalves, vai virar minissérie da Rede Globo." *Revista Fórum*, March 26, 2019. https://revistaforum.com.br/um-defeito-de-cor-de-ana-maria-goncalves-vai-virar-minisserie-da-rede-globo/.

Degler, Carl. *Neither Black nor White: Slavery and Race Relations in Brazil and the United States*. Madison: University of Wisconsin Press, 1971.

DeIuliis, David, and Jeff Lohr. "Rewriting the Narrative: Communicology and the Speculative Discourse of Afrofuturism." In *Afrofuturism 2.0*, edited by Reynaldo Anderson and Charles Jones, 167–184. Lanham, MD: Lexington Books, 2016.

Delgado, Camilo. *Historias, leyendas y tradiciones de Cartagena*. Cartagena: Colombia Mogollón, 1914.

Dennis, Christopher. "The Current and Future State of Afro-Colombian Prose Fiction." *Afro-Hispanic Review* 30, no. 1 (Spring 2011): 81–100.

Dery, Mark. "Black to the Future: Interviews with Samuel R. Delany, Greg Tate, and Tricia Rose." *South Atlantic Quarterly* 92, no. 4 (1993): 735–778.

———, ed. *Flame Wars: The Discourse of Cyberculture*. Durham, NC: Duke University Press, 1994.

———. "Negro para o futuro." *Rizoma.net*, 132–137, 2006. https://issuu.com/rizoma.net/docs/afrofuturismo.

Dhouti, Khamla. "Reconfiguring Mestizaje: Black Identity in the Works of Piri Thomas, Manuel Zapata Olivella, Nicolás Guillén, and Nancy Morejón." PhD dissertation, University of Texas, 2002. https://repositories.lib.utexas.edu/handle/2152/10957.

———. "Rewriting the Other: Manuel Zapata Olivella's *¡Levántate Mulato!*" *Letras Hispanas* 4, no. 2 (Fall 2007): 129–137.

Diaz, Junot. *The Brief, Wondrous Life of Oscar Wao*. New York: Riverhead Books, 2008.

Díaz-Granados, José Luis. "Premio Aplauso." *Afro-Hispanic Review* 20, no. 1 (Spring 2001): 6–12.

Dreher, Martin. *A Igreja Latino-Americana no contexto colonial*. São Leopoldo: Sinodal, 2007.

Du Bois, W. E. B. *The Souls of Black Folk*. Toronto: Dover, 1994.

Duarte, Eduardo de Assis. "Na cartografia do romance brasileiro, *Um defeito de cor*, de Ana Maria Gonçalves." Literafro, October 10, 2018. www.letras.ufmg.br/literafro/arquivos/autoras/anamariacritica03.pdf.

Duarte, Eduardo de Assis, and Maria Nazareth Soares Fonseca, eds. *Literatura e afrodescendência no Brasil: Antologia crítica*. Vols. 1–4. Belo Horizonte: Editora da Universidade Federal de Minas Gerais, 2011.

Dumett Sevilla, Antonio. "Homenaje a Manuel Zapata Olivella and David Sánchez Juliao." *El Universal*, November 19, 2011. www.eluniversal.com.co/suplementos/dominical/homenaje-manuel-zapata-olivella-y-david-sanchez-juliao-53909.

Duncan, Quince. "El afrorealismo: Una dimensión nueva de la literatura latinoamericana." *Istmo* 10 (January 25, 2005). http://istmo.denison.edu/n10/articulos/afrorealismo.html.

Edison, Thomas Wayne. "Restored Roots: *Muntu* as a Healing Agent in *Pelo bueno, pelo malo* by Carmen Montáñez." *Hispania* 100, no. 4 (December 2017): 624–635.

Erickson, Peter. "The Black Atlantic in the Twenty-First Century: Artistic Passages, Circulations, Revisions." *Nka: Journal of Contemporary African Art* 24 (2009): 56–71.

Escobar, Arturo. "Activism as History Making: The Collective and the Personal in Collaborative Research with the Process of Black Communities in Colombia." In *Bridging Scholarship and Activism: Reflections from the Frontlines of Collaborative Research*, edited by Bernd Reiter and Ulrich Oslender, 105–122. East Lansing: Michigan State University Press, 2014.

Espinosa, Germán. "Introduction." In Manuel Zapata Olivella, *Pasión vagabunda*, ix–xxi.

———. "Realidad y pararrealidad de Manuel Zapata Olivella." In *Ensayos completos*, vol. 1, 241–244. Medellín: Fondo Editorial Universidad de Escuela de Administración, Finanzas e Instituto Tecnológico, 2002.

Esquivel-Suárez, Fernando. "The Global War on Drugs." *Global South Studies: A Collective Publication with the Global South*, August 23, 2018. https://globalsouthstudies.as.virginia.edu/key-issues/global-war-drugs.

Evaristo, Conceição. *Ponciá Vicêncio*. Belo Horizonte: Mazza, 2003.

Fanon, Frantz. *Black Skin, White Masks*. Translated by Richard Philcox. New York: Grove Press, 2008.

———. *The Wretched of the Earth.* Translated by Constance Farrington. New York: Grove, 1963.

Farias, P. F. de Moraes. "Africentrism: Between Cross-Cultural Grand Narrative and Relativism." *Journal of African History* 44 (2003): 327–340.

Fernández Ochoa, Adelayda. *La hoguera lame mi piel con cariño de perro.* Havana: Casa de las Américas, 2015.

Ferreira, Lígia Fonseca. *Com a palavra, Luiz Gama: Poemas, artigos, cartas, máximas.* São Paulo: Imprensa Oficial, 2011.

———, ed. *Primeiras trovas burlescas de Getulino.* São Paulo: Martins Fontes, 2000.

Figueredo, Eurídice. "Os brasileiros retornados à África." *Caderno de Letras da UFF* 38 (2009): 51–70. www.uff.br/cadernosdeletrasuff/38/artigo3.pdf.

Figueroa, Víctor. *Prophetic Visions of the Past: Pan-Caribbean Representations of the Haitian Revolution.* Columbus: Ohio State University Press, 2015.

Filho, Adonias. "Introduction." In Olinto, *A casa da água*, 1–6.

Fitz, Earl. *Rediscovering the New World: Inter-American Literature in a Comparative Context.* Iowa City: University of Iowa Press, 1991.

Follett, Richard. "The Spirit of Brazil: Football and Politics of Afro-Brazilian Cultural Identity." In *Recharting the Black Atlantic: Modern Cultures, Local Communities, Global Connections*, edited by Annalisa Oboe and Anna Scacchi, 71–92. New York: Routledge, 2008.

Forgues, Roland. *Palabra en el viento: Ensayos sobre creación e identidad en América Latina.* Paris: Editions Mare et Martin, 2008.

Fox, Patricia. *Being and Blackness in Latin America: Uprootedness and Improvisation.* Gainesville: University Press of Florida, 2008.

Frazier Clemons, Brenda. "Manuel Zapata Olivella's 'Un extraño bajo mi piel': A Study of Repression." *Afro-Hispanic Review* 2, no. 3 (Fall 1983): 5–7.

Freches, Claude-Henri. "La négritude et les problèmes du Noir dans l'oeuvre de Zapata Olivella." *Journal de la Société des Américanistes* 66, no. 1 (1979): 383–385.

Freyre, Gilberto. *Casa-grande e senzala: Formação da família brasileira sob o regime de economia patriarchal.* 48th ed. Recife: Fundação Gilberto Freyre, 2003.

———. *The Portuguese and the Tropics: Suggestions Inspired by the Portuguese Methods of Integrating Autochthonous Peoples and Cultures Differing from the European in a New, or Luso-Tropical Complex of Civilisation.* Translated by Helen M. D'O. Matthew and F. de Mello Moser. Recife: Executive Committee for the Commemoration of the Fifth Centenary of the Death of Prince Henry the Navigator, 1961.

Furtado, Júnia Ferreira. *Chica da Silva: A Brazilian Slave of the Eighteenth Century.* Cambridge: Cambridge University Press, 2009.

Garavito, Julián. "En busca de una identidad cultural colombiana: *Changó, el gran putas* de Manuel Zapata Olivella." *Thesaurus* 52, nos. 1–3 (1997): 320–329. Centro Virtual Cervantes. http://cvc.cervantes.es/lengua/thesaurus/pdf/52/TH_52_123_326_0.pdf.

Garcés González, José Luis. "Breve memoria de Zapata Olivella." *El Espectador*, November 15, 2014. www.elespectador.com/noticias/cultura/breve-memoria-de-zapata-olivella-articulo-527820.

———. *Manuel Zapata Olivella, caminante de la literatura y de la historia.* Bogota: Ministerio de Cultura, 2002.

García-Conde, Luisa. "Jorge Artel: Versos y prosa de un poeta indomulato." In *Si yo fuera tambó: Poesía selecta de Candelario Obeso y Jorge Artel, edición crítica*, edited by

Graciela Maglia, 189–199. Bogota: Editorial de la Pontífica Universidad Javeriana, 2010.

Garland Mahler, Anne. *From the Tricontinental to the Global South: Race, Radicalism, and Transnational Solidarity*. Durham, NC: Duke University Press, 2018.

Gaskins, Nettrice. "Afrofuturisms on Web 3.0: Vernacular Cartography and Augmented Space." In *Afrofuturism 2.0*, edited by Reynaldo Anderson and Charles Jones, 27–44. Lanham, MD: Lexington Books, 2016.

Gibson, Annie. "Vencendo confins: A voz resistente na narrativa de Kehinde em *Um defeito de cor*." *Pterodáctilo*, no. 7 (Fall 2009): 1–23.

Gilroy, Paul. *Against Race: Imagining Political Culture across the Color Line*. Cambridge, MA: Belknap, 2002.

———. *The Black Atlantic: Modernity and Double Consciousness*. New York: Verso, 1993.

———. *Darker Than Blue: On the Moral Economies of Black Atlantic Culture*. Cambridge, MA: Harvard University Press, 2011.

———. "Del Atlántico Negro a la melancolía poscolonial." Interview by Jim Cohen and Jade Lindgaard. *Revista Iberoamericana* 82, nos. 255–56 (April–September 2016): 301–321.

———. "Holberg Laureate Paul Gilroy's Acceptance Speech." *Holberg Prize*, May 31, 2019. www.holbergprisen.no/en/news/holberg-prize/holberg-laureate-paul-gilroys-acceptance-speech.

———. *Postcolonial Melancholia*. New York: Columbia University Press, 2006.

———. *Small Acts*. London: Serpent's Tail, 1993.

Gleason, Judith. *Agontimé, her legend*. New York: Viking Compass Books, 1970.

Glissant, Édouard. *Poetics of Relation*. Translated by Betsy Wing. Ann Arbor: University of Michigan Press, 1997.

Gomes, Flávio. *O alufá Rufino: Tráfico, escravidão e liberdade no Atlântico Negro, c.1822–c. 1853*. Rio de Janeiro: Companhia das Letras, 2010.

Gómez, Pablo. "La colección de Manuel Zapata Olivella." *Revista de Estudios Colombianos* 37–38 (2011): 117–118.

Gonçalves, Aline Najara da Silva. "A saga de Kehinde: Uma representação do protagonismo negro no romance histórico *Um defeito de cor*." *Historien—Revista de História* 4 (June 2011): 143–152. http://revistahistorien.blogspot.com/2011/06/4-edicao-da-revista-historien.html.

Gonçalves, Ana Beatriz, and Clara Alencar Pimentel. "A mulher e a maternidade: Breve leitura do romance *Um defeito de cor* de Ana Maria Gonçalves." *Terra Roxa e Outras Terras: Revista de Estudos Literários* 17, no. 2 (2009): 117–124. www.uel.br/revistas/uel/index.php/terraroxa/article/view/25011.

Gonçalves, Ana Maria. *100 meias confissões de Aninha*. August 1, 2006. http://anamariagoncalves.blogspot.com/.

———. "Ana Maria Gonçalves—New Columnist for the Intercept Brasil." YouTube, December 2, 2016. www.youtube.com/watch?v=FPFj5ToQ9xc.

———. *Ao lado e à margem do que sentes por mim*. August 1, 2006. http://anamariagoncalves.blogspot.com/.

———. "A aula de racismo e machismo à brasileira do secretário de Educação do Rio." *Intercept Brasil*, December 1, 2017. https://theintercept.com/staff/ana-maria-goncalves/.

———. "A Caixa, Machado de Assis e o branqueamento do Brasil." *Forum*, September 18, 2011. www.revistaforum.com.br/idelberavelar/2011/09/18/a-caixa-economica

-federal-a-politica-do-branqueamento-e-a-poupanca-dos-escravos-por-ana-maria-goncalves/.

———. "Carta aberta ao Governador Rui Costa, da Bahia." *Blogueiras negras*, February 27, 2015. http://blogueirasnegras.org/2015/02/27/carta-aberta-ao-governador-da-bahia/.

———. "Caso William Waack: A cumplicidade também é agente do racismo." *Intercept Brasil*, November 11, 2017. https://theintercept.com/staff/ana-maria-goncalves/.

———. "Dear White People liberta a arte negra de referências brancas." *Intercept Brasil*, May 31, 2017. https://theintercept.com/staff/ana-maria-goncalves/.

———. *Um defeito de cor*. Rio de Janeiro: Editora Record, 2006.

———. "Depois de 15 anos e muita pressão, o FLIP finalmente abre espaço para Mulheres e negros na programação." *Intercept Brasil*, July 26, 2018. https://theintercept.com/staff/ana-maria-goncalves/.

———. "É difícil fazer com que os 'bem intencionados' entendam o racismo." *Intercept Brasil*, December 2, 2016. https://theintercept.com/staff/ana-maria-goncalves/.

———. Email correspondence. December 30, 2016.

———. "Esquerda exclui minorias de debate 'promissor' sobre a nação brasileira." *Intercept Brasil*, May 3, 2017. https://theintercept.com/staff/ana-maria-goncalves/.

———. "Falta empatia para entender a revolta dos negros." *Intercept Brasil*, January 11, 2017. https://theintercept.com/staff/ana-maria-goncalves/.

———. "Fateful Hour." Translated by Eric Becker. *Glossolalia* 2 (2016): 41–72.

———. "'History' Insists on Covering Up the Intellectual Production of Black Women, Even in the 21st Century." *Intercept Brasil*, March 12, 2017. https://theintercept.com/staff/ana-maria-goncalves/.

———. "Inspiração e viagens através da diáspora: Uma entrevista com Ana Maria Gonçalves." Interview by John Maddox. *Afro-Hispanic Review* 30, no. 2 (Fall 2011): 167–180.

———. "Longe de Charlottesville, São Paulo também celebra 'o lado errado da história.'" *Intercept Brasil*, August 15, 2017. https://theintercept.com/staff/ana-maria-goncalves/.

———. "Luislinda Valois, Michel Temer e o beija-mão para ser esquecido." *Intercept Brasil*, April 20, 2017. https://theintercept.com/staff/ana-maria-goncalves/.

———. "Marinha agride, intimida e ameaça comunidade quilombola na Bahia." *Intercept Brasil*, February 8, 2017. https://theintercept.com/staff/ana-maria-goncalves/.

———. "O medo sempre nos traz algo de familiar, que é o nosso preconceito." *Intercept Brasil*, March 22, 2017. https://theintercept.com/staff/ana-maria-goncalves/.

———. "Onde andará a boa e velha liberdade?." *Geledés*, May 13, 2013. www.geledes.org.br/onde-andara-boa-e-velha-liberdade/#gs.WwUJ7TM.

———. "Paulo Enrique Amorim, o 'negro de alma branca,' e os demônios de cada um de nós." *Geledés*, February 27, 2012. www.geledes.org.br/paulo-henrique-amorim-o-negro-de-alma-branca-e-os-demonios-de-cada-um-de-nos-por-ana-maria-goncalves/#gs.MwQrZNM.

———. "Na polêmica sobre turbantes, é a branquitude que não quer assumir seu racismo." *Intercept Brasil*, February 15, 2017. https://theintercept.com/staff/ana-maria-goncalves/.

———. "Preface" In Castro and Fraga, *Do outro lado*, 20–22.

———. "Os previlegiados estão preparados para a verdadeira meritocracia?" *Intercept Brasil*, August 9, 2017. https://theintercept.com/staff/ana-maria-goncalves/.

———. "O que a polêimica sobre o filme 'Vazante' nos ensina sobre fragilidade branca." *Intercept Brasil*, November 16, 2017. https://theintercept.com/staff/ana-maria-goncalves/.

———. "Quem é Jocenildo? Em processo." Blog do IMS, Instituto Moreira Salles, July 26, 2017. https://blogdoims.com.br/quem-e-josenildo/.

———. "Slavery and Human Rights in Brazil." Paper presented at the University of Georgia, Athens, May 13, 2013.

———. "Sob olhar branco, sofrimento negro vira espetáculo." *Intercept Brasil*, April 5, 2017. https://theintercept.com/staff/ana-maria-goncalves/.

Gonçalves, Ana Beatriz, and Clara Alencar Pimentel. "A mulher e a maternidade: Breve leitura do romance *Um defeito de cor* de Ana Maria Gonçalves." *Terra Roxa e Outras Terras: Revista de Estudos Literários* 17, no. 2 (2009): 117–124. www.uel.br/revistas/uel/index.php/terraroxa/article/view/25011.

Gonzales, Rodolfo "Corky," and Alberto Urista (Alaurista). "El plan espiritual de Aztlán." *El Grito del Norte* 2, no. 9 (July 6, 1969): 5. https://icaadocs.mfah.org/icaadocs/THEARCHIVE/FullRecord/tabid/88/doc/803398/language/en-US/Default.aspx.

González Cajiao, Fernando. *Teatro colombiano de hoy: Antología*. Mexico: Fondo de Cultura Económica, 1992.

González Echevarría, Roberto. *Myth and Archive: A Theory of Latin American Narrative*. Cambridge: Cambridge University Press, 1990.

González-Wippler, Migene. *Powers of the Orishas: Santería and the Worship of Saints*. New York: Original Publications, 1992.

Goyal, Yogita. "Africa and the Black Atlantic." *Research in African Literatures* 45, no. 3 (Fall 2014): v–xxii.

Greenwald, Glenn. "The Intercept Brasil Welcomes Ana Maria Gonçalves as a Columnist on Race, Politics, and Culture." *Intercept Brasil*, December 2, 2016. https://theintercept.com/2016/12/02/the-intercept-brasil-welcomes-ana-maria-goncalves-as-a-columnist-on-race-politics-and-culture/.

Guevara, Ernesto [Che]. *El socialismo y el hombre en Cuba*. Marxists.org. www.marxists.org/espanol/guevara/65-socyh.htm.

Guicharnaud-Tollis, Michèle. "*Changó, el gran putas* de M. Zapata Olivella, novela del espacio intermedio." In *Historia, espacio e imaginario*, edited by Jacqueline Covo, 275–283. Lille: Septetrion. 1997.

Guillén, Nicolás. "Balada de los abuelos." Centro Virtual Cervantes, 2018. https://cvc.cervantes.es/literatura/escritores/guillen/poemas/poema_11.htm.

Guimarães, Antonio Sérgio Alfredo. "Africanism and Racial Democracy: The Correspondence between Herskovits and Arthur Ramos (1935–1949)." *Estudos Internacionais de América Latina y o Caribe* 19, no. 1 (2008/2009): 53–79. http://eial.tau.ac.il/index.php/eial/article/view/470.

Guzmán Morales, Rodolfo. "Lugar caribeño y textualización de un viaje personal en *Tambores en la noche*." In *Si yo fuera tambó: Poesía selecta de Candelario Obeso y Jorge Artel, edición crítica*, edited by Graciela Maglia, 177–188. Bogota: Editorial de la Pontífica Universidad Javeriana, 2010.

Hanchard, Michael George. *Orpheus and Power: The Movimento Negro of Rio de Janeiro and São Paulo, 1945–1988*. Princeton, NJ: Princeton University Press, 1994.

Hegel, Georg Wilhelm Friedrich. *Phenomenology of Spirit*. Translated by A. V. Miller. Edited by J. N. Findlay. Oxford: Clarendon, 1977.

Helg, Aline. "Oralidad y escritura en la historiografía de los esclavos afrodescendientes." In *Palenque Colombia: Oralidad, identidad y resistencia*, edited by Graciela Maglia and Armin Schwegler, 85–106. Bogota: Editorial Pontífica Universidad Javeriana, 2012.

———. "Simón Bolívar and the Spectre of 'Pardocracia': José Padilla in Post-independence Cartagena." *Journal of Latin American Studies* 35, no. 3 (August 2003): 447–471.

Hellwig, David, ed. *African-American Reflections on Brazil's Racial Paradise*. Philadelphia: Temple University Press, 1992.

Henao Restrepo, Darío. Introduction to *Changó, el gran putas*, by Manuel Zapata Olivella. In *Biblioteca de Literatura Afrocolombiana*, vol. 3, edited by Darío Henao Restrepo, 11–29. Bogota: Ministerio de Cultura, 2010. http://babel.banrepcultural.org/cdm/ref/collection/p17054coll7/id/2.

Hendrix, Jimi. "Voodoo Child (Slight Return)." *Electric Ladyland*. Reprise, 1968.

Henriques, Ricardo. *Desigualdade racial no Brasil: Evolução das condições de vida na década de 90*. Rio de Janeiro: IPEA, 1999.

Henry, Madeleine. "Greece and Africa in *Changó, el gran Putas*." Paper presented at the Classical Association of the Midwest and South, Southern Section, Tallahassee, FL, November 2, 2012.

Hitchcock, Alfred. *Psycho*. Shamley Productions, 1960.

Hofer, Stefan. "Entre la contingencia y la predeterminación: Ritualidad en *Changó el gran putas* de Manuel Zapata Olivella." In *Ritualidades latinoamericanas: Un acercamiento interdisciplinario* / Ritualidades Latino-Americanas: Uma Aproximação Interdisciplinar, 401–416. Frankfurt: Vervuert, 2003.

Hood, Edward Waters. "Manuel Zapata Olivella y Gabriel García Márquez." *Ciberayllu*, January 16, 2004. www.andes.missouri.edu/andes/Cronicas/EWH_Zapata.html.

Hughes, Langston. "Letter to Manuel Zapata Olivella." Unpublished letter, n.d. Vanderbilt Manuel Zapata Olivella Papers, Nashville.

———. "Youth." *Crisis*, January/February 2002, 40. https://books.google.com.

Hurston, Zora Neale. *Barracoon: The Story of the Last "Black Cargo."* New York: Amistad, 2018.

———. "Characteristics of Negro Expression." In *Negro: An Anthology*, edited by Nancy Cunard, 24–31. New York: Frederick Ungar, 1970.

———. *Dust Tracks on a Road: An Autobiography*. 2nd ed. Urbana: University of Illinois Press, 1984.

Institute of Advanced Studies. "Professor Paul Gilroy Appointed Founding Director of Centre for the Study of Race & Racism." University College London, May 21, 2019. www.ucl.ac.uk/institute-of-advanced-studies/news/2019/may/professor-paul-gilroy-appointed-founding-director-centre-study-race-racism.

Jackson, Richard. *Black Literature and Humanism in Latin America*. Athens: University of Georgia Press, 1997.

———. "Myth, History, and Narrative Structure in Manuel Zapata Olivella's *Changó el Gran Putas*." *Revista/Review Interamericana* 13, nos. 1–4 (1983): 108–119.

Jackson, Shirley. "African World View in Five Afro-Hispanic Novels." *Afro-Hispanic Review* 5, nos. 1/3 (1986): 37–42.

Jacobs, Naomi. *The Character of Truth: Historical Figures in Contemporary Fiction*. Carbondale: Southern Illinois University Press, 1990.

Jahn, Janheinz. *Muntu: African Culture and the Western World*. Translated by Marjorie Greene. New York: Grove, 1961.

James, Conrad. *Writing the Afro-Hispanic: Essays on Africa and Africans in the Spanish Caribbean*. London: Adonis and Abbey, 2012.

James González de Allen, Gertrude. "Enrique Dussel and Manuel Zapata Olivella: An Exploration of De-colonial, Diasporic, and Trans-modern Selves and the Politics of Recognition." *World Knowledges Otherwise* 2, no. 1 (2006): 1–12. https://pdfs.semanticscholar.org/4f02/c35de86f84221c670d7d03c5a24de33e6ff5.pdf.

Jaramillo, María Mercedes. "Bojayá in Colombian Theater: Kilele: A Drama of Memory and Resistance." In *Black Writing and the State in Latin America*, edited by Jerome Branche, translated by Emma Freeman, 103–126. Nashville: Vanderbilt University Press, 2015.

———. "*Hotel de vagabundos*: Crisol racial de las Américas." *Revista de Estudios Colombianos* 44 (2014): 13–17.

Jaramillo, María Mercedes, and Lucía Ortiz. *Hijas del Muntu: Biografías críticas de mujeres afrodescendientes de América Latina*. Bogota: Panamericana, 2011.

Johnson, Samuel. *The History of the Yorubas: From the Earliest Times to the Beginning of the British Protectorate*. London: Lowe and Brydone, 1921.

Jones, Nicholas. "Sor Juana's Black Atlantic: Colonial Blackness and the Poetic Subversions of *Habla de negros*." *Hispanic Review* 86, no. 3 (Summer 2018): 265–285.

Kabral, Fábio. *O caçador cibernético da Rua 13*. Rio de Janeiro: Editora Malês, 2017.

———. "Categoria: O caçador cibernético da Rua 13." June 2019. https://fabiokabral.wordpress.com/category/literatura/o-cacador-cibernetico-da-rua-13/.

———. "A diretora analista de mídias oníricas." In *2084: Mundos Cyberpunks*, edited by Lídia Zuin, 30–35. Manaus: Lendare, 2018.

Kaplan, Carla, ed. *Zora Neale Hurston: A Life in Letters*. New York: Doubleday, 2002.

Katzinski, Vera. "Afro-Hispanic American Literature." In *The Cambridge History of Latin American Literature*, vol. 2, edited by Enrique Pupo-Walker and Roberto González Echevarría, 164–194. Cambridge: Cambridge University Press, 1996.

Kraay, Hendrick. "Patriotic Mobilization in Brazil: The Zuavos and Other Black Companies." In *I Die with My Country: Perspectives on the Paraguayan War 1864–1870*, edited by Hendrick Kraay and Thomas Wigham, 61–75. Lincoln: University of Nebraska Press, 2004.

Krakusin, Margarita. "Estructura y técnica en Changó, el gran putas de Manuel Zapata Olivella." *Caribe* 4, no. 2 / 5 (2001–2002): 68–79.

Lamothe, Daphne Mary. *Inventing the New Negro: Narrative, Culture, and Ethnography*. Philadelphia: University of Pennsylvania Press, 2008.

Laó-Montes, Agustín. "Hilos descoloniales: Trans-localizando los espacios de la diáspora africana." *Tabula Rasa* 7 (July–December 2007): 47–79. www.scielo.org.co/pdf/tara/n7/n7a03.pdf.

Lara Ramos, David. "Zapata Olivella, Manuel. Changó, the Biggest Badass." *Revista de Estudios Colombianos* 37/38 (2011): 119–120.

Larkin do Nascimento, Elisa. *O sortilégio da cor*. São Paulo: Selo Negro, 2003.

Lárraga, Maribel. "Los demonios y testimonios en la memoria colectiva de *El fusilamiento del diablo* y *El diablo en Texas*." *Publication of the Afro–Latin American Research Association* 8 (2004): 27–33.

Ledent, Bénédicte, and Pilar Cuder-Domínguez, eds. *New Perspectives on the Black Atlantic*. New York: Peter Lang, 2012.

Lehnen, Leila. "Growing Up to Human Rights: The Bildungsroman and the Discourse of Human Rights in *Um defeito de cor*." In *Literature and Ethics in Contemporary*

Brazil, edited by Vinicius Mariano de Carvalho and Nicola Gavioli. New York: Routledge, 2017, 100–119.

Lewis, Marvin. "*En Chimá nace un santo*: Myth and Violence." *Kentucky Foreign Language Quarterly* 25 (1978): 145–165.

———. "La trayectoria novelística de Manuel Zapata Olivella: De la opresión a la liberación." In *Ensayos de literatura colombiana*, edited by Raymond Williams, 137–148. Bogota: Plaza y Janés, 1985.

Lewis, Marvin, and Edward Mullen, eds. *Afro-Hispanic Review* 20, no. 1 (Spring 2001).

Lima, Dulcilei da Conceição. "Desvendando Luíza Mahin: Um mito libertário no cerne do feminismo negro." Master's thesis, Universidade Presbiteriana MacKenzie, 2011.

Lima Santos, Denilson. "Abdias do Nascimento y Manuel Zapata Olivella: Intelectuales del siglo XX en el sendero de la discursividad ancestral yoruba y bantú." *Estudos de Literatura Brasileira Contemporânea* 44 (October/December 2004): 223–248.

Livre Opinião. "'Tchau, querida!,' texto inédito de Ana Maria Gonçalves, tem leitura dramática no Auditório Ibirapuera com direção de Wagner Moura." *Livre Opinião*, November 22, 2016. https://livreopiniao.com/2016/11/22/tchau-querida-texto-inedito-de-ana-maria-goncalves-tem-leitura-dramatica-no-auditorio-ibirapuera-com-direcao-de-wagner-moura/.

Locke, Alain. "Enter the New Negro." *Survey Graphic*, March 1925, National Humanities Center Toolbox: The Making of African American Identity, vol. 3, 1917–1968. http://nationalhumanitiescenter.org/pds/maai3/migrations/text8/lockenewnegro.pdf.

"Lois Roth Award for a Translation of a Literary Work Winners." Modern Language Association, 2016. www.mla.org/Resources/Career/MLA-Grants-and-Awards/Winners-of-MLA-Prizes/Biennial-Prize-and-Award-Winners/Lois-Roth-Award-for-a-Translation-of-a-Literary-Work-Winners.

Lopes, Nei. *Enciclopédia brasileira da diáspora africana*. São Paulo: Selo Negro, 2011.

———. *Oiobomé: A epopéia de uma nação*. Rio de Janeiro: Agir, 2010.

López, María Adelaida, dir. *Manuel Zapata Olivella: Abridor de caminos*, 2007; Colombia: Azul y Naranja Producciones. YouTube, February 23, 2012. www.youtube.com/watch?v=3Dpc4w2Kp6I.

Loveman, Mara. "The Race to Progress: Census Taking and Nation Making in Brazil (1870–1920)." *Hispanic American Historical Review* 89, no. 3 (August 2009): 435–470.

Luis, William. "Editor's Note." *Afro-Hispanic Review* 25, no. 1 (Spring 2006): 5–7.

———. "Introduction." In *Changó, the Biggest Badass*, by Manuel Zapata Olivella, translated by Jonathan Tittler, xiii–xxxv. Lubbock: Texas Tech University Press, 2009.

Luis, William, and Ann González, eds. *Dictionary of Literary Biography: Modern Latin-American Fiction Writers*. Vol. 113. Detroit: Gale Research, 1992.

Lynch, John. *Simón Bolívar: A Life*. New Haven, CT: Yale University Press, 2006.

Macedo, Joaquim Manuel. *Memórias da Rua do Ouvidor.* Edited by M. Cavalcanti Proença. Rio de Janeiro: Editora Tecnoprint, 1966.

Maddock Dillon, Elizabeth. "Atlantic Practices: Minding the Gap between Literature and History." *William and Mary Quarterly* 65, no. 1 (January 2008): 181–186.

Maddox, John. "Afro-McOndo en *The Brief, Wondrous Life of Oscar Wao*." *Caribe* 14, no. 2 (2011–2012): 27–42.

———. "Aleijadinho at Home and Abroad: 'Discovering' Race and Nation in Brazil." *CR: The New Centennial Review* 12, no. 2 (Fall 2012): 183–216.

———. "Ana Maria Gonçalves." In *Oxford Dictionary of Caribbean and Afro-Latin American Biography*, edited by Franklin Knight and Henry Louis Gates, 115–117. Oxford: Oxford University Press, 2016.

———. "The Black Atlantic Revised: Ana Maria Gonçalves's *Um defeito de cor*." *Callaloo* 40, no. 4 (Fall 2017): 155–173.

———. "Una falla geológica de fallas raciales: El Sur norteamericano en Piri Thomas y Manuel Zapata Olivella." *Visitas al Patio* 10 (2017): 13–40.

Maglia, Graciela, ed. *Si yo fuera tambó: Poesía selecta de Candelario Obeso y Jorge Artel, edición crítica*. Bogota: Editorial de la Pontífica Universidad Javeriana, 2010.

———. "Texto cultural, estética de resistencia y *oralitura* en San Basilio de Palenque (Colombia)." In *Palenque Colombia: Oralidad, identidad y resistencia*, edited by Graciela Maglia and Armin Schwegler, 285–320. Bogota: Editorial Pontífica Universidad Javeriana, 2012.

Maglia, Graciela, and John Maddox. "Introduction." *Afro-Hispanic Review* 36, no. 1 (Spring 2017): 11–20.

Maglia, Graciela, and Armin Schwegler, eds. 2012. *Palenque Colombia: Oralidad, identidad y resistencia*. Bogota: Editorial Pontífica Universidad Javeriana.

Maia, Felipe. "Meet the Brazilian Musicians Leading Bahia's Afrofuturism Movement." *Remezcla*, May 16, 2019. https://remezcla.com/features/music/artists-bahia-afrofuturism/.

Manrique, Luis Esteban. "Vida de Libertador: La poliédrica figura de Simón Bolívar by John Lynch." *Política Exterior* 21, no. 118 (July–August 2007): 205–209.

"Manuel Zapata Olivella." Catálogo Fondo Editorial Casa de las Américas. www.casa.co.cu/catalogoeditorial/fichaautor.php?cod=717.

"Manuel Zapata Olivella." Vanderbilt University Heard Library, 2019. http://mzo.library.vanderbilt.edu/.

Manzano, Juan Francisco. *Autobiografía del esclavo poeta y otros escritos*. Edited by William Luis. Frankfurt: Vervuert, 2007.

Martin, Frank. "Palo and Paleros." Interview by William Luis. *Afro-Hispanic Review* 31, no. 1 (Spring 2012): 159–168.

Martin, Kameelah. *Conjuring Moments in African American Literature: Women, Spirit Work, and Other Such Hoodoo*. New York: Palgrave, 2012.

Masterson, Daniel, and Sayaka Funada-Classen. *The Japanese in Latin America*. Urbana, IL: University of Illinois Press, 2004.

Mate-Kojo, Samuel. "Identity, Solidarity, and Autonomy: African Agency in Manuel Zapata Olivella's *Changó, el Gran Putas*." In *Diasporic Identities within Afro-Hispanic and African Contexts*, edited by Yaw Agawu-Kakraba and Komla Aggor, 51–64. Newcastle upon Tyne: Cambridge Scholars, 2015.

McKay, Claude. *The Banjo*. Harcourt Brace and Company. San Diego, CA: 1957.

Megenney, William. "Time and Space: Africa and America in Manuel Zapata Olivella's *Changó, el gran putas*." In *Studies in Honor of Myron Lichtblau*, edited by Fernando Burgos, 229–249. Statesboro, GA: Juan de la Cuesta, 2000.

Mennucci, Sud. *O precursor do abolicionismo no Brasil. Luiz Gama*. São Paulo: Companhia Editora Nacional, 1938.

Menton, Seymour. *Latin America's New Historical Novel*. Austin: University of Texas Press, 1993.

Meredith, Sarah. "With a Banjo on Her Knee: Gender, Race, Class, and the American Classical Banjo Tradition, 1880–1915." PhD dissertation, Florida State University, 2003.

Merla-Watson, Cathryn Josefina, and B. V. Olguín. "Introduction: ¡Latin@futurism Ahora! Recovering, Remapping, and Recentering the Chican@ and Latin@ Speculative Arts." *Aztlán: A Journal of Chicano Studies* 40, no. 2 (Fall 2015): 135–146.
Mignolo, Walter. *Local Histories / Global Designs: Coloniality, Subaltern Knowledges, and Border Thinking.* Princeton, NJ: Princeton University Press, 2000.
Millán, Isabel. "Engineering Afro-Latina and Mexican Immigrant Heroines: Biopolitics in Borderlands Speculative Literature and Film." *Aztlán: A Journal of Chicano Studies* 40, no. 2 (Fall 2015): 167–185.
Miller, Paul D. "Afro-Futurismo: Uma declaração de intenções—De ponta cabeça, de cabeça para baixo." *Rizoma.net* 16–17 (2006). https://issuu.com/rizoma.net/docs/afrofuturismo.
Mina Aragón, William. "Dos ensayos sobre Manuel Zapata Olivella." *Publication of the Afro-Latin American Research Association* 6 (2002): 26–32.
———, ed. "Introduction." In *El árbol brujo de la libertad: África en Colombia: Orígenes, transculturación, presencia. Ensayo histórico-mítico*, by Manuel Zapata Olivella, 13–20. Bogota: Ediciones Desde Abajo, 2014.
———, ed. *Manuel Zapata Olivella: Un legado intercultural.* Popayán: Universidad del Cauca, 2017.
———. *Manuel Zapata Olivella: Pensador Humanista.* Cali: Artes Gráficas del Valle Editores, 2014.
Moncada Esquivel, Ricardo. "La escritora vallecaucana Adelaida Fernández ganó el premio Casa de las Américas." *El País*, February 12, 2015. www.elpais.com.co/entretenimiento/cultura/la-escritora-vallecaucana-adelaida-fernandez-gano-el-premio-casa-de-las-americas.html.
Montáñez Ochoa, Carmen. *Pelo bueno, pelo malo*. Barcelona: Terra Nova, 2012.
Morrison, Toni. *Beloved*. New York: Knopf, 1987.
Múnera, Alfonso. "Manuel Zapata Olivella y la nación inclusive." In *Por los senderos de sus ancestros*, by Manuel Zapata Olivella, 28–38. Bogota: Ministerio de Cultura, 2011.
Nascimento, Abdias. *Africans in Brazil: A Pan-African Perspective.* Translated by Elisa Larkin Nascimento. Los Angeles: African World Press, 1992.
———. *Quilombismo: Documentos de uma miltância pan-africanista.* Rio de Janeiro: Vozes, 1980.
———. *Sortilégio: Mistério negro*. Rio de Janeiro: Teatro Experimental do Negro, 1959.
———. *Sortilégio II: Mistério negro de Zumbi redivivo.* Rio de Janeiro: Paz e Terra, 1979.
Nascimento, Eugênio. "Nobel." In *Modern Slavery and Water Spirituality: A Critical Debate in Africa and Latin America*, by Ineke Phaf-Rheinberger, 53. New York: Peter Lang, 2017.
Nascimento dos Santos, Daiana. "Atlántico negro: El océano en la narrativa de esclavizados." *Acta Literaria* 54 (2017): 29–50.
———. "História e memoria no romance *Um defeito de cor.*" *Izquierdas* 31 (2016): 162–171.
———. "Imaginarios y respresentaciones en la tradición oral africana y latinoamericana." *Acta Literaria* 42, no. 1 (2011): 145–150.
———. "Memoria y representación del barco y del mar en la travesía y la migración forzada." *Afro-Hispanic Review* 32, no. 1 (Spring 2013): 115–128.
———. "La nueva novela histórica y sus insuficiencias teóricas: El emplazamiento negro africano." *Estudios Africanos* 27 (June 2017): 54–65.

———. *El océano de fronteras invisibles: Relecturas históricas sobre (¿el fin? de) la esclavitud en la novela contemporánea*. Madrid: Verbum, 2016.

———. "Los tambores suenan, la voz del pueblo resuena: La representación del negro en la novela contemporánea." *Revista Alpha* 40 (2015): 165–174.

Navarrete, María Cristina. "Palenques: Cimarrones y castas en el Caribe colombiano—sus relaciones sociales (siglo XVII)." In *Palenque Colombia: Oralidad, identidad y resistencia*, edited by Graciela Maglia and Armin Schwegler, 257–284. Bogota: Editorial Pontífica Universidad Javeriana, 2012.

———. *San Basilio de Palenque: Memoria y tradición*. Cali: Universidad del Valle, 2008.

Neri, Nátaly. "Afrofuturismo: A necessidade de novas utopías." Lecture presented at TEDxPetrópolis, Petropolis, RJ, January 21, 2018. YouTube. www.youtube.com/watch?v=_D1y9yZRpis.

Newman, Judith. "Globalizing Gilroy." *Journal of Commonwealth and Postcolonial Studies* 17, no. 1 (Spring 2011): 93–102.

N'gom, M'bare. "Representaciones de la otredad: Experiencia femenina e identidad en ¡Negras somos!" *Cuadernos de Literatura* 19, no. 38 (2015): 119–136.

"The Nobel Prize in Literature 1993." Nobel Media, 2014. www.nobelprize.org/nobel_prizes/literature/laureates/1993/.

Noticias Uno. "Entrega de titulación de tierras en San Basilio de Palenque." *Noticias Uno*, April 15, 2012. https://canal1.com.co/noticias/entrega-de-titulacion-de-tierras-en-san-basilio-de-palenque-2/.

Oboe, Annalisa, and Anna Scacchi. *Recharting the Black Atlantic: Modern Cultures, Local Communities, Global Connections*. New York: Routledge, 2008.

Olaoluwa, Senayon. "African Diaspora beyond the Black Atlantic: Dynamics and Significance in the Latin American World and Elsewhere." *H-Net*, April 22, 2017. https://networks.h-net.org/node/20292/discussions/176852/african-diaspora-beyond-black-atlantic-dynamics-and-significance.

Oleszkiewicz-Peralba, Malgorzata. *Fierce Feminine Divinities of Eurasia and Latin America*. New York: Palgrave, 2015.

Olinto, Antônio. *A casa da água*. 4th ed. Introduction by Adonias Filho. São Paulo: Difusão Editorial, 1983.

Oliveira, Emanuelle. *Writing Identity: The Politics of Contemporary Afro-Brazilian Literature*. West Lafayette, IN: Purdue University Press, 2008.

Oliveira, Luciano. "Um Prêmio Nobel para Ana Maria Gonçalves—Luciano Oliveira." *Revista Será*, December 3, 2014. http://revistasera.ne10.uol.com.br/um-premio-nobel-para-ana-maria-goncalves-luciano-oliveira/.

"Olivella Acquisition Boosts Library's Latin American Collection." *Acorn Chronicle*, January 13, 2010. www.vanderbilt.edu/acorn-chronicle/2010/01/olivella/.

Olliz Boyd, Antonio. "Manuel Zapata Olivella." In *Dictionary of Literary Biography: Modern Latin-American Fiction Writers*, vol. 113, edited by William Luis and Ann González, 313–322. Detroit: Gale Research, 1992.

Ong, Walter. *Orality and Literacy: The Technologizing of the Word*. New York: Routledge, 2012.

Orozco, Ashanti. "Poética del muntú renaciente." Facebook, June 23, 2019. www.facebook.com/dinahorozco/posts/10156890057737631.

Ortiz, Fernando. *Contrapunteo cubano del tabaco y el azúcar*. Havana: Jesús Montero, 1940.

Ortiz, Lucía. "Chambacú corral de negros de Manuel Zapata Olivella, un capítulo en la lucha por la libertad. In memoriam." *Inti* 63–64 (Spring–Fall 2006): 95–108.

———, ed. *"Chambacú, la historia la escribes tú": Ensayos sobre cultura afrocolombiana*. Frankfurt: Vervuert, 2007.

———. "Conversación con Manuel Zapata Olivella." *Revista de Estudios Colombianos* 21, (2000): 60–66. www.colombianistas.org/Portals/0/Revista/REC-21/15.REC_21_LuciaOrtizEntrevZapataOlivella.pdf.

———. "Nacionalismo y transnacionalismo en Manuel Zapata Olivella." *Boletín Hispánica Helvética* 29 (Spring 2017): 129–142.

———. *La novela colombiana hacia finales del siglo XX. Una nueva aproximación a la historia*. New York: Peter Lang, 1997.

———. "La representación del mestizaje cultural en la literatura afrocolombiana." *Actas XIV Congreso Asociación Internacional de Hispanistas* 4 (July 16–21, 2001): 495–503.

Ortiz de Montellano, Bernard, Gabriel Haslip-Viera, and Warren Barbour. "They Were NOT Here before Columbus: Afrocentric Hyperdiffusionism in the 1990s." *Ethnohistory* 44, no. 2 (Spring 1997): 199–234.

Ossa, Luisa. "*Changó, el gran putas*: Afrocentric Discourse." *Monographic Review / Revista Monográfica* 15 (1999): 248–261.

La Palabra. "El año Manuel Zapata Olivella." *La Palabra*, May 27, 2019. Universidad del Valle. http://lapalabra.univalle.edu.co/editorial-el-ano-manuel-zapata-olivella/?fbclid=IwAR13NEXSnoWWsdwFlRQOTfeOPrYRp_6fYVY9Jy_u4FO8cKzrQqTuyy1NM.

Palacios Córdoba, Elba Mercedes. "Epilogue." In *Demando mi libertad: Mujeres negras y sus estrategias de supervivencia en la Nueva Granada, Venezuela y Cuba*, edited by Aurora Vergara Figueroa and Carmen Luz Cosme, 247–260. Puntiel, Cali: Universidad Instituto Colombiano de Estudios Superiores de Incolda, 2018.

Palacios Palacios, George. "Apuntes sobre la música, el folclor, lo nacional-popular y la literatura en algunos de los escritos tempranos de Manuel Zapata Olivella." *Escritos* 23, no. 51 (2015): 439–470.

Palmer, Brian. "The 'Very Particular' History Being Presented at Confederate Sites." *Fresh Air*, National Public Radio, January 21, 2019. www.npr.org/2019/01/21/686547376/the-very-particular-history-being-presented-at-confederate-sites.

Pastrana Arango, Andrés. "Palabras del señor presidente de la república, Andrés Pastrana Arango, con motivo de la imposición de la Orden de Bocayá a ocho ilustres colombianos por su aporte a la cultura." *Afro-Hispanic Review* 20, no. 1 (Spring 2001): 3–5.

Payán, Miguel Juan. "Black Panther." *Revista Acción*, November 1, 2018. www.scribd.com/article/393009454/Black-Panther.

Paz, Octavio. *El laberinto de la soledad*. Mexico: Fondo de Cultura Económica, 1992. First published 1950 by Cuadernos Americanos (Mexico).

Perkowska, Magdalena. *Historias híbridas: La nueva novela histórica latinoamericana (1985–2000) ante las teorías posmodernas de la historia*. Frankfurt: Vervuert, 2008.

Peters, Christabelle. "Crossing the Black Atlantic to Africa: Research on Race in 'Race-less' Cuba." In *New Perspectives on the Black Atlantic*, edited by Bénédicte Ledent and Pilar Cuder-Domínguez, 83–104. New York: Peter Lang, 2012.

Phaf-Rheinberger, Ineke. "Deux romancièrs afro-brésiliennes: Conceição Evaristo et Ana Maria Gonçalves." *Afrique–Brésil* 43 (2017): 47–60.

———. *Historias enredadas: Representaciones asimétricas con vista al Atlántico.* Berlin: Tranvía-Verlag Walter Frey, 2011.

———. *Modern Slavery and Water Spirituality: A Critical Debate in Africa and Latin America*. New York: Peter Lang, 2017.

———. "Myths of Early Modernity: Historical and Contemporary Narratives on Brazil and Angola." In *AfricAmericas: Itineraries, Dialogues, and Sounds,* edited by Ineke Phaf-Rheinberger and Tiago de Oliveira Pinto, 125–150. Frankfurt: Vervuert, 2008.

Phaf-Rheinberger, Ineke, and Tiago Oliveira de Pinto, eds. *AfricAmericas: Itineraries, Dialogues, and Sounds*. Frankfurt: Vervuert, 2008.

Pierce, Marsha. "Transnational / Transcultural Identities: The Black Atlantic and Pythagoras's Theorem." *Callaloo* 30, no. 2 (2007): 547–554.

Pinho, Patrícia de Santana. *Mapping Diaspora: African American Roots Tourism in Brazil*. Chapel Hill: University of North Carolina Press, 2018.

Pinn, Anthony. *Why Lord? Suffering and Evil in Black Theology*. New York: Continuum, 1999.

Pinto, Tiago Oliveira de. "Crossed Rhythms: African Structures, Brazilian Practices, and Afro-Brazilian Meanings." In *AfricAmericas: Itineraries, Dialogues, and Sounds,* edited by Ineke Phaf-Rheinberger and Tiago Oliveira de Pinto, 165–181. Frankfurt: Vervuert, 2008.

Piot, Charles. "Atlantic Aporias: Africa and Gilroy's Black Atlantic." *South Atlantic Quarterly* 100, no. 1 (2001): 155–170.

Piquero Nouhad, Dorita. "Generales de Changó, jinetes y sus caballos." *Les Langues Néo-Latines* 285 (1993): 100–120.

———. "Introduction." In *Changó, el gran putas*, by Manuel Zapata Olivella, 9–55. Bogota: Grupo Editorial Educar, 2007.

———. "La ruta de Chimá al monte Kenia." Palimpsestus/*Palimpsesto* 5 (2005): 148–166. www.bdigital.unal.edu.co/14250/1/3-8071-PB.pdf.

Plant, Deborah. "Afterword and Additional Materials." In *Barracoon*, by Zora Neale Hurston, 117–169. New York: Amistad, 2018.

———. "Introduction." I *Barracoon*, by Zora Neale Hurston, 5–16. New York: Amistad, 2018.

Pons, María Cristina. *Memorias del olvido: La novela histórica de fines del siglo XX*. Siglo Veintiuno Editores, 1996.

Prescott, Lawrence. "Afro-Norteamérica en los escritos de viaje de Manuel Zapata Olivella: Hacia los orígenes de *He visto la noche*." *Afro-Hispanic Review* 20, no. 1 (Spring 2001): 55–58.

———. "Brother to Brother: The Friendship and Literary Correspondence of Manuel Zapata Olivella and Langston Hughes." *Afro-Hispanic Review* 25, no. 1 (Spring 2006): 87–104.

———. "Journeying through Jim Crow: Spanish American Travelers in the United States during the Age of Segregation." *Latin American Research Review* 42, no. 1 (2007): 3–28. *Informe Académico*. http://lasa-4.univ.pitt.edu/LARR/prot/fulltext/Vol42no1/prescott.pdf.

———. "Liberating Blackness: The Theme of Whitening in Two Colombian Short Stories." *Callaloo* 35, no. 2 (2012): 475–493.

———. "Race, Ethnicity, and Nation in Manuel Zapata Olivella's *¡Levántate mulato!*" In *Race, Colonialism, and Social Transformation in Latin America and the Caribbean,* edited by Jerome Branche, 222–230. Gainesville: University Press of Florida, 2008.

———. *Without Hatred or Fears: Jorge Artel and the Struggle for Black Literary Expression in Colombia*. Detroit: Wayne State University Press, 2000.

Prescott, Lawrence, and Antonio Tillis, eds. *Afro-Hispanic Review* 25, no. 1 (Spring 2006): 9–14.

Prestes, Luciana da Trindade, and Emília Maria da Trindade Prestes. "A literatura como mecanismo de luta pelo reconhecimento social de mulheres negras na obra *Um defeito de cor*." *Afro-Ásia* 56 (2017): 129–146.

Public Enemy. "Fight the Power." Motown, 1989.

Quintero, Ciro Alfonso. *Filosofía antropológica y cultural en el pensamiento de Manuel Zapata Olivella*. Quito: Ediciones Abya-Yala, 1998.

Ramírez, Catherine. "Afrofuturism/Chicanafuturism: Fictive Kin." *Aztlán: A Journal of Chicano Studies* 33, no. 1 (2008): 185–194.

———. "Deus ex machina: Tradition, Technology, and the Chicanafuturist Art of Marion C. Martinez." *Aztlán: A Journal of Chicano Studies* 29, no. 2 (October 2005): 55–93.

Ramírez, Liliana. "Chambacú: heterogeneidad y representación." In *"Chambacú, la historia la escribes tú": Ensayos sobre cultura afrocolombiana*, 171–186. Frankfurt: Vervuert, 2007.

———. *Entre fronteras: Latinoamericanos y literaturas.* Balún Canán, Dreaming in Cuban *y* Chambacú. Bogota: Pontífica Universidad Javeriana, 2006.

Ramos, Arthur. *A aculturação negra no Brasil*. São Paulo: Companhia Editora Nacional, 1942.

———. *O negro na civilização brasileira*. Rio de Janeiro: Guanabara, 1971.

Ramos da Silva, Liliam. "A voz do protagonista afrodescendente em romances históricos hispano-americanos: invisibilidade do texto original e algumas (poucas) obras traduzidas no Brasil." *Cadernos de Literatura em Tradução* 16 (2016): 73–88.

Ramos da Silva, Liliam, Andressa Bastos Paz, and Juliana Bastos Paz. "Vozes negras no romance hispano-americano." In *Proceedings of the Semanário Internacional de Língua, Literatura e Processos Culturais*, Universidade Federal do Rio Grande do Sul, Porto Alegre, RS, May 19–22, 2014, 527–537. www.lume.ufrgs.br/handle/10183/138942.

Redação. "'Um defeito de cor' será a nova supersérie da Globo." O Planeta TV, May 18, 2019. https://oplanetatv.clickgratis.com.br/noticias/bastidores/um-defeito-de-cor-sera-a-nova-superserie-da-globo.html.

Reed, A. L., Jr. *W. E. B. Du Bois and American Political Thought*. Oxford: Oxford University Press, 1997.

Reis, João José. *Rebelião escrava no Brasil: A história do Levante dos Malês em 1835*. São Paulo: Companhia das Letras, 2004.

———. *Slave Rebellion in Brazil: The Muslim Uprising of 1835 in Bahia*. Translated by Arthur Brakel. Baltimore, MD: Johns Hopkins University Press, 1993.

Risério, Antônio. "Um defeito de cor." *Terra*, January 19, 2007. http://terramagazine.terra.com.br/interna/0,,OI1351780-EI6608,00-Um+defeito+de+cor.html.

Robinson Abrahams, Hazel. *No Give Up, Maan*. Bogota: Ministerio de Cultura, 2010.

Rocha, Glauber. *A revolução do Cinema Novo*. Rio de Janeiro: Embrafilme; Alhambra, 1981.

Rodríguez-Cabral, Cristina. "Postmodernismo y postcolonialismo en *El fusilamiento del diablo* de Manuel Zapata Olivella." *CLA Journal* 50, no. 2 (June 2006): 238–251.

Rollins, Andrew. "Afrofuturism and Our Old Ship of Zion: The Black Church in Post-modernity." In *Afrofuturism 2.0*, edited by Reynaldo Anderson and Charles Jones, 127–148. Lanham, MD: Lexington Books, 2016.

Ross, Marlon. "Trans-Atlantic Parochialism." *Callaloo* 39, no. 4 (Fall 2016): 887–897.

Rossbach de Olmos, Lioba. "¿Qué pasa con el Pacífico Negro en el Atlántico Negro? El Atlántico Negro de Paul Gilroy frente a los acontecimientos (afro)colombianos." *Memorias: Revista Digital de Historia y Arqueología desde El Caribe* 11 (July–December 2009): 199–219.

Rössner, Michael. 1999. "De la utopia histórica a la historia utópica: Reflexiones sobre la nueva novela histórica como re-escritura de textos históricos." In *La novela latinoamericana entre historia y utopía*, edited by Sonja Steckbauer, 68–78. Eichstätt: Katholische Universität Eichstätt, 1999.

Rufino, Alzira. "Luiza Mahin." In *Eu, mulher negra, resisto*, 2. Self-published, 2010.

Sáenz de Tejada, Cristina. "Raza y género en la narrativa femenina afro-brasileña." *Revista de Crítica Literaria Latinoamerica* 23, no. 46 (1997): 269–285.

"Saint Peter Claver." *Catholic Encyclopedia*. New York: Appleton, 1913.

Salles, Ricardo. *A Guerra do Paraguai: Memórias e imagens*. Rio de Janeiro: Biblioteca Nacional, 2003.

Sansone, Livio. "Da África ao afro: Uso e abuso da África entre os intelectuais e na cultura popular brasileira durante o século XX." *Rizoma.net*, 2006, 34–45. https://issuu.com/rizoma.net/docs/afrofuturismo.

La Santa Biblia. Versión Reina Valera Antigua. Translated by Cipriano de Valera and Casidorio de Reina. La Societat Bíblica Americana, 1940.

Santí, Enrico Mario. "Introducción." In *Contrapunteo cubano del tabaco y el azúcar*, by Fernando Ortiz. Madrid: Cátedra, 2002, 23–119.

Santiago, Silviano. *As raízes e o laberinto da América Latina*. Rio de Janeiro: Rocco, 2006.

Santos, Cristiano Henrique Ribeiro dos. "O simbolismo da árvore-mundo no candomblé: Conexão entre o mundo dos homens e o mundo dos deuses." *Rizoma.net*, 2006, 144–151. https://issuu.com/rizoma.net/docs/afrofuturismo.

Santos, Eduardo Antônio Estevam. "Luiz Gama e a sátira racial como poesia da transgressão: Poéticas diaspóricas como contranarrativa à ideia de raça." *Almanack* 11 (December 2015): 692–731. www.scielo.br/pdf/alm/n11/pt_2236-4633-alm-11-00707.pdf.

Santos, Luís Carlos dos. *Luiz Gama*. São Paulo: Selo Negro, 2010.

Saramago, José. *Memorial do convento*. Alfragide: Editorial Caminho, 1982.

Schindler, Melissa. "Home, or the Limits of the Black Atlantic." *Research in African Cultures* 45, no. 3 (Fall 2014): 72–90.

Schmidt, Simone Pereira. "Navegando no Atlântico Pardo ou a lusofonia reinventada." *Crítica Cultural* 1, no. 2 (July–December 2006): 1–4. www.portaldeperiodicos.unisul.br/index.php/Critica_Cultural/article/view/94/104.

Schmidt-Nowara, Chris. "'This Rotting Corpse': Spain between the Black Atlantic and the Black Legend." *Arizona Journal of Hispanic Cultural Studies* 5 (2001): 149–160.

Schwegler, Armin. "African Roots in Latin America: Palenque (Colombia)." Lecture at the University of California, Irvine, April 6, 2017, YouTube. www.youtube.com/watch?v=HY4RTVaD9Sg.

———. "Sobre el origen africano de la lengua criolla de Palenque (Colombia)." In *Palenque Colombia: Oralidad, identidad y resistencia*, edited by Graciela Maglia and Armin Schwegler, 107–180. Bogota: Editorial Pontífica Universidad Javeriana, 2012.

Scott, David. "An Obscure Miracle of Connection: Discursive Tradition and Black Diaspora Criticism." *Small Axe* 1 (1997): 19–38.

Sertima, Ivan van. *They Came before Columbus: The African Presence in Ancient America.* New York: Random House, 2003. First published 1976 by Random House (New York).

Sierra Díaz, Diana Carolina. "El Muntu: La diáspora del pensamiento filosófico africano en Changó, el gran putas de Manuel Zapata Olivella." *La Palabra* 29 (July–December 2016): 23–44.

Silva, Alberto da Costa. "Introduction." In *Agudás—Os brasileiros do Benim*, by Milton Guran, ix–xv. Rio de Janeiro: Gama Filho, 1999.

Silva, Fabiana Carneiro da. "Quando o que se discute é a realidade: *Um defeito de cor* como provocação à História." *Afro-Ásia* 55 (2017): 71–109.

Simarra, Víctor. "Palenque de San Basilio hoy." Interview by John Maddox. *Publication of the Afro-Latin American Research Association* 18 (2014): 85–95.

Sinker, Mark. "Amando o alien." *Rizoma.net*, 2006, 110–113. https://issuu.com/rizoma.net/docs/afrofuturismo.

Slauter, Eric. "History, Literature, and the Atlantic World." *William and Mary Quarterly* 65, no. 1 (2008): 135–166.

Smart, Ian. *Amazing Connections: Kemet to Hispanophone Africana Literatures.* Washington, DC: Original World Press, 1996.

———. "*Chango, el gran putas* as Liberation Literature." *CLA Journal* 35, no. 1 (January 1991): 15–30.

———. "*Changó el gran putas* by Manuel Zapata Olivella." *Afro-Hispanic Review* 3, no. 2, (Fall 1984): 31–32.

———. "*Changó, el gran putas*, una nueva novela poemática." In *Ensayos de literatura colombiana*, edited by Raymond Williams, 149–156. Bogota: Editorial Plaza y Janés, 1985.

———. "Introduction: *The Afro-Hispanic Review*." *Afro-Hispanic Review* 21, nos. 1/2 (2002): i–vii.

Sommer, Doris. *Foundational Fictions: The National Romances of Latin American Literature.* Berkeley: University of California Press, 1991.

Stephenson Watson, Sonja. "*Changó, el gran putas*: Contemporary Afro-Hispanic Historical Novel." *Afro-Hispanic Review* 25, no. 1 (Spring 2006): 67–86.

Stevens, Cristina. "(Re)writing Pain. The Theme of Violence in Contemporary Afro-Brazilian Women Novelists." *Krypton* 5/6 (2015): 200–207. http://romatrepress.uniroma3.it/ojs/index.php/krypton/article/view/1060.

Strickrodt, Silke. "The Brazilian Diaspora to West Africa in the Nineteenth Century." In *AfricAmericas: Itineraries, Dialogues, and Sounds*, edited by Ineke Phaf-Rheinberger and Tiago de Oliveira Pinto, 37–68. Frankfurt: Vervuert, 2008.

Studnicki-Gizbert, Daviken. *A Nation upon the Ocean Sea: Portugal's Atlantic Diaspora and the Crisis of the Spanish Empire, 1492–1640*. Oxford: Oxford University Press, 2007.

Süssekind, Flora. *Tal Brasil, qual romance? Uma ideologia estética e sua história: O naturalismo*. Rio de Janeiro: Achiamé, 1984.

Sweet, James. *Domingos Álvares, African Healing, and the Intellectual History of the Atlantic World.* Chapel Hill: University of North Carolina Press, 2011.

———. *Recreating Africa: Culture, Kinship, and Religion in the African-Portuguese World, 1441–1770*. Chapel Hill: University of North Carolina Press, 2004.

Syms, Martine. "The Mundane Afrofuturist Manifesto." *Rhizome*, December 17, 2013. http://rhizome.org/editorial/2013/dec/17/mundane-afrofuturist-manifesto/.

Tatis Guerra, Gustavo. "Bajo el árbol brujo de Zapata Olivella." *El Universal*, May 27, 2018. http://m.eluniversal.com.co/suplementos/facetas/bajo-el-arbol-brujo-de-zapata-olivella-279361.

Teixeira de Andrade, Marcos Roberto. "A visão periférica da História em *Um defeito de cor*, de Ana Maria Gonçalves." *Darandina Revisteletrônica* 1 (2010): 1–16. www.ufjf.br/darandina/files/2010/01/Marcos-Roberto-Teixeira-de-Andrade.pdf.

Tempels, Placide. *Bantu Philosophy*. Translated by A. Rubbens and Collin King. Edited by Honoré Vinck. Centre Aequatoria, November 2006. www.congoforum.be/upldocs/Tempels%20BantuPhil%20English%201959.pdf.

"31 anos." Geledés Instituto da Mulher Negra. www.geledes.org.br/.

Thomaz, Paulo. "Des-Reterritorialização: percursos possíveis do romance afro-brasileiro recente." *Estudos da Literatura Brasileira Contemporânea* 45 (2015): 21–35.

Tillis, Antonio. "*Changó, el gran putas*: A Postmodern Historiographic Metafictional Text." *Afro-Hispanic Review* 20, no. 1 (2000): 15–28.

———. *Manuel Zapata Olivella and the "Darkening" of Latin American Literature*. Columbia: University of Missouri Press, 2005.

Tittler, Jonathan. "Catching the Spirit: 'Changó, el gran putas' in English Translation." *Afro-Hispanic Review* 20, no. 1 (Spring 2001): 73–78.

———. "*Changó* el gran putas de Manuel Zapata Olivella en traducción: Movimiento lateral y pensamiento lateral." In *"Chambacú, la historia la escribes tú": Ensayos sobre cultura afrocolombiana*, 183–196. Frankfurt: Vervuert, 2007.

———. "Mi Manuel." *Guaraguao* 9, no. 20 (Summer 2005): 127–129. www.revistaguaraguao.org/archivo/sumario/20.htm.

———. "Translator's Note and Acknowledgments." In *Changó, the Biggest Badass*, by Manuel Zapata Olivella, translated by Jonathan Tittler, introduction by William Luis, ix–xii. Lubbock: Texas Tech University Press, 2009.

Tosta, Anônio Luciano de Andrade. *Confluence Narratives: Ethnicity, History, and Nation-Making in the Americas*. Lewisburg, PA: Bucknell University Press, 2016.

Trump, Donald. "Full Speech President Trump Rally." Huntsville, AL, September 22, 2017. YouTube. www.youtube.com/watch?v=T8-dr1GU8As.

Truth, Sojourner. "Ain't I a Woman?" In *Internet Modern History Sourcebook*, edited by Paul Halsall. Fordham University, 1997. https://sourcebooks.fordham.edu/mod/sojtruth-woman.asp.

Tunca, Daria. "Away from a Definition of African Literature(s)." In *New Perspectives on the Black Atlantic*, edited by Bénédicte Ledent and Pilar Cuder-Domínguez, 105–124. New York: Peter Lang, 2012.

Valdés, Vanessa. *Diasporic Blackness: The Life and Times of Arturo Alfonso Schomburg*. Albany: State University of New York Press, 2017.

Valencia Solanilla, César. "Changó el gran putas: Mito, lenguaje y transgresión." *Poligramas* 19 (June 2003): 167–179. http://bibliotecadigital.univalle.edu.co/xmlui/bitstream/handle/10893/2858/Poligramas.No.19.p.167-179%2c2003.pdf?sequence=1.

Valero, Silvia. "La construcción del 'sujeto afrodiaspórico' como sujeto político en *Un mensaje de Rosa* (2004) y *El pueblo afrodescendiente* (2012) de Quince Duncan." *Revista de Crítica Literaria Latinoamericana* 41, no. 81 (January 2015): 83–107.

———. "¿De qué hablamos cuando hablamos de 'literatura afrocolombiana'? o los riesgos de las categorizaciones." *Estudios de Literatura Colombiana* 32 (2013): 15–37.

van Veen, tobias c. "The Armageddon Effect: Afrofuturism and the Chronopolitics of Alien Nation." In *Afrofuturism 2.0*, edited by Reynaldo Anderson and Charles Jones, 63–90. Lanham, MD: Lexington Books, 2016.

Vargas Llosa, Mario. *Los cachorros*. Barcelona: Lumen, 1937.

Vasconcelos Calderón, José. *La raza cósmica: Misión de la raza iberoamericana, Argentina y Brasil*. Mexico: Trillas, 2012.

Vasser, Uchenna. "Africanidad and the Representation of Female Characters in Manuel Zapata Olivella." *Revista Convivencia* 1, no. 1 (November 2014): 77–98. www.up.ac.pa/ftp/2010/v_postgrado/publicaciones/Convivencia/Convivencia-Vol1-No1.pdf.

Véras, Bruno. "Projeto Baquaqua." Harriet Tubman Institute, York University, Universidade Federal de Pernambuco, Ministério de Cultura do Brasil, May 2016. www.baquaqua.com.br/fontes-historicas/.

Vergara Figueroa, Aurora, and Carmen Luz Cosme Puntiel, eds. *Demando mi libertad: Mujeres negras y sus estrategias de resistencia en la Nueva Granada, Venezuela y Cuba, 1700–1800*. Cali: Instituto Colombiano de Estudios Superiores de Incolda, 2018.

Verger, Pierre. "Uma rainha africana mãe de santo em São Luís." *Revista USP* 6 (1990): 151–158.

Vianna, Hermano. "Atlântico Negro." *Rizoma.net* 100–102 (2006). https://issuu.com/rizoma.net/docs/afrofuturismo.

Wacquant, Loïc. "The Militarization of Urban Marginality: Lessons from the Brazilian Metropolis." *International Political Sociology* 2 (2008): 56–74.

Wade, Peter. *Blackness and Race Mixture: The Dynamics of Racial Identity in Colombia*. Baltimore: Johns Hopkins University Press, 1993.

Walker, Alice. "Foreword." In *Barracoon*, by Zora Neale Hurston. New York: Amistad, 2018, 7–10.

Weelden, Dirk van. "Religião de rua e magia da matrix." *Rizoma.net*, 66–99 (2006). https://issuu.com/rizoma.net/docs/afrofuturismo.

Weldt-Basson, Helene Carol, ed. *Redefining Latin American Historical Fiction: The Impact of Feminism and Postcolonialism*. New York: Palgrave Macmillan, 2013.

Wheat, David. *Atlantic Africa and the Spanish Caribbean, 1570–1640*. Chapel Hill: University of North Carolina Press, 2016.

Williams, Claire. "Tracing Back Trauma: The Legacy of Slavery in Afro-Brazilian Literature by Women." *Angelaki: Journal of the Theoretical Humanities* 22, no. 1 (March 2017): 103–122.

Williams, Raymond, ed. *Ensayos de literatura colombiana*. Bogota: Editorial Plaza y Janés, 1985.

———. *Novela y poder en Colombia, 1844–1987*. Bogota: Tercer Mundo Editores, 1992.

Wood, Marcus. "Slavery, History, and Satire: The Legacy of Gilberto Freyre." In *Recharting the Black Atlantic: Modern Cultures, Local Communities, Global Connections*, edited by Analisa Oboe and Anna Scacchi, 128–146. New York: Routledge, 2008.

Young's Literal Translation of the Holy Bible. Translated by Robert Young. Grand Rapids: Baker Book House, 1953.

Zapata-Cortés, Diana Catalina. "Mestizaje nacional: Una historia 'negra' por contar." *Memoria y Sociedad* 14, no. 29 (July–December 2010): 91–105. www.scielo.org.co/scielo.php?script=sci_arttext&pid=S0122-51972010000200006.

Zapata Olivella, Manuel. "Aquí en la tierra como en el cielo." Manuscript, n.d. Vanderbilt Manuel Zapata Olivella Papers, Nashville, TN.

———. *El árbol brujo de la libertad*. Edited by William Mina Aragón. Cali: Universidad del Valle, 2009.

———. "Artel, el maestro." *Afro-Hispanic Review* 25, no. 1 (Spring 2006): 147–161.

———. *La Calle 10*. Bogota: El Tiempo, 1960.

———. "Caronte Liberado." In *Teatro*, by Juan Zapata Olivella and Manuel Zapata Olivella, 1–30. Bogota: Intituto Colombiano de Cultura, 1972.

———. *Chambacú, Black Slum*. Translated by Jonathan Tittler. Pittsburgh, PA: Latin American Literary Review Press, 1989.

———. *Chambacú, corral de negros*. Medellin: Editorial Bedout, 1967.

———. "Changó. Revisiones S.F." Unpublished manuscript, n.d. Vanderbilt Manuel Zapata Olivella Papers, Nashville, TN.

———. *Changó, the Biggest Badass*. Translated by Jonathan Tittler. Introduction by William Luis. Lubbock: Texas Tech University Press, 2009.

———. "Changó, el Gran Putas." Unpublished film script, n.d. Vanderbilt Manuel Zapata Olivella Papers, Nashville, TN.

———. *Changó el gran putas*. Introduction by Darío Henao Restrepo. Bogota: Ministerio de Cultura, 2010. http://babel.banrepcultural.org/cdm/ref/collection/p17054coll7/id/2.

———. *Changó el gran putas*. Edited by Dorita Piquero Nouhaud. Bogota: Educar, 2007.

———. "Changó, the Holy Mother. . . ." Unpublished television script, n.d. Vanderbilt Manuel Zapata Olivella Papers, Nashville, TN.

———. "Cien años." Unpublished note, n.d. Vanderbilt Manuel Zapata Olivella Papers, Nashville, TN.

———. *Las claves mágicas de América*. Bogota: Plazas y Janés, 1989.

———. "El código guerrero." *Afro-Hispanic Review* 1, no. 1 (Spring 1982): 16.

———. "Conversación informal con Manuel Zapata Olivella." Interview by Margarita Krakusin. *Afro-Hispanic Review* 20, no. 1 (2001): 15–28.

———. *Cuentos de muerte y libertad*. Bogota: Iqueima, 1961.

———. *Detrás del rostro*. Bogota: Aguilar, 1963.

———. *El fusilamiento del diablo*. Bogota: Plaza y Janés, 1999.

———. "Genealogía de los orichas yorubas." Unpublished paper presented at the Ciclo de religiosidad afro-colombiana, Museo de Arte Religioso, Banco de la República, Bogota, Colombia, n.d. Vanderbilt Manuel Zapata Olivella Papers, Nashville, TN.

———. *He visto la noche. Pasión vagabunda*. Bogota: Ministerio de Cultura, 2000.

———. *Hemingway, el cazador de la muerte*. Bogota: Arango Editores, 1993.

———. "Hemingway, el cazador de la muerte: Kenya en la novela de un afrocolombiano." *Publication of the Afro–Latin American Research Association* 2 (1998): 17–29.

———. *El hombre colombiano*. Bogota: Canal Ramírez-Antares, 1974.

———. *Hotel de vagabundos: Teatro*. Bogota: Ediciones Espiral, 1955.

———. *¡Levántate mulato! Por mi raza hablará el espíritu*. Bogota: REI Andes, 1990.

———. *Lève-toi, mulâtre! L'epirit parlera à travers ma race*. Translated by Claude Couffon and Claude Bourguignon. Paris: Payot, 1987.

———. *Manuel Zapata Olivella: Por los senderos de sus ancestros: Textos escogidos. 1940–2000*. Edited by Alfonso Múnera. 2010. http://babel.banrepcultural.org/cdm/ref/collection/p17054coll7/id/17.

———. "Manuel Zapata Olivella—South America's Voice of African Consciousness." Interview by Ja Johannes. *In Motion Magazine*, August 1993. www.inmotionmagazine.com/ac10/jj_mz.html.

———. "La maraca encantada." Unpublished manuscript, n.d. Vanderbilt Manuel Zapata Olivella Papers, Nashville, TN.

———. "El mestizaje en la nueva novela hispanoamericana." *Afro-Hispanic Review* 25, no. 1 (Spring 2006): 163–170.

———. "El Muntu en América." *Afro-Hispanic Review* 20, no. 1 (Spring 2001): 13–14.

———. "El Muntu en América." In *Bridging Scholarship and Activism: Reflections from the Frontlines of Collaborative Research*, edited by Bernd Reiter and Ulrich Oslender, 99–104. East Lansing: Michigan State University Press, 2014.

———. "Navego." *Afro-Hispanic Review* 1, no. 1 (Spring 1982): 16.

———. *Nuestra Voz: Aportes del habla popular latinoamericana al idioma español.* Bogota: Ecoe, 1987.

———. *Pasión vagabunda*. Bogota: Ministerio de Cultura, 2000.

———. "Los pasos del indio." Unpublished script, n.d. Vanderbilt Manuel Zapata Olivella Papers, Nashville, TN.

———. "Los problemas de identidad de los escritores afro-latinoamericanos." *Afro-Hispanic Review* 25, no. 1 (Spring 2006): 171–173.

———. *¿Quién le dio el fusil a Oswald? y otros cuentos*. Bogota: Editorial Revista Colombiana, 1967.

———. *La rebelión de los genes: El mestizaje americano en la sociedad futura*. Bogota: Altamir, 1997.

———. "El substrato negro en el español de América." Unpublished manuscript, n.d. Vanderbilt Manuel Zapata Olivella Papers, Nashville, TN.

———. "Tambores de América para despertar al Viejo Mundo." Unpublished manuscript, n.d. Vanderbilt Manuel Zapata Olivella Papers, Nashville, TN.

———. *Tierra mojada*. Medellín: Editorial Bedout, 1972.

———. Untitled Scrapbook. 1939–? Vanderbilt Manuel Zapata Olivella Papers, Nashville, TN.

———. "Visión: La travesía." *Afro-Hispanic Review* 1, no. 1 (Spring 1982): 16.

Zapata Olivella, Manuel, and Juan Zapata Olivella. *Teatro*. Bogota: Instituto Colombiano de Cultura, 1972.

Zeleza, Paul Tiyambe. "Rewriting the African Diaspora: Beyond the Black Atlantic." *African Affairs* 104, no. 414 (January 2005): 35–68.

Zoggyie, Haakayoo. *In Search of the Fathers: The poetics of Disalienation in the Narrative of Two Contemporary Afro-Hispanic Writers*. New Orleans: University Press of the South, 2003.

———. "Lengua e identidad en *Changó, el gran putas*, de Manuel Zapata Olivella." *Afro-Hispanic Review* 20, no. 1 (Spring 2001): 90–95.

———. "Lengua e identidad en *Changó, el gran putas*, de Manuel Zapata Olivella." *Estudios de Literatura Colombiana* 7 (2000): 9–19.

Zurbano, Roberto. "Entramos en la pos-resistencia: Del álbum de los muertos al ciudadano del futuro." *AfroCubaWeb.com*, October 10, 2013. Lecture at Connecticut College. www.afrocubaweb.com/zurbano/entramos-en-la-post.pdf.

Index

About the Author

JOHN T. MADDOX IV is an assistant professor of Spanish and African American studies at the University of Alabama at Birmingham. He translated Puerto Rican playwright Alejandro Tapia y Rivera's *La Cuarterona* as *Juliet of the Tropics* (2016). He guest edited a special issue of the *Afro-Hispanic Review* on maroons with Graciela Maglia in 2017. His essays have appeared in *Callaloo*, *Hispania*, and *Latin American Research Review*.